FOREIGN POLICY
AND
U.S. PRESIDENTIAL
ELECTIONS

1952
1960

FOREIGN POLICY
AND
U.S. PRESIDENTIAL
ELECTIONS

1952

1960

BY ROBERT A. DIVINE

NEW VIEWPOINTS
A Division of Franklin Watts, Inc.
New York
1974

To Kirk

Cover design by Nicholas Krenitsky
Book design by Rafael Hernandez

Library of Congress Cataloging in Publication Data
Divine, Robert A.
   Foreign policy and U.S. presidential elections,
1952–1960.

   Bibliography: p.
   1. Presidents—United States—Election—1952.
2. Presidents—United States—Election—1956.
3. Presidents—United States—Election—1960.
4. United States—Foreign relations—1945–1953.
5. United States—Foreign relations—1953–1961.
I. Title.
E816.D58   329′.023′73092   73-11029
ISBN 0-531-05358-X
ISBN 0-531-06496-4 (pbk.)

CONTENTS

PREFACE

The place of foreign policy in American presidential politics changed dramatically with the advent of World War II. The old adage, "politics stop at the water's edge," held true for earlier American experience. In most elections, domestic issues relating to economic well-being, political corruption, or sectional interests dominated the political discussion and influenced the voters' decisions. Only infrequently did foreign policy enter into the election process, as in the 1790's, when the Wars of the French Revolution accentuated the divisions between the Federalists and the Jeffersonian Republicans, or in 1920, when the Democrats tried unsuccessfully to turn the election into a solemn referendum on the League of Nations. Usually the candidates focused instead on domestic issues that touched more directly on the lives of voters, such as race relations, land, or jobs.

World War II brought foreign policy squarely into the presidential election process by raising issues of life and death that clearly affected the American people. In 1940, the war in Europe overshadowed the race between Wendell Willkie and Franklin Roosevelt; voters became absorbed in the foreign conflict, allowing the fall of France and the

Battle of Britain to monopolize their attention. Roosevelt shrewdly played up his skill and experience in diplomacy, portraying himself as the man Hitler feared and respected, while Willkie sought to persuade the people that FDR would lead the nation into war against its will. Four years later, the Democrats again stressed the theme of experience and mature leadership to argue for Roosevelt's reelection as the man best qualified to make a lasting peace. Despite bipartisan agreement on the future United Nations, Dewey proved unable to prevent FDR from capitalizing on the peace issue.

The coming of the Cold War insured the continued prominence of international considerations in American presidential politics. By 1948, the proclamation of the Truman Doctrine and the adoption of the Marshall Plan had institutionalized the conflict with the Soviet Union. Henry Wallace challenged the prevailing consensus with his Progressive party candidacy, but his attacks on containment led only to a successful Democratic effort to picture him as a Communist dupe. On the surface, foreign policy played a very minor role in the 1948 election as the Berlin crisis caused Dewey to avoid a partisan attack on the administration's diplomatic record. The new state of Israel raised the only overt international issue during the campaign, and Truman extended immediate recognition in order to retain the Jewish vote. But from the conventions in June and July until election day in November, the blockade of Berlin and the resulting American airlift helped rally public support for President Truman, who stood out as the man holding back the Soviet tide in Europe. Both in blocking a potential GOP attack and in vindicating containment, the Berlin crisis enabled Truman to exploit foreign policy for his narrow upset victory.

As in my volume covering the elections from 1940–1948, I continue to focus on the way in which foreign policy shaped the political process, beginning in 1952 with Eisenhower's shrewd manipulation of the Korean War through Kennedy's maladroit handling of the Quemoy-Matsu and Cuban issues in 1960. I make no claim that foreign policy alone determined the outcome of these elections—I contend only that foreign policy was a major factor that deserves special treatment. I end this account in 1960, but the story could easily be continued. One could argue that world affairs were largely responsible for the landslide victories of Lyndon Johnson in 1964 and Richard Nixon in 1972, and that it was the disaster in Vietnam that drove LBJ out of the presidential race in 1968 and thereby paved the way for Nixon's first triumph.

I have tried to avoid developing any rigid thesis to explain the role of foreign policy in presidential elections, preferring simply to let the actors in the historical drama speak for themselves. I do believe, however, that American presidential candidates have often behaved irresponsibly in dealing with diplomatic issues. Fearful that the public will not comprehend the subtle intricacies of international affairs, aspirants for the presidency have often reduced complex issues to banal slogans, thereby preventing a rational debate over American foreign policy. Thus in 1952 Eisenhower promised to "go to Korea"; four years later Stevenson raised the specter of nuclear pollution of the atmosphere in calling for a test ban; in 1960 Kennedy belabored the issue of the offshore islands unnecessarily. As a result, foreign-policy experts cringe at election time, wincing at the inevitable distortions and misunderstandings arising from campaign rhetoric and hoping for the time when they can once again conduct diplomacy free from political controversy. Despite the failure of presidential candidates to educate the American people on world affairs, the process has not broken down completely. In selecting men like Eisenhower and

Kennedy, the voters have chosen leaders who possessed the ability and knowledge to guide the nation through the hazards of a world in crisis.

I have incurred many debts in the course of the research and writing of this book. A grant from the Penrose Fund of the American Philosophical Society made it possible for me to examine manuscript collections and presidential libraries; the University of Texas Research Institute provided a semester's leave that enabled me to do most of the writing. I am grateful for the assistance of archivists at the University of Tennessee Library, the Manuscripts Division of the Library of Congress, the Princeton University Library, the Cornell University Library, and especially the extremely helpful and courteous staffs of the Harry S. Truman and Dwight D. Eisenhower presidential libraries. Ralph Lapp and Charles Tyroler kindly granted me interviews which helped clarify the importance of the nuclear-test-ban issue in the 1956 campaign. I wish also to thank the many dedicated librarians at the University of Texas who have served me so competently in the course of my research. I am grateful to Mrs. Laura Bodour for typing the manuscript so efficiently. My wife, Barbara Renick Divine, has sustained an unflagging interest in this project for five years, enduring my absences for research as well as the frequent mental aberrations of a spouse lost in the past. Once again, she has demonstrated her unfailing gift for editorial judgment and thereby helped give this book whatever stylistic grace it may possess.

R. A. D.
Austin, Texas
July, 1973

FOREIGN POLICY
AND
U.S. PRESIDENTIAL
ELECTIONS

1952

1960

1952

123456

The Cold War continued to dominate American life in 1952, but the fear of all-out war that prevailed in 1948 had given way to feelings of frustration as Americans saw before them an apparently endless cycle of Communist aggression and belated American reponse. The United States had scored one substantial Cold War victory. Plans for the formation of the North Altantic Treaty Organization had gone ahead quietly during the 1948 election, culminating in a treaty which the Senate ratified after a brief debate in the spring of 1949. For the first time in history, the United States was committed to defend the nations of Western Europe from aggression.

The Truman administration took the lead in implementing NATO by asking World War II hero General Dwight D. Eisenhower to leave the presidency of Columbia and become Supreme Commander of the multi-national army being created to defend Europe against a Soviet attack. Eisenhower, who believed that American security depended on a free Western Europe, took up his duties in early 1951. He was immediately faced with a critical challenge from Republican isolationists, led by former President Herbert Hoover, who opposed the permanent stationing of American troops in Europe and called instead for abandoning the continent in favor of a retreat to "this Western Hemisphere Gibraltar of Western Civilization." No longer restrained by Arthur Vandenberg, who died early in 1951, GOP senators criticized the administration's plans to send four American divisions to Europe, suggesting instead that the United States rely on its naval and air power to oppose Soviet expansion. Eisenhower flew back from Paris to oppose what some called "the new isolationism," and Governor Dewey urged Republicans to stand behind the bipartisan containment policy. But not until the administration promised to limit the American presence on the continent to four divisions did the Senate finally agree to the troop deployment.[1]

Events in Asia weakened the bipartisan policy even more. Late in 1949, the Communists, led by Mao Tse-tung, completed their conquest of China, forcing Chiang Kai-shek and his demoralized Nationalists to flee to Formosa for refuge. The Republicans, who had not participated in framing Far Eastern policy, immediately accused the Democrats of "losing" China to the Communists. The outbreak of the Korean War in June 1950 briefly quieted the partisan attacks as Republicans supported Truman's decision to commit American troops, technically under United Nations authority, to repel the North Korean invasion. President Truman and Dean Acheson, who replaced Marshall as Secretary of State in 1949, quickly set the stage for a new outburst of political controversy by repeated shifts in their Korean strategy. Pledged originally simply to defend the concept of collective security by driving the Communists out of South Korea, the administration became so enraptured with Douglas MacArthur's sweeping victory at Inchon in September 1950 that it permitted the General to send his troops north of the 38th parallel in pursuit of the fleeing remnants of the North Korean army. Despite warnings, through India, of possible Chinese Communist intervention, the administration sought the unification of Korea by armed force as MacArthur's troops drove toward the Yalu River and Manchuria. In November, the Chinese intervened massively, catching the American forces unprepared and driving them completely out of North Korea before a spring counteroffensive finally stabilized the front a short distance north of the 38th parallel.

General MacArthur, ignoring his own responsibility for this disaster, came forth with proposals to broaden the war against China by using Chiang Kai-shek's troops, by blockading the coast of China, and by bombing Chinese supply centers in Manchuria and thus ending the privileged sanctuary across the Yalu. When the Joint Chiefs rejected these suggestions, MacArthur began to call publicly for escalation, writing Republican Minority Leader Joseph W. Martin, "There is no substitute for victory." Truman finally responded to this flagrant act of insubordination by relieving MacArthur of his command on April 11. Greeted as a conquering hero when he returned home for the first time in fourteen years, MacArthur urged Americans to win the Korean War, while the administration countered by arguing that an all-out effort against China would expose Western Europe to Soviet conquest. The limited-war strategy finally prevailed, but many people resented what they felt to be a futile stalemate in Korea.

On July 11, 1951, truce negotiations began in Kaesong, raising hopes for a quick settlement of the Korean War. The talks soon bogged down in technicalities, but when they resumed in October, after a brief United Nations offensive had gained several strategic points, the two sides agreed on a five-point agenda. In November, the Communists receded from their original demand that the 38th parallel become the cease-fire line, and peace seemed near when the negotiators agreed on a temporary armistice along the existing battle line. But then the talks foundered on the prisoner-of-war issue. The

United States held approximately 132,000 prisoners; 75,000, including 15,600 Chinese, refused to go back to their homelands, and the United States steadfastly upheld their right to resist forcible repatriation. The Communists, infuriated by this blow to their prestige, were equally adamant in insisting on the return of all their captured troops. Truman, despite his great desire for a peaceful settlement, refused to compromise on this crucial issue. He told the nation on May 7, 1952: "To agree to a forced repatriation would be unthinkable. It would be repugnant to the fundamental moral and humanitarian principles which underlie our action in Korea." Though Republicans continued to charge that the administration lacked the will to win the Korean War, it was the President's unyielding determination not to force the prisoners of war to return home to certain punishment and possible death that prolonged the unpopular conflict.[2]

The loss of a nuclear monopoly also contributed to the sense of frustration. Though experts had warned in 1945 that the Soviets would probably develop their own atomic bomb within five years, the American people were shocked when Truman announced on September 23, 1949, that the Russians had exploded an atomic device. Exclusive American possession of the bomb was basic to both military policy and public confidence in the Cold War; the Truman administration moved to bolster both by going ahead with plans to develop the hydrogen bomb, a thousand times more destructive than the weapons that leveled Hiroshima and Nagasaki. After an intense but secret debate which divided the scientific community, by mid-1950 the United States was engaged in a crash thermonuclear program that rivaled the wartime Manhattan Project in scale. A theoretical breakthrough by mathematician Stanislaw Ulam and physicist Edward Teller in the spring of 1951 insured a successful outcome, and the administration went ahead with plans for the first hydrogen bomb test in the fall of 1952.[3]

The panicky reaction to Soviet atomic power was matched by an equally emotional response to the continuing disclosures of Soviet espionage activities in the United States. In January 1950, a jury found Alger Hiss guilty of perjury (the statute of limitations prevented trying him on spy charges) and sent him to jail. A month later, Joseph McCarthy, an obscure junior senator from Wisconsin, told a GOP audience in Wheeling, West Virginia, that he had the names of 205 Communists inside the State Department. In subsequent speeches, the number changed from 205 to 57, 81, 10, 116, and finally to one, Owen Lattimore, a Johns Hopkins professor who was ultimately cleared of any Communist connection. The public, however, already convinced by Truman that the nation was in deadly peril from Communism, embraced McCarthy as a patriot bent on winning the Cold War on the home front. When Senator Millard Tydings of Maryland, who opposed him, went down to defeat in November 1950, McCarthy's power grew immensely as politicians became reluctant to challenge his popular witch-hunt.[4]

These developments at home and abroad destroyed public confidence in the Truman administration. The exhilaration many felt when the Russian threat to Europe was stopped by the Berlin airlift had gradually eroded; the fall of China, the outbreak of the Korean conflict, and the Soviet development of the atomic bomb all helped create a new mood of despair. Revelations that several high officials in the Truman administration had accepted mink coats and deep freezes from groups seeking government favors combined with McCarthyism to create a grim outlook for the Democrats in 1952 on domestic as well as foreign issues. A Gallup poll taken in February revealed that Truman's popularity had fallen to a disastrously low 25 percent. The people clearly yearned for a new, bold leader who would lift them out of their anguish and restore their faith in the nation.[5]

I

Senator Robert A. Taft felt that he was the man who could best capitalize on Truman's unpopularity. Reelected to the Senate in 1950 by a massive 430,000-vote margin, Taft set out on his third attempt at the GOP nomination—convinced that he possessed the popularity, the issues, and the strategy to bring his party back to power for the first time in twenty years. Bitter over Dewey's "me too" campaign in 1948, Taft believed that an all-out partisan attack against Truman on both domestic and foreign policy was essential. Dewey had lost, he reasoned, because he had tried to appeal to independents by taking moderate stands; Taft would win by getting out the full Republican vote. On domestic issues, the senator was willing to tolerate McCarthy, despite a personal distaste for his tactics, because of his success in undermining the Truman administration. With Vandenberg's death, Taft was ready to depart from bipartisanship and make the most of Democratic failure in foreign policy.[6]

Bothered by the isolationist label his opponents had hung on him in the past, Taft set forth his views in a book, *A Foreign Policy for Americans,* published in late 1951. There he demonstrated that he was not a simple-minded isolationist who wanted to retreat back to a Fortress America and ignore the world. His opposition to containment reflected a genuine dislike for a policy built on the threat of military force, a conservative abhorrence for vast government spending, and above all a sophisticated belief that neither American resources nor American ideology justified an attempt to impose a *Pax Americana* on the world. But the main thrust of the book was political, not philosophical. Taft blamed the Cold War on the

Democrats: in six short years the Truman administration had thrown away the victory won by American soldiers in World War II. "The concessions made at Teheran, Yalta, and Potsdam and our later policies in the Far East," he charged, "were such as to build up Soviet Russia to a position of power which today does indeed present a threat to the security of the United States." Praising Vandenberg for his role in developing the containment policy, Taft said the administration finally stopped the Soviet threat in Europe, but it utterly neglected a similar menace in Asia. To document his claim that "the Administration's weak policy invited the Communist attack," he cited Dean Acheson's January 1950 speech stating that Korea was beyond the American defense perimeter. "The Korean War and the problems which arise from it," Taft contended, "are the final result of the continuous sympathy toward communism which inspired American policy."

Taft set forth two alternatives to the policy of containment. The first, implicit in Hoover's 1951 proposal of an American Gibraltar, called for reliance on air and naval power, rather than ground forces, to defend American security. He favored withdrawing U.S. troops from Europe as soon as the continental powers were strong enough to defend themselves; the American role should be limited to air and naval support and never again should the nation's troops fight on foreign soil. "Not only is an all-powerful air force the best possible defense for the United States," Taft argued, "but it is also the best deterrent to war." As a corollary to "massive retaliation" (as his proposal would come to be known), Taft advocated an ideological offensive against Communism, "an affirmative policy which will constantly extend the doctrine and the power of liberty." He suggested a worldwide propaganda campaign beamed at the captive peoples of Eastern Europe and even proposed "an underground war of infiltration in Iron Curtain countries." "While it may be a dangerous undertaking," he added, "I believe that an able and courageous leader could successfully work out a system which would give the Soviet Government something to worry about behind the iron curtain itself." Thus, far from being an isolationist, Taft proposed a strategy of liberation that went far beyond the relatively passive containment policy of the Truman administration.[7]

Taft began his quest for the nomination in the fall of 1951, and this time he concentrated on winning public support in the primaries as well as securing the backing of party leaders. He traveled more than 46,000 miles by plane, bus, auto, and train, giving 534 speeches in 41 states in an effort to prove his ability as a partisan campaigner. Everywhere he went, he put Truman's foreign policy on trial, claiming the Democrats had "built up communism to the point where it is the threat it is to us today." He recited the litany of Teheran, Yalta, and Potsdam in blaming Roosevelt and Truman for the loss of Eastern Europe and China.

Taft focused his heaviest fire on the Korean conflict, which he continually called "Truman's War." He repeated the charge that Acheson "invited" the North Korean aggression and argued that "we could have won this war if we had adopted the proposals of General MacArthur at the time they were made." He called for a blockade of China, bombing of Manchuria, and the use of Chiang's troops "in diversionary raids in South China." Again and again he accused the administration of not wanting "to win the war in Korea," but at the same time he called for a negotiated settlement, saying "a deadlocked peace is better than a deadlocked war." "I think," he added, "we'd better make a deadlocked peace and go on from there." He never mentioned the delicate prisoner-of-war issue, nor explained how he reconciled his advocacy of MacArthur's proposals to escalate the war with his own call for a peaceful settlement.[8]

While Taft stumped the country, Harold Stassen, now president of the University of Pennsylvania, and Earl Warren, still governor of California, declared their candidacies. Both supported the bipartisan foreign policy, but political observers doubted that either could mount an effective challenge to Taft within the Republican party. At the same time, General Douglas MacArthur stood by in case Taft faltered. He issued a public statement saying that he would not "shrink . . . from accepting any public duty to which I might be called by the American people," and in mid-March he told the Mississippi state legislature, "Our failure in Korea will probably mean the ultimate loss of all continental Asia to international Communism," in a speech that many saw as an open bid for political support. Taft continued to run strongly, however, and MacArthur finally realized that the senator had preempted the Republican right wing. When Representative Joseph Martin tried belatedly to arrange a draft movement, MacArthur told him, "I really think the Republican Party owes it to Taft. He should be nominated." [9]

II

The very qualities that endeared Taft to the Republican right alarmed the eastern internationalists who had controlled the choice of GOP candidates since 1940. "He has been wrong on foreign affairs almost 100 percent," commented the *New Republic*'s TRB. "Now he is trying to prove he was right and sell America the New Isolationism." The problem for Republicans who supported bipartisanship was to find a man to beat Taft. After two defeats, Dewey had neither the interest nor the appeal; Stassen and Warren lacked broad national support. The only exciting alternative individual was General Dwight D. Eisenhower, who had successfully resisted Democratic overtures in 1948 and had always insisted that he had no presidential ambitions. [10]

The Democrats were also interested in Eisenhower. Early in 1951, Harry Truman decided privately not to stand for reelection, and after failing to persuade his old friend Fred Vinson to run, he approached Ike when the General returned to Washington for consultations in November 1951. Arthur Krock learned of this conversation from Justice William O. Douglas; though both Truman and Eisenhower vehemently denied it, Krock went ahead and published the story, saying that Ike had turned down the offer because he opposed the Democrats' domestic policy.[11]

The Krock report acted as a catalyst for a movement among eastern Republicans to draft Eisenhower for the GOP nomination. Massachusetts Senator Henry Cabot Lodge had first approached the General in the summer of 1950, while he was still president of Columbia, and though Ike refused to commit himself, Lodge felt he was receptive. Lodge and Governor Thomas Dewey began to support Eisenhower publicly in the fall of 1950, and they were joined by prominent members of the New York banking and legal establishment, who saw in Ike the one candidate who could uphold the bipartisan containment policy against Taft's attack. Lodge traveled to Eisenhower's headquarters in Paris in September 1951 and tried to convince the General that he was the only internationalist who could win in 1952. Ike remained noncommittal, but Lodge went away believing that the General was beginning to weaken. Lodge began working for Ike's nomination with a small Washington group including Senators Frank Carlson of Kansas, Irving Ives of New York, James Duff of Pennsylvania, and Governor Dewey and his chief political adviser, Herbert Brownell. General Lucius Clay, wartime associate of Ike and now a partner in a Wall Street investment firm, met with the group in November and agreed to serve as go-between for the politicians. On November 11, they chose Lodge as the informal campaign manager; all that remained was to secure Ike's formal consent to accept the nomination if it were offered him.[12]

Legend has it that Ike was a reluctant candidate in 1952.

Certainly he had the air of a man who preferred not to run and who would do nothing in his own behalf; yet that is precisely how most Americans want their prospective presidents to act. Murray Kempton has written that Ike's greatest gift was his ability to disguise his intentions. Kempton compared him to Edward Lear's "Quangle Wangle" who hid his face behind a beaver hat. "Innocence was Eisenhower's beaver hat," Kempton wrote, adding that he used an impish grin and an unbelievably confusing syntax to hide his shrewd intelligence and lofty ambitions. Robert Murphy, who worked with Ike all through the war, recalled what Patton said, after Eisenhower removed him from his command for slapping a soldier: "Ike wants to be President so much you can taste it." Cyrus Sulzberger, the *New York Times* foreign correspondent, came to know Ike quite well in Paris by becoming one of his regular bridge partners. Though Ike told him he would never "work" to get the presidency, by September 1951 Sulzberger was writing in his diary, "I have an increasing feeling that the general definitely wants to be elected President on a Republican ticket. I cannot prove this, but I know him well enough to feel my instinct is correct." [13]

In his memoirs, Ike claims it was the pull of duty, and above all his belief that Taft would sabotage the containment policy, which finally caused him to run. In the spring of 1951, when he was back in Washington to respond to isolationist attacks on American troops in Europe, Ike held a secret meeting with Senator Taft in his Pentagon office. He had prepared a statement renouncing all intention of running in 1952 and he planned to release it if the senator would simply agree to support the idea of collective security in Europe. When Taft refused, Ike tore up the statement and left the future open. The men seeking to draft Ike played up their fear that Taft would reverse the bipartisan foreign policy, and evidently they influenced the General with this argument. While Ike still refused to commit himself fully, in late 1951 he led Lucius Clay to believe that if they went ahead, he would not disown them. In a letter to Clay on December 21, Eisenhower asked him to serve as an "intermediary" with the professional politicians and then added, "As you know, I think that the effort to produce collective security must succeed—otherwise, I see nothing but a bleak future for our country." A few days earlier, he had told Sulzberger that Taft lacked any comprehension of world issues and that if the Republicans could not find someone else to oppose the Ohio senator, he would accept a genuine draft. But, Ike added sternly, he would make no move himself.[14]

Lodge decided it was time to act. The filing deadline was approaching for the New Hampshire primary and unless Ike was on the ballot, Taft could claim an easy victory. On Sunday, January 5, Lodge called a press conference at the Shoreham Hotel in Washington to disclose that Eisenhower was a Republican and to announce that he had written to Governor Sherman Adams to have Ike's name entered in New Hampshire. "I have assured Governor Adams that General Eisenhower is in to the finish," Lodge added confidently. Skeptical reporters approached Ike the next day in Paris, and after a brief pause he confirmed Lodge's statement that he was a Republican and said he had agreed to be a candidate in New Hampshire. But he insisted that he would not campaign actively for the presidency, telling reporters, "I shall continue to devote my full attention and energies to the performance of the vital task to which I am assigned." [15]

The press greeted Ike's hesitant entry into politics with warm applause. The *New York Times* led the rush of editorial support for his candidacy, and even such liberal journals as the *New Republic* and the *Nation* backed the draft-Ike movement, though they warned against stampeding for him until he gave his views on all outstanding issues. "The General should be asked to resign his command immediately, return home, and start answering questions," suggested Freda Kirchwey. His friends agreed, and throughout January and February they bombarded him with requests to campaign actively for the GOP nomination. They warned him that Taft had a big head start, that his own absence was taken as a sign of reluctance to run, and that Republican professionals, remembering unhappy experiences with Willkie, still had to be converted. "There is a growing feeling," wrote Paul Hoffman, president of the Ford Foundation and former administrator of the Marshall Plan, "that failure on your part to participate personally in the campaign may put your nomination in jeopardy." William Robinson and Clifford Roberts, two of Ike's wealthy golf partners, finally proposed that he accept an invitation to dedicate a war memorial in Abilene, Kansas, his boyhood home, as a means of appearing before the voters in person.[16]

"This spring doesn't seem to bring me any reason for getting up and dancing around the Maypole," Ike confided to Hoffman. "I am constantly hounded, advised, counselled, and sometimes just scolded." Although Eisenhower continued to insist that he had to give his NATO duties priority, he began to weaken. In mid-February, Clay met with him in London, where both men were attending the funeral of King George VI. Armed with letters from Robinson and Roberts, Clay again put the case for an early return, and this time Ike finally relented. He told Clay he would come back to dedicate the Abilene memorial and to campaign in person, but he was vague on the timing—disappointing Clay, who wanted him to return before the Republican convention in July.[17]

In New Hampshire, Ike's supporters went all-out to defeat Taft, who spent several weeks campaigning in person, trying to exploit a Gallup poll which showed him narrowly ahead of Ike among Republican voters in the nation—34 percent to 33 percent. Governor Sherman Adams and senators Lodge and Duff joined with television celebrity Tex McCrary and band leader Fred Waring in campaigning for Ike. Thanks to their efforts, Eisenhower won a solid victory, defeating Taft by more than 10,000 votes out of 80,000 cast, and winning all fourteen delegates. "Eisenhower now seems to be leading the Republican race for the first time since November," commented *Time*. Two weeks later, a last-minute write-in campaign by his supporters in Minnesota gained him 106,946 votes, almost as many as Harold Stassen, the only candidate on the ballot, and five times the number of write-ins that Taft received. The Ohio senator, shocked by Ike's sudden show of strength, withdrew his name from the New Jersey primary and concentrated his efforts on the Midwest, where his foreign policy views had the greatest support.[18]

Eisenhower found his showing in the primaries very encouraging. After New Hampshire, Clay flew to Paris and found Ike "visibly eager" to win the nomination; on March 20, the General told Cyrus Sulzberger that he had decided to return to the United States in late May or early June. Eisenhower gave Lodge the good news in early April, and the Massachusetts senator responded by overhauling the draft-Eisenhower organization. Walter Williams, a Seattle businessman, headed a new body called Citizens for Eisenhower; he was assisted by Paul Hoffman, who took a leave from the presidency of the Ford Foundation to give full time to the campaign. Lodge continued as campaign manager, working within the Republican party with Herbert Brownell to secure delegate support in those states without primaries, while Lucius Clay continued to coordinate the movement and keep in close touch with Eisenhower himself. Citizens for Eisenhower would underwrite all the campaign costs and Clifford Roberts offered to pay Ike's personal expenses when he resigned from the Army to seek the nomination. Ike accepted gratefully, telling Roberts, "The only thing I insist upon is that anything done for me be completely legal and ethical." [19]

On April 11, General Eisenhower told a crowded press

conference at his headquarters in Paris that President Truman had approved his request to be relieved of his NATO command and to be placed on inactive status without pay, effective June 1. He would return to the United States in early June to seek the GOP nomination in person, he declared, and if he was successful, he would then resign his army commission. Taft was one of the first to hail Ike's announcement, saying that he was delighted that the General would now be able to speak out and give his views on the many issues confronting the nation. The Ohio senator proved he was still a formidable challenger by defeating both Earl Warren and Harold Stassen in the Wisconsin primary. In Nebraska, Taft won a write-in victory over Ike, 76,556 to 61,592, and in Illinois he secured nearly a million votes against 135,000 write-ins for Ike.[20]

By May, the Republican contest had settled down into a close two-man race between Taft and Eisenhower. Ike won a major victory in Massachusetts, beating the senator by more than 150,000 votes to demonstrate his popularity in the East, and later in the month the General easily defeated Warren in the Oregon primary. The Gallup poll showed Eisenhower moving ahead of Taft, 37 percent to 34 percent, and *Newsweek*'s board of experts predicted, by a vote of 35 to 11, that Ike would win the Republican nomination. But Taft still controlled more than 500 delegates to the convention and could appeal powerfully to rank-and-file Republicans who resented the tight hold that eastern internationalists had maintained on the party in the past. As Ike's advisers had foreseen, it would take all his charm and a major personal effort to overcome Taft's determined opposition.[21]

III

In contrast to the sharply drawn contest for the GOP nomination, the Democrats engaged in a free-for-all marked by confusion, uncertainty, and near-chaos. President Truman tried to control the situation, but all his efforts failed. Rebuffed by Vinson and Eisenhower in 1951, he settled on Governor Adlai E. Stevenson of Illinois as the best-qualified Democratic candidate in 1952. In January, the President invited Stevenson, whose name had already been frequently mentioned as a presidential possibility, to meet secretly with him at Blair House, where Truman was living while the White House underwent major repairs. To Truman's great surprise, Stevenson declined his offer of support for the Democratic nomination, telling the President that he was already committed to run for a second term as governor of Illinois. Privately, Stevenson told George Ball that he refused because he did not want to be Harry Truman's candidate. "If I do have to run," Stevenson said, "I must run on my own, with no one telling me what to do or say." In early March, Truman tried once more to persuade Stevenson, but again the governor politely turned him down.[22]

The President was now on the spot. Estes Kefauver, the Tennessee senator who had won national fame for his crime probe and then criticized the administration for corruption, had entered the New Hampshire primary and was certain to win unless Truman opposed him. The President's supporters in New Hampshire placed his name on the ballot, but on January 31 Truman ordered it taken off, telling reporters, "All these primaries are just eyewash." The public outcry at this disparaging remark led the President to reconsider, and on February 5 he announced that he would permit his candidacy to stand but would not campaign actively for delegates in New Hampshire. Despite a strenuous Kefauver effort, political experts predicted a sweeping Truman victory in the state as administration supporters campaigned for him. But the Tennessee senator pulled off a major upset, defeating the President narrowly in the popular vote and gaining all twelve delegates. Two weeks later, Truman startled a Jefferson-Jackson Day Dinner in Washington by announcing, "I shall not be a candidate for reelection." As cries of "Oh, my God!" and "Oh, no!" went up from the audience, the President continued, "I shall not accept a renomination. I do not feel that it is my duty to spend another four years in the White House." [23]

Estes Kefauver was the immediate beneficiary of Truman's announcement. A tall, long-faced man, Kefauver had developed the reputation of being a loner in his six years in the House and four years in the Senate. Kefauver had alienated the Democratic leadership with his investigation of crime, revealing participation of such party leaders as Mayor William O'Dwyer of New York City and Senator Scott Lucas of Illinois in underworld activities. Slow and humorless in manner, and apparently incapable of forming close personal relationships, Kefauver was a poor speaker who read his speeches, as one newsman commented, "with all the gusto of one who is seeing the text for the first time." Yet his sincerity and genuine concern for the welfare of the individual led people to identify with him easily. He developed a highly personal campaign style, walking up and down the streets of communities shaking each person's hand slowly as he stared into his eyes. His attractive wife, Nancy, always accompanied him on these hand-shaking trips, and her beauty and charm helped offset his rural awkwardness. To the amazement of professional politicians, Kefauver's person-to-person techniques caught on with the party's rank-and-file, and people came away impressed with his dedication and commitment. Shrewd observers also noted the deep sense of self-righteousness and the flaming ambition that burned deep behind his impassive exterior.

Though the Tennessee senator had antagonized the President by charging the administration with corruption, he stood squarely within the party's mainstream. A liberal on economic issues, he had supported nearly all of Harry Truman's Fair Deal measures, and in the process had cut himself off from fellow southerners who resented his support for civil rights legislation. Kefauver was equally orthodox on foreign policy, voting consistently for the containment policies, foreign aid, and Truman's stand in Korea. He enthusiastically supported the Atlantic Union movement to achieve greater political unity among the NATO allies, and during the spring primaries he briefly departed from the administration's position by advocating limited bombing of Chinese bases in Manchuria as a way to break the stalemated peace negotiations on Korea. But his appeal was primarily based on domestic issues, not foreign policy; he stood forth as the man who could clean up the mess in Washington yet continue Truman's policies at home and abroad.[24]

Kefauver swept through the spring primaries against only token opposition from pro-administration candidates. His only defeat came in Florida, where Georgia Senator Richard Russell beat him narrowly by appealing to segregationist sentiment. By the end of May, Kefauver had won ten of eleven primaries and had received more than two of the three million votes cast. Liberals, who at first had regarded him as "a TV clown, a handshaker, a headline hunter" now began to see him as a courageous challenger, and many began to support him after Illinois Senator Paul Douglas proclaimed, "I am in Kefauver's army. I'm enlisted for the duration." Gael Sullivan, former acting chairman of the Democratic National Committee, became his campaign manager and gave the Kefauver movement the professional air it needed. The candidate himself remained aloof and enigmatic, but his coonskin cap, symbolic of his refusal to be Boss Crump's pet coon, became a familiar sight throughout the country, and his air of mystery intrigued voters who were ready for a change in 1952.[25]

Political observers still felt that Adlai Stevenson remained the most likely Democratic nominee. A group of his Illinois supporters, led by University of Chicago historian Walter Johnson, began a concerted movement for his candidacy in February, and, after Truman withdrew, they grew optimistic. Stevenson dimmed their hopes, however, when he announced in mid-April that he was running for governor of Illinois and thus "could not accept the nomination for any other office this summer." Johnson and his committee refused to give up, but Truman and most party leaders began to look for other alternatives.[26]

Stevenson's credentials for the presidency were impressive. As a Princeton-educated Chicago lawyer, he had entered government service with Frank Knox in 1941, serving as special assistant to the Secretary of the Navy until Knox's death in 1944. Then he had moved to the State Department, playing a key role as an adviser at the San Francisco Conference that created the United Nations and later serving as adviser and alternate delegate to the General Assembly. In his first try at elective office, he won the governorship of Illinois in 1948 by an amazing 572,067-vote margin. Urbane and sophisticated, in contrast to Kefauver's country-boy manner, Stevenson possessed a delightful sense of humor, a mellow speaking voice, and a deep sense of public service. He had an intellectual's distaste for simplistic solutions, and his tendency to see the complexity of problems facing the nation reinforced his natural caution. As a result, he often created the impression of indecision and, at times, of weakness.

Stevenson stood slightly to the right of Kefauver and Truman on domestic issues, being more concerned with efficiency in government than with righting the wrongs in American society. But his great passion was foreign policy. He was an ardent Cold Warrior who believed that "the Soviet objective is one world—one Communist world." He shared the prevailing belief in Soviet duplicity, and he was convinced that containment was the only way to protect American security. Above all, he believed in collective security, and he defended the Korean War as "a historic achievement" in checking aggression. If Truman had not fought, "Munich would follow Munich" and the result would be "to surrender all positions of strength, to enfeeble the grand alliance of the free." Deeply resentful of

Taft's attacks, Stevenson wrote, "To call Korea 'Truman's war' distorts the entire historical significance of our prompt response through the United Nations to the cynical challenge to the whole concept of collective peace and security." [27] Stevenson was genuinely torn in 1952. He disliked Truman and the corruption of his administration, but like Eisenhower he feared that Taft would lead the nation back into isolationism. He was reluctant to run, yet he recognized the call of duty. Many party leaders, watching him speak extensively across the nation while disclaiming his candidacy, concluded that he simply wanted to be drafted so that he could run independent of Truman and not be saddled with defense of the administration's mistakes. George Ball believed that he was prepared to run only against Taft, since Stevenson told him that he thought Ike "might not make a bad President." His closest friends were not sure of his inner feelings, and all the evidence indicates that, unlike Eisenhower, Stevenson was a truly reluctant candidate. "I have felt strangely isolated of late—what with so many persistent pressures in directions that are distasteful," he wrote to Eric Sevareid in June. "I hope I can find the way to do the right thing. I had hoped that circumstances and the pre-convention contest would have resolved the problem long since," Stevenson lamented. [28]

As the time approached for the convention, the situation became even more confused. With Truman's encouragement, Averell Harriman, the long-time diplomat and public servant, announced his candidacy. Despite his big-business background, Harriman took a strongly liberal position on domestic issues in a bid for labor support. He was an even more ardent Cold Warrior than Stevenson, but his lack of political experience and his inept campaign style kept him from developing popular appeal beyond his own New York delegation. Richard Russell commanded the support of the South, but his racial views made him a regional candidate who planned to use his strength to block a nominee hostile to the South. A deadlocked convention loomed, with Kefauver, Harriman, and Russell controlling about 300 delegates apiece, far short of the 616 needed to win. It seemed likely that the party would be forced to choose one of the dark horses, such as Vice-President Alben Barkley or Oklahoma Senator Robert Kerr, and face nearly certain defeat in the fall—unless Stevenson's supporters could mount a successful draft for their reluctant candidate.[29]

IV

In the spring of 1952, John Foster Dulles emerged as a key figure in the increasingly bitter contest between Senator Taft and General Eisenhower. After the 1948 election, Governor Dewey had appointed Dulles to the Senate to fill a vacancy and he had served until the fall of 1949, when Herbert Lehman defeated him in a special election to fill out the term. In March, Secretary of State Dean Acheson persuaded Truman to appoint Dulles as a State Department consultant, and Acheson then commissioned Dulles to negotiate a final peace settlement with Japan. Dulles carried out this delicate assignment with great skill while the Korean War raged, earning Acheson's and Truman's favor by keeping the Japanese negotiations out of politics. The United States and Japan signed the peace treaty in September 1951, and after the Senate ratified it, in March 1952, Dulles resigned from the State Department. For the first time in two years, he was free to speak out publicly on foreign policy.

"I look forward to the possibility of expressing my views about foreign policy under conditions which will not risk embarrassment either to the administration or to any presidential candidate," Dulles announced upon reentering private life. He went on to reaffirm his commitment to bipartisanship, saying that "accord on basic foreign policy issues" was "necessary to save our nation from mortal danger." He kept silent about his presidential preferences, giving the Taft forces reason to believe he might back the Ohio senator despite his close ties with Dewey, who was pushing hard for Eisenhower. Influenced by a desire to be on the winning side so that he could fulfill his lifelong ambition to be Secretary of State, Dulles moved cautiously to keep foreign policy out of the preconvention contest. Beyond that, he searched for common ground on which all Republicans could unite.[30]

During the spring, Dulles came forward with two major foreign policy suggestions for the Republicans to pursue in the coming election—massive retaliation and liberation. Both reflected his disenchantment with the Truman administration's emphasis on military containment, and both were elaborations of ideas Taft had presented in his book, *A Foreign Policy for America*. Massive retaliation was a logical outgrowth of Taft's argument that the United States should rely upon its superior air and naval power to balance off huge Communist ground forces. When Russia or China committed an act of aggression, Dulles argued, the United States should respond "with *weapons* of its choosing against *targets* of its choosing at *times* of its choosing." Such a strategy clearly relied on the threat of atomic attack, but Dulles never specifically mentioned nuclear weapons, preferring to talk about "community punishing force" and "deterrent power." Massive retaliation, he contended, would prevent the free world from becoming a victim of the "twin evils of militarism and bankruptcy" by ending the need for local defense forces all around the Communist perimeter. The certainty of a prompt American response would act as a deterrent. "If a potential aggressor knew in advance that his aggression would bring that answer," he claimed, "then I am convinced that he would not commit aggression." [31]

Dulles' second proposal was more radical. Critical of the passive, defensive nature of containment, he wanted the United States to take the moral and spiritual offensive in the

Cold War by challenging Soviet domination of Eastern Europe. Dulles first outlined liberation in 1950, when he suggested in his book *War or Peace* that America should devise ways "to carry hope and truth and the prospect of liberty to the peoples who are the prisoners of Soviet Communism." Like Taft, he felt that the United States should rekindle hope among the captive peoples by making it *"publicly known that it wants and expects liberation to occur,"* but he stressed the need to pursue peaceful means so as to avoid "a series of bloody uprisings and reprisals." He advocated measures to encourage people to escape from the Iron Curtain, extensive radio propaganda beamed at Eastern Europe, and the proclamation with our allies of "a great new Declaration of Independence" for the Soviet satellites. He warned that liberation might take a decade to occur, but that in the long run the ideas of freedom and democracy would wear down Soviet despotism. Above all, such a program "would recommit our nation to the universal cause of human liberty and just government." Calling upon Americans to bring out the best in their heritage, Dulles asserted, "We have always been, as we always should be, the despair of the oppressor and the hope of the oppressed." [32]

Dulles presented his views in a series of speeches and a widely publicized article in *Life* that appeared in mid-May. Emmet John Hughes, the editor *Life* assigned to work with Dulles, tried to sharpen Dulles' vague prose, especially on the crucial issue of liberation. "We would chase this proposition around and around and around," Hughes commented, "but it never acquired substance beyond his affirming the desirability of it." Yet however imprecise, liberation had great political appeal, offering as it did the illusion of success in the Cold War without sacrifice or strain. Its greatest advantage was in offering Republicans a unifying slogan that effectively disguised the differences between isolationists and internationalists. [33]

Lucius Clay read an early draft of Dulles' *Life* article, and was so impressed that he sent a copy to Eisenhower in Paris. Ike, who had met Dulles casually while serving as president of Columbia University but had never known him well, wrote to Dulles in early April to tell him that he "was as deeply impressed as ever with the directness and simplicity of your approach to such complex problems." Liberation apparently met with Ike's approval, but he objected to massive retaliation, asking what steps Dulles would advocate in case of indirect Soviet political aggression, citing Czechoslovakia as an example. Despite this reservation, Ike asked Clay to arrange for Dulles to fly to Paris so that the two men could have a full exchange of their foreign policy views.[34]

On May 3, Dulles met with Eisenhower for three hours, and two days later, after Dulles delivered a speech to the French National Political Science Institute, they conferred again. The two men hit it off well, according to Eisenhower, who quizzed Dulles closely on his commitment to collective security. Dulles thought Ike tended to neglect Asia in his concern for European security, but on the whole he found the General's views "satisfactory." At the end of their first conversation, Dulles told Ike that he planned to support him for the nomination, but said he would delay any public announcement until he had a chance to explain his position to Taft.[35]

A week after Dulles returned from Paris, Senator Taft approached him with an unusual request. Aware that Dulles was moving into the Eisenhower camp, Taft expressed his admiration for Dulles' recent foreign policy pronouncements and said he hoped very much to avoid a fight over foreign policy that would split the GOP. When Dulles said he had already decided to support Ike, Taft asked him to delay any public announcement and to prepare a draft foreign policy plank embodying the ideas he had presented in *Life*. Taft said he would be willing to back Dulles' draft and do everything possible to have it accepted by the convention. After conferring with Dewey, Brownell, and Clay, Dulles accepted this assignment with some misgivings. "I am not sure that I can succeed in this mission," he wrote Eisenhower, "even though Taft initially sponsors it. He may not be able to control his followers and it may be merely, or partly, a ruse to keep me tied up for the time being."

Ike had no objections, and on June 1 the Republican National Committee announced that Dulles would serve as the chief foreign policy adviser to the platform committee. It was a shrewd move by Taft, who wanted desperately to escape the isolationist label his opponents kept pinning on him. Recognizing how close Dulles' views were to his own, the Ohio senator hoped to blunt the internationalists' argument that Eisenhower was the only GOP candidate who could continue the policy of containment. For Dulles, it was an opportunity to preserve unity within the party and commit the Republicans to his new doctrine of liberation as a substitute for Vandenberg's outmoded bipartisanship.[36]

V

"Soon I shall be coming home and I really dread—for the first time in my life—the prospect of coming back to my own country," Eisenhower wrote on May 19 to Clifford Roberts, who had made the arrangements for Ike to launch his quest for the nomination in Abilene, Kansas. After a brief stop in Washington, where he reported on the status of NATO to Truman, Eisenhower arrived in Abilene on June 4. In the morning, he gave a brief and moving extemporaneous speech as he laid the cornerstone of a museum planned in his honor, and then prepared for a major address to be broadcast nationally on radio and television. Heavy rains kept the crowd far below the 50,000 the sponsors expected, but Ike gamely went ahead with his outdoor speech when the downpour slackened. Reading ponderously from a text prepared in Paris, Eisenhower disappointed not only his drenched listeners but the millions more around the country who had looked forward so eagerly to his first political effort. In trite, almost banal phrases, he stated his opposition to bureaucracy, high taxes, and inflation as he concentrated on domestic issues. He never mentioned Taft's name, and his only references to foreign policy came in brief attacks on Yalta and the loss of China. The hostile Chicago *Tribune* dismissed it as "five-star generalities," and the *New Republic*'s TRB called it "devout, platitudinous and dull," concluding, "It probably lost him a million votes." [37]

The next morning, Eisenhower proved far more effective when he moved on to the stage of the Plaza movie theater in Abilene for his first political news conference. Carefully coached by press secretary James Hagerty, Ike fielded the questions with ease and confidence, displaying an ability, which he raised to a high art, to answer at length without clarifying the issues. Reporters were surprised at how conservative he appeared to be on domestic matters, even to the right of Taft on some points. On foreign policy, he stated his views cautiously, upholding the containment policy in Europe and refusing to blame the Democrats for the loss of China. Most significantly, he defended the Truman administration's refusal to widen the conflict in Korea and its attempt to seek an armistice through negotiation. "I do not believe that in the present situation," he stated forthrightly, "there is any clear-cut answer to bringing the Korean War to a successful conclusion." [38]

From Abilene, Eisenhower went to New York, where he began a series of meetings with state delegations to the forthcoming GOP convention. Much more impressive in small groups than on the platform, Ike used his charm to woo undecided delegates. He avoided formal speeches; in a nationally broadcast appearance in Detroit, he discarded a prepared text and instead answered what he called the questions most often asked him in private. He delighted his audience, when asked why he did not object at the time to the decisions reached at Teheran, Yalta, and Potsdam, by answering, "Well, some of you men out there were second lieutenants. Did they ask you?" Then in mid-June he retired to Denver to rest up for the convention, pleased at the warm reception given him by a crowd of 100,000 but troubled by the refusal of many Republicans to greet him with open arms.[39]

The experts gave Ike barely passing marks for his first venture into politics. "General Eisenhower's most vivid characteristic is his transparent sincerity and honesty," commented James Reston, while Edwin Lahey praised him for his "infinite wholesomeness." He had done a good job of discarding his military background and appealing to the people on a simple, down-to-earth basis. But he also displayed a very thin skin, bridling quickly at hostile questions and acting hurt whenever he felt the slightest criticism. He wanted to be liked by everyone, and he seemed puzzled at the failure of the people to rally enthusiastically upon his return home and grant him the nomination without further ado. Though he continued to lead Taft in the Gallup poll, 43 percent to 36 percent, he lost the South Dakota primary, the last before the convention, by a small margin, and *Newsweek*'s political experts gave Taft a slight edge in the upcoming convention. Ike, ready to accept the nomination from a grateful and admiring public, now found himself immersed in a no-holds-barred political fight.[40]

Taft greeted Eisenhower's belated entry into the political arena with a blistering foreign policy speech on June 1, the day the General arrived back in the United States. Accusing the Democrats of pursuing "disastrous" policies at Yalta and Potsdam, Taft condemned bipartisanship and insisted that the Republicans would have to make foreign policy a major campaign issue. In an obvious reference to Eisenhower, Taft commented, "We cannot afford to nominate a candidate who will not condemn the utter failure of Mr. Truman's administration." Then he proceeded to elaborate on the themes of massive retaliation and liberation. Reiterating his belief in security through air power rather than ground forces, Taft called for "the building of an Air Force sufficiently large to control the air over this country, over the oceans which surround this continent, and able to deliver atom bombs on Russian cities and manufacturing plants." At the same time, he rejected containment and proposed instead a "crusade against totalitarianism" in order to win "the battle against Communism in the minds of men." Citing Dulles' *Life* article several times, Taft deliberately sought to throw off the isolationist label and identify himself with the leading Republican Cold Warrior.[41]

Throughout the month of June, Taft virtually ignored domestic issues as he presented himself to the Republican voters as the only man who could challenge the Democrats on foreign policy. He played down his former opposition to stationing troops in Europe, saying that he accepted this commitment, and instead accused Ike of ignoring the Communist danger in Asia and especially the Korean War. "I would think that he has shown no indication of criticizing in any way the policy which has involved us in what I think is an unnecessary war," Taft told a New York City press conference. Claiming that Ike was portraying him as "a straw man in the form of an isolationist," Taft told a Pennsylvania audience, "I had been hoping that he would develop a policy of attacking Democrats." Repeatedly, Taft accused General Marshall of cutting off aid to Chiang Kai-shek, and Dean Acheson of inviting the Reds to invade South Korea; then he demanded that Eisenhower join him in condemning "the people who built up the Russian threat." "We can't soft pedal foreign policy," Taft argued in asking people to reject Ike. "We can't fail to point out the tremendously disastrous result of the policy of the last five years which has lost the peace after we won the war." [42]

The men around Eisenhower, realizing that Taft was trying to play down the differences between the contenders, urged the General to direct his fire at Taft, not at the Truman administration. In a supposedly off-the-record luncheon with newsmen on June 23, Ike tried to avoid mentioning Taft, but when reporters kept asking why he was in the race, he burst out, "All right, I'll tell you why I'm running for the Presidency. I'm running because Taft is an isolationist. His election would be a disaster." Later that day, the General toned down his remarks in a nationally broadcast speech, saying simply that he was running "because I believe that peace may well be at stake." He struck out hard at massive retaliation, calling air-power advocates "false prophets" who were preaching a new form of isolationism. Though he never mentioned Taft by name, it was clear he had his opponent in mind when he warned that there was "no easy way to peace" and said that those who believed that the United States could meet the Communist threat by itself were taking "an unjustified gamble with peace." [43]

John Foster Dulles, caught in this crossfire, continued to do all he could to reconcile the foreign policy conflict between Taft and Eisenhower. Working with the GOP Resolutions Committee, he wrote to Ike on June 17 to report "that we can probably get an acceptable foreign policy plank without an open fight." Ike's advisers, who were banking on a major showdown with the Taft forces on foreign policy, so as to win over uncommitted delegates, found this optimism disturbing. On June 21, Arthur Vandenberg, Jr., serving as an aide to Lodge, informed Dulles that the General was sending him a letter, which was to be made public, calling for a strongly internationalist platform plank. When Dulles replied that he thought there would be no difficulty in achieving that goal, Vandenberg carefully explained to him that "the General's political advisers thought it useful to keep this issue alive." Eisenhower's letter to Dulles, which was made public on June 24, stressed the importance of a platform plank calling for "positive, forward looking action and leadership in the promotion of collective security" and not one just giving "lip service or begrudging approval." "We must face facts," Ike concluded, "which means that any thought of 'retiring within our own borders' will certainly lead to disaster for the U.S.A." Dulles, finally getting the point, threw away a draft reply, saying, "I do not think that the forthcoming Republican platform will compromise such views," and instead made public a one-sentence letter to Eisenhower: "It is most helpful to me, as adviser to the Resolutions Committee, to have this expression of your views." [44]

Only once did Eisenhower come out and join Taft in an attack upon the Democrats. In a radio address to American youth on June 26, the General blamed the loss of China, the division of Germany, and the outbreak of the Korean War on the Truman administration. The Democrats had been "too ready for too long to trust a godless dictatorship," Ike maintained. But the rest of the time, he continued to warn against Taft's isolationism, and his supporters went even further in trying to exploit the Cold War attitudes of most Americans. Paul Hoffman declared that Eisenhower was "the last man Stalin wants to see elected President of the United States," while Clare Booth Luce claimed that the defeat of Ike "would give Stalin the only real political victory he has had in Europe." Internationalist editorial writers agreed; such widely different journals as the *New York Times* and the *New Republic* called upon the Republican party to ignore Taft's "last-minute promises" and select Eisenhower, who had supported Truman's containment policy in Europe without being identified with the President's failures in Asia. [45]

VI

As the convention approached, the ground swell that many had expected to develop when Ike returned to the United States failed to take place. Instead, Taft continued to lead in pledged delegates, 464 to 392, and though the Eisenhower forces hoped to pick up second-round support from backers of

Stassen and Warren, Taft had firm control of the all-important convention machinery. Ike's only advantage lay in the public opinion polls, which showed that he could easily defeat any Democratic candidate, while Taft trailed both Stevenson and Kefauver in trial heats. Raising the specter of isolationism had not stampeded Republicans into the Eisenhower camp; Taft remained the favorite of the party faithful, who ignored the argument that only the popular General could appeal to the independents and Democrats needed for a GOP victory in the fall. Eisenhower, who had planned to wait in Denver for the news of victory from Chicago, finally agreed to attend the convention and join personally in the last-minute search for delegates.[46]

The mood of the Republicans in Chicago as the convention opened was highly nationalistic. Taft's supporters used their control of the machinery to invite General Douglas MacArthur and former President Herbert Hoover, "the two most distinguished residents of the Waldorf Towers," who represented the "dinosaur wing" of the party according to one Ike-backer, to address the gathering. In his keynote speech, MacArthur blasted the Democrats for their failures at Teheran, Yalta, and Potsdam, calling them "those reckless men who, yielding to international intrigue, set the stage for Soviet ascendancy as a world power and our own relative decline." The Republicans gave him a seven-minute ovation, and they went all-out the next night when Hoover spent more than an hour indicting the Democrats for their Cold War mistakes. Seventy-one times the delirious delegates interrupted the aging Hoover as he reiterated his own concept of an American Gibraltar as a substitute for containment, which he claimed could lead only "to the bankruptcy which is Stalin's greatest hope." Repeating the arguments of Dulles and Taft, he advocated massive retaliation by saying, "The sure defense of London, New York, and Paris is the fear of counterattack on Moscow from the air." The most dramatic manifestation of the rank-and-file resentment over eastern domination of the party came on the third day, when Senator Everett McKinley Dirksen of Illinois, a staunch Taft supporter, pointed his limp finger at Thomas Dewey in the New York delegation and charged, "We followed you before and you took us down the road to defeat," as boos welled up from the approving audience.[47]

The Republican platform reflected the intensely partisan feelings that prevailed at the convention. Dulles wrote the original draft and submitted it to Colorado Senator Eugene Millikin, head of the Resolutions Committee, who urged him to strengthen its vague and idealistic language. Though Dulles began with a brief description of postwar Soviet expansion, he made no effort to blame it on the Democrats. Instead he focused on support for NATO and the UN and set forth his liberation policy as a Republican alternative to containment. After his arrival in Chicago on July 1, Dulles began toughening up the opening section under prodding from Millikin. The Resolutions Committee finally rewrote the Dulles draft, keeping the commitment to collective security and the proposals for liberation, but adding a stinging indictment of the Truman administration. With considerable reluctance, Eisenhower joined with Taft in approving the plank before the convention opened.[48]

The platform statement on foreign policy began by charging that the Democrats had "squandered the unprecedented power and prestige which were ours at the close of World War II." It accused Truman of abandoning Poland, Lithuania, Estonia, Latvia, Czechoslovakia, and finally China to Communist rule. "Teheran, Yalta, and Potsdam were the scenes of those tragic blunders with others to follow," the platform declared. Asserting that the Korean conflict could have been avoided "with foresight," the Republicans accused the Democrats of waging war with "no hope of victory," but they offered no positive alternatives. The most striking part of the platform was the promise to "repudiate all commitments contained in secret understandings such as those of Yalta which aid Communist enslavement" and the pledge to achieve "the genuine independence of those captive peoples." In language far broader than any Dulles had suggested, the platform condemned "the negative, futile and immoral policy of 'containment' which abandons countless human beings to a despotism and godless terrorism," and proposed instead to "revive the contagious, liberating influences which are inherent in freedom" in order to "set up strains and stresses within the captive world which will make the rulers impotent to continue in their monstrous ways." Nowhere did the platform say how this magical liberation was to take place, and in the following section the party recorded its continued support for "regional security treaties," the heart of containment.[49]

Most commentators accepted the denunciation of the Democrats as the price Dulles had to pay in order to commit the party to an internationalist platform. Eisenhower himself said privately that the platform was "a bit savage," but he liked the section on collective security; Anne O'Hare McCormick noted that "in some respects, indeed, it seems to advocate more intervention than the sharply scored policy of the Democrats." The *New Republic* took a more hostile view, seeing the platform as "a rewriting of history which would earn failing marks for an eighth-grade school boy." The editors were particularly critical of liberation. "Promises to help enslaved peoples mean nothing and risk terrible misunderstandings," they wrote, "or they mean something and risk war." [50]

Eisenhower accepted liberation, but he firmly rejected massive retaliation, which some Taft supporters tried to interject into the national security plank. The original draft included a statement affirming "such a retaliatory striking power as to deter sudden attack or promptly and decisively defeat it." Eisenhower saw in this phrase the exclusive reliance on air power which Taft had emphasized and which implied acceptance of Hoover's American Gibraltar strategy. The General informed Dulles that he could never run on such a platform, and Dulles finally prevailed on Senator Millikin to drop the word "retaliatory" in favor of a simple call for "a force in being, as distinguished from paper plans, of such power as to deter sudden attack or promptly and decisively defeat it." [51]

With the platform accepted, the long-awaited showdown between the Eisenhower and Taft forces finally occurred. Ike's advisers had already scored a crucial victory by challenging Taft's control of southern Republican delegations, especially in Texas, where former Democrats had turned out in mass to choose delegates pledged to Ike. Meeting in rump session, the regular Texas Republicans sent a group bound to Taft to Chicago, confident that the old-guard credentials committee would throw out the upstarts. The Eisenhower forces, sensing a moral issue on which they could put Taft on the defensive, insisted that no disputed delegates could vote on the question of seating rival delegations and then, on the third day, succeeded in overturning the report of the credentials committee on the floor of the convention by a vote of 607 to 531. The next day, Ike led Taft at the end of the first roll call and was only nine votes short of the nomination when Minnesota switched from Stassen to give him the victory. Bricker then went to the podium for Taft and asked the convention to make the nomination of Eisenhower unanimous. "My God, I love him," one delegate said of Taft. "It kills me to have to do this to him." [52]

The next day Eisenhower brushed aside his brother Milton's suggestion that he offer Taft the vice-presidency; instead he followed the advice of Lodge, Dewey, and Brownell in selecting Senator Richard M. Nixon, who had won the respect of the old guard for his role in exposing Alger Hiss yet had consistently supported an internationalist foreign policy. Then Ike came before the convention and delivered one of his most forceful and successful public addresses. He gave no specifics on foreign policy, but he set forth a stirring campaign theme when he promised "to lead a great crusade for Freedom in America and Freedom in the World." [53]

Foreign observers, fearful from the MacArthur and Hoover speeches that the United States would turn inward under Republican leadership, breathed a sigh of relief at Ike's nomination. "It is now certain," commented the *Times* of London, "that the broad stream of American leadership in the world will not be diverted or dry up." At home, Ernest Lindley saw Ike's victory as a triumph for collective security and a defeat for "Gibraltarists" and "Asia-firsters." William S. White thought that Taft had lost because his stands on foreign policy "had frightened beyond recall too many." But despite the frantic efforts of Ike's advisers to promote a foreign policy dispute between their candidate and Taft, there is no evidence that international issues influenced the final choice. A majority of the delegates, Richard Rovere noted, favored Taft over Ike. "Preparing to embrace Eisenhower, they poured contempt upon his friends," Rovere wrote; "preparing to repudiate Taft, they embraced him." Eisenhower's selection revealed that realism triumphed over sentiment in the GOP; out of power for twenty years, the delegates discarded the man they most admired to choose a candidate they believed could bring them to victory in November.[54]

VII

When the Democrats assembled in Chicago two weeks later, uncertainty still prevailed. Kefauver led in number of delegates, but the opposition of party leaders, most of all Harry Truman, doomed his chances. Senator Richard Russell commanded a southern bloc and Averell Harriman counted on the powerful New York delegation, yet there was no evidence that either man could win broad national support. Vice-President Alben Barkley's brief candidacy as a dark horse ended on the first day of the convention, after labor leaders vetoed him on grounds of age. Adlai Stevenson remained coy, saying that the only office he sought was governor of Illinois while his friends kept insisting that he would accept a genuine draft. As governor of the host state, he gave the welcoming address, and when he transformed what was usually a perfunctory speech into an eloquent statement of his views, many delegates began to look upon him with new respect. The amateurs running the draft-Stevenson movement began to receive professional help as word spread that Stevenson was Truman's choice. But Stevenson, more reluctant than ever to run now that Ike was the GOP candidate, refused to do anything to advance his own cause.[55]

Foreign affairs played a minor role in the Democratic proceedings. "The outside world has hardly intruded on this meeting," commented Anne O'Hare McCormick, noting that the only platform fight came over civil rights. The foreign policy plank, adopted unanimously by the Resolutions Committee and the full convention, called for "peace with honor," "strong, balanced defense forces for this country—land, sea and air," and "the Wilsonian principle of the right of national self-determination." The platform praised the record of the Truman administration in containing Soviet aggression and claimed a victory for collective security in Korea, asserting, "The Communist aggressor has been hurled back from South Korea." There was even an echo of liberation in a pledge not to "abandon the once-free peoples of Central and Eastern Europe who suffer now under the Kremlin's tyranny in violation of the Soviet Union's most solemn pledges at Teheran, Yalta, and Potsdam," but no call to action beyond expanding the Voice of America broadcasts behind the Iron Curtain.[56]

A strong defensive tone ran through the convention oratory on international issues. Governor Paul Dever of Massachusetts gave a hackneyed keynote speech in which he blamed Cold War losses on "Soviet perfidy," and declared, "The courageous and decisive action taken in Korea may well have halted the outbreak of a third world war." Senator Paul Douglas of Illinois revealed growing Democratic fears that the Republicans would mount an all-out political attack on the Korean War. In an hour-long speech, he pointed out that Republicans shared the responsibility for the war, citing evidence that Eisenhower, as Army Chief of Staff in 1947, had recommended withdrawal of American troops from South Korea and that it was Dulles who advocated this removal in the UN two years later. The war, Douglas then asserted, was not a mistake. If the United States had not fought, "we would have lost all of Asia with its billion people," he argued; ". . . if we had allowed the Communists to take Korea, it would have started an avalanche which in all probability would have quickly imperiled our safety." The next day, in the emotional highlight of the convention, Eleanor Roosevelt took the same position. Greeted with a spontaneous ovation that lasted a full fifteen minutes, she said that American appeasement in Korea "would have led to World War III just as the appeasement of Czechoslovakia led to World War II." Then she quoted a Korean War ace who had told her, "Our men are there so that they will not fight in the streets of their home towns." [57]

The balloting began on the fourth day of the convention, and though Kefauver led for the first two rounds, Stevenson displayed increasing strength despite his personal reticence. Behind the scenes, Stevenson called Truman to ask if it would embarrass the President if he finally became a candidate, and Truman, hiding his irritation at the governor's indecision, persuaded Harriman to drop out of the race so that the New York delegation could break for Stevenson. The Illinois governor was only two and a half votes short of nomination at the end of the third ballot; Kefauver and Russell then withdrew and the delegates nominated Stevenson unanimously. A smiling Truman entered the hall, proclaimed Stevenson "a winner," and announced, to the candidate's dismay, "I am going to take my coat off and do everything I can to help him win." [58]

Stevenson moved quickly to take charge of the Democratic party. In an effort to please the South, he chose Alabama Senator John Sparkman, a liberal on all but the race issue, as his running mate, and then set the theme for his campaign in a moving acceptance speech by promising to "talk sense to the American people." He made no direct reference to foreign policy, but he seemed to have liberation in mind when he asked the Democrats to support "a long, patient, costly struggle which alone can assure triumph over the great enemies of man—war, poverty and tyranny." Liberals, already disenchanted with Eisenhower's concessions to the Republican old guard, were ecstatic over their new spokesman. "WE'RE FOR STEVENSON!" proclaimed the editors of the *New Republic.* "What Eisenhower hoped to be, Stevenson may well become." TRB commented that hard-bitten reporters turned to each other at the end of his speech to ask each other, "Could Stevenson be as good as he sounded?" Even the gamblers were impressed, dropping the odds on a Republican victory from 8 to 5 to even money. "I didn't know what he was saying," one bookmaker explained, "but it sure sounded like Franklin D. Roosevelt all over again." [59]

Others were not so overwhelmed. Secretary of State Dean Acheson, who had worked with Stevenson during the war, dismissed him privately as "a good staff officer but without the stuff of command." Eisenhower withheld any comment, but Richard Nixon told reporters that the Democrats had chosen "some new faces, but the same old deal." The GOP vice-presidential candidate went on to identify Stevenson and Sparkman with Truman and to suggest that foreign policy would be "the big issue of the campaign." "General Eisenhower can offer new leadership in foreign affairs but Governor Stevenson must accept the Administration's foreign policy," Nixon concluded. [60]

More objective observers felt that foreign policy was not likely to loom so large in the fall campaign. Europeans felt that both candidates were likely to carry on containment, and while they knew Ike better, they tended to trust the Democrats on foreign policy. UN observers pointed out Stevenson's contributions to the formation of that international organization and concluded that the election was not likely to affect American diplomacy. McGeorge Bundy summed up the conventional wisdom by arguing in *Foreign Affairs* that Taft had represented the only serious threat to the containment policy; Eisenhower's nomination had insured continuity, since the General firmly opposed any retreat from world responsibilities while Stevenson stood squarely in the internationalist tradition. "Taken together, the differences between the two candidates remain small," Bundy asserted. He knew that the campaign might exaggerate them, he concluded, "but it is fair to hope that the candidates themselves may have the wisdom and courage to accept and even emphasize their basic agreement on what we have called the national imperatives." Ignoring the sharp attacks in the Republican platform and discounting rising public discontent with the Korean War, Bundy failed to anticipate the all-out attack on Truman's foreign policy that Nixon was predicting.[61]

2 3456

The past haunted the Republicans as they prepared for the 1952 campaign. Many party regulars viewed Eisenhower as another Willkie, a political amateur who would become lost and confused in the heat of the presidential race. Others feared above all else a repetition of 1948, when Dewey's failure to attack the Democrats, they felt, cost them certain victory. After the convention, Ike retreated to a fishing camp high in the Rockies, and there he decided to ask Sherman Adams, the governor of New Hampshire, to serve as his "chief-of-staff." Adams would direct the presidential campaign and coordinate the efforts of the GOP National Committee, which would concentrate on Congressional races under Chairman Arthur Summerfield of Michigan, and the Citizens Committee for Eisenhower-Nixon, which would focus on wooing dissident Democrats and independents. Henry Cabot Lodge had to return to Massachusetts to face the challenge of Representative John F. Kennedy for his Senate seat, but the men he had brought into the Eisenhower movement, especially Arthur Vandenberg, Jr., James Hagerty, and Gabriel Hauge, would continue to play vital roles in the campaign. With Sherman Adams—a taciturn, hard-bitten professional—in charge, efficiency became the hallmark of the Republican effort, ending any worry of another Willkie-style disaster.[1]

Professionalism also characterized the GOP campaign strategy. Robert Humphreys, the public relations director of the National Committee, presented a comprehensive plan to Eisenhower and his associates in a meeting at the Brown Hotel in Denver on August 1. Deliberately rejecting Dewey's "me too" attempt to win Democratic and independent votes, Humphreys instead proposed that Ike concentrate on getting out the full support of the 20 million loyal Republicans, and then build his margin of victory from the estimated 45 million potential voters who rarely went to the polls. Describing these stay-at-homes as "those who vote only when discontent stirs them to vote against current conditions," Humphreys argued that the Republicans had to drive them to the polls by stressing the terrible state of the nation. This meant constant attacks on the Truman administration—a deliberate play on voters' emotions, with special stress on "an international situation today that causes Americans . . . *to fear for their national security and lives."* The Republicans would then offer General Eisenhower as the only alternative—the man who could provide "real leadership and real statesmanship."

The Humphreys' plan was a conscious attempt to adapt to Republican purposes the successful give-'em-hell techniques that Truman had used in 1948. Aware of television's growing importance in American life, Humphreys proposed a heavy reliance on TV, especially for informal appearances by the General and for brief spot announcements. He also suggested concentrating on twenty-five states where crucial Senate contests were being waged, so that Ike could not only win these 314 electoral votes but insure a GOP Congress as well. Stevenson was to be ignored; Truman was the target, and the Democratic nominee was always to be referred to as Truman's candidate or Truman's successor. This aggressive attack on the Democrats, capitalizing on public discontent with corruption, Communism, and Korea, was designed to bring to the polls people who had never voted before—to cast their ballots for Eisenhower, the war hero who had reluctantly entered politics to save the nation from disaster.[2]

A week after Eisenhower approved this overall plan, John Foster Dulles flew to Denver to confer with Ike and Nixon on the role of foreign policy in the coming campaign. One of the few men who could bypass Sherman Adams to deal directly with the General, Dulles met with the candidates for two days, and then emerged to talk to the press. Foreign policy, he announced, would be "the major issue" in the fall campaign. "The trend of present foreign policies is to put our nation in the greatest peril it has ever been in in the entire course of our national history," Dulles declared. Stevenson lacked the qualities needed in a time of such grave crisis; only Eisenhower, according to Dulles, had "the experience, the stature, and power of decision in great world matters which is necessary to save our nation." When reporters asked him how the Republicans differed from the Democrats on foreign affairs, Dulles replied, "We will abandon the policy of mere containment, and will actively develop hope and a resistance spirit within the captive peoples which, in my opinion, is the only alternative to a general war." The next day Ike modestly told a press conference that he was not "a messiah," but he went on to confirm Dulles' contention that foreign policy would be "the overshadowing issue" in the election.[3]

Pamphlets prepared for the Republican National Committee and Citizens for Eisenhower-Nixon revealed how far the GOP was prepared to go in rejecting bipartisanship. Identifying Stevenson as "the Truman candidate" pledged to carry on "Acheson's disastrous foreign policy," Republicans claimed, "We can thank the political party in power that one third of all the people in the world are now under Communist domination." In contrast, Eisenhower had proved he could handle the Communists and turn back their aggression "without spilling blood." "If any man can bring the Korean horror to an honorable end," the GOP boasted, "that man is Eisenhower." "Ike's worldwide prestige and experience make him the man most feared by Russia," another pamphlet asserted. "He is our best hope of preventing World War III." As one of the General's aides told a reporter, "Let's face it: The only excuse for Ike's candidacy is that he's the man best qualified to deal with Stalin." [4]

The only disagreement inside the Republican high command developed over how to deal with the Korean War. A speech entitled "War or Peace," which Dulles sent to Eisenhower in mid-August, made no mention of Korea. When this oversight was pointed out, Dulles added a brief section in which the General promised "to stop the killing in Korea," but said he would refrain from discussing the war for fear of jeopardizing the current armistice negotiations. Others advised an all-out effort to exploit the public's distaste for the war in Asia. "Korea looms big in this campaign," wrote Virgil Pinkley, editor of the Los Angeles *Mirror,* to Paul Hoffman, who passed the letter along to Eisenhower. "Isn't it reasonable that General Eisenhower, as an outstanding military leader, one of the world's top diplomats and negotiators," Pinkley continued, ". . . can bring about the best possible solution at the earliest date for Korea?" One of Sherman Adams' New Hampshire friends was blunter in his advice. "Ike is a military man," he wrote. "This is a military matter. In the eyes of many, Ike will rise or fall on his position on Korea." [5]

Dulles, leery of taking up the Korean War, which had been Taft's main issue in the spring, finally advised Eisenhower to propose showering North Korea with propaganda pamphlets extolling life in the free world. Such psychological warfare, Dulles argued, would show "your own determination to win peace by methods of peace." Republican regulars, however, wanted to go much further, suggesting that the candidate back

MacArthur's call for escalation. In a meeting with midwestern leaders in Kansas City, Eisenhower firmly rejected this advice. "We would be going into a Chinese war," he declared, "and starting another war far more difficult to stop than the one we are in now." He admitted the Truman administration had made some "really terrible blunders" in Asia, but he defended the decision to fight in Korea, commenting, "if we had not reacted against the Communistic forces, we would already be involved in a very much greater and more serious thing than we are today." [6]

At the outset, at least, Eisenhower was determined to set limits on the exploitation of foreign policy issues for political expediency. He acquiesced to the politicians' desire to capitalize on his wartime fame and portray him as the only man who could retrieve America s prestige in the world. He was willing to go along with Dulles in offering liberation as a substitute for the containment policy he had helped implement in Europe. But he refused to repudiate his belief that Harry Truman had acted in the national interest in fighting a limited war in Korea to halt Communist aggression without triggering World War III. How long he could maintain this high resolve became a major question that only the fall campaign could answer.

I

". . . [Now] the appalling responsibility that has suddenly fallen to my unwilling lot leaves me in great anxiety," Adlai Stevenson confessed to Bernard Baruch on July 29, 1952. The next day, aware that his agonizing indecision had weakened his candidacy, Stevenson told a press conference that he had overcome his reluctance and was eager to challenge Eisenhower. He also made it clear that he would run his own campaign, saying he would decide whether or not Truman would speak in his behalf. When a reporter asked him if he intended to retain Acheson as Secretary of State, Stevenson ducked, commenting only that he would not discuss Cabinet choices until the election was over.[7]

Stevenson believed that Truman's support was his greatest obstacle, and he moved quickly to try to disassociate himself from the administration. On August 1, he announced the appointment of Wilson W. Wyatt, former head of Americans for Democratic Action who had served as mayor of Louisville, Kentucky, during the war, as his campaign manager. In a direct snub of Truman, Wyatt revealed that the Stevenson campaign would operate out of Springfield, Illinois, instead of the traditional Washington base. A week later, Stevenson chose Stephen A. Mitchell, a reform-minded Chicago attorney, to head the Democratic National Committee. Not only was Mitchell's appointment made over Truman's strong objections, but it was widely interpreted as a slap in the President's face, since Mitchell most recently had served as counsel for a House Judiciary subcommittee probe into irregularities in the Department of Justice.[8]

Stevenson stressed his independence of the administration in rounding out his campaign staff. Two of his Chicago law partners, William Blair and George Ball, along with two Northwestern University law professors, Carl McGowan and Willard Wirtz, formed the inner circle of advisers. He chose Arthur Schlesinger, Jr., Harvard historian and liberal propagandist, to head a speech-writing team which included journalist John Bartlow Martin and economist John Kenneth Galbraith. None of these men had ever served in the Truman administration; they represented the liberal ADA forces that had tried to unseat Truman in 1948 and viewed the President as a handicap rather than an asset in the forthcoming campaign.[9]

In rejecting Truman's guidance, however, Stevenson did not renounce the President's foreign policy. Instead, he announced his support for the much-maligned containment policy and promised that he would say nothing in the campaign "to diminish the allegiance of our Allies." At the same time, he emphasized the lack of agreement on international issues within the Republican party and tried hard to play up the split between eastern internationalists and midwestern isolationists. When President Eisenhower said that he would support all Republican candidates for reelection, even those with whom he disagreed on foreign policy, Stevenson charged that Ike had become the prisoner of Senator Taft and the Republican isolationists. "Can the General be serious when he implies that it makes no difference to him and his 'crusade' whether the Republicans in Congress are for or against international cooperation, for or against the United Nations, for or against strengthening ourselves and the free world?" Stevenson asked mockingly. If so, he commented, then the nation had better be prepared for "a return to isolationism and 'the good old days of Herbert Hoover.' " [10]

Truman watched Stevenson organize his campaign with considerable misgivings. "I have to be exceedingly careful not to use the Presidential Office to overshadow the Presidential Candidate," he confided to Senator William Benton. "It is going to be somewhat of a tightrope walk to keep that from happening." In an effort to prevent a breach, the President invited Stevenson to the White House to attend a Cabinet meeting and receive a briefing on world affairs. Stevenson accepted, and on August 12 the two men tried to straighten out their relationship prior to the Cabinet session. Truman seemed to ignore Stevenson's polite hints that the President refrain from engaging in whistle-stop campaigning on his behalf; they finally agreed that Truman would give a Labor Day address at Milwaukee but wait for a future request from the candidate before making any additional speeches. In a conciliatory gesture, Stevenson accepted the "loan" of two White House aides, Clayton Fritchey and David Bell, to help out in his campaign. Then the President and General Omar Bradley, CIA Director Walter Bedell Smith, and Secretary of State Acheson gave Stevenson a twenty-minute briefing on the state of the world.[11]

The Republicans immediately seized on the meeting, and especially the intelligence briefing, to charge that Stevenson was Truman's "puppet." Ike decried the way the President had used the General's wartime associates, Bradley and Smith, for political purposes, while Nixon charged bluntly, "Adlai Stevenson is part and parcel of the Truman gang." When the President responded by inviting Eisenhower to attend a Cabinet luncheon the next week and receive a similar briefing, Ike declined, saying self-righteously, "It is my duty to remain free to analyze publicly the policies and acts of the present Administration." The General did agree, however, to receive weekly CIA reports, with the understanding that they would in no way restrict his freedom to criticize administration policy.[12]

The rapprochement between Truman and Stevenson proved short-lived. In mid-August, the Oregon *Journal,* a Portland newspaper, asked Stevenson what he planned to do to "clean up the mess in Washington." In his reply, the Democratic candidate tactlessly repeated the phrase "mess in Washington," saying that he would stand on his record in cleaning up a similar situation in Illinois as governor. When reporters asked Truman about Stevenson's use of the offending phrase at his next press conference, the President testily refused to comment, and then added, "I am the key of the campaign." The Democratic candidate, he explained, had no choice; he had to run on the record compiled by the Roosevelt-Truman administrations.[13]

The President was right. However much Stevenson wanted to ignore the administration, as the Democratic candidate he was compelled to defend its policies and programs. He would have been better off if he had accepted this fact of political life gracefully, trying to use the power of the presidency and Harry Truman's proven political talents as campaign assets that might balance off the resentment that had built up during the President's second term. As it was, the more Stevenson tried to separate himself from his fellow Democrat, the more Eisenhower and the Republicans played up his embarrassing predicament.

II

Republicans had their share of dissension. While Eisenhower leisurely prepared for the fall campaign in Denver, Taft supporters in the party revealed their continued disenchantment with the GOP candidate. Colonel Robert McCormick, publisher of the right-wing Chicago *Tribune,* suggested that his readers form "the American party" so that they could oppose both "Truman Democrats" and "Truman Republicans." Senator Taft, who had gone to his summer retreat in Canada after the GOP convention, remained silent, creating speculation that he would not campaign for Eisenhower in the fall. Stories of these possible defections, coupled with the General's apparent inactivity, finally led the Scripps-Howard newspaper chain to print a front-page editorial on August 25 warning Eisenhower that he was "running like a dry creek." Eager for the candidate to come out swinging at the Truman administration, the editors asked in a banner headline, "IKE, WHEN DO WE START?" [14]

The General gave his answer later that day in an address to an American Legion convention in New York City. Devoting himself exclusively to foreign policy, Ike set forth the Taft-Dulles liberation theme with all its rhetorical flourishes. The United States, he declared, "is threatened by a great tyranny —a tyranny that is brutal in its primitiveness . . . a tyranny that has brought thousands, millions of people into slave camps and is attempting to make all humankind its chattel." After reciting the roll of countries lost to Communism, Eisenhower proclaimed, "All these people are blood kin to us. . . . The American conscience can never know peace until these peoples are restored again to being masters of their own fate."

Without ever defining specific measures, Ike called upon the American people to join with him in rolling back the Communist tide in a great moral crusade. "We must tell the Kremlin that never shall we desist in our aid to every man and woman of those shackled lands who seeks refuge with us, any man who keeps burning among his own people the flame of freedom or who is dedicated to the liberation of his fellows." [15]

John Foster Dulles, who had sold the professionals directing Eisenhower's campaign on the liberation strategy, moved quickly to broaden the candidate's stand. In a press conference on August 26, he accused the Truman administration of bringing the United States from a position of "complete security" in 1945 to one of "deadly peril" today. Only Eisenhower could reverse this dangerous trend, Dulles argued. "What we should do is try to split the satellite states away from the control of a few men in Moscow. The only way to stop a head-on collision with the Soviet Union is to break it up from within," he maintained. "It will not stop itself, and a head-on collision means World War III." The next day, in a speech to political scientists in Buffalo, Dulles became more specific in advocating "passive resistance, slow-downs and non-cooperation" by the captive peoples to achieve "disintegration from within" of "the empire of Soviet Communism." In a press conference afterward, he developed the scenario of liberation: first we would stir up resistance through Voice of America broadcasts; then we would air-drop supplies to the freedom fighters rising up against their Soviet masters; finally we would welcome the liberated countries into the free world when the Russians withdrew from the unequal struggle. [16]

Europeans were horrified. Eisenhower and Dulles were "offering a new American foreign policy that no European statesman could follow," commented Harold Callender from Paris. The Manchester *Guardian* lamented the transformation of the "prudent General" the British had known and trusted into "St. Ike the crusader against the Communist dragon and liberator of the captive peoples"; the London *Daily Mirror* accused Eisenhower of "almost out-MacArthuring MacArthur." Some sophisticated continental observers pointed out that the Republicans were engaging in campaign oratory aimed primarily at the Democrats, not the Russians, but even so, they believed that a GOP victory would mean a tougher anti-Communist line, if not actual liberation of Eastern Europe. The Russians played it coolly. Deputy Foreign Minister Jacob Malik dismissed Ike as a "warmonger," while *Pravda,* referring to "threats of Eisenhower against the Soviet Union," told the world that "the Soviet people can only laugh at them as they laughed in their time at threats of Hitler." [17]

The domestic reaction was even more predictable. The *New Republic* placed all the blame on Dulles, warning that "no nation can afford to enter into commitments unless it is prepared to employ all available means to carry them out. . . . His commitment to liberate Europe can be carried out for certain by only one means—a third world war." The editors of *Time,* on the other hand, praised Eisenhower for his stand on liberation. "A great American soldier disclosed political greatness this week," they asserted, "and rediscovered courage as a policy for the nation." [18]

The Democrats, sensing that Eisenhower had gone too far, hit back hard. On Labor Day, Stevenson chose the overwhelmingly Polish-American city of Hamtramck, Michigan, to charge that Ike was raising false hopes of freedom for the people of Poland and Eastern Europe. Accusing Ike of engaging in "loose talk" and "idle threats," the Democratic candidate claimed that the Republican policy risked a war which would "liberate only broken, silent and empty lands." "Action for action's sake," he continued, "is the last resort of mentally and morally exhausted men." Expressing his own concern for the people in the satellites, Stevenson stated his intention "to negotiate in good faith with the Soviet Union," adding, "to close the door to the conference room is to open a door to action." The next day, Truman went even further, accusing the "snollygosters" around Ike of persuading the General to play "cruel, gutter politics with the lives of countless good men and women behind the Iron Curtain." Claiming that it was Russian treachery, not Democratic carelessness, that had created the problem, Truman gave the most solemn warning of all: "To try to liberate these enslaved people at this time might well mean turning these lands into atomic battlefields." [19]

Dulles delivered a scathing counterattack. The Democrats, he charged, "barter away freedom in order to appease the Russian rulers," and condemn "millions to despair, despotism and genocide" by refusing "to try new methods of solving international problems." Calling suggestions that Ike wanted armed revolts "absurd," Dulles stressed "the countless peaceful ways" in which liberation could occur, with Yugoslavia a prime example of how a nation could be detached from the Soviet empire short of war.

Eisenhower, far more concerned than Dulles by the European reaction, went out of his way in a major foreign policy speech in Philadelphia on September 4 to reassure the world that he had no intention of launching a nuclear war to free the captive peoples. Restating the liberation theme, Ike said he intended "to aid by every peaceful means, but only by peaceful means, the right to live in freedom." Rejecting both appeasement and truculence, he spoke in very general terms of the need "to bring hope and every peaceful aid to the world's enslaved people." Above all, he promised to work for peace, saying, "The one—the only—way to win World War III is to prevent it." [20]

Liberation had clearly backfired on the Republicans. Dulles had sold Eisenhower on the policy as a sure way to win the votes of ethnic minorities normally loyal to the Democrats, and especially as a device to win over the right-wing Republicans who were so reluctant to join Eisenhower's crusade. Apparently Eisenhower was never fully convinced. After the Buffalo speech calling for rebellion in the satellites, an angry Ike telephoned Dulles and berated him for omitting the crucial words "by all peaceful means." The European response troubled him deeply, and when Stevenson and Truman accused him of fomenting war, he felt compelled to retreat. The Philadelphia speech, drafted originally by Dulles but toned down considerably by Ike before delivery, marked the watershed. From this time on, Dulles began to fade out of the Republican campaign as Eisenhower turned to new advisers more congenial to his world view.[21]

Two of Henry Luce's ablest journalists, C. D. Jackson and Emmet John Hughes, now took charge of foreign policy speech-writing for Eisenhower. Hughes, who had taken an intense dislike to Dulles when editing his *Life* article in the spring, concentrated on keeping liberation out of all future Eisenhower speeches. He succeeded in this endeavor. Ike never used the word again, and only once, on Pulaski Day (October 11), did the candidate associate himself with the idea. Then, under great pressure from party leaders, Ike issued a statement repeating the platform repudiation of the Yalta agreement on Poland and voicing his own prayers "for the independence of Poland, now captive under Communist domination." C. D. Jackson tried hard to block this statement, warning those close to Ike that "Yalta is a very, very complicated business—for instance, what is Yalta poison for the Poles is Yalta meat for the Hungarians." Ike acted only after Arthur Bliss Lane, the former ambassador to Poland who was heading GOP efforts to woo ethnic minorities, boarded the campaign train and told him "that if a statement were not made we would stand to lose the Polish-American vote." [22]

Though the candidate dropped liberation from his campaign, the Republicans continued to stress it at the local level. Lane supervised the printing and distribution of thousands of pamphlets aimed at the thirteen nationality groups in East Europe "betrayed by the Democratic Administration during the past decade," and he organized committees "to lift the Iron Curtain" and hold "Liberation Rallies and Liberation Weeks" among minorities in the cities of the Northeast and Middle West. Lane concentrated on Polish Americans, telling them that containment was a policy of "acquiescence in the enslavement of Poland," and promising that the Republicans would free their kinsmen without going to war. Senator Irving Ives of New York called openly for "giving every possible aid to underground movements within the Iron Curtain," and Richard Nixon, reviewing a Pulaski Day parade in New York City, denounced Yalta and proclaimed, "We must give hope to the people of Poland for their eventual freedom." [23]

The Democrats, satisfied with forcing Eisenhower to go on the defensive, left liberation alone. Instead they tried to appeal to minorities by accusing the Republicans of discriminating against East Europeans in voting for the McCarran-Walter immigration bill, which perpetuated the national-origins quota system. Since the quotas kept immigration from behind the Iron Curtain down to a trickle, this proved to be an effective argument in halting ethnic defections from the Democratic party. [24]

Liberation thus did not play the major role Dulles had conceived for it in the presidential election. Eisenhower, backed by eastern internationalists within the party, refused to exploit an issue which frightened our European allies and which alienated many Democrats and independents who were leaning toward the General. The party used it as a subordinate theme to attract minority votes, but it disappeared from the national contest by early September and never emerged again.

In this case, Eisenhower, after a brief flirtation, remained true to his own convictions and refrained from espousing what was essentially Taft's alternative to containment.

III

The Eisenhower campaign moved into high gear in mid-September when the candidate embarked on a five-week tour of the nation. Sherman Adams headed an entourage that included senators Frank Carlson of Kansas and Fred Seaton of Nebraska, GOP National Chairman Arthur Summerfield, who worked largely with local Congressional candidates, and James Hagerty, the press secretary. A team of speech-writers led by Jackson and Hughes worked in the campaign headquarters at the Hotel Commodore in New York City, getting occasional help from such diverse individuals as Harold Stassen, Herbert Brownell, and Stanley High, a former Protestant minister and speech-writer for FDR. Jackson would send the speech texts to Gabriel Hauge aboard the campaign train, usually only a day or two before they were to be used. Then Hauge and Robert Cutler, a Boston banker whom Henry Cabot Lodge had loaned to Ike as a "man Friday," transposed the high-toned prose into what Cutler called "campaign speech English" and reporters dismissed as "synthetic banalities" and "meaningless platitudes." Eisenhower would give the text a final polishing, removing any fancy rhetoric in a constant striving, as Hughes saw it, "to reduce all issues to some bare essence, starkly seen and graphically stated." [25]

The General traveled in the last car of the train, shielded from the public by his advisers, who occupied the next unit. Local dignitaries would board the train along the way, sitting in a conference car and waiting for the brief appearance, the handshake, and the magnetic smile of the candidate. Cutler would hand Ike his schedule at precisely eight o'clock each morning, and then Hauge would give him a series of 6-by-3-

inch cards to use in the half-dozen rear-platform talks he made each day. Ike referred to these cards for local issues; then he gave his standard whistle-stop speech in which he hit hard at such domestic issues as inflation and government spending. He took an almost childish delight in simple illustrations. Reporters groaned each time he held up an egg to point out that there were no less than sixty-eight separate taxes on it; or when he displayed a piece of scrap lumber almost sawn through in two places and broke off a piece to show how the dollar had shrunk under Roosevelt, then split the remnant, finally holding aloft the last third as triumphant proof of Truman's devaluation of the dollar. But the crowds loved it. Just the sight of Eisenhower, arms held high in a huge V, bald pate gleaming above his smiling face, brought forth roars of approval from the people who gathered at the train stations. In larger cities there would be a motorcade, with Ike standing in the back seat of an open car graciously accepting the homage the crowds lavished on him. "Few care what he says," commented the *New Republic*'s TRB; "they want to see him and show their trust in this genial, kindly, fatherly figure."

Behind the scenes, the General's advisers worried and fretted, never free of the memory of Dewey's defeat. Ike's tendency to let his words get away from him, like a balloon breaking "loose from its grammatical moorings" terrified them. They came to fear the General's shifting moods, never sure when, sensing a hostile crowd, he would suddenly turn off his charm and deliver a flat and listless speech. They kept the candidate on a murderous schedule, allowing him only one two-day rest from September 14 to October 18 and asking him to give more than fifty major speeches. When Ike's rimless glasses made him appear even older than he was, they had him wear new, dark-rimmed ones. The General took everything in stride, confident that he was leading the American people on a great crusade to redeem the nation from Truman's errors. His own serene self-assurance, together with a powerful sense of indignation that he communicated to all who heard him, gave his campaign a tone that raised it above the manipulations of the professionals and touched the American people as no one had since FDR.[26]

The Gallup polls reflected the surge to Eisenhower. After the conventions, he led Stevenson 47 percent to 41 percent, with 12 percent undecided. By the end of September, Ike had won the support of more than half those polled, recording 51 percent, while Stevenson had gained only one percentage point. He was winning over the undecideds, those who in 1948 had gone 4 to 1 for Truman and thus confounded the pollsters' projections. Political journalists, remembering 1948 and the heavy Democratic edge in registration, continued to predict a narrow Stevenson victory. Yet the huge, enthusiastic crowds the General attracted—even in the South, where no Republican had campaigned before—made even the most skeptical wonder if Eisenhower was not in fact carrying out a political revolution by inducing millions of new voters to join his great crusade.[27]

IV

The Republican old guard remained Eisenhower's gravest problem. Although Taft had promised to support Ike after the GOP convention, the senator had retreated to Canada and refused to participate in the campaign. "Until Bob Taft blows the bugle," declared Indiana's state GOP Chairman, "a lot of us aren't going to fight in the army." When Chicago *Daily News* reporter Edwin Lahey interviewed Taft at his summer home and concluded that Ike's chances of winning his support were "about zero," the General asked Senator Carlson and Arthur Summerfield to sound Taft out through his intermediaries, Senators Dirksen and Bricker. Aware that he needed the party regulars to win, Eisenhower made it clear that he was willing to meet any reasonable demands that Taft might make.

At seven-thirty on the morning of September 12, Taft slipped quietly into Ike's Morningside Heights home in New York City, close to the Columbia University campus. Two hours later, a beaming Taft emerged to read a statement to the press. The senator disclosed that the two men had discussed a summary of Republican principles that Taft had prepared, and, after a few changes, Eisenhower had signed it. The joint statement dealt mainly with domestic issues, and was surprisingly conservative in tone. Ike agreed with Taft in condemning "creeping socialization in every domestic field" and in calling for drastic reductions in federal taxation and spending. Taft admitted that he disagreed with Eisenhower on foreign policy, but he quickly added, "I think it is fair to say that our differences are differences of degree."

The press immediately dubbed the compromise "the surrender of Morningside Heights," and many eastern liberals claimed that Ike had sold out to the midwestern isolationists. The Democrats began referring to the General as "Taft's captive," and Adlai Stevenson quipped, "It looks as if Taft lost the nomination but won the nominee." Dewey warned the Eisenhower people that in New York the deal was causing Jewish voters to fall away from the GOP like "autumn leaves." But Ike and his advisers ignored all the protests. They had united the party, an achievement vital to the overall plan of building from a solid base of Republican votes to capture the stay-at-homes. Taft threw himself into the campaign, speaking not only in Ohio but across the nation to rally the party faithful to Ike's crusade. Though deep divisions remained, Eisenhower succeeded in bringing together the two wings of the Republican party for the first time since 1940.[28]

The same considerations lay behind Eisenhower's decision to support the reelection of senators William Jenner of Indiana and Joseph McCarthy of Wisconsin. Both men were Republicans, and both exploited the anti-Communist sentiment at home for partisan advantage. Moreover, both had attacked General George C. Marshall, Ike's wartime sponsor and mentor, as "a traitor" and "a living lie." In August, when a reporter asked Eisenhower if he agreed with a statement by Nixon endorsing all GOP candidates, the General replied affirmatively, saying that he would back McCarthy "as a member of the Republican organization." A reporter then asked him how he could do so in view of the Wisconsin senator's attacks on Marshall. Flushed with anger, Ike rose from his chair to praise General Marshall as "a perfect example of patriotism and loyal servant of the United States," all the while carefully refraining from any direct repudiation of McCarthy.[29]

Eisenhower and his aides were bombarded with conflicting advice on how to deal with the Republican extremists. Henry Cabot Lodge warned against embracing McCarthy and Jenner, claiming they could cost Ike "that vast element symbolized by the *New York Times, New York Herald Tribune,* Washington *Post*," while Indianapolis publisher Eugene C. Pulliam argued that it would be "a tragic mistake" to repudiate McCarthy because he "has the confidence of literally millions of people who think he is being directed by God in his campaign." Governor Walter J. Kohler of Wisconsin advised Sherman Adams to have the General remain quiet about McCarthy, who, he predicted, was virtually certain to win renomination in the September party primary.[30]

Eisenhower played it by ear when he stumped Indiana in early September. Introduced by Jenner at an Indianapolis rally, Ike urged voters to support all the party's nominees in November without singling out Jenner by name, but he winced visibly when the senator threw his arm around him afterward. The next day, Sherman Adams expressed his disgust in a letter to Kohler. "I am still most disturbed about how to handle McCarthy as a person," he confessed. "My experience in Indiana indicates that the person whom we least desire to embrace literally monopolizes the General in his public appearances, which is, to say the least, most embarrassing." [31]

McCarthy won his primary handily, and when Eisenhower's campaign train came to Wisconsin in early October, Adams was still not sure how to proceed. McCarthy boarded the train and introduced the candidate in Appleton, the senator's home town. Ike treated him coolly and went ahead with his plans to denounce McCarthy's methods and praise Marshall in a major Milwaukee address. Governor Kohler, however, finally convinced a harried Sherman Adams that if Ike persisted, the Republicans would lose in Wisconsin. Adams then persuaded Eisenhower to drop the offending passage. News of this deliberate omission of the planned defense of Marshall leaked to the press and created an uproar in the East. "Do I need to tell you that I am sick at heart?" cabled *New York Times* publisher Arthur Hays Sulzberger to Eisenhower. The General ignored the uproar; his only concession came in Newark, New Jersey, later in October when he added George Marshall's name to a list of "great American patriots." [32]

There was one compromise Dwight Eisenhower refused to make. At the time of the Republican convention, Douglas MacArthur announced that he was forsaking politics as well as soldiering to become chairman of the board of Remington Rand, Inc. "I will take no part in the political campaign," he announced. "I will not be a part of the political picture." Nevertheless, Gerald L. K. Smith's Christian Nationalist party nominated MacArthur for the presidency, and right-wing extremists succeeded in placing his name on the November ballot in several states. General MacArthur ignored this development, apparently hoping that his silence would be sufficient to kill it. [33]

As the campaign progressed, it seemed likely that MacArthur would receive a substantial number of votes in a half-dozen states where Eisenhower and Stevenson were running neck and neck. Republican officials began pressuring Ike to ask MacArthur for a public statement repudiating the splinter movement and endorsing Eisenhower for the presidency. "You ought to get MacArthur into the picture," Joe Martin told Eisenhower when he spoke in Massachusetts. "A lot of people believe in him." One GOP official arranged a meeting between Arthur Summerfield and a Remington Rand vice-president to set the ground rules for a conference between the two generals. The face-to-face encounter never took place; Ike apparently refused to go hat in hand to his old commander and ask for his endorsement, although his research service recommended on October 28 that "a typically dramatic MacArthur announcement might well be the turning point of the campaign, winning the election for Eisenhower." Ike was willing to appease the old guard politicians, but he drew the line at humbling himself before a fellow officer.[34]

V

The gravest threat to Eisenhower's candidacy came in mid-September when the New York *Post* revealed that Richard Nixon had access to a fund of over $18,000 contributed by wealthy Californians to help pay his political expenses as a senator. This disclosure hit the Republicans with devastating impact, since Eisenhower had seized on the scandals of the Truman administration in promising that a Republican government would be "as clean as a hound's tooth." Nixon immediately labeled the charges a Communist smear, but eastern Republicans took them seriously. Thomas Dewey, Lucius Clay, and Herbert Brownell and the major metropolitan dailies in the East advised Ike to drop Nixon from the ticket. Bernard Baruch suggested that Nixon issue a statement saying he was retiring in order to insure Ike's victory in November; the Eisenhower-Nixon research service advised Sherman Adams to tell Nixon to "move fast, withdraw personally, irrevocably, unequivocally, and immediately." [35]

Eisenhower refused to be rushed. Following Robert Cutler's advice, he asked Nixon for a full report on the fund and had a Los Angeles law firm conduct an independent investigation which concluded that Nixon's activities were completely legal. Robert Taft and Senator William Knowland of California came to Nixon's defense, denying that he had done anything wrong and urging Ike to retain him as the vice-presidential candidate. Eisenhower finally agreed to let Nixon make his own case to the American people in a nationally televised speech. Ike watched Nixon's appeal to the nation and seemed to be moved by his young colleague's emotional baring of his meager resources and by his resourceful appeal to sentiment when he asked if his critics wanted him to give up his dog, Checkers, a recent gift to his children.[36]

The speech rallied the nation behind Nixon, but to the senator's surprise and growing anger, Ike ordered him to fly east to give Eisenhower a personal explanation. Nixon at first refused to undergo this humiliation, but finally he relented and journeyed to Wheeling, West Virginia, where Ike greeted him cordially at the airport and said, "You're my boy." In a limousine on the way to a nearby stadium, Ike grilled Nixon on his fund; then, when they arrived, he told the expectant audience that he was proud to have Richard Nixon as his running mate. "This is probably the greatest moment in my life," Nixon declared, and then broke into tears as Bill Knowland came over to shake his hand.[37]

The fund incident transformed Richard Nixon into a political celebrity in his own right, adding strength to the ticket and reassuring party regulars who feared a takeover by Dewey and the eastern establishment. The Taft wing of the party now felt it had its own man at the top, and in the remainder of the campaign, Nixon spoke out more and more boldly along the lines Taft had pioneered in the spring. He focused on foreign policy, repeating the various changes on the liberation line. Nixon accused Truman of "losing" 600,000,000 people to Communism; he cited Stevenson's support of Alger Hiss as proof of the Democratic candidate's softness on Communism; he claimed that "nothing would please the Kremlin more" than Stevenson's election. Above all, he kept up a steady attack on the administration's foreign policy. He asserted that a Democratic victory would mean "the awful prospect of still more wars under the Truman-Acheson and now Stevenson–Alice-in-Wonderland policy of Communist containment." Stevenson became "Adlai the Appeaser," a Ph.D. graduate of "Dean Acheson's Cowardly College of Communist Containment." By contrast, Nixon called Eisenhower "the one man in the world most hated and feared by the masters of the Kremlin and their satellites," the man who "will take us off the defensive and on the offensive." [38]

Thus Richard Nixon used his moment of greatest adversity to become the leading disciple of the Taft-Dulles attack on the bipartisan foreign policy. Eisenhower, the very symbol of that joint endeavor in Europe, kept silent, accepting Nixon as he had Taft, Jenner, and McCarthy (though not MacArthur) as part of the price he felt he had to pay in order to restore integrity and decency to American government. The General was proving to be a far more astute politician than his admirers had thought possible: he had flawed his own great crusade in search of political victory.

VI

Adlai Stevenson's campaign started slowly. Virtually unknown to the American people, the Democratic candidate failed to attract large or enthusiastic crowds as he traveled across the nation. Intent on setting forth his views on the major issues, he stinted on whistle-stop appearances in order to devote more time to polishing and rewriting the formal speeches that Arthur Schlesinger, Jr., and his aides prepared for him. He tried to cut down on the tours of the hinterlands, referring to his campaign managers as "tormentors" and insisting on frequent returns to Springfield, where he could rest and reflect on the ideas he wanted to share with the American people. His determination to reshape all his speeches so that they would bear his own distinctive style, often done at the expense of handshaking and other traditional campaign pursuits, led one aide to remark, "He would rather write than be President." [39]

Stevenson was at his best in large, formal speeches. Unimpressive physically, with a slight paunch and a receding hairline, he spoke with authority and often a poetic eloquence that touched many of his listeners deeply. He found Eisenhower an easy target for his sharp wit and he probed relentlessly at the heavy-handed, humorless campaign being waged by Ike, Nixon, and Taft. David Lilienthal thought that Stevenson was "putting on one of the greatest performances in public life in my recollection," calling his speeches "gems of wisdom and wit and sense." TRB saw him as "a Woodrow Wilson with a sense of humor," while John Mason Brown commented on his ability to awaken an audience "as if a giant switch were thrown on," as "Stevenson's personality and strength blazed forth in their full light." But politicians noted that Stevenson's appeal seemed limited; his cool, dispassionate analysis of the ills facing America failed to move most Americans, many of whom resented his schoolmasterly style and his cultivated air of disdain for the masses. Stevenson talked over the heads of the people, the professionals complained, leading Stewart Alsop to suggest that Stevenson had become the candidate of the "eggheads," the liberal writers, artists, and college professors who formed the nation's intellectual establishment but who represented only a tiny fraction of the electorate.[40]

In August, Stevenson spoke out boldly in an effort to offset his reputation as a hesitant, indecisive leader. In an address to the American Legion convention in New York, two days after Eisenhower had spoken, he attacked Joseph McCarthy for his smear of General Marshall. Claiming that the Red-baiters fitted Samuel Johnson's definition of patriotism as "the last refuge of scoundrels," he told the astonished Legionnaires, "Patriotism with us is not the hatred of Russia; it is the love of this Republic," and won an ovation surpassing that given to Ike. Everywhere he went, he defended Truman's conduct of the Korean War, telling audiences that if the U.S. had not fought, "we would not only have lost Korea but we would have invited the Soviet Union to pursue aggression elsewhere." The Democrats, he claimed, had "checked Soviet aggression and perhaps saved the world from a third world war." He hit hardest at the liberation theme, condemning Eisenhower and Dulles for engaging in "a cynical and transparent attempt, drenched in crocodile tears, to play upon the anxieties of foreign nationality groups in this country." Stevenson defended the policy of containment and pointed out that the Republican alternative called for "civil war in the satellite countries" and thus risked "the initiation of a third world war." [41]

The Democratic candidate discussed world affairs most fully in a nationally televised address at the Veterans Memorial Auditorium in San Francisco, where the United Nations had been founded seven years before. With the Korean War uppermost in his mind, Stevenson counseled a policy of coexistence, calling repeatedly for "patience," "compromise," "adjustment," and "negotiation." He denied that such forbearance meant giving in to the Communists. "It is waging the contest between freedom and tyranny by peaceful means," he asserted. "It will involve negotiation and adjustment—compromise but not appeasement—and I will never shrink from these if they would advance the world toward a secure peace." He labeled the Korean War "a turning point in history" and supported the administration's effort to resolve it by armistice talks.

"A wise man does not try to hurry history," he concluded. "Many wars have been avoided by patience and many have been precipitated by reckless haste." [42]

Stevenson's conciliatory approach to the Cold War brought mixed responses. Raymond Moley condemned his "sentimental" ideas, dismissing them as "appeasement of Communism," and Kenneth Royall, Truman's Secretary of the Army in the late 1940's, defected to the Republicans. The *Reporter*, originally for Ike, switched to Stevenson on foreign policy issues, and Oregon Senator Wayne Morse, a liberal Republican, announced that he could not campaign for Eisenhower. The *Nation* summed up liberal feelings when it endorsed Stevenson and his policy of "peaceful coexistence." A Republican victory, the editors announced, would be "a disaster for the country and perhaps the world," since it would be taken "as an indication that the United States had ruled out the possibility of a peaceful settlement of the cold war." [43]

Despite Stevenson's soft line, he remained a Cold Warrior, speaking frequently about the differences between the "free world" and Communism. He accepted the support of Dean Acheson, the outspoken Secretary of State who insisted that the United States could negotiate with the Russians only from positions of strength. Acheson gave two major political addresses for Stevenson, bristling with attacks on the Soviet Union as well as on the Republicans; and he ignored requests from India Edwards, a leading member of the Democratic National Committee, and Stephen Mitchell, the party's national chairman, to announce that he would retire as Secretary of State after the election. Though Stevenson permitted National Committeeman Jacob Arvey, his backer in Illinois, to predict that Acheson would be dropped as Secretary of State, the Democratic candidate refused to repudiate the man who symbolized the policy of containment. His failure to do so weakened his call for peaceful negotiations to end the Cold War.[44]

VII

Harry Truman brought Stevenson's faltering campaign to life. In late September, the President began a whistle-stop tour of the nation that generated the excitement and enthusiasm the Democrats so desperately needed. Drawing even bigger crowds than Ike, Truman blasted the General as a "puppet" of an "unholy crew" of Republican isolationists. The President kept up a steady attack on the GOP as incompetent to handle American diplomacy. "They haven't had a single constructive idea about foreign policy since Senator Vandenberg died," he asserted, and he warned that a Republican victory would mean an "isolationist Congress." He defended his decision to fight in Korea, expanding the explanation of an air force officer from Kansas by saying, "We are fighting in Korea so we won't have to fight in Wichita, or in Chicago, or in New Orleans, or on San Francisco Bay." He compared his defense of Korea with the failure of England and France to stand up to Hitler at Munich: "By meeting aggression in Korea, we have saved the free nations of Asia from catastrophe." [45]

Truman's most valuable contribution to Stevenson's cause was to take on Eisenhower personally, and thus end the pretense that the General stood above partisan politics. The President pointed out that Ike had said in November 1945 that the Russians wanted only friendship with the United States. "Perhaps if he had given us better advice in 1945," Truman added, "we wouldn't have had so much trouble in waking up the country to the danger of Communist imperialism in 1946, 1947, and 1948." He charged that Ike was responsible for the failure to secure access rights to Berlin from the Soviets at the war's end, and he revealed that Eisenhower, as Army Chief of Staff, had recommended the withdrawal of American troops from South Korea in 1947. Eisenhower, according to Truman, had fallen "into the hands of the Republican snollygasters," and, as a result, "he is now going around the country

campaigning against his own record, and his own principles."
Truman delivered his lowest blow when he accused Ike of
supporting the discriminatory McCarran-Walter Immigration
Act and thus endorsing "the very practice that identified the
so-called 'master race' " in Nazi Germany.[46]

Rabbi Abba Silver immediately issued a statement expressing his "shock" at the President's attack, and both Washington
Post publisher Eugene Meyer and Bernard Baruch rallied to
the General's defense. *Time* compared Truman to Joe McCarthy with his wild charges, but political observers noted a sharp
upswing in the Democratic campaign as voters began to react
to Truman's lively assaults. A Gallup poll taken in early October showed Stevenson narrowing Eisenhower's lead to 4 percentage points (49 to 45), and the Republican research service
warned Sherman Adams that the renewed Democratic interest
"poses a grave threat" to Ike's chances. "There is little doubt
that Truman is responsible for this alarming shift of public
opinion," the report concluded. Although, as TRB noted, "the
raw pigments of Truman" made Stevenson seem "like a pastel
candidate," the President's fiery entry into the campaign gave
the Democrats their first real excitement and at least the glim-
mer of possible victory.[47]

VIII

The Republicans, worried by their rivals' sudden resurgence, responded by making the Korean War a major issue.
The peace talks at Panmunjon had been going on for over a
year without any significant progress, and though the casualties were light as both sides refrained from heavy fighting,
popular discontent with the stalemate was building up in the
United States. Gerard Lambert, a Princeton public opinion
expert conducting special surveys for Sherman Adams, was
the first to note the trend. On September 16, he informed
Adams that to his surprise the American people were deeply

disturbed by the war in Korea, ranking it second only to government waste and bureaucracy as a matter of grave concern. Lambert did a series of special surveys in twenty-seven major states which confirmed his original finding and revealed that, among independent voters, Korea ranked as the primary issue. Published polls revealed how the war could be turned to the GOP's advantage. Elmo Roper found that frustration with the peace negotiations being conducted by the Democrats led 53 percent of those surveyed to recommend a new offensive to win the conflict, compared to 22 percent who favored continued talks and 12 percent who preferred total withdrawal. When George Gallup asked voters which candidate they thought "could handle the Korean situation best," 67 percent responded "Eisenhower" and only 9 percent "Stevenson." [48]

Despite pressure from the Taft wing of the party, Eisenhower had left the war alone in the early stages of the campaign. In his Philadelphia foreign policy speech on September 4, Ike had blamed the war on the Democrats, saying that they had failed to arm the South Koreans properly and that they had "abandoned China to the Communists," but he neither questioned the decision to fight in 1950 nor offered any solution to the current impasse. Two weeks later, after his aides had studied the public opinion surveys, Eisenhower hit hard at the war issue in a major speech in Cincinnati, Robert Taft's home town. He cited Dean Acheson's January 1950 speech declaring that Korea lay outside the American defense perimeter in the Pacific, then charged, "Five months later Communist tanks were rolling over the Thirty-Eighth parallel to assault South Korea." Again, he accepted the decision to fight, but he accused the Truman administration of bungling, saying, "Our servicemen were summoned to snatch military victory from political defeat." The noisy audience roared its approval as Taft beamed, happy that Ike now agreed with him on Korea. [49]

Eisenhower took a much more significant step while whistle-stopping through Illinois on October 3. Speaking to a college audience at Champaign, he referred again to the "bungling" by the Democrats that forced "young farm boys" and "students" to fight in Korea. It made no sense, he went on, for Americans to bear the brunt of battle. "That is a job for the Koreans. . . . If there must be a war there, let it be Asians against Asians, with our support on the side of freedom."

Ike's call for Koreans to go it alone, with its racist overtones, horrified United Nations observers, who quickly pointed out that South Korean forces now manned nearly half the battle line. C. D. Jackson immediately cabled the campaign train to express his displeasure, pointing out, "The way it sounded here was that the General thought it was a fine [idea] to have Asians killing Asians, while we could remain safe on the sidelines giving a loud cheer to the team we liked best." But leading Republican spokesmen embraced Ike's suggestion eagerly. Governor Dewey termed it "a brilliant contribution," saying that within a year 90 percent of the front-line troops would be South Koreans, while Senator Taft praised Ike for acknowledging his belief that "we cannot permanently maintain American troops on the continent of Asia." [50]

Eisenhower's advisers decided that it was good politics to exploit the public's disgust over American casualties in Korea, and in subsequent speeches the General continued to call for replacing American boys with Koreans on the battlefield. He went one step further in San Francisco on October 8, by attacking the Truman administration for entering into the deadlocked truce negotiations. Citing Truman's 1948 remark that he liked "old Joe Stalin," the General charged that a naive President had fallen into a "bear pit" in accepting a cease-fire that enabled the exhausted Communists to regroup and prepare for new offensives. Though he refrained from any specifics, Eisenhower promised that if elected he would give "full dedication to the job of finding an intelligent and honorable way to end the tragic toll of American casualties in Korea," which he listed at "120,000 Americans killed, wounded or missing." [51]

Two days before Eisenhower spoke, the Communists began a bloody assault on White Horse Hill, a key outpost manned primarily by South Koreans. The Republic of Korea forces acquitted themselves well, throwing back the Chinese attackers in the fiercest fighting in six months. The United States responded by suspending the truce talks, still stalled on the prisoner-of-war issue, and then, using American troops, launched a counterattack in an effort to take high ground in the "Iron Triangle" area. Several hundred GI's died in the bloody hand-to-hand combat, and the names of those killed appeared on the front pages of Scripps-Howard newspapers across the country. "And now with fresh blood on the first snows on the hills of Korea, . . . a sense of danger grows," commented Raymond Moley. "In such a moment people seek integrity and character. They find it in Eisenhower." [52]

The Democrats realized how damaging the Korean issue could be politically, and they fought desperately to state their case to the American people. Ignoring the pleas of liberal supporters for withdrawal, Stevenson stood firmly behind the administration in a speech in Louisville answering Ike's Cincinnati address. He defended Dean Acheson, pointing out that both Eisenhower and MacArthur had recommended pulling American troops out of Korea before 1950. Turning to the attack, he accused Ike of trying to milk votes out of "our ugly, miserable, bloody ordeal" in Korea, and he charged that the General had forsaken his own foreign policy ideas in taking up Taft's position. Stevenson ridiculed Taft's Morningside Heights statement that his differences with Ike were only a matter of degree, asking, "Is it a difference of degree to blame the Korean War on Stalin or on our own President?" Reaffirming his own support for the principle of collective security, he concluded, "I call upon America to reject the new isolationism." [53]

Stevenson responded to Ike's call for substituting Asian boys for Americans in a nationally televised fireside speech on October 16. Eisenhower, he asserted, had missed the significance of the Korean conflict. It was not a local civil war—the Communist attack was aimed at the whole free world. "Today we are defending America in Korea," he declared. "The Korean War is not a war that concerns just Koreans. It is our war too, because—and there should be no mistake about this—world domination is the ultimate target of the communist rulers, and world domination includes us." Truman had averted World War III by fighting in Korea, Stevenson concluded, but the candidate offered no solution other than continued fighting and negotiation until the Communists stopped their aggression.

In effect, Stevenson was enunciating what later came to be known as the domino theory: halt Communist aggression when it first breaks out, or else it will knock over the free nations and ultimately imperil the United States. The day before, Averell Harriman had voiced the same idea in Boston, warning that withdrawal of American troops from Korea would "open the floodgates of Communist aggression to sweep down and across all of Southeast Asia and Formosa, isolate Japan, put India in a pinchers and undermine the Middle East." In his whistle-stop campaign, Truman again and again paraphrased his favorite line from the Korean War ace by asserting that if we did not defend Korea, we would have to fight in Wichita, or Kansas City, or . . . , supplying the name of whatever community he happened to be in on that day. Stevenson put it most eloquently at the Alamo on October 18, when he said the American men fighting and dying across the Pacific knew that "tyranny must be halted, at whatever cost, whenever it marches or creeps or crawls against the liberties of free men." Then, warning that there were no "cheap and painless shortcuts" to peace, he summed up his own Cold War ideology as the ultimate reason for fighting in Korea: "God has set for us an awesome mission: nothing less than the leadership of the free world." [54]

In his own earthy way, Harry Truman fought back against the Republican onslaught. He accused Eisenhower of selling out to the isolationists, of swallowing "Senator Taft's policy hook, line and sinker," of throwing "his reputation and his record to the winds, sidestepping or repudiating all the things that we thought he stood for." Then, in a speech in Hartford, he laid down the gauntlet. Thinking that he was calling Ike's bluff, Truman challenged Eisenhower and "his snollygoster foreign state advisers" to tell the nation how he would end the Korean conflict. "If he knows a remedy and a method for that situation, it is his duty to come and tell me what it is—and save lives—right now," Truman asserted. For the next few days, Truman repeated his dare to the Republican candidate, mocking him for his silence and accusing him of making "a political football" out of Korea.[55]

Eisenhower gave his answer in a speech at Detroit on October 24. "In this anxious autumn for America, one fact looms above all others in our people's mind," he began. "One tragedy challenges all men dedicated to the work of peace. One word shouts denial to those who foolishly pretend that ours is not a nation at war. This fact, this tragedy, this word is: Korea." He went on to blame Truman and Acheson for exposing South Korea to Communist attack and commented, "The old Administration cannot be expected to repair what it failed to prevent." Then he came to his dramatic climax:

> That job requires a personal trip to Korea. I shall make that trip. Only in that way could I learn how best to serve the American people in the cause of peace.
> I shall go to Korea.[56]

"That does it—Ike is in," reporters told Sherman Adams. Virtually all political commentators agreed. *Newsweek* asserted that Ike's campaign "hit its peak in a single sentence uttered in Detroit," while Associated Press reporter Jack Bell wrote, "For all practical purposes, the contest ended that night." Even the editors of the *New Republic* admitted that "twelve million parents found it hard to turn down a five-star General who assured them he would protect their sons from enemy fire." No one seemed to worry over Eisenhower's failure to say what he would do in Korea—the simple fact of his going, as the leading military figure of his day, was enough. "This was what most of us had wanted to hear," commented Marquis Childs. "He was a great soldier, and we could trust what he told us after he had had a firsthand look at the long-stalemated front in Korea. . . . He would find a way to bring peace." [57]

The promise to go to Korea was the logical culmination of a Republican effort to capitalize on public disenchantment with the limited war. Several men, including *Newsweek* foreign affairs editor Harry F. Kern and Frank Hilton, director of the GOP's veterans division, had suggested such a statement to the national committee early in the campaign, but Ike's advisers kept postponing a decision until the time was right. Meanwhile, the idea that Ike had unique qualifications to end the conflict began to take hold. Kenneth Royall telegraphed the General on October 22 to express his belief that he was "the one person in the world whom Stalin and his group most respect and fear," and he concluded, "Your election would be our surest guarantee that we could shorten the Korean tragedy." Darryl Zanuck sent in a slogan on the day of the Detroit speech that one of his Hollywood co-workers had coined: "Our country was founded by a general; now let's save it with one."

Emmet Hughes, who wrote the Detroit speech, had thought

up the idea of having Ike promise to go to Korea in mid-September. At first he dismissed it as too obvious, but then he decided to save it for a Korea speech late in the campaign. His main objective, he wrote later, was to insure that Eisenhower maintained a flexible position on the war and did not succumb to right-wing pressures for MacArthur-style escalation. When Truman issued his challenge for Eisenhower to make his solution public, Robert P. Burroughs, a public relations man with the GOP National Committee, passed along a suggestion by Ralph Cake that Ike pledge to go to Korea, and with it the comment, "What about saving this for the speech the night before the election?" Unaware of this proposal, C. D. Jackson took the text of the speech Hughes had prepared to Sherman Adams, who immediately approved it. The two men feared that Ike might reject the idea on grounds of principle, but they need not have worried. When Adams showed Ike the text, his eyes lit up as he read it. He reached for a pencil, made a few changes to sharpen the impact of the key sentence, and then gave his approval. His only doubts, according to Hughes, came later—after Bernard Baruch warned him that it would be a dangerous and reckless thing to risk his life by traveling to the battleground. "I just don't know about that speech, now," Ike told Hughes. "We may have won—or we may have *lost*—the whole election right there." [58]

IX

The anguished howls of the Democrats indicated that the speech had drawn blood. National Chairman Stephen Mitchell called it "a grandstand play to get votes"; Averell Harriman dismissed it as "a snare and a delusion"; Wayne Morse wanted to know, "What miracles does he think he can perform?" Estes Kefauver, campaigning in Pennsylvania, took up Truman's taunts by stating, "I want to urge him to go now, tonight. Let's not even wait for tomorrow. . . . If the General has a feasible solution, why didn't he mention it in the last two and a half years?" In Los Angeles, vice-presidential candidate John Sparkman asked more sober questions: "Is he willing to send those prisoners back to the Reds and is he willing to expand the war?" Senator Fulbright feared that Ike had in mind a showdown with the Russians. "An ultimatum at this juncture," the Arkansas senator told a Virginia audience, "could well mean catastrophe for the whole world." [59]

In August, Adlai Stevenson had decided that if he won the election, he would take a trip to Korea, Japan, and India to get a personal grasp of Asian issues before his inauguration. He and his advisers had kept plans for the journey secret, he later wrote, "fearful that it might be construed as a political gesture." Now several of his aides suggested that he reveal his own proposed trip, but Stevenson rejected the idea, pointing out that he lacked the military standing that made Ike's pledge so effective. Instead, he answered Eisenhower on October 25 by adding a section to a speech he gave in Boston; he reiterated his contention that unless the United States defeated the Communists in Korea, American troops would have to fight "on our own beaches and in our own streets and cities." The only way to end the Korean War, he asserted, would be for all Americans to unite and support the administration's quest for an honorable peace.[60]

Once again it was Harry Truman who carried the fight back to Eisenhower. Throughout the last week of the campaign, the President attacked the General personally, accusing him of advocating "Republican isolationist policies of withdrawal, of feeble half measures, of appeasement and surrender." In Detroit, Truman charged that Eisenhower had "slurred and belittled the efforts of our allies. He has put fear in the hearts of free people all over the world by his loose talk about the fighting in Korea." On October 27, Truman released a long statement showing that in 1947 the General, then the Army Chief of Staff, recommended to Truman that

American troops be withdrawn from Korea. Two days before the election, the President released the text of the Joint Chiefs' recommendation for withdrawal that Eisenhower had signed on September 26, 1947. In his final campaign speech in St. Louis, Truman referred to the General's change of heart, and then commented, "I knew him; I trusted him. At one time, I thought he was qualified to be President." Then Truman claimed that politics had transformed him. "I cannot but conclude that it would be disastrous for us to elect as President a man who shows so great a willingness to do the purely expedient thing in matters that vitally concern our national survival." [61]

Meanwhile, Stevenson still groped for an effective reply to Eisenhower's Korean pledge. He tried ridicule, saying the speech was foisted on a naive candidate by "a speech writer from a slick magazine" and comparing the General's suggestion that Asians fight Asians to isolationists in 1940 wanting only Europeans to fight Europeans. He tried an appeal to reason, asserting that the real enemy was in Moscow, not Korea, and that the only way to end the war by negotiation would be to deal directly with the Kremlin. Stevenson even questioned Ike's integrity. "It's hard to know which general to believe," he told a New York audience, "the one who damned Taft in June or the one who embraced him in September; the general who praised George C. Marshall in New Jersey, or the general who declined to praise him in Wisconsin."

Ultimately, Stevenson had no choice but to reiterate his defense of the administration's policy. In an address at the Brooklyn Academy of Music on October 31, he carefully examined the alternatives in Korea. He ruled out withdrawal as a return to isolation and he rejected escalation as risking World War III. He then explained how the current truce negotiations had become bogged down on the prisoner-of-war issue, and he vowed that, much as he wanted peace, he would never force unwilling captives to return to their Communist homelands to face certain punishment and possible death. Having taken his stand with Truman, Stevenson then condemned Eisenhower. "There is no greater cruelty, in my judgment, than the raising of false hopes—no greater arrogance than playing politics with peace and war," Stevenson declared. "Rather than exploit human hopes and fears, rather than provide glib solutions and false assurances, I would gladly lose this presidential election." [62]

Stevenson had never been more eloquent, but there was no way he could turn the Korean War against Eisenhower. Refusal to repatriate prisoners of war was a noble position that most Americans supported, but the fate of Chinese and North Korean captives did not match the emotional appeal of ending the war and saving American lives. The savage fighting that broke out in early October continued throughout the month, and even though South Korean troops bore the brunt of battle, American casualties ran to nearly one thousand a week as General James Van Fleet committed regiment after regiment to hold the high ground in the Iron Triangle. As Stevenson pointed out, Stalin and his associates in the Kremlin held the decision for peace in their hands, and at this time they were apparently willing to let the Chinese and North Koreans continue fighting. The American people, tired of war and distrustful of the administration, were ready to follow the man who promised to stake his own great reputation on ending the conflict. [63]

X

Though many Republicans felt that the Detroit speech had clinched the election, the party leaders spared no effort in keeping the Democrats on the defensive during the campaign's climax. Richard Nixon, the man who had exposed Alger Hiss, gave a nationally broadcast address reminding the voters that Adlai Stevenson had testified in the traitor's behalf. "Can such a man as Stevenson," Nixon asked, "be trusted to lead our crusade against communism?" To make sure that everyone knew the right answer, Senator Joseph McCarthy told a nationwide radio and television audience that Stevenson had actively aided and abetted the Communist cause, referring to the Democratic candidate twice as "Alger" Stevenson.[64]

Eisenhower disassociated himself from these smear tactics, but he pretended great indignation at the Democratic criticism of his "go to Korea" pledge. "If by going out there we can improve our plans by so much as to save the life of one single American boy," he declared self-righteously, ". . . then the meeting is worthwhile and, in any event, I am going." He answered Stevenson's suggestion that he should go to Moscow rather than Korea to end the war by comparing such a journey to Yalta and Potsdam. "It is the cry of men whose whole formula for dealing with Soviet aggression has been openly stated in terms of 'give' and 'concede.' " In a major address telecast from New York City, Eisenhower read a letter from General Van Fleet complaining that the Pentagon was impeding his plans to replace American troops with South Korean soldiers. Our boys, Ike declared, "do not belong in the front lines whenever there are Koreans willing and anxious" to fight. He kept repeating his promise to go to Korea, though he was careful to point out that he had "no magic military wand to bring that war to an end." And in his final campaign appearance, a radio and television address from Boston Garden, he called loftily for national unity while asking rhetorically, "Is our age cursed to live under some inexorable law that decrees—whatever soldiers win, statesmen must surrender?" [65]

Despite the extremely effective way Ike had exploited the war, the experts, remembering 1948, forecast a very close election. Eisenhower had taken an early lead, they contended, but his compromises with Taft, McCarthy, and Jenner had hurt him, allowing Stevenson to draw even by mid-October. The editors of *Time* thought that Eisenhower had pulled ahead again with the Korean issue, but *Newsweek*'s board of experts predicted a Democratic victory by the very close margin of 267 electoral votes for Stevenson to 264 for Ike. The pollsters were extremely wary; Elmo Roper claimed that the election was too close to predict, and although George Gallup's final survey showed Ike leading, 47 to 40 percent, he gave Stevenson nearly all the undecideds and called it a toss-up.[66]

Perhaps the contrasting mood of the rival camps offered the best indication of the likely outcome. James Reston reported that the Democrats were downcast, fearing that the Korean issue had beaten them. On the Republican side, John Foster Dulles revealed the optimism that prevailed among Ike's advisers on the eve of the election. Dulles spent one evening with Lucius Clay, discussing procedures for the orderly transfer of power, and on the day before the election, he wrote to Eisenhower, "I go [to the polls] serenely confident of the outcome." Praising the General for his "superb campaign," Dulles said he knew Ike was glad "to have this one behind you and be moving on from the phase of words to the phase of deeds." [67]

XI

The suspense did not last very long on election night. Eisenhower swept New England in the early returns, cracked the supposedly solid South with wins in Virginia, Florida, and Texas, and by midnight had carried such major northern industrial states as New York and Pennsylvania. Stevenson issued a gracious concession at Springfield, expressing his hope that Ike would become "the servant and guardian of peace," and shortly before two A.M. the General appeared at his headquarters in the Hotel Commodore to claim victory.

When the full returns came in the next day, it became clear that Eisenhower had scored a great personal triumph. He carried 39 states with 33 million votes, compared to Stevenson's nine states and 27 million popular votes. The basic campaign plan paid off handsomely; over 61 million people went to the polls, 11 million more than the previous high in 1940, as Ike's great crusade brought out the stay-at-homes in droves. Sixty-one percent of the electorate voted, as opposed to 52 percent in 1948. Stevenson actually received three million more votes than Truman did in his great upset, but the amazing surge of new voters for Eisenhower insured his defeat.[68]

The New Deal coalition that Roosevelt had forged and Truman had maintained did not collapse altogether. Eisenhower won over nearly 20 percent of the Democrats, but labor, farmers, and members of minority groups voted for Stevenson, even if by reduced margins. Roman Catholics, particularly Irish followers of Joseph McCarthy and Poles attracted by the promise of liberation, defected heavily from the Democratic ranks. Most Jews and Negroes remained loyal to their party, and liberal intellectuals voted even more heavily for Stevenson than they had for Truman, leading Murray Kempton to comment, "The knuckleheads have beaten the eggheads." [69]

The best indication of continued Democratic vitality came in the Congressional results. Despite Eisenhower's broad appeal, the Republicans barely carried the House and gained control of the Senate by a single seat. McCarthy won reelection easily in Wisconsin, but by a margin much smaller than Eisenhower's, Jenner just squeaked through in Indiana, and in Massachusetts Henry Cabot Lodge was defeated by Representative John F. Kennedy. Eisenhower's coattails were virtually nonexistent; his popularity transcended traditional party lines and made the Republican triumph extremely shaky.[70]

Virtually all the commentators cited the Korean War in explaining Eisenhower's victory. They pointed to the way the conflict had dominated the last two weeks of the campaign, and they cited the General's promise to go to the battlefield as the clinching argument. "Millions of Americans saw in Eisenhower the candidate most likely to find some way out," commented *Newsweek*. Stevenson's aides agreed. Interior Secretary Oscar Chapman summed up their feelings when, asked by a reporter why the Democrats had lost, he replied, "Korea, more than anything else." The sense of national frustration over the stalemated war had built up to dangerous proportions and the public was in a vengeful mood, Stuart Brown wrote. "Stalin was too remote to be punished or to serve as a useful scapegoat," he pointed out. *"Someone* had to be blamed because *everyone* was to blame." Stevenson, trapped by Truman's record and convinced that there was no other way out, ended up as the sacrificial lamb.[71]

Korea became the decisive issue because it represented a deep feeling of malaise about the course of the Cold War. The editors of the *Nation* spoke of "the feeling of insecurity that pervades the American electorate" in noting that Eisenhower alone seemed to offer hope for a brighter future. "The American people saw Eisenhower and a sweeping change as the likeliest means of getting relief from the tensions generated by Korea and the Cold War," commented labor leader Hugo Ernst. After interviewing voters in Massachusetts, James MacGregor Burns and Philip Hastings reported that people backed Eisenhower as "a man deeply experienced in foreign affairs." "He served as a symbol of national security much as Roosevelt served as a symbol of economic security in the 1930's," they concluded. The University of Michigan survey research team came to similar conclusions after analyzing voters' attitudes. Those interviewed preferred the Democrats on domestic issues, especially economic ones, and though they distrusted the Republican party on foreign policy because of its isolationist past, they turned to Ike in the belief that he had unique qualifications "to handle the foreign situation." This faith in Eisenhower, symbol of victory in World War II, explains why he ran so far ahead of his party. The people, as Sherman

Adams observed, voted for the man they felt was "best quali-
fied to deal with the Communist menace and to bring peace in
Korea and the world." The fact that he was running on the
Republican ticket was irrelevant.[72]

Liberation had little to do with Ike's victory. It may, as
Louis Gerson argues, have "set the tone of the campaign," at
least in the beginning, but Eisenhower recognized its limitations quite early and dropped it after his Philadelphia speech
in September. The Democratic charge that liberation would
lead to nuclear war more than offset the aura of change the
slogan evoked. Its only specific contribution to Ike's victory
was to reduce the Democratic Polish vote, normally 70 percent, to approximately 50 percent and to add slightly to Eisenhower's appeal to other anti-Communist minorities, especially the Irish and the Germans. Both groups were largely
composed of former isolationists whom Truman had won
back to the Democratic party with his Cold War rhetoric in
1948 and who now backed Eisenhower as they had Willkie in
1940.[73]

What the election demonstrated above all else was Eisenhower's consummate skill as a politician. The General, whom the
pros regarded as a rank amateur in the early months of 1952,
proved to be, as Samuel Lubell remarked, "as compleat a political angler as ever fished the White House." He did everything right. He made the right compromises, bringing Taft
into the campaign when he needed him most and exploiting
the powerful sentiment for McCarthy among Americans from
all walks of life. He handled the Nixon fund episode adroitly,
avoiding the demands for dumping the vice-presidential candidate from the ticket without damaging the high moral tone he
had set for his crusade. Korea was the supreme test of his political maturity. He developed the issue slowly, stating his
views with increasing vigor as the fighting intensified and timing his final pledge perfectly. And even then, with the help of
Emmet Hughes, he maintained his flexibility by taking a posi-

tion that left him complete freedom in dealing with Korea as President. His promise to go to the battlefront committed him neither to escalation nor to withdrawal; in office, he would be able to carry out the very administration policies he condemned in the campaign.[74]

It is doubtful that Eisenhower ever sat down and consciously plotted out his campaign moves. Unlike Dewey, he was not a political strategist. Rather, he was an instinctive politician, a man who trusted his own shrewd insights into the public mood and reacted accordingly. He liked to portray himself as a man of rigid principle, in the mold of Herbert Hoover, but in reality he had much more in common with the pragmatic Franklin Roosevelt. Starting out as the reluctant candidate asked to save the bipartisan containment policy, he proceeded systematically to embrace every one of the foreign policy positions advocated by Robert Taft—except for massive retaliation, which he would adopt once in office. The eastern establishment could chide him, as did the *New York Times* and Walter Lippmann, for abandoning some of their cherished ideals, but they could hardly drop the man they had begged to enter the political arena as their champion.[75] By attacking containment and above all by exploiting the Korean War, Eisenhower won over the Taft supporters who had never trusted Dewey. Thus he overcame the old isolationist-interventionist split that had weakened the GOP since 1940 and reached out to the independents and stay-at-homes with solid Republican backing. All the while, he encouraged the myth that he was a novice in politics. Hiding his cleverness from public view, he let Herbert Brownell and Sherman Adams gain the plaudits, and Richard Nixon and John Foster Dulles take the responsibility for any mistakes. Eisenhower's greatness as a political leader lay precisely in his ability to create the impression that he was above politics. In 1952, Americans chose him because they really believed he would be President of all the people.

1956

3456

Dwight D. Eisenhower proved to be a highly popular President. He delegated authority freely, allowing such strong-minded Cabinet members as Secretary of State John Foster Dulles, Treasury Secretary George Humphrey, and Secretary of Defense Charles E. Wilson to run their departments independently and to appear to determine the administration's major policies. As a result, these men, and not the President, bore the burden of any criticism, while Eisenhower kept a careful eye on what they were doing through his effective and loyal White House staff, headed by Sherman Adams. He kept above partisan quarrels, letting Nixon lead the fight against the Democrats in Congressional elections. Although intellectuals and pundits caricatured him as a lazy, part-time President who spent too many days on the golf course or vacationing at Palm Springs and Camp David, the people liked the calm, relaxed leadership he provided.

As a party leader, Ike was much less successful. Senator McCarthy continued his irresponsible attacks on government officials despite the Republican victory in 1952. Eisenhower refused to enter into a gutter brawl with the Wisconsin senator, preferring to wait for him to fall victim to his own excesses. In

1954, McCarthy took on the United States Army and, in the course of televised hearings, exposed his warped values and demeaning tactics to the entire nation—which led finally to a Senate vote of censure. Senator Robert Taft, who had agreed to assist the administration as majority leader, died in 1953; his death made White House relations with the Republican right wing much more difficult. The new GOP leader in the Senate, William Knowland of California, took a hard line on Communism, especially in Asia, and backed the Bricker amendment—an attempt to place severe constitutional limits on presidential authority in treaty-making. Eisenhower found it much easier to work with the Democrats, who controlled both houses after 1954, and especially with the two Texas leaders, Speaker Sam Rayburn and Senate majority leader Lyndon B. Johnson. To the growing resentment of many liberal Democrats, Rayburn and Johnson cooperated closely with the President in winning Congressional approval for both his foreign and domestic measures.[1]

By mid-1955, it seemed that the next presidential election would be a very routine and humdrum affair. Ike's popularity was at an all-time high; the Republicans had fulfilled their promises of peace and prosperity and had ended the bitterness and sense of frustration that had characterized Truman's last years in office. In the early fall, Eisenhower was relaxing at Denver on one of his frequent vacations; on September 23 he played eighteen holes of golf and then, after lunch with some friends, returned to the course for another nine. He complained of indigestion, but his playing partners dismissed it lightly, chiding him for eating raw onions so freely. He went to bed early that evening, and then awoke in the night with chest pains. His doctor quietly moved him to a Denver hospital the next morning, and twelve hours later Press Secretary James Hagerty revealed that the President had suffered a severe heart attack. For the next few days, Ike fought for his life, but when it became clear that he would survive, most political commentators assumed that he would retire to private life after his term expired.

Speculation about Ike's probable successor began to flourish, centering on Vice-President Richard Nixon. Nixon acted with restraint, refusing to talk about his political future. He presided at several Cabinet meetings, but the White House staff, headed by Sherman Adams, jealously protected the presidential prerogatives, either making decisions themselves or taking issues directly to the recuperating Eisenhower. As the President's health improved, he went to his farm at Gettysburg, a place which his wife loved but which he found tedious, to convalesce. His strength came back quickly, and he soon became impatient with his restricted life. As some of his aides undoubtedly hoped, he found inactivity hard to bear. By mid-January, after a trip to Key West, he returned to the White House to resume his duties and already half-resolved to seek reelection.[2]

The pressures on Eisenhower to run again were building up. After surveying the other possible choices, a group of Ike's 1952 backers, including Lucius Clay, Thomas Dewey, Paul Hoffman, and Henry Cabot Lodge, announced that they were ready to reactivate Citizens for Eisenhower. On January 13, the President had dinner with twelve of his leading advisers—among them John Foster Dulles, Sherman Adams, Herbert Brownell, and Henry Cabot Lodge—and canvassed them on the question of his candidacy. All spoke out favorably, stressing his unique qualifications in the field of foreign policy and the absence of any other attractive GOP candidate. The President gave no firm indication of his decision, but his guests went away confident that he had been won over. If Ike had any doubts of the public's desires, the February Gallup poll erased them. Seventy-seven percent of the people expressed their approval of his handling of the presidency; 61 percent wanted him to run again, compared to 25 percent opposed and 11 percent with no opinion.[3]

On February 29, the President appeared before a press conference relaxed and tanned after ten days spent hunting and playing golf in Georgia. Before reporters could ask him the usual question, he announced that he had decided to run again and that he would explain his reasons to the American people that evening on radio and television. He talked candidly about his health that night, explaining that the doctors had given him an encouraging report but also noting that he would have to rest at least ten hours out of every twenty-four. He admitted talking with many friends and advisers, but he added, "In the last analysis, however, this decision was my own." "As of this moment," he asserted, "there is not the slightest doubt that I can perform, as well as I ever have, all of the important duties of the Presidency." He wanted to use his energy to serve the nation as its President, not as presidential candidate, and therefore he announced, "I shall, in general, wage no political campaign in the customary manner." But he would give regular talks by radio and television, and he expressed confidence that the record of his administration would insure a Republican victory in November.[4]

At the morning press conference, a reporter asked Eisenhower if he would retain Richard Nixon as his running mate. To everyone's surprise, the President hedged, expressing his "admiration" for Nixon but claiming that it would be inappropriate for him to discuss his choice for the vice-presidency until the party had selected him again as their presidential candidate. When a reporter asked pointedly if Nixon was in fact his choice, Ike replied, "I am very fond of him, but I am going to say no more about it." Actually, Eisenhower had called Nixon in for a private talk the day before, revealed his own decision to run again, and then suggested to the Vice-President that he consider accepting a Cabinet post, on the grounds that such a position would boost his chances for the presidency in 1960. The President may well have believed that Nixon would advance his own career by stepping out of the vice-presidency, but at the same time Ike was under pressure from Lucius Clay and other advisers to drop Nixon as a divisive figure who would weaken the ticket.

Whatever Ike's motivation, journalists had a field day speculating on the vice-presidency. At subsequent press conferences, they raised the question of Nixon's future, until finally Ike said, "The only thing I have asked him to do is to chart his own course and tell me what he would like to do." Reporters quickly pointed out that Nixon could hardly decide on his own without knowing Ike's wishes, and the President responded at his next news conference by saying that he would be "happy to be on any political ticket in which I was a candidate" with Nixon. The Vice-President hesitated for several weeks, thinking seriously about resigning, but then, encouraged by National Chairman Leonard Hall, he finally went to Ike and said he wished to run again. James Hagerty called a news conference at which Nixon announced that he was "available" for the vice-presidential nomination if the convention chose him, and Hagerty added, "The President has asked me to tell you gentlemen that he was delighted." Reporters still wondered, however, why Ike had let Nixon go through this agonizing process and then had not even given him his blessing in person. Some attributed it to the President's lack of political experience, but others saw it as a shrewd move to test out Nixon's popularity and drop him from the ticket if he proved vulnerable. Only when the Vice-President proved he had strength within the party did Eisenhower relent.[5]

I

Adlai Stevenson, the reluctant candidate in 1952, openly sought the nomination in 1956. Instead of retiring to private life after his defeat, he stayed in the public eye with well-publicized trips abroad, where he met with world leaders, and with frequent speaking engagements at home. He pitched in to help pay off the party's campaign debts and he worked hard to elect a Democratic Congress in 1954. Behind the scenes, he met at regular intervals with a study group composed of former government officials and college professors and headed by Thomas Finletter, Truman's Secretary of the Air Force. Stevenson used this brains trust, which included Arthur Schlesinger, Jr., John Kenneth Galbraith, and Chester Bowles, to help him formulate his positions on major national issues. Early in 1955, a group of his political supporters, led by former Democratic National Chairman Stephen Mitchell, organized a steering committee for Stevenson's candidacy, and in June they opened an office in Chicago with $50,000 they had raised from his loyal supporters.[6]

In the spring of 1955, Stevenson apparently told those close to him that he would run again, but he felt it wise to avoid an early public announcement. When he refused to commit himself to Harry Truman in a July meeting between the two men, the former President, remembering Stevenson's hesitation in 1952, began to throw his support to Averell Harriman, who had won the governorship of New York in 1954. Stevenson quietly lined up support from a majority of the other Democratic governors, and in early September he decided to make his formal announcement at a meeting of the Democratic National Committee in Chicago in mid-November. Eisenhower's heart attack suddenly made the Democratic nomination more attractive and Stevenson stepped up his activities. By the time he declared his candidacy on November 15, most of the party's leaders, except for Truman, had rallied to his side. Gallup polls showed him as the choice of a majority of Democratic voters, and by the end of 1955 *Life* believed he was so far ahead that the editors headlined a story, "It's Adlai versus Stevenson for the Democratic Nomination." [7]

Estes Kefauver remained unconvinced. The Tennessee senator still had his eye on the White House and, despite the overwhelming odds, he threw his coonskin cap in the ring on December 16, 1955. Though he could no longer exploit public discontent with Truman, he used the professionals' support of Stevenson to portray himself once again as the underdog fighting the party bosses. He announced his intention of entering all the major primaries, planning to appeal directly to the rank-and-file with his folksy, engaging handshaking tactics. Liberals, dismayed by Stevenson's accent on moderation and compromises with southern as well as northern party leaders, greeted Kefauver with new interest, if not encouragement. The *Reporter* and the *Nation* announced that they would withhold any endorsement of Stevenson pending the outcome of the primaries. Governor Harriman remained in the wings, keeping silent about his plans but ready to enter the contest openly if Stevenson faltered.[8]

Kefauver quickly proved that Stevenson was vulnerable. In New Hampshire, the state where he had embarrassed Truman in 1952, he swept to victory against only token opposition. To the experts' surprise, he decided to challenge the front runner in Minnesota, where strong backing from Senator Hubert Humphrey and Governor Orville Freeman made Stevenson appear unbeatable. Kefauver waged one of his most dogged campaigns, touring the state for eleven days; his slashing attacks on Eisenhower's farm policies, in contrast to Stevenson's well-modulated but abstract speeches, impressed the voters. Helped by a large Republican cross-over vote, Kefauver won a stunning victory, beating Stevenson by over 50,000 votes and winning twenty-six of the thirty delegates. "Senator Kefauver's weakness is that he has nobody for him but people," quipped James Reston. For Stevenson, it was no laughing matter. He had lost his status as front runner; now he would have to abandon his aloof posture and fight for the nomination.[9]

II

In his first four years in office, Dwight D. Eisenhower achieved a remarkably successful record in foreign policy. He fulfilled his major campaign commitment by going to Korea in December 1952 and bringing that limited war to an end seven months later. The death of Stalin in March 1953 undoubtedly influenced the Russians and Chinese, but the Eisenhower administration's threat to use nuclear weapons to break the stalemate apparently persuaded the Communist negotiators to give way on the prisoner-of-war issue and sign an agreement similar to the one Truman had sought unsuccessfully for nearly two years. When the Chinese then shifted their support southward to aid the Viet Minh rebels who had been fighting against the French in Indo-China since 1947, the President acted with remarkable restraint, vetoing a plan for American air strikes to aid the beleaguered French garrison at Dien Bien Phu. Instead of intervening militarily, the United States participated in the Geneva conference that led to French withdrawal and the temporary division of Vietnam at the 17th parallel. In the Formosa Straits, President Eisenhower took a firmer stand, committing the United States to protect Chiang Kai-shek's regime on Taiwan and securing Congressional authorization to defend not only the main Nationalist island but "closely related" areas such as the islands of Quemoy and Matsu, just off the coast of China. Eisenhower refused to commit himself publicly on the offshore islands, but the ambiguous American stand discouraged the Communist Chinese from launching an all-out attack in 1955.[10]

Eisenhower was proudest of his attempt to liquidate the Cold War by direct negotiations with the Soviets. In July 1955, he met at Geneva with the two men who had emerged from the power struggle in the Kremlin that followed Stalin's death, Nikolai Bulganin and Nikita Khrushchev. Bulganin held the title of premier, but it was Khrushchev, as first secretary of the Communist party, who wielded the real power. The summit meeting failed to resolve the major issues between the two rivals: the United States refused to consider Soviet proposals for West German disarmament as a precondition for unification of Germany, while the Soviets dismissed Eisenhower's "open skies" proposal as a first step toward arms control. Despite these setbacks, the President returned from Geneva convinced he had opened up a dialogue with the Soviet leaders that promised a more genuine detente in the future. The American people, basking in the "spirit of Geneva," seemed to agree.[11]

While Eisenhower pursued his mandate for peace, Secretary of State John Foster Dulles reassured those Americans who feared too soft a policy toward the Russians. It was Dulles who proposed intervention in Indo-China in 1954 to save the French, Dulles who wanted to fight to defend Quemoy and Matsu, Dulles who opposed the Geneva summit and persuaded Ike to take an unyielding stand on the crucial German issue. As Secretary, Dulles did drop the liberation rhetoric, especially after the ruthless Soviet suppression of an East German uprising in July 1953, and he acquiesced in the administration's decision not to repudiate the Yalta agreements. He scored his major victory when he sold the President on massive retaliation as the only way the United States could meet its global commitments without bankrupting itself. In a major speech in January 1954, Dulles announced that the administration would in the future avoid limited wars like the one in Korea and instead would defend the free world by relying "primarily upon a great capacity to retaliate, instantly, by means and at places of our own choosing."[12]

Dulles spelled out the implications of massive retaliation in a controversial interview published by *Life* in January 1956. Reviewing administration policy in Korea, the Formosa Straits, and Indo-China, Dulles claimed that three times the United States had gone to the brink of war to keep the peace.

"You have to take chances for peace, just as you take chances in war, . . ." Dulles told author James Shepley. "The ability to get to the verge without getting into the war is the necessary art. If you cannot master it, you inevitably get into war. If you try to run away from it, if you are scared to go to the brink, you are lost," he concluded. Though the Secretary admitted that Eisenhower made the ultimate decisions, *Life* headlined the story, "Three Times at Brink of War: How Dulles Gambled and Won." [13]

The article touched off a furious debate. Adlai Stevenson led the Democratic charge, saying, "I am shocked that the Secretary of State is willing to play Russian roulette with the life of our nation." Journalists condemned Dulles for his arrogance as well as his foolhardiness. James Reston was especially critical, claiming that Dulles had added "something new to the art of diplomatic blundering": "He doesn't stumble into booby traps," Reston mocked, "he digs them to size, studies them carefully, and then jumps." The violent criticism finally led *Life* publisher Henry R. Luce to state that Dulles had not approved the article nor read it in advance. Luce apologized for the lurid headline and argued that most of the comments centered on one paragraph in the original story that had been taken out of context. "[T]here is nothing in Secretary Dulles' words which is contrary to common sense," Luce argued. "For the Secretary is stating in vivid terms the perils of appeasement which should be understood by free men everywhere." Dulles called a special press conference to clarify his views, saying that it was the Communists, not the United States, who had brought the world to the brink of war. President Eisenhower told newsmen that he had not read the article, but announced that he had "complete faith in Mr. Dulles." "He is a man of great professional skill in the field," the President commented, "and to my mind, the best Secretary of State I have ever known." [14]

Privately, however, the President must have regretted the

political embarrassment Dulles had caused him with the "brinksmanship" label. At a time when the President defined his policies as "waging peace," and was trying above all else to keep his diplomacy out of partisan politics, Dulles gave the Democrats an opening they were certain to exploit. "You do make it extremely difficult for your friends and for those whose whole disposition is to support the administration," Lewis Douglas, a leading Democrat for Ike, wrote to Dulles. "Particularly you make it difficult for the great mass of independent people, and for the large number who crossed from the shore of one party to the shore of another in 1952," Douglas commented. Sherman Adams agreed, calling the *Life* article "most unfortunate." [15]

A sudden shift in Soviet foreign policy made Dulles' rigid approach seem particularly inadequate. Unlike Stalin, Khrushchev realized the importance of the newly emerging nations of the world; he now adopted a softer, more flexible approach, designed to appeal to the former colonial peoples. In the fall of 1955, he and Bulganin had made a tour of Asia, stopping off in Afghanistan, Burma, and India. They spoke in peaceful accents and began offering economic and technical aid to the underdeveloped countries. A much more startling change took place at the 20th Party Congress in Moscow in February 1956. In his major public address, Khrushchev announced his commitment to "the Leninist principle of peaceful coexistence of states with different social systems" and then proceeded to assert that Communism could triumph over capitalism in the world without a great war. "Peaceful coexistence" meant less reliance on force and violence and greater use of economic and diplomatic forms of competiton. In a secret speech that leaked to the West later, Khrushchev denounced Stalin and his crimes, raising hopes that the new Soviet foreign policy marked a genuine shift and not merely a temporary change in tactics.[16]

Dulles greeted the new Soviet foreign policy line as a victory for the Eisenhower administration. "The unity and firmness and resolution of the free nations during the past few years have caused the Soviet policy to fail," he told the Senate Foreign Relations Committee on February 24, "and today they are trying to figure out how they are going to get a better one." Two days later, Dulles told a Philadelphia audience that the Soviets adopted a new foreign policy "because they have been thwarted by the free world." In April, he dismissed the denunciation of Stalin by pointing out that the Soviet Union was still a dictatorship bent on world conquest. Having shown the Kremlin "the futility of their policies of violence," Dulles contended that "it would be folly for the free nations to consider that they can safely lower their guard and fall apart." [17]

Most American commentators disagreed with Dulles' analysis. Ernest Lindley warned that our allies were deeply troubled by the new initiative the Soviet Union had taken in world affairs. Walter Lippmann complained that American policy "remained frozen and inflexible." James Reston reported from Washington, "There is more apprehension in the capital today about the conduct of foreign policy than at any time since the Korean War." The *New Republic* linked the sluggish American response to Eisenhower's heart attack, pointing out that the Russians had been gaining steadily in the world since September. "In these months the Soviet Union has broken out of its self-imposed isolation," the editors commented. "The United States has not responded to these new threats. We have not yet shown an awareness of the changed conditions which the Communists have grasped and are determined to exploit." [18]

What the *New York Times* now labeled "a potentially great debate on the fundamental direction of American foreign policy" reached a climax when both Adlai Stevenson and President Eisenhower addressed the American Society of Newspaper Editors in Washington on April 21. Speaking first, Stevenson bluntly charged that under Eisenhower "the United States has come dangerously close to losing, if indeed it has not lost, its leadership in the world—economically, militarily, and worst of all, morally." He accused the administration of "sterility" and charged that a "rigid, unimaginative" foreign policy had enabled Russia to make impressive gains among the new nations. The United States, he asserted, must win back the decent respect of the world by abandoning massive retaliation, by channeling its foreign aid through the United Nations rather than military alliance systems, and, above all, by taking the first step toward arms control through a suspension of hydrogen bomb tests. "It is time to regain the initiative," Stevenson concluded, "to release the warm, creative energies of this mighty land; it is time to resume the onward progress of mankind in pursuit of peace and freedom." [19]

A few hours later, Eisenhower spoke from the same podium. He ignored Stevenson's criticism, telling the editors that "we have reason for cautious hope that a new, a fruitful, a peaceful era for mankind can emerge from a haunted decade. The world breathes a little more easily today." He took credit for ending the Korean War and made a strong plea for an expanded foreign aid program for the underdeveloped nations. He discounted the recent changes in Soviet policy, echoing Dulles in saying that Russia remained a "dictatorship." In informal remarks at the end of his speech, he told the newsmen that the Soviets had not changed: "Their basic aim is to conquer the world, through world revolution if possible, but in any way." [20]

The editors, despite their overwhelmingly Republican makeup, found Stevenson's description of the international situation more perceptive. In a poll taken before the two speeches, fifty-four newspapermen said that they thought the United States was "losing the Cold War," compared to twenty-four who did not. The important guests at the convention, including congressmen, Supreme Court justices, and Cabinet members, also believed that the Cold War was going against the United States, though the margin was closer, 43 to 26.

The leading Democratic contender had clearly found an unexpected Republican weakness. With Eisenhower's leadership in doubt after his heart attack, Stevenson could exploit Dulles' stereotyped response to the new Soviet peace offensive and make foreign policy a major issue in 1956, thus neutralizing the GOP's greatest asset.[21]

III

Stevenson's call for a ban on the testing of hydrogen bombs, offered to the newspaper editors as an example of his more constructive approach to world issues, touched on an issue of vital national concern. The world had entered the thermonuclear age on November 1, 1952, just three days before Eisenhower's election, when American scientists detonated a primitive hydrogen device a thousand times more powerful than the bomb that destroyed Hiroshima. The Soviets exploded their first hydrogen bomb on August 12, 1953; seven months later, on March 1, 1954, at Bikini atoll the United States tested a hydrogen bomb which released more than fifteen megatons of explosive energy. With the advent of these thermonuclear weapons, the United States lost its atomic advantage over the Soviet Union; each of the superpowers now possessed the capacity to destroy the other.

The hydrogen bomb was a logical outgrowth of the original atomic bomb, whose explosive force came from the splitting apart of heavy atoms of either uranium-235 or plutonium. As early as 1943 scientists realized that the tremendous heat generated by this fission process could be used to fuse together the light atoms of tritium, a rare form of hydrogen, and lead to a much vaster release of energy. In developing this fusion process, American scientists found a shortcut that would reduce greatly the amount of tritium needed: they wrapped a layer of common uranium, a cheap and plentiful element in contrast to U-235, around a core consisting of an atomic bomb and a quantity of lithium deuteride, which released tritium to fuel the fusion reaction when the atomic trigger was detonated. The fusion of tritium created fast neutrons that then split apart the ordinary uranium to produce a massive fission explosion. Thus the so-called hydrogen bomb was actually a fission-fusion-fission weapon that drew more than half its explosive energy from the splitting apart of ordinary uranium.

The nature of the hydrogen bomb led to serious fallout hazards. A true fusion bomb would be extremely clean, leaving virtually no radioactive particles to contaminate the atmosphere. But a fission bomb results both in local fallout, caused by the ground debris, and global fallout, as radioactive byproducts such as strontium-90 are sucked up into the atmosphere and then gradually fall back to earth. Strontium-90 has a half-life of twenty-eight years. When it reaches the earth, it enters the food supply, most often in cow's milk, and ultimately lodges in human bones, where it can cause cancer. The first warning of this new danger to mankind came by accident. In March 1954, a small Japanese fishing boat, the *Lucky Dragon,* received a heavy coat of fallout from the American hydrogen bomb test at Bikini. Several of the Japanese fishermen became ill; one crew member died after the boat returned to Japan, and several of the others developed tumors. Ralph Lapp, a nuclear physicist who first explained the "dirty" nature of the American hydrogen bomb, publicized the *Lucky Dragon* case and warned that repeated nuclear testing could in time so contaminate the planet as to endanger all human life.[22]

Many scientists began to advocate a suspension of nuclear testing on humanitarian grounds—to stop the fallout; others saw a test ban as the best and simplest way to halt the spiraling arms race. Until 1955, the United States and Russia had concentrated on the problem of eliminating nuclear weapons in their disarmament proposals. When a new subcommittee of the United Nations Disarmament Commission began meeting in early 1955, the United States shifted its emphasis to ways of trying to control and limit the use of nuclear weapons rather than to do away with them. The American proposals, culminating in Eisenhower's open-skies plan, received little encouragement from the Russians, who continued to press for a total ban on the use of atomic and hydrogen bombs. Khrushchev and Bulganin, during their visit to India in December 1955, joined with Prime Minister Nehru in calling for an end to nuclear tests as a first step toward controlling the arms race. At nearly the same time, the Pope, in a year-end message to mankind, also advocated a test ban as part of a broader disarmament proposal. In his public address to the 20th Party Congress in February, Nikita Khrushchev put forth the idea of a test ban, saying it would provide the basis for subsequent disarmament negotiations with the United States.[23]

The United States failed to respond to the Soviet initiative on a test moratorium. In January, Dulles told a press conference, "We have not yet found any basis which would seem to warrant us in suspending hydrogen bomb tests," adding that test suspension could only be considered as part of an overall disarmament agreement, with proper safeguards to protect against violations. When the UN disarmament subcommittee resumed its meetings in London in March 1956, the chief American negotiator, Harold Stassen, ignored the test ban concept in putting forth a proposal for a limited open-skies arrangement with Russia. The Soviets countered with a plan to freeze and gradually reduce all conventional forces and to outlaw all future nuclear tests.[24]

Thomas Murray, a member of the Atomic Energy Commission, provided the impetus for Stevenson's test ban proposal. In testimony before a Senate subcommittee on April 12, Murray, a Truman appointee, proposed a ban on "multimegaton thermonuclear weapons," arguing that we had already perfected these huge bombs and did not need to test them further.

Murray professed not to be overly concerned with the radiation hazards, stressing instead the need to concentrate on testing and developing small nuclear bombs that could be used in limited wars. Stevenson, in his address to the newspaper editors two weeks later, cited Murray's remarks in setting forth his own test ban proposal. "As a layman I hope I can question the sense in multiplying and enlarging weapons of a destructive power already almost incomprehensible," Stevenson declared. Like Murray, Stevenson made no mention of the fallout hazard, focusing instead on the need to achieve progress toward arms control. The United States, Stevenson suggested, should act unilaterally, but if the Soviet Union did not respond, then "we can reconsider our policy." A test ban, he affirmed, would be "a step which, it seems to me, we might now take, a step which would reflect our determination never to plunge the world into nuclear holocaust, a step which would reaffirm our purpose to act with humility and a decent concern for world opinion." [25]

Two days later, Nikita Khrushchev, while touring England with Bulganin, undercut Stevenson's appeal for a test ban. In a speech in Birmingham, the Soviet leader boasted of Russian scientific and technical progress, and then asserted, "I am quite sure that we will have a guided missile with a hydrogen bomb that can fall anywhere in the world." Khrushchev's reference to a soon-to-be-perfected ICBM (Inter-Continental Ballistic Missile) sent shivers up the spines of the American people. Democrats, led by Senator Stuart Symington, had for several months been charging that the Eisenhower administration was lagging in the race to build these new weapons. When reporters asked Stevenson how he felt about Khrushchev's boast, he surprised them by saying that he felt Eisenhower had been "dangerously dilatory" in developing the new missiles. He reaffirmed his test ban proposal, but he quickly added, "the means of delivery, by guided missiles or airplanes, is another question and it is evident that we must renew our efforts in the whole area so that we shall not find ourselves subject to power-political blackmail." [26]

Reporters eagerly sought President Eisenhower's reaction to Khrushchev's ICBM boast and to Stevenson's test ban proposal in his weekly press conference on April 25. The President confessed he had no reason to doubt that Russia had the ability to perfect an intercontinental missile, but he noted that it was a huge leap to move from laboratory tests to actual deployment of such a weapon. Then he linked the ICBM with the test ban. "It is a little bit of a paradox to urge that we work just as hard as we know how on the guided missile and that we stop all research on the hydrogen bomb, because one without the other is rather useless," the President commented. He went on to defend testing as essential, not to develop bigger bombs but to create more versatile weapons with less fallout that could be used for defensive purposes. Testing of the hydrogen bomb, he continued, was necessary "to make it more of a military weapon and less one just of mass destruction." [27]

In May, despite protests from the Soviet and Japanese governments, as well as from American pacifists, the administration went ahead with a planned series of nuclear tests in the Marshall Islands. The first and most spectacular blast took place on May 21, when a B-52 dropped a ten-megaton bomb over Namu Island in Bikini atoll. This first American hydrogen bomb to be dropped from an airplane missed the target by nearly four miles; but the huge fireball, exploding 15,000 feet above the earth's surface, created very little local fallout and there was no repetition of the *Lucky Dragon* incident. The Atomic Energy Commission refused to release details of other explosions, but Japanese scientists who monitored the series reported seven more test shots, including one of an H-bomb warhead which exploded at an altitude of 100,000 feet. In a press conference on May 23, Eisenhower referred only to the ten-megaton explosion in telling newsmen that the AEC had achieved its stated purpose of testing a smaller H-bomb with substantially less fallout; he made no mention of a successful test of an ICBM warhead.[28]

The developing public concern over fallout received new impetus with the simultaneous release of American and British scientific reports on radiation dangers on June 12. In the United States, a committee of the National Academy of Science concluded that fallout had little appreciable effect on food supplies, though it admitted that the long-term effects of strontium-90 were difficult to determine and it called for further study of this problem. The gravest danger, the committee concluded, was genetic. The American people were accumulating dangerously high levels of radiation which could affect future generations by causing serious mutations. The scientists put the major blame on medical and dental X rays, not fallout, and they called for strict standards to limit exposure to diagnostic X rays. The present level of fallout was not dangerous, they concluded, but they called for further study and warned that an increase in testing might create human hazards. The British Medical Research Council findings were almost identical. There was virtually "no pathological danger from fallout," the English scientists found, but they expressed deep concern about the long-term effects of strontium-90, "which is beginning to accumulate in bone." [29]

The administration treated the scientific reports as evidence that testing did not create a serious health problem. The American ambassador to the United Nations Disarmament Commission, James Wadsworth, cited the report of the National Academy in arguing against an Indian proposal for a test ban treaty. "Properly conducted nuclear tests," Wadsworth argued, "do not constitute a hazard to human health and safety." Ralph Lapp, however, disputed the Academy's findings. In a *New Republic* article, he maintained that for the next fifty years strontium-90 from nuclear tests could continue falling to the earth, where it would be absorbed into the grass eaten by cows and would eventually contaminate the milk children drank. Calling on the superpowers to enact an immediate test ban, Lapp declared, "Russia and America have an equal stake in avoiding radioactive recklessness." Other scientists—notably Eugene Rabinowitch, editor of the *Bulletin of the Atomic Scientists,* and David Inglis, a nuclear physicist—backed Lapp's call for a test ban. Rather than radiation dangers, however, they emphasized the need to halt the arms race before the development of an ICBM.[30]

Testimony made public in late June by General James M. Gavin, chief of the Army's research and development, to a Senate armed forces subcommittee in late June presented a much more shocking view of the fallout problem. Speaking of the possibility of a nuclear war between Russia and the United States, General Gavin commented that "several hundred millions" would be killed, including many millions in Western Europe. When senators asked why friendly populations would perish as a result of an American atomic attack on the Soviet Union, Gavin explained that if the wind blew the wrong way, the fallout would kill people as far west as the British Isles. Another Pentagon spokesman, who preferred to remain unidentified, said that if the winds were "unfavorable," the death toll could be as high as 500 million.[31]

In an effort to offset this alarming news, Admiral Lewis Strauss, the chairman of the AEC, announced on July 19 that the recent Pacific tests had proved that the United States had developed a much cleaner hydrogen bomb with relatively little fallout. "We are convinced that mass hazard from fallout is not a necessary complement to the use of large nuclear weapons," Strauss concluded, adding that the cleaner bomb marked a step forward "not only from a military point of view but from a humanitarian aspect." Liberal editors quickly attacked Strauss for publicizing "humanitarian bombs" as "a sedative to calm public nerves." Eugene Rabinowitch pointed out that Strauss's statement invited "misinterpretation," since the American people had no guarantee that the Soviets would use a clean bomb if they attacked the United States. Ralph Lapp said bluntly: "War is a dirty business. Science has not succeeded in making it any cleaner. Part of the madness of our time is that adult men can use a word like humanitarian to describe an H-bomb." [32]

Stevenson remained silent on his original proposal, except for one brief defense of the test ban in a primary debate in Florida with Senator Kefauver. Yet the idea he had brought into the political arena with his April 21 speech continued to gain adherents in the scientific and intellectual communities. The Federation of American Scientists came out in favor of a "worldwide ban on further tests of nuclear weapons" in June, and two months later, on the eleventh anniversary of the bombing of Hiroshima, the editors of the *Nation* called on President Eisenhower "to make a unilateral announcement that we will make no further H-bomb tests, the commitment to stand only as long as other nations also refrain from making tests." "There is no risk," the editors explained, "in such a declaration and there might be great advantage." Although the administration continued to ignore this rising wave of protest, the test ban had become a significant political issue, one which aroused such deep public concern that it could not be postponed indefinitely.[33]

IV

Adlai Stevenson was too busy trying to beat back Kefauver's challenge in the spring of 1956 to pay much attention to foreign policy. Shocked by the Minnesota outcome, his advisers urged him to abandon his "lofty position in the eyes of the ordinary citizen" and pursue the personal tactics that worked so well for Kefauver. Stephen Mitchell told Stevenson to present himself to the people "as a human being," suggesting that he drop his set speeches in favor of informal question-and-answer sessions with the voters. Reluctantly, Stevenson decided to accept this advice and to campaign on his personality rather than on the issues in two critical primaries—Florida and California. In his first Florida stop in mid-April, Stevenson shed his coat and took to the streets, stopping people, shaking hands, and saying, "I'm Adlai Stevenson and I need your support." [34]

Kefauver responded by redoubling his personal efforts in these two widely separated states, and the campaign soon took on a bitter, feuding air. Both men virtually ignored foreign policy, save for a few digs at John Foster Dulles, whose brinksmanship made him the obvious straw man for all Democrats to attack. Kefauver expressed the hope that Dulles would take the nation "to the brink of peace"; Stevenson warned that the Secretary of State was "bringing us to the edge of the nuclear abyss." The two candidates spent most of their time on the segregation issue, each striving hard to convince California voters that he backed the Supreme Court decision on school integration while telling Floridians that he opposed the use of force to achieve desegregation. The lack of issues between Kefauver and Stevenson made their one face-to-face encounter—a televised debate in Miami—a bland one. The only time sparks flew was when Kefauver accused his opponent of advocating unilateral disarmament in his test ban proposal, and pointed up the inconsistency of stopping tests while developing the ICBM. Stevenson heatedly denied wanting to halt missile progress and said he only wished to end the testing of the H-bomb, "the most lethal, the most terrible, the most devastating, the most ghastly weapon that has been developed on the face of the earth." [35]

Stevenson won a narrow victory in Florida, barely nosing out Kefauver with 51 percent of the vote. Reporters found apathy the most significant feature of the primary, noting that the two presidential contenders attracted only half the number of voters who had cast ballots three weeks before in a hotly contested governor's race. In California a week later, Stevenson, with the backing of the state's party leaders, won a sweeping triumph. He received over a million votes, as against less than 700,000 for the Tennessee senator. After California, Kefauver's candidacy was doomed, but Stevenson was still not certain of the nomination. Governor Averell Harriman of New York, who had found Kefauver a useful stalking horse, now entered the contest openly. Backed by Northern liberals and machine bosses, as well as by Harry Truman (who said there was no man in the country "I think more highly of"), Harriman was a formidable opponent who disagreed sharply with Stevenson's foreign policy views. Privately the New York governor complained that Stevenson was "soft on communism," and publicly he criticized the Eisenhower administration for letting down its guard against the Russians. "It is clear now," Harriman contended in May, "that the 'spirit of Geneva' was a smoke screen behind which the Russians have made a major break-through." [36]

In addition to Harriman, Stevenson faced a new threat in the "favorite son" candidacy of Senate Majority Leader Lyndon Johnson. Put forward by the Texas delegation in the spring, Johnson began to attract support across the South, replacing Richard Russell as that region's candidate in the forthcoming national convention. Stevenson, however, remained relatively popular in the South because of his moderate stand on the race issue, and overall he had regained his initial position as front runner. But in the process he had lost some of his original appeal as a fresh, courageous voice in American politics. In taking to the streets to defeat Kefauver and in moderating his liberal views to placate the South, Stevenson seemed to be just another ambitious politician. Yet his loyal enthusiasts still hoped that the "old" Stevenson would return. "We have too vivid and grateful a memory of the leadership Adlai Stevenson offered our nation four years ago," commented the

Reporter, "and we cannot give up hoping and praying that once the silly season of primaries is over, the same voice that we found so stirring will make itself heard again." [37]

V

In the spring, as President Eisenhower recovered fully from his heart attack, he began to look forward to the coming election. He expressed astonishment to reporters at his continued extraordinary popularity, reflected in the Gallup poll (in mid-May, the survey showed 71 percent approved of Ike as President); and he announced in late May that he would expand his campaign activities in the fall in order to help elect a Republican Congress. National Chairman Leonard Hall expressed his pleasure at Ike's display of enthusiasm, commenting on the steady stream of memos he was receiving from the White House about how the GOP should conduct the fall campaign.[38]

John Foster Dulles remained the Republicans' most serious liability. When the Soviets announced a dramatic reduction of 1.2 million men in their armed forces in early May, the Secretary of State told incredulous reporters that the move would actually strengthen, not weaken, Soviet military power. The Russians needed the men in industry and agriculture, Dulles explained, adding that "there is nothing to prevent the speedy recall and equipping of large units of thoroughly trained reserves." Asked if the United States would make similar reductions in military manpower, Dulles said no, commenting, "It would be very foolish for us to drop our guard." A month later, addressing a Kiwanis International convention in San Francisco, Dulles repeated his hard-line view of the recent changes in Soviet foreign policy. He dismissed Khrushchev's denunciation of Stalin, calling the present Soviet leader "a despot" who had failed to oppose his predecessor's crimes. He went on to warn that the Soviets might soon resort again to violence, which he described as "the classic and natural tactic of Soviet communism." He doubted that the Russians would long continue a policy of "peaceful coexistence" which permitted the world to judge "the most dramatic contrast between the dynamic liberalism of free societies and the brutal reactionism of those who glorify physical power." Thus, despite the significant changes taking place behind the Iron Curtain, Dulles continued to preach a pure form of Cold War theology.[39]

The Secretary's moralistic views proved embarrassing to the President, who sought a more flexible position. On June 6, Eisenhower told reporters that the United States would no longer insist that recipients of American aid join military alliances against the Soviet Union. "If you are waging peace," the President explained, "you can't be too particular sometimes about the special attitudes that different countries take." He went on to point out that the United States had taken a neutral stance as a young nation, and said he saw nothing wrong with uncommitted nations today choosing neutralism to avoid military involvement in the quarrels of other countries.[40]

Dulles, bombarded with protests from American allies around the world, hurried to the White House the next day. After a long conference with the President, the White House released a new statement clarifying Eisenhower's position on neutralism. It affirmed his support for American allies abroad, and then stated that while the President believed there were "special conditions which justify political neutrality," he felt that "no nation has the right to be indifferent to the fate of another." Eisenhower was unavailable for further comment, and, in a speech at Iowa State College later in the week, Dulles attacked neutralism as "an obsolete conception, and, except under very exceptional circumstances, . . . an immoral and shortsighted conception." Vice-President Nixon was one of the many who were confused by the administration's flip-flop. In a speech at Lafayette College early in the week, he advocated a flexible policy toward uncommitted nations, but after Dulles clarified the issue, he attacked neutralism for making "no moral distinction between the Communist world and the free world." "Is democracy to be equated with dictatorship?" Nixon asked rhetorically. "Is freedom the same as tyranny?" Democrats, delighted at the Republican mix-up, responded by portraying Ike as a captive of Dulles' inflexible policy and poked fun at the Secretary of State. "Dulles has again upheld his reputation as the only bull who carries his own China around with him," commented the *Nation*.[41]

In the midst of the neutralism flap, Eisenhower suddenly suffered a severe attack of ileitis, a digestive disorder that required a two-hour operation to remove a section of his intestines. This major surgery, coming so soon after his heart attack, raised serious doubts about his candidacy, but Republican spokesmen, notably Leonard Hall and Press Secretary Jim Hagerty, released a series of optimistic statements indicating that Eisenhower would run for reelection after a quick recovery. The President left the hospital after three weeks, and, while recuperating at Gettysburg in July, he announced through Senator Knowland that he had not changed his mind about running, claiming that he was in better shape than when he made his original decision in February. Democrats complained about asking the people to elect a part-time leader and "a kind of President Emeritus," hinting darkly that "a vote for Mr. Eisenhower was in reality a vote for Richard M. Nixon for President." When Eisenhower finally returned to the White House in late July, reporters were shocked by his gaunt, haggard appearance. He had lost seven pounds, and he confessed to Cyrus Sulzberger in early August that he still felt weak from his recent ordeal. Republicans scoffed at these reports. National Chairman Leonard Hall announced that Ike felt fit and would campaign vigorously in the fall, giving five or six major speeches in different parts of the country. But most commentators believed that the President's health remained a major issue, and one that kept the forthcoming election from becoming a shoo-in for the GOP.[42]

VI

While Eisenhower slowly recovered from his operation, dramatic events in Eastern Europe and the Middle East threw a long shadow over American politics. The first ominous news came from Poland. On June 28, workers in the city of Poznan left their factories and paraded through the streets shouting "Bread!" and "Out with the Russians!" Apparently Khrushchev's attacks on Stalin encouraged the Polish workers to believe that Russia was loosening its grip on the satellites. They seized a radio station, overran the local Communist party headquarters, and freed a group of political prisoners from a secret police jail. The Polish government rushed in troops, and after three days of bitter fighting, in which fifty-three insurgents were killed and more than two hundred wounded, the army put down the spontaneous uprising. The United States stood quietly by, despite the rioters' appeals to Americans visiting a trade fair in Poznan for help from the West. John Foster Dulles scrupulously avoided any talk of liberation in a special press conference he held on July 11 after returning from a ten-day vacation. "I believe that the most we can do is to adhere to the old historic American tradition of setting an example of the good fruits of freedom," the Secretary said. "The idea that we can help along by direct interference is, I think, a false idea." The administration did offer some surplus food stocks to the Polish people, but the Warsaw government brusquely rejected this aid.[43]

The Poznan riots, however, rekindled Republican thinking about ways to appeal again to Eastern European minority groups within the United States. Back in December, President Eisenhower had affirmed his commitment to "peaceful liberation" in a special Christmas message to those behind the Iron

Curtain. "The American people recognize the trials under which you are suffering," the President declared, ". . . and share your faith that right in the end will prevail to bring you once again among the free nations of the world." Though refugee groups praised Ike for these encouraging words, Arizona publisher William R. Mathews expressed a common view when he wrote the President that there was no such thing as "peaceful liberation," saying, "This policy will gradually take us into another war." Eisenhower made no further references to liberation, but in March, A. B. Hermann, a Republican who had worked in the party's nationalities division in 1952, had urged Leonard Hall to reactivate this group. Hermann pointed out that 85 percent of the voters of European ethnic origin lived in just 17 states with a combined electoral vote of 302, more than enough to cinch the election. He listed the 17 states and the percentage of nationalities in each, and then in May sent a second memorandum to White House aide Howard Pyle, telling him that he faced a "terrific problem" in reactivating the various nationality groups "which were allowed to lie dormant practically since 1952." [44]

Chairman Hall appointed Hermann director of the revived nationalities division of the party, and by June Hermann was sending out press releases in twelve different foreign languages to newspapers. The Poznan riots quickened Republican interest in ethnic minorities, and in late July Hermann arranged a meeting between his Nationalities Advisory Committee and Senator Prescott Bush of Connecticut, chairman of the Republican Platform Committee. But the Republicans did not push the liberation theme openly, as they had in 1952; they focused instead on proposals to liberalize immigration policies for refugees from behind the Iron Curtain. The abortive uprisings in East Germany and Poznan served as grim reminders of how dangerous it was to raise false hopes in the satellite nations in the quest for votes at home. [45]

The second crisis began in Washington on July 19, when

Secretary of State John Foster Dulles met with the Egyptian ambassador to discuss an offer the United States had extended in December 1955, in cooperation with Great Britain and the World Bank, to finance the Aswan Dam on the Nile. In surprisingly blunt diplomatic language, Dulles informed the ambassador that the United States was withdrawing its offer on the grounds that Egypt lacked the financial stability to support the vast project. President Gamal Abdel Nasser, who had been conferring in Yugoslavia with India's Prime Minister Nehru and President Tito, returned to Egypt and a week later replied to Dulles in a four-hour speech from Cairo. The Egyptian government, Nasser declared, would build the dam by nationalizing the Suez Canal and using its $100 million in annual revenue to finance the project. With this action, the world was plunged into the most serious crisis it had faced since the end of the Korean War.[46]

The Suez crisis had been developing for more than a year. In 1955, Dulles, fearful of Soviet penetration into the strategic Middle East, had taken the lead in forming the Baghdad Pact, a defensive alliance consisting of Turkey, Pakistan, Iraq (the only Arab member), England, and France. The United States, in an attempt to preserve the goodwill of Egypt and Syria, Iraq's traditional rivals, did not join the Pact. The American action, however, led President Nasser, who had come to power in Egypt after an army-led coup had overthrown King Farouk in 1952, to turn to the Soviet Union for support. In late 1955, the Soviets concluded a large arms deal with the Egyptians, agreeing to supply the leading Arab country with Czech guns, tanks, and airplanes that could overturn the uneasy balance of power in the Middle East. The Israelis countered by asking the United States to sell them weapons so that they could defend themselves against an expected Egyptian attack. Secretary Dulles refused, saying that such open sales would touch off a dangerous arms race, but he encouraged England and France to sell Israel tanks and jet fighters.

In April, the rising tension led to heavy fighting between Egypt and Israel in the Gaza strip—which ended only after UN Secretary General Dag Hammarskjöld undertook a personal peace-keeping mission.[47]

Throughout the spring, Dulles overrode British and French objections and pursued a conciliatory policy toward Nasser. But he became furious in May, when the Egyptian leader recognized Communist China and concluded a trade deal by selling Peking $28 million worth of surplus cotton. Then in June, Dmitri T. Shepilov, the new Soviet Foreign Minister, made an ostentatious visit to Cairo just as the last British troops were leaving the Suez under an agreement negotiated in 1955. Rumors spread that Shepilov brought with him a Russian offer to finance the Aswan Dam; in reality, he concluded another arms deal with Nasser that mortgaged the entire Egyptian cotton crop to the Soviet Union. With many congressmen and senators saying that they could no longer vote for aid to Egypt, Dulles decided that the latest Soviet arms deal had made the Egyptians economically and politically dependent on the Soviet Union. With Eisenhower's approval, but without informing the British, Dulles went ahead on July 19 with his abrupt withdrawal of the offer to finance the huge dam.[48]

Most Americans applauded Dulles' action. *Newsweek* praised him for showing all neutral nations "that it was no longer profitable to play the East against the West for economic aid," while *Time* called it a "gambit that took the breath of professionals for its daring and won the assent of kibitzers for its instinctive rightness." Eisenhower developed second thoughts, writing in his memoirs that "we might have been undiplomatic in the way the cancellation was handled," but Dulles quickly assured him that the opposition in Congress would have forced the administration to take the same action in the long run. "As it was," Dulles argued, "we retained some flexibility." [49]

No one in Washington was prepared for the Egyptian re-

sponse. Eisenhower admitted afterward that he was "astonished" when Nasser seized the Suez Canal, commenting, "We
hadn't thought of it." Dulles was off on a goodwill trip to
Peru, apparently assured by his brother, CIA Director Allen W. Dulles, that Nasser would take the withdrawal lying
down. The British, who concurred in the cancellation but were
angry about not being consulted in advance, reacted strongly.
The Suez had traditionally been the English lifeline to Singapore
and the East, and it was the route for most of the oil that fueled
the economy of Britain and all Western Europe. Though Nasser promised to run the canal efficiently, England, along with
France, felt the need to protect the rights of its citizens who
owned stock in the Universal Suez Canal Company, expropri-
ated by the Egyptians. Above all, Prime Minister Anthony
Eden feared the precedent that Nasser was establishing. England had suffered from the consequences of appeasing Adolf
Hitler in the 1930's. "It was 1938 over again," Harold Macmillan reported Eden as saying. "He would not be party to
any new appeasement." [50]

"My colleagues and I are convinced that we must be ready,
in the last resort, to use force to bring Nasser to his senses,"
Eden cabled President Eisenhower on July 27. "For our part
we are prepared to do so. I have this morning instructed our
Chiefs of Staff to prepare a military plan accordingly."
Alarmed, Eisenhower immediately replied by urging the British not to use force except as a last, desperate resort. "I personally feel sure that the American reaction would be severe
and that great areas of the world would share that reaction,"
Ike told Eden. In his memoirs, the President said his greatest
fear was that precipitate British action would destroy the
United Nations. He made no mention of political considerations, but certainly he must have been aware that a Middle
Eastern war would undercut his plans to run for reelection on
a platform of peace and prosperity. In any case, instead of
waiting for Dulles to return from Peru, he dispatched Robert

Murphy, a veteran diplomat, to London with instructions to discourage "impulsive armed action." Beyond that, the President simply told Murphy, "Just go over and hold the fort." Publicly, Eisenhower played the crisis coolly, telling a press conference on August 1 that the West faced "a very grave issue" and adding, "It is something to be handled with care." [51]

Murphy arrived in London to find that the British were determined to use force to thwart Nasser's seizure of the canal. Though he tried to make it clear to Eden that the United States opposed a military solution, the British Prime Minister remained adamant. "As Eden expressed it," Murphy wrote later, "there was no thought of asking the United States for anything, 'but we hope you will take care of the Bear!'" In other words, England wanted the United States to warn the Soviet Union off so that the British and the French could handle Nasser on their own. Two days later, Dulles finally arrived in London. From the outset, according to Murphy, the Secretary's goal was to avert military action, since he "was acutely aware that a commitment to support hostilities could have a disastrous effect on Eisenhower's candidacy that year for reelection as President." Dulles' main tactic was to stall for time in the hope that he could at least postpone an armed showdown until after the elections. Accordingly, he prevailed upon the British and the French to shelve their plans for intervention and instead convene a conference of twenty-four nations that used the Suez Canal. Dulles tried to placate America's allies by denouncing Nasser's grab of the canal as "an angry act of retaliation against fancied grievances," but he also commented, "We do not want to meet violence with violence." Lord Beaverbrook's London *Daily Express* reported in disgust, "This is an appalling reminder that Dulles—and Ike himself—are interested mainly in . . . the coming Presidential elections." [52]

Dulles returned to the United States on August 3, and that

evening he appeared on national television with the President to report to the American people on the crisis. The Secretary outlined the plans for a canal users' conference, scheduled for mid-August in London, and stressed the international character of the canal by arguing that no one nation should determine its fate. He expressed the hope that the moral force of world opinion would dictate a peaceful solution, and when he was asked what the United States would do if moral suasion failed, Dulles replied, "We have given no commitments at any time as to what the U.S. would do in that unhappy contingency." In a press conference a few days later, Eisenhower reinforced the Secretary's views, saying, "I can't conceive of military force being a good solution." But when a journalist tried to get the President to say that he opposed the use of military force "under any circumstances," Ike burst out, "I didn't say that. I was very careful not to say that. . . . I don't mean to say that anyone was to surrender rights without using everything they can to preserve their rights." Privately, Eisenhower boasted to Cyrus Sulzberger that when events appeared to be moving toward war, "I put my foot down and stopped the drift." He expressed confidence in a peaceful solution, adding that Khrushchev, whom he likened to "a drunken railway hand," did not want war but was only "fishing in the troubled waters of the Middle East." [53]

The political ramifications of the Middle East crisis could never have been far from the President's mind. He received a steady stream of telegrams and letters from domestic pressure groups, pointing up the varied American interests at stake. Zionists called upon him to prevent Nasser from closing the canal to the Israelis. The National Association of Federations of Syrian and Lebanese American Clubs pleaded with him to prevent the use of force against Egypt. Exporters and oil executives urged the President to stand firmly against the attempt to interfere with world commerce. [54]

The President referred these petitioners to the State Department, but he did undertake one significant political step himself. On August 12, the Sunday before the Democratic national convention was scheduled to open in Chicago, Eisenhower asked a bipartisan Congressional delegation to meet with him and Dulles at the White House for a briefing on the Suez crisis. Some twenty-two representatives and senators attended, including nine Democrats who flew back from Chicago for the conference. For an hour and a half, Eisenhower, Dulles, and Admiral Radford, Chairman of the Joint Chiefs of Staff, outlined the situation to the legislators. They stressed American opposition to the use of force and said that the United States would restrict itself to keeping the Russians out if fighting erupted. The members of Congress refused to commit themselves to anything more than a general statement recognizing "the importance of dependable operation of the Canal as a major artery of world traffic." Majority Leader Lyndon Johnson did tell the press afterward, "Politics stop at the water's edge when the security of our country is at stake," but neither the Texas senator nor any other prominent Democrat would accept the President's invitation to accompany Dulles to the forthcoming London conference.[55]

The Suez crisis, bursting with such suddenness, ended the long period of calm that had prevailed since the Geneva summit conference in mid-1955. A new and ominous sense of impending peril replaced it, creating a potentially dangerous situation for the Republicans, who had hoped to capitalize on Eisenhower's success in ending the Korean conflict and reducing Cold War tensions. In acting quickly and efficiently in the crisis, the President dispelled speculation that his ill health prevented him from giving effective leadership, and reassured those who had voted for him in 1952 in the belief that he was uniquely equipped to deal with world problems. His insistence on a peaceful solution distressed the British, who foolishly believed that their old wartime comrade would stand by them in a showdown. They failed to realize that Eisenhower's primary concern in 1956 was in "waging peace"; his personal abhorrence of war coincided with the political necessity of keeping the world at peace during the forthcoming election campaign.

VII

Despite the outbreak of the Suez crisis, foreign policy did not play a prominent role at the Democratic convention. As the platform committee began its deliberations in Chicago in early August, there was little disagreement on the foreign policy plank. A group of the party's diplomatic specialists, led by Dean Acheson, Chester Bowles, Paul Nitze, Ben Cohen, and Senator William Fulbright, prepared a draft plank which the politicians overhauled in an attempt to appeal more directly for domestic votes. Zionists appeared at the committee's hearings to plead for arms for Israel; the Federation of American Scientists made a strong case for including a nuclear test ban in the platform; while Thomas Finletter urged the party to attack Eisenhower for failing to maintain "air-atomic supremacy" vis-à-vis the Soviet Union. The committee quickly reached agreement on a revised foreign policy plank, which the convention accepted without dissent.[56]

The platform opened with a general indictment of Eisenhower's record in foreign affairs. Citing the administration's confusion over neutralism, its undue reliance on nuclear weapons, and above all Dulles' dangerous tactic of brinkmanship, the Democrats claimed that true peace "may be destroyed without a shot being fired." They homed in on the Suez crisis, charging that it was "a consequence of inept and vacillating Republican policy." "Our Government's mistakes have placed us in a position in the Middle East which threatens the free world with a loss of power and prestige, potentially more dangerous than any we have suffered in the past decade."

When they turned to constructive alternatives to Republican

policies, the Democrats put forth a series of unconnected and often contradictory proposals designed to offer something for everybody. They pledged support for Chiang Kai-shek and promised never to recognize Communist China (which led Adlai Stevenson to comment, "Oh, my God!"). They went after the Jewish vote by endorsing the sale of arms to Israel "to redress the dangerous imbalance of arms in the area resulting from the shipment of Communist arms to Egypt." They even mimicked the 1952 Republican call for liberation of Eastern Europe by proclaiming, "We look forward to the day when the liberties of all captive nations will be restored to them and they can again take their rightful place in the community of free nations." The platform ducked the crucial issue of nuclear testing with a statement calling simply for "a comprehensive survey of radiation hazards from bomb tests . . . in order to determine what additional measures are required to protect existing and future generations from these invisible dangers." Most observers dismissed the platform as a blatant attempt to play politics with foreign policy. "The assumption seems to be that Americans vote as minorities—not as Americans," concluded Cyrus Sulzberger, while the *New Republic* called the plank "a dishonest conglomeration of irrelevancies and inaccuracies which no administration could live by in the hydrogen age." [57]

Stevenson ignored the party's foreign policy statements as he concentrated on the nomination. On July 31, he received a great boost when Estes Kefauver finally withdrew from the race and urged his delegates to back Stevenson. Harriman stepped up his belated efforts to stop Stevenson, making clear his desire for stronger Cold War policies against Russia and focusing particularly on his opponent's moderate civil rights stand. Just before the convention opened, Lyndon Johnson announced his formal candidacy, but few observers felt that either Harriman or Johnson could prevent Stevenson's nomination on the first ballot.[58]

Harry Truman finally breathed life into what seemed to be a drab and routine convention. On his arrival in Chicago, he told reporters he opposed Stevenson's nomination, but kept them dangling when they asked if he would back Harriman publicly. Then on Saturday, August 11, the former President called a news conference at the Sheraton-Blackstone. Before a jammed audience, with television cameras whirring away, Truman endorsed Harriman as the more experienced candidate in a time of "mounting crises in the world." "[T]he convention must name a man who has the experience and the ability to act as President immediately upon assuming that office," Truman declared, "without risking a period of costly and dangerous trial and error." Harriman's supporters gave a great roar of approval, "and all of a sudden," commented the *New Republic*'s TRB, "it was a grand old-fashioned rowdy, wildly improbable, Democratic convention again, with everybody yelling, communicative, bellicose and happy." [59]

Truman's dramatic move failed to swing the nomination to Harriman. Popular and colorful as he was with the rank-and-file, Truman could no longer influence the powerful party leaders who controlled the large delegations. The Stevenson forces quickly countered with a warm endorsement from Eleanor Roosevelt; and Jim Finnegan and Hy Raskin completed their careful wooing of undecided delegates to insure Stevenson's first ballot triumph. In some ways, Truman's action probably relieved Stevenson. Ever since the 1952 campaign, he had been trying to get out from under Truman's shadow and prove his independence. Now at last, the *New Republic* commented, "he will be free to act as his own man, free as few candidates for President have been in our own time." [60]

On the first roll call, Stevenson swept to an easy victory, securing 905½ votes to 210 for Harriman and 80 for Johnson. Then, in an unprecedented move, the candidate renounced his prerogative of naming his running mate and asked the convention to choose the vice-presidential nominee. In the free-for-all that followed, Estes Kefauver narrowly defeated Senator John F. Kennedy—who had placed Stevenson's name in nomination—and thus joined his former rival on the ticket, adding strength in the rural regions where Stevenson's sophisticated style had little appeal.[61]

Harry Truman took his defeat with good grace. Appearing at the convention's last session, he endorsed Stevenson, saying that Adlai had given him a "pretty good licking, and he's going to give Eisenhower a better one." The candidate then gave an eloquent acceptance speech in which he outlined his vision of a "New America." Stevenson stressed domestic issues, promising an end to poverty and discrimination in American society, but he also called for new initiatives abroad "to meet the challenge of the vast social revolution that is sweeping the world." In blunt terms, he denied Eisenhower's claim that all was well in the world. "The truth is not that our policy abroad has the Communists on the run," Stevenson declared. "The truth is that we are losing the cold war." Yet he failed to offer any specific solutions, saying simply that the United States must "reverse the spread of Communism" and "launch new programs." In words foreshadowing John F. Kennedy's theme in 1960, Stevenson proclaimed, "I say it is time to get up and get moving again." Nowhere in the speech, however, did Stevenson say how he would achieve this objective.[62]

"Stevenson has a terribly difficult role to play," commented TRB. "He has to tell the nation that peace and prosperity aren't enough—that the time calls for greatness." The *New Republic* columnist had pinpointed the Democratic candidate's agonizing dilemma. Eisenhower had ended the Korean War and kept the nation at peace for four years without bringing on the depression that Democrats kept predicting. The weaknesses in America's world position that Stevenson perceived—the failure to appeal to new nations, the refusal to take the initiative in ending the arms race—had not become apparent to the American people. Eisenhower's quick action in damping down the Suez crisis won the public's admiration and prevented any serious political repercussions. Many Americans admired Stevenson for his moderation and intelligence, but there was little likelihood that the people would vote to change leaders as long as Eisenhower kept the nation affluent and at peace.[63]

VIII

While the Democrats were meeting, Secretary Dulles departed for London to attend the conference of canal users. He was fully aware that the Suez crisis cast "a darkening shadow" over the upcoming Republican convention, and he was not at all sure that he could achieve a peaceful solution. "Every day that goes by without some outbreak is a gain, and I just keep trying to buy that day," he told Emmet Hughes. "I don't know anything to do but keep improvising." When he arrived in London, he released a statement of principles which included both a promise that Egypt's sovereign right would be respected and a pledge that the canal would be operated efficiently as "an international waterway." Nasser's orderly administration of the canal, which prevented any interruption of normal commerce, strengthened Dulles' appeal to the British and French to postpone any resort to force while peaceful negotiations continued. On the last day of the Republican convention, the London conference finally adopted Dulles' proposal for a committee of five, headed by Australia's Robert G. Menzies, to go to Cairo and seek Nasser's agreement to international operation of the canal. Even liberal critics were impressed by the Secretary's achievement. "Mr. Dulles should be given his due," commented the *New Republic*. "He employed moderation, a sensitivity to others and a lawyer's clarity to bring into focus several basic facts about the new world situation." [64]

The Republicans tried to ignore the Suez crisis in preparing their platform. The original draft, prepared by Dulles' staff in January 1956, stressed the way in which the Eisenhower administration had checked the Communist tide throughout the world, and boasted about the role the United States had played in getting the British to evacuate their Suez base and thus avert war between England and Egypt. In drafts which Dulles sent to Platform Committee Chairman Prescott Bush and President Eisenhower in mid-July, all references to Suez were dropped, and none were added after Nasser's seizure of the canal on July 26. While Dulles was in London in late July, conferring with the English, Bush told one of the Secretary's aides he "hoped that recent events in the Middle East would not force us to modify the favorable language which had earlier been worked out with reference to Middle East problems." Dulles concurred, allowing Under Secretary of State Herbert Hoover, Jr., who represented him at the convention, to make only one change in the State Department draft to acknowledge the existence of the Suez crisis: the preamble was altered to read, "In a world fraught with peril . . ." [65]

The foreign policy plank which Hoover presented to the Republicans at San Francisco, and which the convention approved unanimously, stressed Eisenhower's success in ending the Korean War and maintaining world peace. "One leader in the world today towers above all others and inspires the trust, admiration, confidence and good will of all the peoples of every nation—Dwight D. Eisenhower," the platform declared. "Under his leadership, the Republican Administration has carried out foreign policies which have enabled our people to enjoy in peace the blessings of liberty." After citing a string of diplomatic victories ranging from Iran to Guatemala, the platform promised continued support for the United Nations, for foreign aid, and for regional defense systems like NATO. On the Middle East, the Republicans addressed themselves solely to the Arab-Israeli dispute, and, while they refused to advocate the sale of arms to Israel, they did promise to protect that country "against armed aggression." Other promises included support for Chiang and continued nonrecognition of Red China and a mild reaffirmation of peaceful liberation of "the oppressed peoples and nations" of Eastern Europe. The press accepted the GOP platform as the expected defense of the party's foreign policy record, but Adlai Stevenson immediately accused the Republicans of deception, scoring them for their failure even to mention the Suez crisis.[66]

When the Republican convention opened in San Francisco on August 20, the delegates were in a passive mood, ready to renominate Eisenhower and Nixon without fanfare. Harold Stassen provided the only real interest. In July he had called a press conference to announce that, after studying a poll indicating that Nixon would cost Eisenhower a great many votes in November, he had decided to back Massachusetts Governor Christian Herter for the vice-presidential nomination. Eisenhower carefully kept hands off this attempt to dump Nixon from the ticket, though he did ask Stassen to take a leave from his duties as presidential disarmament adviser. Leonard Hall rallied the party leaders behind Nixon, and Herter himself deflated Stassen's maneuver when he announced that he would personally place Nixon's name in nomination at San Francisco. Stassen persisted in his efforts until the convention opened, and then, after a conference with the President, he permitted Eisenhower to tell the press he was convinced that a majority of the delegates favored Nixon, and that accordingly Stassen would end his opposition and give a seconding speech for Nixon. When reporters again asked Eisenhower if he wanted Nixon as his running mate, the President answered ambiguously, "I think he is as good a man as you can get." [67]

With all suspense ended, the convention went off with "multi-jewel precision," *Time* commented. "At the flick of a hand from Hollywood's George Murphy, the convention entertainment director, singers of all shapes and sizes appeared to entertain the delegates." When Eisenhower arrived a day ahead of schedule, he received a dizzying reception. Looking ruddy and much healthier, he gave his famous grin and raised his arms over his head to form a huge V for victory. In the Cow Palace, speaker after speaker praised the President until finally I. F. Stone commented, "Not since Stalin passed away has any people had such a paragon for a leader." Thomas E. Dewey pulled out all the stops in lauding Ike for ending the Korean War, declaring, "The name Eisenhower was again enshrined in the hearts of the grateful American people—and I am sure they will never forget it." [68]

The convention renominated Eisenhower by acclamation and then chose Richard Nixon as his running mate with only one dissenting vote—a Nebraska delegate who stubbornly insisted on casting his lonely ballot for a fictitious "Joe Smith." In a vague, platitudinous acceptance speech, the President called the Republicans the party of the future and promised to end the Cold War by bridging "the great chasm that separates us from the peoples under communist rule." Murray Kempton marveled at the waves of applause that followed the speech. "Dwight Eisenhower has somewhere learned to play the nonsense of our political carnival the way Ben Hogan plays Pebble Beach," he wrote. When the applause died down, Kempton continued, "the President led us all in singing 'God Bless America' and the angels came down and he and Mrs. Eisenhower were transported off in a cloud of dreamdust." [69]

"We appear to be afflicted with a cult of Eisenhower," agreed George Dangerfield. The genial President, standing above his party and beyond partisan controversy, was ready to lead the Republicans to victory on a surefire platform of peace and prosperity. The American people seemed ready to follow his leadership, completely apathetic to a steadily worsening world situation. "Throughout the Midwest," concluded a *Newsweek* survey, "one could go for days without hearing mention of the Kremlin, or, for that matter, of the

H-bomb." Dismissing the change in Soviet foreign policy, an Atlanta banker told one of the magazine's reporters, "Nobody talks about the Russians but professors." Yet, as Emmet Hughes commented, two issues darkened the overall outlook for the Republicans. The first was the President's health—one bad cold that sent him to bed could lose the election. The other was the Suez crisis, which Hughes likened to "the soft and rhythmic ticking of a time bomb." If it exploded before November, it could "shatter most Republican pretensions in foreign policy, as well as validate much Democratic criticism of the strategy and behavior of Dulles." No one understood this better than the Secretary of State, who was determined to drag out the crisis until his chief was safely reelected.[70]

456

Adlai Stevenson set out in 1956 to prove that he was a very different man from the reticent candidate who had been buried under the Eisenhower landslide four years before. This time he had sought the nomination eagerly and won it after a strenuous primary contest in which he had developed a new down-to-earth political style. Gone were the lofty speeches lecturing the American people on their duties and responsibilities. Instead of using his rapier wit to ridicule Republican foibles, the new Stevenson planned a hard-hitting political attack that would expose the ineffectiveness of Eisenhower's leadership in order to re-create the old Democratic majorities. Stevenson's days as an amateur were over. He would now prove he was a professional politician who could find and exploit the gut issues and thereby confound the pollsters and experts who were predicting an easy victory for the President.

His appointment of James Finnegan as campaign manager signified Stevenson's coldblooded approach to the 1956 campaign. Finnegan, an old pro who had engineered the overthrow of traditional Republican control in Philadelphia, set up Stevenson's headquarters in Washington and immediately began coordinating the national campaign with the various state party efforts. Realizing that elections were won at the precinct level, Finnegan had Stevenson and Kefauver take a swing around the nation in late August to meet with local party leaders in a series of regional conferences. The oddly contrasting candidates, Adlai short and elegant, Estes tall and folksy, avoided any public appearances as they met with influential Democrats in Santa Fe, Vancouver, Sioux City, Knoxville, and Chicago. Instead they listened to local grievances, heard state chairmen tell them what issues to stress, and tried to overcome the prevailing defeatism by displaying confidence in their ability to wage a successful campaign.[1]

All the party leaders, from Finnegan down, urged Stevenson to ignore foreign policy and concentrate on domestic issues. Eisenhower, they argued, had preempted the peace issue by ending the Korean War and reducing tensions with the Soviets at Geneva. Despite the uneasiness of the experts over the new flexible tactics Khrushchev was pursuing, the politicians realized that the American people believed Eisenhower had eased world tensions to the point where they felt less threatened by events abroad than at any time since the rise of Hitler. Any effort to appeal to voters on foreign policy could only play into the hands of the Republicans. Instead, the advisers told Stevenson to focus on domestic issues in an effort to rebuild the shattered New Deal coalition: economic appeals to special-interest groups, an attack on the close ties between corporations and the Eisenhower administration, and, above all, a personal assault on Richard Nixon as the likely successor to Eisenhower, in 1960 if not earlier.

The intellectuals around the candidate went along with the new strategy. Though they preferred the eloquent Stevenson who took the high road in 1952, men like Arthur Schlesinger, Jr., John Bartlow Martin, and Willard Wirtz accepted the need for political pragmatism as the guiding force behind the 1956 campaign. They tried to keep a measure of the old eloquence and lofty idealism in his speeches, but they acquiesced in the need to present Stevenson as a man deeply concerned about the daily problems of the average American. Sensitive to the charge that they were eggheads, these intellectuals tried to be even more hard-boiled in their approach than Finnegan himself. They accepted the prevailing view that the American people were apathetic toward world affairs and thus confirmed the decision to forgo attacks on Eisenhower's foreign policy. When one idealist objected to Stevenson's failure to criticize the Eisenhower-Dulles massive retaliation policy and call instead for more reliance on conventional forces, John Bartlow Martin shot back sarcastically: "You want the Governor to claim that he knows more about war than Eisenhower, and then come out in favor of an increased draft, plus a few hundred thousand aircraft workers laid off on the West Coast, and all this in order to get ready for another Korea. Somehow, I don't think it will work." [2]

Stevenson yearned to make foreign policy a central campaign issue. Tired of the domestic problems he had hammered away on during the primaries, he looked forward to taking up the international issues on which he was convinced Eisenhower had misled the American people. But his awakened political ambitions overcame his best instincts, and he reluctantly agreed to subordinate foreign policy in an effort to make the most effective possible challenge to Eisenhower. Yet in doing so, he only added to the great handicaps already facing him. Stevenson's basic appeal lay in his high idealism and his conviction that the United States could do much more to fulfill its world mission. Four years before, he had won the respect of millions of Americans with his freshness, his enthusiasm, and his unquenchable belief in national greatness. Now he seemed to be just another politician, moved only by the desire to advance his personal fortunes. When he opened his campaign with a nationally televised speech from Harrisburg, Pennsylvania, in mid-September, he seemed nervous and ill at ease, lacking in self-confidence and obviously not putting his heart into the effort. "There is always a part of Stevenson standing aside and watching the other half," commented TRB, and this time, one could almost sense Stevenson's better half expressing anguished disapproval. "Four years ago he wanted to win high-mindedly," commented James Reston; "this year he wants to win." [3]

I

In contrast, Eisenhower was much more at ease campaigning in 1956 than he had been four years before. "Actually, I find this business of relying on the record of the Administration much less distasteful . . . than I did the type of campaign we had to wage in 1952," he wrote to a friend. "I am proud of what we have done." With the Korean War ended and the economy booming, the President was content to rely on the party slogan, "Peace and Prosperity." The Gallup poll in August showed him leading Stevenson by a huge margin, 61 to 37 percent; the Las Vegas gamblers were quoting odds of 3–1; and in Moscow Nikolai Bulganin supposedly quipped, "Ike could win even with Molotov as a running mate." Yet the President did not take the election for granted. When George Gallup sent Vice-President Nixon a proposal that each GOP county chairman be asked to secure 10 percent more votes in his area than had been cast for Ike in 1952, Eisenhower embraced the idea enthusiastically and asked each local leader to achieve his new quota. He also asked each member of the Cabinet to participate in the campaign by undertaking speaking tours arranged by Sherman Adams in which they were to rebut all charges made by Stevenson and Kefauver. Dulles tried to beg off from this partisan duty, but he finally agreed to appear on one of the party's special television programs to discuss the administration's record in foreign policy.[4]

The Republican National Committee, headed by Leonard Hall, did everything possible to exploit the peace theme. The

GOP printed up leaflets with Ike's picture and the caption, "He ended the Korean War and has kept America out of war." At the height of the campaign, the party distributed more than a million copies of a comic book extolling the President's contributions to world peace. One panel showed a wounded veteran in bed saying, "Isn't one war in a man's lifetime more than enough!" Another had a young woman saying, "When Ike flew to Korea in '52 as he promised, I didn't dare let myself believe that he could accomplish anything. . . . But a few months later, our wedding bells rang—right after Jim came home from Korea—that was Ike's wedding present to us." Citizens for Eisenhower, the volunteer committee operating independently of the National Committee, stressed the same theme. "Since the summer of 1953," ran one of their pamphlets, "the Korean War ended, not one United States soldier has been killed or wounded in combat—we have been at peace. Republicans wage peace." [5]

Emmet John Hughes, the man who had drafted the "go to Korea" speech in 1952, returned to the President's staff in September and tried to pitch Eisenhower's campaign on a higher level. In his memoirs, Hughes contends that Ike chewed out the party leaders for oversimplifying the peace issue and told Hughes that, while he was proud of his record, "we have got to do a hell of a lot *more* in the next four years than we've been able to in the last four." Leonard Hall and Sherman Adams, however, the men who ran Ike's campaign, ignored his disclaimers as they exploited the ending of the Korean War and the easing of Cold War tensions.[6]

The plan called for Richard Nixon to carry on the day-to-day speaking chores, expounding on the Republican record and answering all the charges made by the Democrats. In the campaign kickoff, an elaborate picnic for five hundred party workers at Gettysburg, Eisenhower limited himself to introducing Nixon, praising his running mate highly. He then sat back to hear the Vice-President lambaste the Democrats for their claim that the Republicans were losing the Cold War. "It may not be surprising that those who defend an administration which never recognized there was a war in Korea may not know the difference between war and peace," Nixon commented. "But believe me—believe me—the American people do."

With Nixon bearing the brunt of the campaign, the GOP leaders planned to restrict Eisenhower's appearance to a series of carefully spaced television speeches in cities around the nation. The President would fly in from Washington, ride in a motorcade from the airport to a central auditorium, address a group of the party faithful, and then return to his duties in the White House. "Ike is a kind of icon," explained TRB to his *New Republic* readers. "He is now to be paraded by the GOP as a sort of sacred relic in troubled spots: a statue that is wheeled into a community, to whom songs are sung almost reverent in tone, to whose views Nixon appeals to silence all opposition, to whom support is invited as a duty." [7]

II

Despite the decision not to give foreign policy high priority, Stevenson did not ignore world affairs during the first month of his campaign. In nearly every speech, he made at least one or two references to the state of the world, usually suggesting that the present calm was deceptive and charging that the Republicans were losing the Cold War through a policy of drift. "Why don't they tell us the truth?" he asked in San Francisco. "Why don't they tell us that the menace of Communism has been growing, that neutralism is spreading, that the realities are grim and that we can lose the cold war without even firing a shot?" He never pressed his point home, however, contenting himself with the general indictment but failing to detail the specific ways in which Eisenhower had weakened America's position in the world. He spent more time rebutting the

GOP charge that the Democrats were the party of war. In indignant tones, he told an American Legion audience that "peace is not an issue in this election," and called the Republican attempt to blame the Korean War on the Democrats "as miserable a fraud as has ever been used by a political party." "There is no peace party in the United States, just as there is no war party," he told a group of Iowa farmers. "No American wants war." Stung by the way the Republicans tried to monopolize the peace theme, Stevenson asked the GOP if they wanted to disavow America's role in the two world wars and Korea. "We fought these wars," he declared, "not as Democrats nor as Republicans, but as Americans." [8]

His address to the American Legion convention in Los Angeles on September 5 was the only one devoted exclusively to foreign affairs, and it was here that he made two statements the Republicans seized upon to elevate into major campaign issues. The first was Stevenson's call for an early end to the draft. Aware of rumors that the Eisenhower administration contemplated abolishing conscription as part of armed forces modernization, and fearful that the President would make such an announcement at the height of the campaign, Stevenson decided to strike first. To the surprise of the Legionnaires, and to the alarm of many of his advisers, he declared that the requirements of technology in the atomic age necessitated smaller but more professional armed forces rather than large numbers of unskilled soldiers. "We can now anticipate the possibility hopefully but responsibly that within the foreseeable future we can maintain the military forces we need without the draft," Stevenson contended. "I think it is the national will, shared equally by every American candidate or voter, Democrat or Republican, that the draft be ended at the earliest possible moment, consistent with the national safety."

The veterans applauded politely, but the next day they showed their real feelings when they gave an ovation to Richard Nixon. The Vice-President dismissed Stevenson's ideas on the draft as a cheap political maneuver, reminding his audience that "in international affairs, particularly, the easy way is seldom the right way. This is no time to suggest to our friends or our possible opponents abroad that America is getting soft and tired and is looking for an easy way out of world responsibilities." Other Republicans were more outspoken in their criticism. Senate Minority Leader William Knowland called Stevenson's proposal "a blatant attempt to get votes," while Thomas Dewey, once again playing an active role in a GOP campaign, commented, "If this country should ever elect a man who threatens to undermine our defenses, that day we will lose all our allies and we will be naked and alone in a hostile world." [9]

Public opinion reacted strongly against Stevenson's suggestion. The *New York Times,* spokesman for eastern internationalists, claimed that his remarks would "encourage neutralist sentiment elsewhere in Europe and play into the hands of those people everywhere who would like to slow up or let down in the Western military effort." The *Reporter* lamented their candidate's stand, pointing out that one-third of American military manpower still came from selective service. In a nationwide poll, *Newsweek* found that most people viewed the draft as a "necessary evil" and only one in seven backed Stevenson's stand. Realizing the opposition he had stirred up, Stevenson called a press conference in mid-September to clarify his position. He pointed out that he was referring to the future, not the present, when he advocated ending the draft, and he promised that he would only go ahead after careful study and assurance that an all-volunteer army would best serve the national defense. Despite the outcry, however, Stevenson at first refused to reverse himself. In a speech at Minneapolis on September 29, he likened the Republican criticism to "Maginot Line" thinking, as he pointed out, "Nothing is more hazardous in military policy than rigid adherence to obsolete ideas." But the issue continued to work against him, and he finally accepted the advice of the professionals and dropped it from his speeches.[10]

His second statement to the Legion convention created even greater controversy and eventually became a dominant issue in the campaign. While discussing his ideas on national security, Stevenson briefly referred to his April call for a nuclear test ban. "I regret that the Administration chose to casually dismiss my proposal last spring to halt further testing of large nuclear devices, conditioned upon adherence by the other atomic powers to a similar policy," he commented. "I call attention to the fact that these other nations have subsequently announced their willingness to limit such tests."

In his rebuttal the next day, Nixon singled out the test ban reference for special criticism. To stop testing, the Vice-President asserted, "would have been not only naïve but dangerous to our national security. To have taken such action would have been like telling police officials that they should discard their weapons provided the lawbreakers would offer to throw away the machine-guns." Then, referring to both the test ban and draft proposals, Nixon slyly concluded, "It is time that we realize that well-intentioned but mistaken men can be as great a threat to the nation's security as admitted Communists or fellow-travelers." [11]

Stevenson was surprised by the vehemence of Nixon's attack. He had not intended to make the test ban proposal a major campaign issue, and he apparently only raised it because he understood that the National Security Council was planning a similar proposal. The Soviets had just begun a series of H-bomb tests, revealed with considerable fanfare by AEC Chairman Lewis Strauss and President Eisenhower after evidence of each shot; and the British had just announced plans for additional atomic bomb tests in the Pacific. The Soviets justified their explosions on the grounds that the United States had refused their offer to enter into a test ban agreement as the first step toward "banning and destroying atomic weapons." After the election, Stevenson revealed that his advisers had urged him not to refer again to the test ban idea, telling him that it was "unwise politics" and would cost him votes. He went ahead, he explained, only because of his intense desire for the United States to take the initiative in bringing the nuclear arms race under control.[12]

Stevenson's advisers were undoubtedly right in their warning; the Soviets immediately made his position especially precarious when Premier Bulganin sent President Eisenhower a letter on September 11 renewing the Russian offer for a ban on H-bomb tests as "the first important step toward the unconditional prohibition of these types of mass destruction weapons, which is in full accordance with the hopes and desires of all mankind." Stevenson, now seemingly the advocate of a major Soviet diplomatic move, kept silent, but the damage had been done. Emmet Hughes could not believe that Stevenson would bungle so badly. Instead of attacking the Republicans at their vulnerable spots, such as Dulles' policy of brinkmanship, massive retaliation, and the Suez crisis, the Democratic candidate had instead chosen to challenge the President on issues of national defense, where he was virtually impregnable. Given Eisenhower's standing as the foremost military leader of his generation, the Republicans would have little difficulty in discrediting Stevenson's proposals and turning them to the advantage of the GOP.[13]

The President moved quickly to capitalize on the openings Stevenson had left him. In his first campaign speech, drafted by Hughes and delivered over national television, Eisenhower cited with great pride his record of accomplishments—ending the Korean War, helping West Germany become independent, negotiating the Austrian peace treaty, freeing Guatemala from Communist control. "We have seen an end to the old pattern of tragedy: not a single nation has been surrendered to aggression," Eisenhower asserted. "We have maintained this defense of freedom without recourse to war." He never mentioned Stevenson by name, but he dismissed both of his rival's proposals brusquely. "We cannot prove wise and strong by any such simple device as suspending, unilaterally, our H-bomb tests," the President declared. "Our atomic knowledge and power have formed the saving shield of freedom." Then he stated categorically that ending the draft would "weaken our armed forces," as well as dishearten our allies. "We cannot—in short—face the future simply by walking into the past—backwards," Eisenhower concluded.

The nation's press applauded the President for standing above partisanship in his quest for peace. Even liberal journals realized how successful Eisenhower had been in appropriating "the major issue of the campaign." "The word, he said, was peace," the *Nation* commented. "And so it is." One of Stevenson's aides later told Emmet Hughes: "The night of the President's first speech I decided to destroy six speeches I'd outlined for Adlai. Eisenhower *gave* the speech I had been trying to get our boy to give for weeks." [14]

In subsequent addresses, the President simply reiterated the themes he had laid down in the first television broadcast. "Not only is this Administration dedicated to peace," he told a Cleveland rally on October 1, "but we have established a record in behalf of peace that all the world respects." That same day he reminded students at the University of Kentucky, "In Korea, long since, the guns have stilled—and in America, the casualty lists have ended. . . . And there have been no more Koreas—anywhere in the world." He continued his oblique attack on Stevenson's proposals, refusing to debate either the draft or the test ban issues on their merits, but instead condemning them categorically. He told a Pittsburgh audience on October 9 that national strength was imperative to discourage aggressors, and then added, "Now I, my friends, as your President and Commander-in-Chief of the Armed Forces, cannot and will not make proposals contrary to national interest—

nor offer you attractive prospects if they are unjustified by world realities." [15]

Eisenhower's belief that Stevenson put forth his proposals purely as political ploys gave his denunciations an air of outraged sincerity. When reporters asked him if his administration had any plans to end the draft in the near future, he became irate, saying that the draft was necessary for "carrying out the responsibilities for the security of this country." He apparently never credited Stevenson with an honest effort to modernize the American military system, and when the Democrat refused to back down, the President released a statement affirming the need to continue the draft. He cited the fact that he had been able to reduce the number of men conscripted each year from over 500,000 to 136,000, but he then claimed that any further reduction would be "hurtful to America's security interests throughout the world." "The Free World looks to the United States for leadership in standing firm against the Communist push," he concluded. "We must not now betray that leadership by loose talk of soon ending the draft." [16]

The President was even angrier at Stevenson for bringing up the test ban proposal. Eisenhower considered nuclear questions far too complex and sophisticated for the public to understand, and he did not want any aspect of arms control made the subject of political debate, where matters of life and death could easily be oversimplified or distorted. Accordingly, he tried to avoid discussing the test ban, but when reporters brought it up at a news conference on October 5, he told them his main objection was the unilateral nature of Stevenson's proposal. While it was true that the United States could detect a Soviet violation, it would then take "months and months" before America could respond with new tests of its own. As a result, the President warned, the Russians "could make tremendous advances where we would be standing still." The next day, Eisenhower spelled out his objections at length in a second presidential statement. In essence, his position was that testing could not be separated from the broader issue of control of nuclear weapons, and the United States insisted as a matter of national policy that any disarmament plan would have to contain specific and absolutely foolproof inspection safeguards. He repeated his argument that a violator of an unsupervised test ban would gain an invaluable head start, and he revealed his own deepest convictions when he contended, "This specific matter is manifestly not a subject for detailed public discussion—for obvious security reasons." [17]

Eisenhower picked up valuable support for his position when Harry Truman, campaigning in Detroit for Stevenson, told reporters that he could not go along with the test ban idea. "We should retain our advantage and if that means testing bombs, well okay," Truman told a press conference, adding that he had turned down similar proposals when he was in the White House. The former President tried to play down his disagreement with Stevenson in subsequent statements, but he never retracted his opposition to a test ban, telling reporters, "We can't possibly quit till this Russian business is under control."

The President, genuinely alarmed lest the issue of nuclear testing become a political football, hoped the discussion would now end. When reporters brought up both testing and the draft at a news conference on October 11, asking if stories that the administration had been considering both proposals before Stevenson advocated them were true, Ike became furious. He heatedly denied that anyone in his administration had suggested ending the draft, and then he said flatly, "Now, I tell you frankly, I have said my last words on these subjects." The President's anger, always one of his most impressive weapons in exchanges with newsmen, disguised the fact that he had not included the test ban in his disclaimer, leaving open the possibility that the National Security Council had indeed been at least contemplating such a move prior to Stevenson's American Legion speech.[18]

One final Stevenson initiative in September gave the President an even better opportunity to display his righteous indignation. On September 25, in the course of a speech in Miami, the Democratic candidate charged that, at the urging of his brother Milton, President Eisenhower had approved loans of more than $100 million to Argentine dictator Juan Perón. The State Department quickly checked and found that the loans, which totaled over $130 million, were extended in 1950 and 1951 by the Truman administration. When reporters brought up the charge at a presidential news conference on September 27, Eisenhower, smiling broadly, informed reporters, "It was the Democratic government" which had loaned Perón the money, adding that his administration had withheld all credits from Perón until he was overthrown in 1955. "Our opponents," Eisenhower wrote later, "had made the mistake of peering into the barrel of their own gun when they pulled the trigger." [19]

The Perón boomerang marked the culmination of Stevenson's inept handling of foreign policy issues in the first month of the campaign. As Arthur Krock pointed out, "in a campaign where strategy called for incessant and developing attack," Stevenson had enabled the President to put him on the defensive. The people, asked to choose on matters of national security between the opinions of the architect of victory in Europe in World War II and a man wholly without military experience, came down heavily on the President's side. The Democratic candidate had raised significant questions in regard to both the draft and nuclear testing, but Eisenhower had been able to avoid meaningful public debate without alienating any voters. The majority of the American people accepted the President's assurances that all was well in the world and that the Cold War was gradually fading away.

His failure to draw Eisenhower into a dialogue on foreign policy issues troubled Stevenson deeply. As he went about the country stressing domestic concerns, he seemed strangely ill at ease and uncomfortable. "He slaps but he doesn't punch," noted James Reston. "He has the words but somehow he doesn't have the melody." Sympathetic reporters noted that he seemed tired and listless, "like a man desperately sick of his own voice." In constantly repeating pragmatic political arguments, he had lost his zest for the campaign; he desperately yearned for the opportunity to cut through the bland clichés of the Eisenhower regime to expose the perils facing America in the world. Despite his weariness and frustration, he still sought a way to arouse the American people from their complacency, not just to win an election, but to redeem his own sense of leadership.[20]

III

As the campaign progressed, the Suez time bomb kept ticking away. Day after day, headlines in American newspapers recited the moves and countermoves of the diplomats who sought a peaceful settlement. John Foster Dulles was in the forefront, striving with all his skill and cunning to placate the outraged English and French and negotiate a compromise settlement with the increasingly intransigent Gamal Nasser. Even the usually hostile *New Republic* was impressed with his energetic diplomacy, comparing him to the Scarlet Pimpernel: "He is here, he is there, he is everywhere." Fear accounted for the Secretary of State's frantic activity. He was afraid that the canal crisis would disrupt his obsessive crusade against Soviet Communism by forcing the United States to back its Western allies and thus alienate the new nations in Asia, Africa, and the Middle East. He was even more concerned about the possible domestic political consequences. The Republicans had based Eisenhower's reelection campaign on the theme of peace; if England and France resorted to force to regain control of the canal, it would make a mockery of the President's words. Accordingly, Dulles was determined to master the crisis and prevent a military showdown, at least until Eisenhower was safely reelected.[21]

In early September, Dulles awaited the outcome of the Menzies mission. At the London conference in late August, eighteen nations had agreed to send a five-man negotiating team, headed by Australian Prime Minister Robert Menzies, to present a plan to Nasser for international operation of the Suez Canal. Few expected Nasser to accept it, since it denied his main contention—that Egypt had both the legal right and the technical ability to run the canal. Nasser received the Menzies group politely, but tension increased as England and France began building up their armed forces on the nearby island of Cyprus. Privately, English Prime Minister Anthony Eden informed Eisenhower of how seriously his government viewed the canal seizure, comparing Nasser to Hitler and vowing that once again England was prepared to lead "Europe in the fight for freedom" rather than "perish by degrees." Deeply troubled, Eisenhower immediately wrote back to Eden, expressing his misgivings about the use of force and warning that it "might cause a serious misunderstanding between our two countries." The next day, September 9, the Menzies mission ended in failure, and the world moved one step closer to war. In a press conference on September 11, the President repeated an earlier statement that the United States was "dedicated to a peaceful solution of the Suez controversy." He refused to say what the United States would do if our allies finally did use force, but he made clear his fundamental objections to a military solution by saying, "We established the United Nations to abolish aggression, and I am not going to be a party to aggression if it is humanly possible to avoid it or I can detect it before it occurs." [22]

"The gun is loaded, aimed and the finger is on the trigger,

but the U.S. is the safety catch," *Time* quoted a Cairo observer as saying. Dulles, realizing that unless he intervened, England and France would invade Egypt, suddenly put forth a new proposal for a Suez Canal Users' Association which would take over the operation of the canal without Egyptian cooperation or consent. With great reluctance, the English government decided to go along with Dulles' scheme, and Eden had the unenviable task of defending the Users' Association to Parliament. When members asked the crucial question—what would happen if Egypt tried to prevent ships from coming through the canal?—the Prime Minister took refuge in the ambiguous wording of Dulles' proposal: the nations concerned "will be free to take such further steps as seem to be required either through the United Nations, or by other means for the assertion of their rights." The next day, Dulles undercut the implication that the Western nations would use force if necessary to keep the canal open. "We do not intend to shoot our way through . . . ," Dulles told reporters. "If we are met by force, we do not intend to get into a shooting war." Though he spoke only for the United States, noting that each nation would have to decide for itself, his words robbed the Users' Association of all effectiveness. He refused even to advocate economic pressure against Egypt, saying that he preferred the alternative of sending ships around the Cape of Good Hope if Nasser refused to let the association operate the canal.[23]

Amid a growing sense of pessimism, Dulles flew to London for a conference to implement his plan. Nasser, emboldened by Dulles' refusal to take a strong stand, now denounced the new Western move and indicated his country would resist any international effort to take over the canal. Even more ominously, the Soviets called the plan "a great provocation" against Egypt and hinted at their intention of backing Nasser in a showdown. Nevertheless, the Secretary of State pushed ahead, securing British and French acceptance of his Users' Association and agreeing to their proposal to take the whole matter before the Security Council as a threat to world peace. On his return from London, Dulles exuded confidence, telling reporters that the conference had "registered solid gains" and expressing his belief that Egypt would ultimately accept international operation of the waterway.[24]

The consensus among objective observers was far less optimistic. They interpreted the Anglo-French decision to submit the dispute to the Security Council as a calculated step to exhaust the last legal recourse while the two nations went ahead with plans for an invasion. The fact that Egypt had proved able to run the canal efficiently—using hastily trained volunteer pilots, including many from behind the Iron Curtain, after Western personnel quit in mid-September—greatly weakened the British and French arguments for international operation. Equally important, the possibility of Nasser's accepting a political compromise had become increasingly remote. Once he had seized the canal and weathered the storm of Western protest, the Egyptian leader had become a hero in the Third World, a David who had challenged Goliath and survived. The Soviets, impressed with his success, moved cautiously to his side as they realized that the United States was not going to take a firm stand behind its Western allies. The English and French, now convinced they had been betrayed by Dulles, were determined not to continue giving in to Nasser. They went along with further diplomatic procrastination only as a convenient cover for their developing plans to solve the crisis through military force.[25]

Adlai Stevenson carefully avoided the worsening Suez situation in the early stages of the campaign. In a press conference on August 31, he indicated that he was "unfamiliar with the delicate diplomatic negotiations" taking place in London, and he told reporters he would welcome secret CIA briefings if the administration would only offer them. Eisenhower acted quickly on the hint, extending the briefings to the Democratic candidate on a weekly basis and reminding him that they "would be of a secret character and exclusively for your personal knowledge." Stevenson received the first briefing in Washington on September 14. Three days later, he called a special press conference to announce that he would leave Suez alone during the campaign, saying, "I do not think that any comment by me at this crucial moment would serve a constructive purpose." He reminded reporters of his long-standing criticism of the way Dulles had handled Middle Eastern problems, but he expressed the desire not "to add to the difficulties of the President and the Secretary of State in this delicate situation."

Stevenson's forbearance, so reminiscent of Dewey's decision not to exploit the Berlin crisis in 1948, was squarely in the bipartisan tradition pioneered by Vandenberg and Dulles. Some of Stevenson's advisers, while appreciative of the patriotic motive behind his move, questioned its political wisdom. On September 24, Arthur Schlesinger drafted a statement critical of Dulles' handling of the Middle Eastern situation that circulated through the Stevenson and Kefauver camps. The Schlesinger memorandum condemned Dulles for taking too hard a line against Nasser and proposed that if Eisenhower would take personal charge of the negotiations and work for Western acceptance of a nationalized canal, then Stevenson would back him fully. Nothing came of this proposal to make the Secretary of State a political target; Stevenson apparently decided to stick to his resolve not to play politics with the Suez crisis.[26]

Some Republicans, in contrast, searched for ways to turn the dangerous international situation to their partisan advantage. On October 9, Gabriel Hauge suggested to Sherman Adams that he arrange some meetings between the President and "leading foreign ministers" attending the UN debate on the canal. "There ought to be some way to use this to support the leadership point in the campaign," Hauge argued. C. D. Jackson, *Time* executive and former presidential assistant, suggested that Eisenhower reassure the Jewish community, alarmed by the growth of Nasser's power during the Suez crisis, by authorizing a large loan to Israel by the Export-Import Bank or, if that seemed too blatant, by "making a small symbolic contribution of five planes to Israel to round out Israel's defensive position." Adams temporized by announcing a special mission to Israel to gather data to support a loan, but Dulles killed off the plane transfer, telling Adams that "the 'symbolic' contribution would in effect constitute a distinct change in policy." Eisenhower deeply resented any attempts to intrude politics into his conduct of foreign policy. When Senator Knowland came to the White House to urge him not to let Britain "drag us into another one of their wars," Ike exclaimed to Emmet Hughes, "If that isn't the silliest damn kind of talk!" [27]

The President tried his best to avoid any public comment on the course of the crisis, putting off reporters by simply reiterating his hopes for a peaceful solution each time they brought it up. His resolve to keep the issue out of the campaign finally broke, however, when it seemed that the Security Council had worked out a viable solution. On October 12, UN Secretary General Dag Hammarskjöld secured agreement among the British, French, and Egyptian foreign ministers to a set of six principles designed to govern future canal operations. Elated by this apparent triumph for his peaceful policy, the President told a televised meeting with campaign workers that he had "the best announcement that I think I could possibly make to America tonight." He went on to describe the progress made at the UN and then concluded, "It looks like here is a very great crisis that is behind us." The next day, however, England and France raised difficult questions about how the six principles were to be implemented, and the agreement quickly broke down on specifics. The Security Council finally voted unanimously to adopt the six principles, but the Soviet Union vetoed a subsequent Anglo-French resolution which tried to give them substance. Far from being over, the crisis now entered its most dangerous phase—all recourse to peaceful settlement had been exhausted and neither side was willing to back down. Outwardly, all was calm as the flurry of diplomatic activity ended, but behind the scenes the British and French stepped up their invasion plans.[28]

The Democrats were slow to react to Eisenhower's mistake. On October 16, Estes Kefauver, who had been campaigning in rural areas of the West, came to New York City and charged Dulles with "bungling" the Suez situation. In an appeal to Jewish voters, he denounced the administration for appeasing Nasser and for placing "oil above principle in the Middle East." Stevenson waited to end his silence on Suez until a major foreign policy speech in Cincinnati on October 19. Addressing a highly partisan crowd, Stevenson drew heavy applause by accusing Dulles of "describing every defeat as a victory and every setback as a triumph." He went on to say that he had deliberately avoided mention of Suez, but after the President brought it into the campaign "in a highly misleading way," he could no longer keep quiet. But instead of a full critique of the administration's policy, ranging back to the withdrawal of the Aswan dam offer through Dulles' transatlantic diplomacy, the Democratic candidate simply condemned the Republicans for permitting the Soviets to penetrate into a vital strategic region. "Russian power and influence have moved into the Middle East—the oil tank of Europe and Asia and the great bridge between the East and West." Then he went on to other topics, refusing to take a stand on the issues in the crisis or to outline alternative lines of policy. Though the audience cheered him mightily, it was a disappointing performance.[29]

Stevenson had missed one of the few opportunities he had had to narrow Eisenhower's commanding lead. Suez was the GOP's most vulnerable point, and a hard-hitting attack on the way American policy was splitting apart the Western alliance would have given the Democrats the issue they needed to discredit the Republican claim that all was well in the world. Stevenson undoubtedly thought that he was acting in the national interest, but he would have served the nation far better had he attempted to bring the whole range of options on Suez into the public discussion. Not only did he hurt his own cause by adhering to the old bipartisan tradition, but he kept the American people in the dark when, above all, they needed illumination on the perils that lay ahead in the Middle East.

IV

The Republicans, uneasy over the course of the Suez crisis, tried to keep the Democrats on the defensive by continuing their attack on Stevenson's proposed ban on H-bomb testing. Though President Eisenhower had reportedly spoken his "last words" on that subject, more partisan GOP campaigners hit hard at the nuclear issue. Senator Karl Mundt, leading a Republican "truth squad" that followed Stevenson around the country, called the test ban proposal "a disservice" to the country, while Attorney General Herbert Brownell charged that the cessation of nuclear tests could only "bring joy to the hearts of those who expect to wipe out the free nations one by one." Former candidate Thomas Dewey cited the H-bomb issue in a nationally televised speech to question Stevenson's capacity for leadership. "In these troubled times we don't dare risk an impulsive, ill-informed man in the White House," he warned. ". . . One act of weakness, one act based on misinformation, could plunge this world into another war." As usual, it was Richard Nixon who made the fiercest attacks. Calling Stevenson's test ban proposal "catastrophic nonsense" in a Philadelphia speech, the Vice-President likened it to "playing Russian roulette but with only the Russians knowing which chamber had the fatal bullet in it." "Mr. Stevenson has raised grave doubts," Nixon concluded, "as to whether he has the judgment, the responsibility, and the temperament to lead the United States and the free world in this critical period." [30]

Stung by these attacks, Stevenson began to reconsider his earlier decision not to press the H-bomb issue. Strong expressions of support from leading scientists—notably Ralph Lapp and Charles C. Price, director of the Federation of American Scientists—along with a new statement on September 21 by AEC Commissioner Thomas Murray, reiterating his belief that the U.S. already possessed more than enough huge H-bombs, encouraged the Democratic candidate to explore the question more thoroughly. On October 3, he had his press secretary ask David Lilienthal, former chairman of the AEC, to submit his ideas on the test ban. A hectic debate developed between Stevenson's advisers; the political pros warned against taking on President Eisenhower on a matter of national security, while the amateurs, sensing that Stevenson needed a moral issue to lift his flagging campaign, urged him to answer the Republican attacks on the test ban.[31]

Troubled by the conflicting advice, Stevenson decided to sound out public reaction in a swing along the West Coast. In Seattle on October 9, he denounced the Republicans for ridiculing "attempts to save man from the greatest horror his ingenuity has ever devised," and he was surprised at the sustained applause he received. He repeated his advocacy of a test ban at Portland, evoking a wave of cheers, and again at Oakland, where he won an ovation. "It was the biggest and longest spontaneous demonstration he has had at any time on any issue since the start of the campaign," commented Harrison Salisbury. At his final stop in San Diego, Stevenson expressed his contempt for Eisenhower's refusal to debate the H-bomb question. "I say that there can be no 'last word' on this fateful subject until mankind is freed of the menace of incineration."

Stevenson returned from the Pacific Coast convinced that he had found the issue he needed to reverse his declining fortunes. Jim Finnegan was still skeptical, but the idealists like

John Bartlow Martin and Arthur Schlesinger, Jr., could now argue that Stevenson had hit upon a sleeper with great political potential. It is unlikely that this pragmatic consideration was uppermost in Stevenson's mind; he was attracted most by the opportunity to take his stand on a matter of conscience and thus restore the sense of mission that had been missing from his campaign. "There are worse things that can happen to a man than losing an election," he told Newton Minow. "The worst thing is to lose one's convictions and not tell the people the truth."

On Friday, October 12, Stevenson announced that he would make a nationally televised address on the test ban issue on the following Monday, and then retired to the seclusion of his Libertyville farm to prepare his remarks. Geochemist Harrison Brown of Cal Tech flew in to brief the candidate on the technical aspects of the test ban proposal. Clinton Anderson, chairman of the Joint Congressional Committee on Atomic Energy, who had earlier been cool to Stevenson's proposal, agreed to appear on the program along with hawkish Senator Stuart Symington of Missouri. Contrary to the usual procedure, there was no advance text for journalists; Stevenson released only the title, "The Greatest Menace the World Has Ever Known." [32]

Stevenson began by reviewing the arms race, "which threatens mankind with stark, merciless, bleak catastrophe." Speaking from a small television studio in Chicago, he blamed the Russians for previous failures at nuclear disarmament, but he insisted that the United States take the initiative in breaking the stalemate. He repeated his familiar arguments that a test ban did not require elaborate inspection procedures, commenting, "You can't hide the explosion any more than you can hide an earthquake," and pointed out that a test ban could help control the arms race by preventing the spread of H-bombs to other nations. Then, for the first time, he stressed the danger to mankind from radioactive fallout. Strontium-90, "the most dreadful poison in the world," was already showing up in the bones of human beings, Stevenson asserted. "I do not wish to be an alarmist and I am not asserting that the present levels of radioactivity are dangerous," he continued. "Scientists do not know exactly how dangerous the threat is. But they know the threat will increase if we go on testing."

After raising this emotional issue, Stevenson returned to his primary point: bringing the arms race under control. He cited British and Russian expressions of willingness to join in a test ban, and asked, "What are we waiting for?" If elected President, he promised, he would make a nuclear test treaty "the first order of business." He then turned to Senators Anderson and Symington, who soberly assured the nation that a test ban would not endanger national security. Stevenson concluded with an attack on Eisenhower for his refusal to discuss the testing issue and with a call to action. "This is one matter on which the defeatist view that nothing can be done must be rejected," he declared. "I say that something can be done, that the deadlock can be broken, that the world can make a new beginning toward peace." [33]

Over the next two weeks, Stevenson and his running mate stressed the test ban issue in speeches across the country. Though they tried to stick to the essential idea of limiting the arms race, inevitably they appealed to the emotions in their rhetoric, often distorting the scientific issues in the process. Stevenson told a cheering throng of 18,000 Democrats in Madison Square Garden on October 23 that "the transcending question before humanity is whether there will be any tomorrow at all," and then, after an oblique reference to Ike's health, added, "I don't think this nation wants the great decisions about the H-bomb entrusted to Richard M. Nixon." Three days later, the Democratic candidate told an Illinois audience that if the arms race continued, the next step would be a "cobalt bomb." "But this is madness—this policy of trying to preserve peace by a preponderance of terror," Stevenson concluded. "And what is it going to do to mankind in the process—bone cancer, deformed children, sterility?" [34]

Estes Kefauver was even more careless in exploiting the test ban issue. On October 16, he astonished a group of reporters in New York City by telling them that the explosive force from hydrogen bombs was "sufficient to blow the earth off its axis by 16 degrees, which would affect the seasons." Responsible scientists called the remark "incredible," and the vice-presidential candidate's staff made a desperate search for corroboration as Kefauver's statement became the butt of GOP jibes. Undaunted by this slip of the tongue, Kefauver took the advice of his publicity director and focused on the danger of strontium-90 fallout to children. Again and again he talked about bone cancer, stillbirths, and genetic damage as he told audiences, "Your vote on November 6 may help decide whether the human race will live or die." In a nationally televised talk from Los Angeles, Kefauver claimed that only a test ban could halt an "epidemic" of nuclear tests that could lead to international "suicide" through radioactive fallout. Then, as the screen lit up with a film clip of an H-bomb explosion, the candidate commented, "Poison from these clouds will be falling for the next 30 to 40 years." [35]

The scientific community quickly divided over the wisdom of Stevenson's test ban proposal. Many scientists, disturbed by the apathy of the American people toward the spiraling arms race, welcomed the new public interest. Prominent scholars, including Nobel laureates Carl D. Anderson and H. J. Muller, issued statements supporting the test ban. The Federation of American Scientists endorsed Stevenson's stand, though the organization carefully refrained from backing his candidacy. The Democrats publicized the favorable comments widely and arranged for Dr. Benjamin Spock, the noted pediatrician, to give a five-minute television talk on the hazards of fallout for children. At the same time, many scientists opposed the test ban idea, and the White House had no difficulty in getting twelve leading academicians, headed by physicist John Dunning of Columbia University, to sign a statement regretting "the injection into a political campaign of statements and conclusions which extend beyond the limits of existing scientific evidence."

Radioactivity provoked the greatest amount of controversy. Administration supporters pointed to the reports of British and American experts released in June that minimized the danger of fallout to human health. A report by AEC Commissioner Willard Libby, released three days before Stevenson's October 15 telecast, claimed that the amount of strontium-90 in the human body in fifteen years "probably will be substantially the same as it is today." Though many scientists, led by Ralph Lapp, challenged Libby's finding, the Republicans relied on it heavily to rebut the fallout arguments. Several scholars who supported Stevenson's proposal expressed regret at his emphasis on radioactivity, noting that there was not yet enough evidence to permit drawing any valid conclusions about the extent and nature of the fallout hazards. The real danger, argued Eugene Rabinowitch, editor of the *Bulletin of the Atomic Scientists,* lay in the millions who would die in a nuclear war, not the possibility of damage from a few tests. Rabinowitch, along with H. J. Muller and David R. Inglis, called on Stevenson to stop playing on emotions with the fallout argument and instead to emphasize the need to halt testing as the best way to slow down the arms race.[36]

President Eisenhower, disturbed by the growing controversy over what he considered a delicate subject, tried to avoid the public dialogue Stevenson sought. He refused to make any immediate comment on the test ban issue, asking instead that John Foster Dulles and Lewis L. Strauss, chairman of the AEC, prepare a thorough brief defending administration policy. When Dulles realized that preparing such a document would take at least a week, he drafted an interim presidential statement that minimized the fallout issue by stating, "From a health standpoint, there is greater danger from wearing a wrist watch with a luminous dial." The President vetoed this statement, but in the course of a West Coast speaking tour, Eisenhower did break the vow that he had uttered his "last words" on the test ban question. With icy contempt, he told campaign workers in Portland to disregard "pie in the sky promises and wishful thinking" and then warned a public gathering that "the road to surrender is paved with good intentions." At Los Angeles on October 19, the President linked the test ban with Stevenson's plan to end the draft as "a strange new formula" for national defense that defied "ordinary common sense." In New York a week later, he made his most direct reply to the Democratic candidate when he declared, "The compelling challenge before the world is not the matter of testing nuclear weapons—but of making impossible their use in any nuclear war." [37]

Other Republicans were eager to discuss the test ban proposal. In Flint, Michigan, Tom Dewey labeled Stevenson's suggestion "an invitation to national suicide," reminding his audience of Pearl Harbor as he warned, "Our greatest cities could be wiped out by the hydrogen bomb in eighty seconds." In a CBS interview the next day, Dewey said that nuclear weapons were "too delicate and dangerous" to be discussed in a political campaign, and then went on to call Stevenson's test ban "dangerously irresponsible scaremongering." Richard Nixon made a similar charge, telling an Illinois audience that the Democrats "have attempted to capitalize on terror and fear." The Vice-President stressed the administration's concern for national defense, warning the American people that if they chose Stevenson, they "would be taking a fearful risk with their own security." And once again he questioned Stevenson's loyalty as he told a Baltimore audience on October 19 that if the United States accepted a test ban, "we will be doing exactly what Khrushchev and Bulganin want us to do." [38]

On the day Nixon spoke, the State Department transmitted

a letter from Nikolai Bulganin to President Eisenhower that gave substance to his charge. In very heavy-handed prose, the Russian leader reminded Eisenhower of his September 11 offer to negotiate a test ban agreement. "We fully share the opinion recently expressed by certain prominent public figures in the United States concerning the necessity and the possibility of concluding an agreement on the matter of prohibiting atomic weapon tests," Bulganin wrote. The President, furious at the Soviets for meddling in American politics, immediately had the White House release a statement denouncing the letter, which the Russians made public, as "a propaganda exercise." Then on October 21, Eisenhower replied in a public letter which the *New York Times* called "one of the most strongly worded diplomatic communicatons in recent years." The President bluntly told Bulganin that his letter constituted "interference by a foreign nation in our internal affairs." He made no reference to the merits of a test ban agreement, but instead restated the American position that effective arms control requires "systems of inspection and control, both of which your Government has steadfastly refused to accept." [39]

Bulganin's letter caught both Stevenson and Kefauver off guard. When the news first broke, Kefauver urged Eisenhower to enter into formal negotiations with the Russians for a test ban, saying we had nothing to lose and everything to gain. Stevenson rebuked the President for rejecting the Russian proposal "out of hand," warning that the United States could not "afford to let them continuously appear before the rest of the world as more devoted to peace and disarmament than we are." After reading Eisenhower's reply to Bulganin, Stevenson expressed his own resentment at the way the Russians had interfered in the campaign, but then he added: "The real issue is not Mr. Bulganin's manners or Russian views about American politics. The real issue is what we are going to do to save the world from hydrogen disaster." [40]

The Republicans made the most of the Bulganin letter. Senator Knowland called on Stevenson to disavow his proposal and join in "a united front" to repudiate "the unwarranted interference of Premier Bulganin of the Soviet Union in our free American elections." Dewey accused the Democratic candidate of walking into a "Communist mousetrap," and Nixon compared Stevenson's suggestion to the concessions Neville Chamberlain made to Hitler at Munich. "I believe that all of us who are supporting the Eisenhower ticket," the Vice-President told a group of Los Angeles campaign workers, "have a responsibility not to let the voters forget Mr. Stevenson's ill-advised and terribly dangerous scheme which would play so disastrously into the Communists' hands." [41]

Most observers shared the Republican feeling that the test ban issue had boomeranged against Stevenson. When President Eisenhower released his five-page statement prepared by Dulles and Strauss, the nation's press accepted the arguments that testing did not endanger national health and that, in the absence of any agreement on controls or inspection, its cessation would imperil the security of the United States. The *New York Times* concluded, "We are confident that as between Mr. Stevenson's proposals and President Eisenhower's 'safety first' procedure, American opinion will sustain the President." Bernard Baruch—author of the first American plan to control nuclear weapons, and a Democrat—broke his usual silence during presidential campaigns to warn against any step toward disarmament without a rigid inspection system. "It is better to be safe than sorry," the park-bench philosopher advised. Arthur Krock joined in the condemnation of Stevenson's proposal, and even James Reston, though he saw merit in the test ban, agreed that the Democratic candidate had failed to persuade the American people that he knew more about nuclear arms than General Eisenhower. The only dissenting view came from liberal journals. The *New Republic* praised Stevenson for taking "a first step to putting the malevolent genie back in its bottle," while Max Ascoli applauded the Democratic candidate for returning to the high ground of 1952. The *Nation* even believed that he had brought his campaign to life and thus had struck political "pay dirt" on the H-bomb issue.[42]

Though *Newsweek* reported that the test ban proposal had cost Stevenson votes among the undecideds, an analysis of the campaign mail suggests a very different public response. The aide in charge of Stevenson's incoming mail noted a sudden upsurge; more than a thousand letters a day were arriving at the candidate's Washington headquarters by late October. More than half of them dealt exclusively with the H-bomb issue, and nearly all the writers endorsed Stevenson's stand. The letters came primarily from the large urban areas, often from suburbs normally Republican, and a breakdown indicated that most of the correspondents were professional men —doctors, lawyers, and college professors. A sampling of the incoming White House mail confirms this pattern. Letter after letter arrived during the last two weeks of October from Republicans unhappy with Eisenhower for his refusal to heed Stevenson's test ban ideas. "As a registered Republican I urge you to agree stopping hydrogen bomb tests," wired a Californian. "We want our children to beget normal, healthy children," telegraphed a Philadelphia couple; "Stop H-bomb tests and debate the issue with Stevenson." "Dear Mr. President, Your testing of H-bombs is juvenile and shocking," wrote an Ohio mother. "Why are we even toying with the idea of continuing to test these double-edged weapons when there is even the slightest possibility that our children can suffer from the insidious long-range effects." Almost all the telegrams and letters reflected individual sentiments; there were no form postcards and no indications of an organized letter-writing campaign. Thousands of Americans, alarmed by the fear of fallout and the danger of nuclear war, pleaded with their President to adopt Stevenson's test ban proposal.[43]

The evidence is too contradictory to allow a clear-cut conclusion, but it does seem that Stevenson had hit a sensitive public nerve with his test ban concept. The American government had never revealed the reasons behind the decision to build a hydrogen bomb in 1951, nor explained to the people the nature of the subsequent deadlock between the United States and the Soviet Union over these awesome new weapons. In putting forth his test ban idea, Stevenson confronted the American people with vital issues that should have been aired years before. The immediate political impact was negative; the people tended to rally behind Dwight D. Eisenhower and to accept his authoritative reassurances. Nevertheless, Stevenson had alerted millions of Americans to the perils of the nuclear age and had begun to neutralize the Republican mastery of the peace issue.

V

A series of foreign crises erupted during the last two weeks of the campaign that completely overshadowed domestic issues and brought the world ominously close to a nuclear war. The first outbreak came in Poland, where there had been growing restlessness at Soviet domination since the Poznan riots in June. Wladyslaw Gomulka, a Communist leader who had been purged and imprisoned under Stalin, emerged as the new spokesman for Polish independence. On October 19, the Central Committee of the Polish Communist party convened in Warsaw prepared to make Gomulka the First Secretary and demand that the Russians remove Marshal Konstantin K. Rokossovsky from his position as Defense Minister. In a surprise move, Khrushchev, Molotov, Mikoyan, and other prominent Russian leaders flew to Warsaw for a face-to-face meeting with the Poles. Though Russian army units surrounded the Polish capital, Gomulka and his associates held firm, insisting that they were good Communists and demanding only the right to run Poland's internal affairs free of Soviet interference. Impressed by the Poles' determination, the Russian leaders finally agreed to a compromise: Gomulka would become First Secretary, but Rokossovsky and the Soviet troops would stay, at least for the time being. Incredibly, Khrushchev appeared to be willing to loosen the tight Soviet grip on a nation vital to Russian security.[44]

Americans watched the unfolding Polish drama with profound concern. When President Eisenhower first learned of the crisis on October 20, he issued a statement of sympathy for the Poles, saying, "Our hearts go out to them, that they at last may have that opportunity to live under governments of their own choosing." On the same day, former President Truman tried to exploit events in Warsaw for the Democrats. He blamed the Eisenhower administration for a "failure to perceive" the plight of Poland and other countries "crushed under the heel of Communist terror." Adlai Stevenson had similar inclinations, but after consulting Governor Averell Harriman of New York, the Democrat's most experienced expert on the Soviet Union, he restricted himself to an innocuous statement of sympathy for the Poles as they struggled for freedom. "With imagination and ingenuity this country and the free world should be able to help this process," he commented.[45]

The Polish crisis brought the old issue of liberation again to the fore. During 1956, in contrast to 1952, the Republicans had been careful to subordinate the promise of freedom to the satellite countries, confining their appeals to specific ethnic groups. A reactivated Republican Nationalities Division ordered "I Like Ike" buttons in ten foreign languages, distributed 500,000 pamphlets entitled, *Republican Policy of Liberation,* and prepared press releases stressing the Eisenhower administration's commitment to the captive peoples. But Eisenhower and Nixon avoided mention of liberation in their speeches, and even John Foster Dulles, sobered by the futile riots in East Germany in 1953 and in Poznan more recently, refrained from calling for an end to the Iron Curtain.[46]

As it became clear that the Russians had backed down, the administration moved cautiously toward support for the Gomulka government. President Eisenhower, acting on the advice of Averell Harriman, as relayed to him by General Lucius Clay, authorized Dulles to inform the Poles that the United States was willing to extend economic aid without fanfare. In the course of a political speech on October 23, the President reiterated his admiration for the Poles in their quest for independence, and announced that he considered it America's responsibility "to help those freedom-loving people who need and want and can profitably use our aid." The Republicans wisely avoided any public effort to exploit the apparent victory in Poland, but Dulles did tell the press that he thought the world was "seeing the beginning of Polish independence." [47]

The unrest behind the Iron Curtain quickly spread to Hungary, where rebellious youth began calling for the ouster of Prime Minister Mátyás Rákosi and the removal of all Russian troops from the country. On October 23, the Hungarian security police fired on a crowd of demonstrators, and though the Russians responded by replacing Rákosi with the more popular Imre Nagy, the situation soon deteriorated into the senseless violence the Poles had so carefully avoided. At the request of the Nagy government, Russian army units entered Budapest, and the Hungarian rebels, using rocks and Molotov cocktails, fought back with great heroism against the Red troops and tanks. The gallant freedom fighters prevented a rapid Soviet takeover of the capital as the hapless Nagy sought desperately for a compromise that would end the bloodshed.[48]

"Poor fellows, poor fellows," Eisenhower said privately of the Hungarian rebels. "I think about them all the time. I wish there were some way of helping them." He knew there was little the United States could do, but he expressed his contempt for the Russians in a public statement on October 25. "The United States deplores the intervention of Soviet military forces . . . ," the President declared. "The heart of America goes out to the people of Hungary." The next day, he explored every aspect of the situation in a National Security Council meeting, telling his advisers that if the United States took any action, the Russians might "be tempted to resort to extreme measures, even to start a world war." At his request, the NSC drew up a position paper which proposed reassuring the Soviets that the U.S. would make no effort to transform either Poland or Hungary into military allies, but also warning them that America would support UN action, "including the use of force," to stop the invasion of Hungary—a meaningless threat since the Russians could veto any such UN decision.

Secretary of State Dulles finally set forth the administration's policy toward Poland and Hungary in the course of a nonpartisan speech to the Dallas Council on World Affairs on October 27. In a text Eisenhower had approved in advance, Dulles expressed American concern for the struggling "captive peoples." "They must know that they can draw upon our abundance to tide themselves over the period of economic adjustment which is inevitable." But then Dulles carefully hedged this offer of economic assistance by assuring the Russians that the U.S. had "no ulterior purpose in desiring the independence of the satellite countries." "We do not look upon these nations as potential military allies," Dulles declared. "We see them as friends and as part of a new and friendly and no longer divided Europe." Two days later, to make sure the Russians got the message, Eisenhower approved a Dulles suggestion to have American diplomats call this paragraph of the speech to the attention of the Kremlin.[49]

Just when things looked bleakest, news of a great victory reached the United States. On October 30, the Russians signed an agreement to remove their troops from Hungary and promised to enter into negotiations with all the satellite countries to reexamine their political, military, and economic relations with the Soviet Union. Nagy quickly negotiated an armistice with the rebels in Budapest as joyous bands of young people began demanding that Hungary withdraw from the Warsaw Pact and become a neutral nation.[50]

"In six days the Hungarian people made history—six days that shook the world," *Time* boasted. *Newsweek* praised the rebels in equally extravagant terms and declared that "the cracks in the Soviet 'monolith' can never be healed." *Time* hailed Dulles as the architect of the successful liberation of Poland and Hungary, and Republican orators were quick to make the same point. Speaking in New Haven, Thomas Dewey claimed that Republican policies were "bearing historic fruit by the spontaneous self-liberation of the enslaved peoples" of Poland and Hungary. Richard Nixon trod more carefully in speeches to Polish and Hungarian groups in Chicago on October 26, but when the outlook improved on October 29, he told a Los Angeles audience that the uprisings in the satellites could be "fused into a victory for the free world" by Eisenhower's reelection. The President, in his campaign appearances, tried to avoid commenting on the developments in Eastern Europe. He wanted to devote himself exclusively to the foreign crisis, but when his advisers pointed out that a sudden change in plans would alarm the public, he agreed to continue giving political speeches. As he interrupted sessions of the National Security Council to talk with a delegation of Republican women from Pennsylvania and to tape a message to drought-stricken Texas farmers, he could not escape thinking of the "possibility that Russia might start a military movement to put down her rebellious satellites which could develop to the proportions of a major war." Relieved by the good news on October 30, he made his one public reference to the Hungarian crisis the next day when he boasted to the American people that his administration had worked constantly "to keep alive the hope of these peoples for freedom" and then declared optimistically, "a new Hungary is rising from this struggle." [51]

VI

Whatever satisfaction the administration received from the uprisings in the satellites was more than offset by the violent renewal of the Suez crisis. After the end of the United Nations debate in mid-October, the Middle East situation remained unnaturally quiet. Rumors of the buildup of British and French forces in Cyprus worried the CIA, and Secretary of State Dulles became even more concerned as he realized that he had heard nothing from the British or French for over a week. When President Eisenhower received reports that the Israelis were mobilizing for an assault on Egypt, he sent a private message to Prime Minister David Ben-Gurion warning him that despite the election at home, the administration would oppose any act of aggression by Israel. On October 28, the President issued a statement informing the public that he had sent a second message to Ben-Gurion protesting Israeli military preparations and "expressing my grave concern . . . that no forcible initiative be taken which would endanger the peace." The next morning, with some misgivings, Eisenhower set out on a quick aerial tour of the South to begin his last active week of campaigning.[52]

A huge crowd cheered Eisenhower at the Miami airport, his first stop. He dealt mainly with domestic issues, but near the end he bore down heavily on world affairs, declaring, "We shall press our search for peace from a position of strength— spiritual, intellectual, economic, military strength." He gave a similar talk at Jacksonville, and as he prepared to board his plane for the day's last appearance, an aide informed him that Israeli troops had invaded the Sinai peninsula a few hours earlier. "Well, this is war," he remarked immediately. Murray Kempton, observing the conversation from a distance but unaware of what was being said, noted that the President drew up his lips "above and below his teeth in a moment's trace of surprise and trouble." Eisenhower went on to Richmond and gave his prepared address without informing the audience of the alarming news from the Middle East, but then he flew back to Washington, canceling plans for appearances in Tennessee, Oklahoma, and Texas the next day.[53]

At eight that evening, Eisenhower convened a hastily called meeting of his principal foreign policy advisers: Secretary of State Dulles; his brother, CIA Director Allen W. Dulles, Arthur Radford, chairman of the Joint Chiefs, Secretary of Defense Charles E. Wilson, and Under Secretary of State Herbert Hoover, Jr. For several hours they discussed the situation with the President. "Everybody at the meeting agreed that if Russia came openly to Nasser's assistance," reported Sherman Adams, "a war was inevitable." The President, convinced that the British and French were behind the Israeli attack, decided to ask the UN Security Council to condemn the Jews for an act of aggression, though he realized such a course was bound to split apart the Western alliance.[54]

The next day England and France entered directly into the crisis. Anthony Eden, after twice refusing Eisenhower's request that his country support the resolution against Israel in the Security Council, informed the President that his government had joined with France in sending Israel and Egypt an ultimatum demanding that they pull their forces back ten miles from Suez within twelve hours or face Anglo-French seizure of the canal. The Israeli thrust into the Sinai was obviously more than a unilateral act of aggression; the invasion of Egypt was part of a larger plan aimed at undoing Nasser's occupation of the Suez Canal.[55]

Eisenhower's aides were furious at the duplicity of England and France. "What your friends won't do to you behind your back!" Sherman Adams kept muttering. Emmet Hughes, called in to help draft a speech to the nation on the crisis, was appalled at the mood in the White House. Looking only to the possible effect of the Suez crisis on the election, the men around the President wanted him to denounce the British and French. One aide even suggested a threat to drop an atomic bomb on the Middle East unless all sides ceased firing immediately! The President, fortunately, took a more dispassionate view. Instead of anger, he expressed disappointment in the behavior of America's allies. Sir John Slessor, a marshal in the Royal Air Force who saw Eisenhower on October 31, reported that the President's reaction was "one of amazed stupefaction at the rashness of our unilateral use of force, involving at least the risk of general war, without consultation with our major ally." Ike expressed the same sentiments to Hughes. "I've just never seen great powers make such a complete *mess* and *botch* of things," he told his speech-writer on October 30. "Of course, there's nobody, in a war, I'd rather have fighting alongside me than the British. . . . But this thing! My God!" Unlike Dulles, who took the Anglo-French action as a personal insult to be avenged, Eisenhower viewed his allies' rash action as a terrible mistake and then set about to do all he could to right the situation.[56]

The President now took personal command of American policy. He canceled all further campaign appearances save one in Philadelphia, and he relegated Dulles to a secondary role, asking him to prepare a draft of a speech to the nation that Eisenhower planned to give on national television on October 31. When the text arrived in the White House only a few hours before air time, both Eisenhower and Hughes felt it was too vague and rambling as well as too hard on England and France. The President asked Hughes to rewrite it, and while the speech-writer raced to meet the approaching deadline, with Dulles in the next room going over the revised text, Ike relaxed by hitting golf balls across the White House lawn.

Hughes finished the text only an hour before the telecast was to begin—the President received the typed copy just ten minutes before he went on the air.

In somber tones, the President reviewed the recent events in the Middle East, culminating with the Israeli attack on Egypt and the British-French ultimatum. "The United States was not consulted in any way about any phase of these actions," the President informed the American people. "We believed these actions to have been taken in error," he continued, saying that the United States would now work through the UN to try to stop the aggression and negotiate a peaceful solution. Though the President was obviously distressed to have to act against England and France, he expressed his belief that a higher principle than loyalty to allies was involved. "There can be no peace—without law," Eisenhower insisted. "And there can be no law—if we were to invoke one code of international conduct for those who oppose us—and another for our friends." [57]

While the President spoke, the members of the Security Council debated a resolution introduced by American representative Henry Cabot Lodge, calling for Israel to halt its invasion and for all UN members to refrain from using force in the Middle East. Seven nations, including the Soviet Union, voted for the American resolution, whereupon England and France cast vetoes to prevent the United Nations from interfering with their plans to recapture Suez. The Anglo-French ultimatum expired on the morning of November 1, five days before the election, and a few hours later British and French planes began bombing Egyptian military targets in a prelude to a full-scale invasion.

Regretfully, the President ordered Secretary Dulles to bring the Suez dispute before an emergency session of the General Assembly under the Uniting-for-Peace procedure, and to take the lead in organizing international opposition to the Anglo-French aggression. "It was in many ways the hardest decision

. . . that the President and I ever had to take," Dulles said afterward. Despite nagging stomach cramps, the first sign of the intestinal cancer that would eventually take his life, Dulles flew to New York to take personal charge of the American effort to secure a cease-fire in the Middle East. "I doubt that any delegate ever spoke from this forum with as heavy a heart as I have brought here tonight," he told the General Assembly, and then the Secretary proceeded to plead for concerted action to halt the aggression. "I believe that the first thing is to stop the fighting as rapidly as possible lest it become a conflagration which would endanger us all," Dulles asserted. The debate lasted all evening and into the early hours of November 2; finally, at three in the morning, the General Assembly adopted the American cease-fire resolution by a vote of 64 to 5, with six nations abstaining. After the vote, Dulles returned to Washington and the next day he entered Walter Reed hospital to undergo a major abdominal operation.[58]

VII

The disastrous turn of events in the Middle East finally persuaded Adlai Stevenson to attack the administration's Suez policy. When he learned of the Sinai invasion on October 29, Stevenson accused Eisenhower of giving the American people reassurances that "have been tragically less than the truth." In subsequent speeches, he described Ike as a "part-time President" who let men like Dulles and Nixon make "incredible blunders" which had "helped the Communists in a few months gain the foothold in the Middle East sought by the Czars in vain for centuries." He sent a public telegram to the White House urging Eisenhower to assure the country that he would not "commit us to any precipitate military action," adding, "I believe that most Americans have grave doubts over any policy that links us with Communist Russia and President Nasser."

Stevenson gave his fullest indictment of the administration's Suez policy in a nationally televised speech from Buffalo on November 1. Replying to the President's talk to the country the night before, the Democratic candidate recited the catalogue of Republican errors, which ranged from acceptance of Russian arms sales to Egypt, through the withdrawal of the Aswan Dam offer, to Dulles' actions in splitting the Western alliance. "We have lost every point in the game," Stevenson charged. "I doubt if ever before in our diplomatic history has any policy been such an abysmal, such a complete and such a catastrophic failure." Above all, Stevenson denounced Eisenhower and Dulles for aligning the United States in the UN "with Soviet Russia and the dictator of Egypt against the democracies of Britain, France and Israel." He offered no suggestions on how the United States could deal with the immediate crisis, and though in later speeches he outlined such long-range goals as a security pact for Israel, resettlement of Palestine refugees, and international control of the canal, he never revealed how he expected to achieve these goals. Instead, he simply hammered away at the embarrassing position the administration had got into, hoping that the voters would turn in disgust and ask the Democrats to restore America's sagging world prestige.[59]

Eisenhower was furious at Stevenson for his attacks. "I just cannot figure out," he exclaimed to Emmet Hughes, "how that darn fool has the nerve to attack our foreign policy in this situation—with all the work and all the thought that have been put into it." A few prominent Republicans panicked, telling Eisenhower that his policy would antagonize Jewish voters and cost him the election. The President ignored these warnings and refused to let partisan politics interfere with his handling of the crisis.[60]

Out on the hustings, Richard Nixon sought to turn the outbreak of fighting in the Middle East to Republican advantage. Instead of boosting Eisenhower as the man of peace, the

Vice-President talked of him as "the greatest Commander-in-Chief America has ever had" and as an experienced statesman who "knows how to maintain the military strength necessary to deter aggression by the men in the Kremlin and Peiping." In contrast, he described Stevenson as "a jittery, inexperienced novice who is eager to have the job but who is utterly unqualified to make the great decisions demanded by the times." Stevenson was simply not in the same league with Ike when it came to a world crisis, Nixon explained to a Harlem audience. "The butchers of the Kremlin would make mincemeat of Stevenson over a conference table." Nixon's most astonishing about-face came in a November 2 speech in Hershey, Pennsylvania. Using a text prepared in the State Department and approved by Dulles, the Vice-President described the American break with England and France in the UN over Suez as a "declaration of independence that has had an electrifying effect thoughout the world." By at last rejecting European colonialism, Nixon claimed, the United States had gained the respect of the new nations of Asia and Africa and won "a worldwide vote of confidence." [61]

Nixon's arguments struck a responsive chord among the American people. Though James Reston summed up the feelings of foreign policy experts when he wrote on November 1, "The United States has lost control of events in areas vital to its security," there was a noticeable shift of public sentiment toward the President. The natural tendency of the people to rally behind the President in a crisis was reinforced by the enormous respect most Americans had for Eisenhower's judgment in military affairs. Kenneth Royall, Truman's Secretary of the Army who had switched parties in 1952, expressed this in a television broadcast a few days before the election: after citing Eisenhower's experience, he concluded, "God has blessed us with the right man at the right time." [62]

The only apparent headway Stevenson made with his attacks on the administration's handling of the Suez crisis was among Jewish voters. Zionists bombarded the White House with messages of protest. A Boston Congressman begged presidential aide Robert Cutler to have Eisenhower qualify his opposition to Israel's invasion of Egypt, pointing out that nearly all the Jews in his district were supporting Stevenson. Movie producer David Wolper wired Eisenhower from Hollywood on November 2, "You've lost my vote and my yearly 10,000 dollar contribution to the Republican Party because of your misguided stand on the Israel question." The Republicans, however, aware that Jews normally voted Democratic, could write off their vote without undue concern that it would endanger Eisenhower's chances for reelection.[63]

In the long run, the most serious effect of the foreign crises on Stevenson's campaign was to displace the nuclear test ban issue on which the Democrats had been making some progress. Stevenson dropped references to the test ban from most of his speeches, and though on October 29 he released a long position paper challenging the administration's stand, it went virtually unnoticed in the furor over Hungary and the Suez. More important, the events in Eastern Europe and the Middle East cast doubt on the wisdom of Stevenson's idealistic quest for peace through mutual trust. The Russian tanks in Budapest and the British bombing of Egypt reminded American voters how important military strength is in foreign affairs. "In the midst of such grave threats to world peace," commented the *New York Times,* "it is not conceivable that a United States Administration would weaken its arsenal, or, . . . if it did, that the American people would support the action." Unable to make headway early in the campaign against the Eisenhower peace blitz, Stevenson found that the sudden threat of war, instead of proving his case, made it even harder for him to challenge the President's leadership. "Someone observed," commented a Stevenson biographer, "that it was impossible to defeat a president whose aces in the hole were peace, prosperity—and war." [64]

Out of desperation, Stevenson in the last days of the campaign turned to attack the one target left open to him—Richard Nixon. In Los Angeles on October 27, Stevenson suggested that Eisenhower's frail health would enable the Vice-President to play a dominant role if the Republicans won the election, then went on to express his fear of "Richard Nixon's hand on the trigger of the H-bomb." Two days later, in Boston, he made the same point even more bluntly when he asked: "Above all, are we seriously asked to entrust the destiny of America—the future of our children—the decision over the hydrogen bomb—to the Vice-President of the United States, Richard M. Nixon?" He repeated this question in Chicago on November 3, pointedly commenting that the President's age and health record "makes it inevitable that the dominant figure in the Republican party under a second Eisenhower term would be Richard Nixon." In his final campaign speech, televised to the nation from Boston on the night before the election, Stevenson stated openly his belief that Ike would not survive a second term in office, and then added, "I recoil at the prospect of Mr. Nixon as the custodian of this nation's future, as guardian of the hydrogen bomb." Stevenson's most ardent admirers regretted this last-minute descent into what they considered gutter politics. Jim Finnegan, on the other hand, thought that if Stevenson had concentrated on Ike's health and Nixon's likely succession throughout the campaign, he would have made it a much closer contest.[65]

VIII

On the eve of the election, forecasters predicted an overwhelming triumph for President Eisenhower. Though Stevenson had closed the gap in the public opinion polls slightly in October, by the end of the month Gallup still found that 60 percent of the American electorate favored Eisenhower. Forty-seven of fifty political experts polled by *Newsweek* picked the Republican candidate to win, and most commentators expected Eisenhower to receive at least 380 electoral votes, far more than the 266 needed for reelection.[66]

Dramatic events abroad, which began the weekend before the election, killed whatever slight hopes the Democrats still had of victory. On Sunday, November 4, the Soviet Union intervened with massive force in Hungary. Two hundred and fifty thousand troops, spearheaded by columns of tanks, burst into Budapest, and despite gallant resistance from the freedom fighters, quickly seized control of the capital and replaced Nagy with János Kádár, a hard-line Communist loyal to Moscow. Hungarian groups in the United States bombarded the White House with appeals for help, calling on Eisenhower to intervene with armed force and thus become "the savior of Hungary and also the champion of the free world against this newest Russian aggression." The freedom fighters, one telegram pointed out, "have given their lives for the same principles which you, sir, have so often stressed in your public declarations." "This would be madness," Dulles commented on the proposals to intervene. "The only way we can save Hungary at this time would be through all-out nuclear war." Stevenson, deciding against a special address to the nation on Hungary, contented himself with a telegram to the President suggesting that the United States call on the UN to send a team of neutral observers into Poland and the other satellites to save them from undergoing Hungary's ordeal.[67]

Eisenhower felt utterly frustrated. He wanted to aid the Hungarians, but there was no way he could get American help to that landlocked country. "Sending United States troops alone into Hungary through hostile or neutral territory would have involved us in a general war," he wrote afterward. So instead he sent a letter to Bulganin urging the Russians "in the name of humanity" to withdraw their forces from Budapest immediately and "permit the Hungarian people to enjoy and exercise the human rights and fundamental freedoms affirmed for all peoples in the United Nations Charter." When the Soviets ignored this request, the United States asked the Security Council to order a Russian withdrawal from Hungary, only to meet with a Soviet veto. The General Assembly finally adopted the American resolution by a vote of 50 to 8, but the Russians ignored the world body as their troops completed the conquest and subjugation of Hungary. On November 6, the day of the election, the rebellion in Budapest was over and the surviving freedom fighters were streaming into neutral Austria, sadly disillusioned by the passive role the United States had played.[68]

On Monday, November 5, the first detachments of British and French troops landed in Egypt, several days behind schedule. Paratroopers began to surround Port Said, the northern terminus of the Suez Canal, only to encounter fierce Egyptian resistance. In the United Nations, the General Assembly voted 59 to 0—with England, France, and Israel abstaining—to create an international peace-keeping force under the direction of Secretary General Dag Hammarskjöld to supervise a cease-fire in the Middle East. Later in the day, the British and the French received a more ominous warning from the Kremlin. "We are fully determined to crush the aggressor and restore peace in the East through the use of force," threatened Bulganin, hinting that the Soviets were prepared to launch rocket attacks at England and France as well as send "volunteers" to help Egypt defend the canal. In a separate message to Eisenhower, Bulganin took note of American opposition to the Suez venture to suggest a joint Russian-American expedition to halt the Anglo-French invasion. Khrushchev, who was responsible for this provocative proposal, dismissed the objections of Molotov, who argued that Eisenhower was sure to reject it, by saying, "We'll make him put his money where his mouth is." [69]

"It would be difficult to exaggerate the extreme tension that gripped the United States Government between about 6 o'clock last night and 1 o'clock this afternoon," Edwin L. Dale wrote in the *New York Times* on election day. "It goes without saying that the thought of nuclear war was urgently in many minds." The President, fearful that the Bulganin note was "the opening gambit of an ultimatum," told Emmet Hughes that "if those fellows start something, we may have to hit 'em—and, if necessary, with *everything* in the bucket." Taking no chances, Eisenhower placed the Air Defense Command on emergency status and issued a precautionary alert to the Sixth Fleet in the Mediterranean. Then, to reassure the American people as well as the European allies, he released a statement denouncing Bulganin's proposal for joint military action as an "unthinkable suggestion" designed "to divert world attention from the Hungarian tragedy." The United States, the President declared, would support the UN cease-fire effort and was prepared to oppose any Soviet military intervention in the Middle East.[70]

Political considerations took a relatively low priority for the President on election day. He began the morning with a conference on Suez with Allen Dulles and Acting Secretary of State Herbert Hoover, Jr., telling them that if the Soviets moved against England and France, "we would of course be in a major war." He then motored to Gettysburg with Mamie to vote and to spend the day relaxing, but he was soon called back to Washington for another urgent series of consultations on the Middle East. Shortly after noon, he called Anthony Eden to urge him to accept the proposed UN cease-fire. To his relief, the Prime Minister informed him that England and France had agreed to stop their invasion effective at midnight and withdraw from Egypt upon the arrival of the UN peace-keeping force. Then Eden asked Ike how the campaign had gone. "I don't give a darn about the election," the President commented; "I guess it will be all right." [71]

It was more than all right. In what James Reston termed "the most spectacular Presidential election victory since

Franklin D. Roosevelt submerged Alfred M. Landon in 1936," Eisenhower decisively won a second term in office. He improved on his 1952 showing, carrying 41 states and receiving nearly 58 percent of the popular vote, compared to 39 states and 55 percent four years before. Most impressive was the widespread nature of his victory. He carried six states in the South, cracked the Democratic grip on the big cities by winning Chicago and narrowing Stevenson's margin in New York to less than 100,000 votes, and cut substantially into the Negro vote. Above all, it was a personal triumph for Ike, the man who placed himself above party. The Republicans failed to carry either the House or the Senate, and the Democrats increased their lead in the nation's statehouses.[72]

Nearly all commentators agreed that the foreign crises at the climax of the campaign magnified the dimensions of Eisenhower's victory. Political analyst Louis H. Bean estimated that as many as three and a half million voters shifted from Stevenson to Eisenhower during the last two weeks of the campaign, transforming a close election into a landslide. "In a time of great international tension," Bean explained, "the man in the White House—whether Republican or Democrat—is bound to win." Jim Finnegan agreed, indicating that his figures revealed a shift of from 4 to 7 percent of the vote to Eisenhower as a result of the events in Hungary and the Middle East. "Peace was the dominant issue of the election," commented *Newsweek* on Eisenhower's victory. "Millions credit him with ending the fighting in Korea; millions believe that he knows how to deal firmly and fairly and effectively with the Russians." Eisenhower won big, Eric Sevareid argued, because the people turned to him as a man they could trust in a time of grave crisis. "It was a kind of drawing together of the great majority," he explained, "in a manifestation to a threatening world that we are one people." [73]

The Democrats were understandably bitter that Eisenhower won reelection because of foreign problems his administration had helped create. "Apparently all you have to do to win elections is to make fatal mistakes in foreign policy," commented one of Stevenson's aides. The defeated candidate himself thought it ironic that at the campaign's climax "millions of voters turned to the Eisenhower Administration for security from the Eisenhower Administration's mistakes." Stevenson could accept defeat, but he found it difficult to understand, as he explained to Eric Sevareid, "the overwhelming endorsement of an administration whose errors were freshly revealed." What saddened him most was "the massive ignorance of our people about our situation abroad, and the extent to which the Administration has successfully contributed to this delinquency." "To ratify failure is bad enough," he told Herbert Lehman, "but the ignorance it discloses is more serious." [74]

Stevenson's failure in 1956 was doubly tragic. On one level, he went against his own best instincts in following the advice of the political pragmatists who told him to ignore foreign policy. Stevenson's great attractiveness lay precisely in his ability to rise above petty politics and appeal to the American conscience by trying to illuminate and educate the people on the great issues of the day. In avoiding foreign policy early in the campaign and in focusing on Nixon and on Eisenhower's health, he revealed himself as just another ambitious politician on the make. Even his proposals to end the draft and to ban H-bomb testing seemed to be political gimmicks—deft attempts to appeal to the emotions rather than to reason. He later said that his greatest disappointment in the 1956 campaign was the "failure to evoke any real debate of issues." "In the climate of opinion which then prevailed," he noted, "it was easy—and politically astute—for my opponents to brush them aside." [75]

Even worse, his accommodation to the conventional political wisdom proved to be poor politics. As it turned out, events overseas played a major role in the election. If Stevenson had challenged Eisenhower's conduct of foreign policy from the outset, and particularly if he had attacked Dulles' handling of the Suez controversy, he would have been in an excellent position to reap the full political benefit from the Middle East explosion at the climax of the campaign. A comprehensive indictment of Eisenhower's Cold War policies would also have placed his draft and H-bomb proposals in a far better perspective and made them seem much less like expedient maneuvers. Stevenson genuinely felt that the Republicans were losing the Cold War through rigid, inflexible, and outdated policies that ignored the perils of the H-bomb stalemate and the opportunities opened up by the emergence of the nations of the third world. If he had built up his case with the eloquence and fervor he had shown in 1952, he still might not have won; but at least he would have offered the American people viable alternatives that could have narrowed Eisenhower's margin of victory substantially. As it was, he tarnished the bright reputation he had achieved in 1952 and went down to a disastrous political defeat.[76]

1960

56

Almost everything went wrong during Eisenhower's second term in office. The prosperity that had helped win him reelection ended abruptly in 1957 with a recession that lasted more than a year. Though the economy eventually recovered, the Democrats took advantage of the decline to score an impressive victory in the 1958 elections, widening their control of the House to over 100 seats and gaining a majority of 64 to 34 in the Senate. Among his close associates, Eisenhower suffered two deep personal losses. In 1958, Sherman Adams resigned after it was revealed that he had received gifts, most notably a vicuna coat, from Boston businessman Bernard Goldfine; the next spring, John Foster Dulles finally succumbed to the cancer that had stricken him at the height of the Suez crisis. The President, his influence already diminished by his lame-duck status, now had to face crucial problems at home and abroad without the assistance of the two men he had relied upon most heavily in the past.

The Cold War continued to pose the most serious dilemmas facing Eisenhower. The Middle East situation remained potentially explosive, but American intervention in Lebanon in 1958 helped restore an element of stability there. A graver threat to world peace began in November 1958, when Nikita Khrushchev suddenly reopened the long-dormant German problem by threatening to give East Germany control of access rights to Berlin within six months unless the Western powers agreed to evacuate their forces and make Berlin a free city. The United States responded by rejecting Khrushchev's demands and announcing that it was prepared to use force if necessary to defend its position in Berlin. The Soviet leader warned that such steps would lead to World War III, but he modified his time limit when the Western powers agreed to discuss the whole German problem in a Foreign Ministers Conference at Geneva. Christian Herter, who replaced Dulles as Secretary of State, represented the United States at this meeting, which dragged on for several months only to end in a stalemate.[1]

In the Western Hemisphere an equally serious problem emerged in the late 1950's. On January 1, 1959, Fidel Castro climaxed his three-year struggle to oust the Batista regime: he entered Havana in triumph to begin a sweeping revolution that soon brought the United States and Cuba on a collision course. Though many Americans had sympathized with Castro's movement, his blatant anti-Americanism, the wholesale execution of his political opponents, and the increasingly important role of Communists within his government quickly turned American opinion strongly against him. President Eisenhower, fearful of alienating the other Latin American nations by unilateral action, tried to pursue a conciliatory policy toward the new Cuban government. But Castro's boasts of spreading his revolution throughout Latin America began to worry the administration, and in March 1960 Eisenhower issued a secret order for the CIA to begin training Cuba's exiles for a possible invasion of the island.[2]

The greatest blow to American confidence in the Cold War came in October 1957, when the Soviet Union astonished the world by orbiting Sputnik, the first artificial earth satellite.

Americans, accustomed to unquestioned leadership in science and technology, found it difficult to believe that their rival had beaten them into space. After several humiliating failures, the United States launched its first successful satellite in early 1958. Its much smaller size, however, indicated that the Soviets had taken an impressive lead in developing rocket engines strong enough to power intercontinental ballistic missiles, the next ominous step in the arms race. Although the Eisenhower administration had a well-rounded missile program under way —including medium-range Thor and Jupiter rockets deployed in Western Europe in 1958, Atlas ICBM's which became operational in late 1959, and Polaris submarine missiles which were scheduled for 1960—Democratic critics in Congress, led by Senator Stuart Symington of Missouri, charged that the Soviet Union had opened up a missile gap over the United States that would imperil the nation's security by the early 1960's. Using data leaked by the Pentagon, the administration's critics claimed that by 1962 the Russians would have one thousand ICBM's, compared to only three hundred for the U.S. President Eisenhower and Secretary of Defense Neil H. McElroy assured the nation that American superiority in bombers and the planned Polaris missile, a weapon the Soviets had not yet developed, gave the United States a secure deterrent. Yet public concern over the Russian gains in the arms race continued to grow.[3]

Confronted by these problems, President Eisenhower decided to take personal charge of American diplomacy. Reversing his previous reluctance to enter into summit meetings, in July 1959, he invited Nikita Khrushchev to visit the United States and engage in a private discussion on all outstanding issues between the two superpowers. Aware that his invitation would disturb America's allies, the President embarked on a trip to England, Germany, and France, conferring with Western leaders and receiving enthusiastic public receptions that encouraged him to engage in more personal diplomacy. In

September, Khrushchev arrived in the United States and toured the country under the watchful guidance of UN Ambassador Henry Cabot Lodge. At the end of his visit, the Soviet leader met for several days with Eisenhower at Camp David, the President's retreat in the Maryland mountains. They failed to resolve any outstanding issues, but Eisenhower felt that he scored a major victory when he persuaded Khrushchev to issue a statement withdrawing any time limit for the settlement of the Berlin situation. In return, the President agreed to attend a formal summit conference, which would include the British and French leaders, in the spring of 1960, and to visit the Soviet Union afterward. The meeting at Camp David had eased the tension over Berlin and opened up the possibility for a genuine détente in the Cold War.[4]

Eisenhower took equally bold steps in an effort to bring the arms race under control. Heartened by a meeting of technical experts in Geneva in the summer of 1958, which indicated Russian willingness to accept inspection controls, the President reversed his stand on nuclear testing. On August 22, 1958, he announced that the United States, which had recently completed an extensive series of H-bomb tests, would voluntarily suspend further nuclear explosions for a year, beginning October 31, provided the Russians would also refrain from testing. Although the Soviets never made a similar declaration, they entered into a new round of arms talks in the fall and, after one brief series in early November, apparently gave up nuclear tests. The initial optimism over an early test ban agreement faded when Russia renewed its objections to an extensive system of inspection and when the United States discovered that underground nuclear tests would be much more difficult to detect than had been previously thought. In 1959, the President proposed to the Soviets a limited test ban—a treaty outlawing tests in the atmosphere, where violations were easy to detect—while negotiations continued on ways to monitor tests conducted underground and in outer space. When the

Soviets responded with a broad proposal to outlaw all nuclear weapons within four years, the United States announced the end of its voluntary suspension, but Eisenhower refrained from actually holding tests until the Soviets did so. In February 1960, the Russians suddenly agreed to enter into negotiations for a limited test ban treaty, provided the United States and Britain would not conduct underground tests for the next four or five years, while the three nations explored ways of broadening the ban to include all weapons tests. Despite opposition from American military men, who felt underground explosions were vital to the perfecting of warheads for new types of missiles, Eisenhower announced in late March that he and British Prime Minister Harold Macmillan had agreed to go along with the Soviet plan. The President expressed the hope that negotiations for a ban on atmospheric nuclear tests could be completed before the summit conference, now scheduled for Paris on May 16. Once a limited test ban treaty was signed, Eisenhower added, the United States would not engage in underground testing for the remainder of his administration —noting that he could not bind his successor on this vital issue.[5]

Eisenhower's vigorous diplomacy undoubtedly helped reassure the American people at a time when their confidence was badly shaken. His popularity climbed to new heights after the Camp David meeting, and he helped win support abroad with a 22,370-mile trip to the Mediterranean and South Asia, highlighted by a triumphant reception in India. The American people had always believed that Eisenhower was a great world leader; now, with Dulles gone, he was at last taking personal charge of American foreign policy. He had yet to solve any fundamental issues, but he had entered into direct negotiations with the Soviets and stirred the hope that he could end the Cold War before he left office.

At the same time, a sense of deep malaise still gripped the American public. The belief that the United States was falling behind the Soviet Union, touched off by Sputnik and encouraged by talk of a missile gap, led to a widespread questioning of the vitality and direction of American society. Walter Lippmann began to ask if the United States had lost its sense of national purpose, and even President Eisenhower felt concerned enough to appoint a Commission on National Goals, charging the distinguished group "to sound a call for greatness." In hearings before a Senate committee in late February 1960, such leading members of the establishment as Robert A. Lovett and Thomas J. Watson warned that the United States was falling behind the Russians in rate of economic growth as well as missiles and satellites. "I feel that we are doing less than our best," asserted Lovett. Many Americans agreed with his assessment, and though most felt the United States was still ahead of its rival in the Cold War, they worried about the future. "The great question that stalks the '60's," commented *Time,* "is whether the U.S. has the plan and purpose to hold its lead against the threats of the Soviet Union." [6]

I

The Democrats were convinced that 1960 was their year. The decline in American world prestige and the widening missile gap gave them ready-made issues to use against the incumbent Republicans. The recurring recessions of the 1950's, and the loss of public confidence after Sputnik, added to their sense of anticipation. Their sweeping victory in the 1958 Congressional elections seemed to point to the capture of the White House in 1960. Above all, they knew that this time they would not have to face Dwight D. Eisenhower, the candidate who stood above his party and won by cutting deeply into Democratic ranks.

The party did not lack for attractive candidates. Adlai Stevenson, at sixty still young enough to be a strong contender, retained his loyal following, but he vowed to make no effort to seek the nomination. He told his friends that he stood ready to accept a genuine draft, as he had in 1952, but he underlined his sincerity in not wishing to run by leaving for a two-month tour of Latin America at the beginning of the primary season. Senator Hubert Humphrey of Minnesota very much wanted the nomination, and hoped to inherit Stevenson's liberal support. Though he had alienated many dedicated progressives by muting his own beliefs to work closely with the ruling clique of southern conservatives in the Senate, Humphrey had a liberal voting record on domestic affairs and a reputation as a confirmed Cold Warrior. He was the first candidate to announce, telling a press conference on December 31, 1959, that he would enter the primaries as the champion of the little people against Republican privilege and wealth.[7]

At the other end of the political spectrum, Senate Majority Leader Lyndon B. Johnson avoided an open declaration and subsequent involvement in the primaries. Instead, Johnson hoped to use his record of legislative accomplishment as the basis for a claim to national leadership. Partisan Democrats resented the way LBJ had ingratiated himself with Eisenhower and they wondered how well he could carry the fight to the Republicans in the fall. The fact that Johnson was from the South hurt him as a national candidate, and his lack of experience in foreign policy raised serious questions about his qualifications for the presidency.

Another senator, Stuart Symington of Missouri, hoped to win the nomination as a dark horse on the single issue of the missile gap. A handsome, affable man, Symington had been a successful St. Louis businessman and later Secretary of the Air Force before entering the Senate. One of the first to question the Eisenhower defense program, he billed himself as "a missile man for a missile age." Coming from a border state and enjoying the strong backing of Harry Truman, Symington planned to stay out of the primaries and offer himself as a compromise candidate if a deadlock developed at the Democratic convention.[8]

In early 1960, John F. Kennedy was way out in front of all other Democrats. The young Massachusetts senator had first won national attention in 1952, when he defeated Henry Cabot Lodge to move from the House to the Senate. In 1956, he had impressed many Americans with his eloquent nominating speech for Adlai Stevenson and with his graciousness in bowing out to Estes Kefauver after a hectic struggle for the vice-presidential nomination. Encouraged by the favorable public response, he began pointing toward 1960 by engaging in speaking tours across the country to build up support among the party's rank-and-file. On April 1, 1959, in a meeting with his close advisers—Larry O'Brien, Kenny O'Donnell, Theodore Sorensen, and his father, former ambassador Joseph P. Kennedy—Kennedy made the decision to run. Pierre Salinger joined the candidate's team in September, setting up headquarters in Washington and doing everything possible to increase Kennedy's visibility in the media. Kennedy made his formal announcement on January 2. With his attractive wife Jackie by his side, he told the press he could offer the dynamic leadership the United States needed to reverse its declining position in the world. "I have developed an image of America as fulfilling a noble and historic role as the defender of freedom in a time of maximum peril—and of the American people as confident, courageous and persevering," he declared. "It is with this image that I begin this campaign." [9]

Kennedy's basic strategy was to win the nomination by sweeping the primaries. He realized that Kefauver had twice failed with this approach, but he had little choice. Stevenson's followers distrusted him, considering him too young, too cool, and too uncommitted to follow in Adlai's footsteps. Liberals never forgave him for his failure to fight McCarthy, and they remained deeply suspicious of his father. The big city bosses of the North were equally antagonistic, skeptical of Kennedy's youth and preferring a more experienced and dependable politician. Kennedy had won considerable southern backing in his vice-presidential contest in 1956, but Johnson had virtually locked up the southern delegations as a regional favorite son. So Kennedy pursued the primary route, knowing that he had advantages of money, image, and issues that Kefauver had lacked.[10]

Kennedy's greatest asset in 1960 was his magnetic appeal. Not since Franklin Roosevelt had a man won so strong a public response on the basis of his personal qualities. Somewhat aloof in his personal relations, Kennedy came across before groups and on television as a warm, sensitive, and attractive individual. The disheveled hair, the boyish grin, even the high-pitched voice and awkward gestures, gave him an air of sincerity and conviction. His keen, analytical mind and firm grasp of details on complex national issues impressed those who saw him and helped offset the worry that he was too young to be President. Aside from his youth, only his religion worked against him, as people remembered the fate of Al Smith in 1928; but even this supposed handicap was an asset in the populous, industrial states of the Northeast and Middle West where presidential elections are won. Eisenhower had cut deeply into the usually Democratic Catholic vote; Kennedy could be counted on to win back many of his wayward coreligionists, and thus rebuild the old New Deal coalition.[11]

Despite his youth and relative inexperience, Kennedy realized from the outset that foreign policy would be crucial in the 1960 election. After interviewing him in December 1959, Cyrus Sulzberger wrote in his diary, "He thinks foreign policy will be the main electoral issue in the sense that the Republicans will be attacked for letting the United States slip backward in the power race." Kennedy had been one of the first to speak out on the missile gap, telling the Senate in August 1958 that within two years the United States would lose "its superiority in nuclear striking power." He called repeatedly for crash programs and extra appropriations to protect American security and "prepare us for the most serious test in our nation's history, which will be impending in the next five years." Early in 1960, Kennedy arranged for Allan Nevins, the distinguished historian, to edit his foreign policy speeches from the fifties under the title *The Strategy of Peace*. This collection revealed Kennedy as an orthodox Cold Warrior who favored the defense of South Vietnam, encouragement for the captive peoples of Eastern Europe, and a tough line against the Soviet Union. In a postscript written on January 2, 1960, Kennedy bemoaned the sense of weakness that had crept into American life in the last few years and issued a call to arms to halt it. "In this next decade there are not going to be any easy answers," he declared. ". . . There are no lazy ways to place the blame and burden on anyone else. It is all up to us—up to each and every one of us."

Kennedy sounded the same theme in his first major address after announcing his candidacy. Speaking to the National Press Club in Washington, he indirectly attacked Eisenhower by saying that the times required an active President in the White House. The American people, Kennedy contended, "demand a man capable of acting as the Commander-in-Chief of the grand alliance, not merely a bookkeeper who feels that his work is done when the numbers on the balance sheet come out even." Convinced that he was in tune with a growing public desire for more vigorous national policies, Kennedy set out to convince the American people that he was the man who could bring America out of its recent lethargy and regain its lost position of world leadership.[12]

II

During Eisenhower's second term, Richard M. Nixon emerged as the General's logical political heir. Hurt by Ike's condescending treatment of him in 1956, Nixon sought to transform his image as a controversial, partisan scrapper into one of a mature leader who could continue Eisenhower's wise policies of peace and prosperity. In an effort to build up his claim to experience in international affairs, he took a highly publicized trip to Latin America in the spring of 1958 that began with heady cheers in Argentina and ended abruptly in Venezuela when an angry, shouting mob smashed and nearly overturned his car. In the fall, he suffered a greater setback when the Democrats swept the Congressional elections despite Nixon's active campaigning for Republican candidates across the country. In the midst of the GOP debacle, Nelson Rockefeller emerged as the one bright light. Having defeated Averell Harriman for the governorship of New York by more than half a million votes, he became Nixon's leading rival for the Republican nomination in 1960.

Three days after the mid-term election, Nixon met with former National Chairman Leonard Hall, an ex-congressman from New York and bitter enemy of Rockefeller, to discuss the future. The outlook could not have been more bleak—the Republican party was in disarray, Rockefeller was fresh from a personal triumph, and Nixon trailed Kennedy in a Gallup poll, 41 to 59 percent. The Vice-President nevertheless told Hall he would fight for the nomination, and the two men proceeded to map out plans for the campaign. Hall took charge of lining up the support of Republican regulars while Nixon brought in two Californians: Robert Finch, a Los Angeles attorney, to direct his campaign and newsman Herbert Klein to manage his press relations. Finch opened an office a few blocks from the White House, and for the next year and a half waged a quiet but very effective effort to ensure Nixon's nomination.[13]

Travel abroad, so embarrassing to the Vice-President in 1958, proved to be his salvation the next year. After Deputy Premier Frol Kozlov visited the United States to open a Soviet trade exhibit in New York, President Eisenhower decided to send Nixon on a tour of Russia, accompanying a similar American exposition in Moscow. On July 23, the Vice-President arrived in Russia, to be greeted by a furious Nikita Khrushchev. Only five days before, Eisenhower had signed a routine Congressional resolution proclaiming Captive Nations Week and bemoaning the fate of the satellite nations of Eastern Europe. In a private meeting in his Kremlin office, the Soviet leader berated Nixon for this insult. The Vice-President tried to bury the issue with a soft answer, but when the two men went on to Sokolniki Park, Khrushchev continued the argument despite Nixon's courteous replies. With American television cameras recording the scene on tape, Khrushchev and Nixon stepped into the kitchen of a model home at the American exhibit. The Soviet leader ridiculed the idea that the average American worker could live in such luxury, and then began a furious denunciation of the United States. Stung by this attack, Nixon could no longer restrain himself. He began shouting back at the Russian, denying his charges and taking the offensive as he repeatedly shook his finger at Khrushchev. The two men finally broke off this exchange, and the remainder of Nixon's trip went smoothly, culminating in a dramatic appearance in Warsaw where several hundred thousand Poles gave him a moving reception.

When Nixon returned to the United States, he suddenly found himself a national hero. Though the actual words in the "kitchen debate" had not been recorded, the cameras had caught the Vice-President standing toe to toe with the Soviet leader, his finger in the Russian's face, defending American honor and integrity in an admirable fashion. Public opinion polls showed that this trip alone had narrowed Kennedy's lead to a slim 4 percent, and by the late fall of 1959 Nixon had gone ahead of his Democratic rival for the first time, 53 to 47 percent. The lesson was clear to Nixon. The GOP was a minority party; to win, the Vice-President would have to gain half the independent vote and persuade at least five million Democrats who had switched to Ike in the 1950's to continue voting Republican in 1960. Eisenhower's great appeal had been in foreign policy, as the man with the experience and stature to handle grave world issues. Nixon would have to forge a similar reputation out of his "kitchen debate" with Khrushchev and out of his eight years of apprenticeship with Eisenhower. A foreign policy appeal that transcended partisan squabbling over domestic issues—here, Nixon realized, lay his best chance to win the prize that only a year before had seemed so far beyond his reach.[14]

The Vice-President's resurgence hurt Rockefeller badly. Throughout 1959, the New York governor traveled across the nation, conferring with party leaders and speaking out on national problems. His years of experience with foreign policy, first as coordinator of Inter-American Affairs and Assistant Secretary of State under Roosevelt and Truman, then as national security adviser to Eisenhower, had made him an ardent advocate of Cold War policies. Rockefeller shared the concern of many Democrats that the Eisenhower administration had failed to take the Russian missile threat seriously enough, and he began calling for a massive increase in defense spending to protect America's security. Rockefeller's ideas appealed to many independents and liberal Republicans, but they were anathema to old guard GOP leaders, who resented both the attacks on the Eisenhower administration and the call for heavy federal spending. Realizing he had little chance to overcome this resistance, Rockefeller announced in December 1959 that he would not be an active contender for the GOP nomination. He did not endorse Nixon, however. Instead, the governor said that he would continue speaking out on the issues in order to keep the voters informed of the perils facing the nation. Insiders hinted that Rockefeller dropped out when private polls showed him trailing Nixon 75 to 15 percent in the forthcoming New Hampshire primary. The governor claimed that party leaders committed to Nixon had convinced him that the convention would be rigged for the Vice-President.[15]

Nixon was disappointed by Rockefeller's withdrawal. He had looked forward to trouncing him in primary contests to be decided by the Republican rank-and-file. Now the Vice-President had no opponent, and thus no easy way to demonstrate his political appeal and maintain a high profile in the press. Accordingly Nixon decided to lie low, in an effort to avoid the personal controversy and debate that had always hindered his political activities in the past. Instead of announcing his own candidacy in a televised news conference, he asked Herbert Klein to inform reporters that he would let his name be entered in the primaries. The Vice-President would not campaign actively in these contests, Klein explained, since his "main concern in the months ahead will be working with the President on tasks of the Administration." This time Eisenhower did not draw back when Nixon tried to stand in his shadow. He sent Nixon a private message of support in January, and in April endorsed him publicly, saying he realized that the Vice-President would have to form his own policies for the future. Nixon, aware of polls that showed only 30 percent of the electorate saying they were Republicans, compared to 47 percent affirming Democratic status, carefully refrained from using the freedom Eisenhower offered him. Instead, he kept silent on controversial issues such as the missile gap, simply repeating the administration's position and giving the impression that he agreed completely with the President.[16]

Nixon's uncharacteristic efforts to avoid attention and controversy led to an immediate decline in his popularity. By March, he had dropped behind Kennedy again, trailing the Democratic front runner in the Gallup poll, 53 to 47 percent. The liberal journals that detested him found his behavior inexplicable; they were baffled by the new, bland Nixon who avoided all personal attacks and contented himself with having his picture taken with prominent athletes. "He reeks of respectability," complained the *New Republic;* "he's Dwight Eisenhower without the charm. . . . this all-American Boy who wants to be the all-American father leading an all-American team is nauseating." [17]

Nixon's listless performance in the spring of 1960 surprised even his Republican supporters. "Nixon is like a man who got on an elevator and found himself on the top floor by mistake," commented one GOP columnist. What Nixon lacked was a strong opponent. Throughout his career, he had relished hard-fought contests which brought out his competitive qualities. Now he drifted in a vacuum, without anyone to attack. By nature a lonely, introspective man, he conferred from time to time with Leonard Hall and with the two men close to him in the Eisenhower administration, Attorney General William Rogers and White House aide General Wilton B. Persons. But he spent most of those long months before the convention brooding about the future and the tough battle he knew lay ahead.[18]

III

John F. Kennedy monopolized the political news in the first few months of 1960. He began his attempt to win the nomination in New Hampshire, campaigning vigorously against the token opposition of a minor candidate. He swept to an impressive victory in March, rolling up twice as many votes as any Democrat had ever gained in this normally Republican state. Then he moved on to Wisconsin, where he challenged Hubert Humphrey close to his home ground. Though many observers thought Humphrey held an advantage, particularly with his more attractive record on farm issues, Kennedy waged an all-out blitz, saturating the state with members of his family and displaying the youthful energy and charm that had become his hallmark. Bobby Kennedy planned the assault with great organizational skill: Rose, the candidate's mother, his three sisters and two brothers, accompanied by a loudspeaker truck playing Frank Sinatra's rendition of the song "High Hopes," appeared in all ten Wisconsin Congressional districts. Kennedy hoped for a decisive victory, but he had to settle for a modest one. He won 56 percent of the vote and led in six districts, taking 20½ delegates to 10½ for Humphrey. More important, political analysts claimed afterward that only a massive turnout of Catholic voters in a state where they made up 30 percent of the electorate had enabled Kennedy to triumph.[19]

Determined to prove that he could win without the support of his fellow religionists, Kennedy entered the West Virginia primary in a two-man race against Hubert Humphrey. Though an early private poll showed Kennedy leading in this overwhelmingly Protestant state, where poverty and social welfare issues predominated, the press played up his constant claim of being the underdog. Humphrey, aided quietly by backers of Johnson and Symington, waged a heroic one-man campaign through the coal-mining towns and villages, but he could not match the far more expensive efforts of the Kennedy family. In early May, the West Virginia voters gave Senator Kennedy the impressive victory he sought, proving that a Catholic could win in a Protestant area. Humphrey gave up his lonely quest for the nomination, muttering, "You can't beat a billion dollars." Despite rumors of massive vote-buying, most experts conceded that Kennedy had demonstrated remarkable political appeal. Noting that reporters referred to him off the record as "Jack the knife," TRB commented on the contradiction between the senator's warm public image and his private personality. "The fact is there is a tough, not to say ruthless quality," he wrote, "about the young, self-possessed glamorous figure." [20]

Despite his primary victories, Kennedy realized that he had not yet clinched the nomination. Lyndon Johnson remained a powerful obstacle, with his solid block of southern delegates and his influential position as Senate Majority Leader. Stuart Symington had finally declared himself on the eve of the Wisconsin primary, and though he failed to attract a significant following, he had the support of Truman and many midwestern leaders. Kennedy's greatest concern, however, was the still uncommitted Adlai Stevenson. He told Arthur Schlesinger, Jr., in 1959 that he regarded "Stevenson's sleeping candidacy" as "his greatest threat," and Adlai's subsequent behavior had done nothing to ease Kennedy's mind. In April, Stevenson returned from his two-month jaunt to Latin America and immediately announced a series of six major speeches to discuss pressing national issues. The first address, given at the University of Virginia in late April, was an eloquent attack on Eisenhower's foreign policy that reminded many Democrats of Stevenson's availability and once again touched off a movement to draft him for the nomination.

Kennedy hoped to head off a contest with Stevenson by winning him over to his side. Earlier, he had persuaded such strong Stevenson workers as Arthur Schlesinger and Chester Bowles to join his camp, Schlesinger as speech-writer and Bowles, former ambassador to India, as foreign policy adviser. After winning yet another primary victory in Oregon in mid-May, the senator decided to approach Stevenson directly and try to gain his public endorsement. Stopping off in Illinois to visit Adlai at his farm, Kennedy considered offering him the post of Secretary of State, but dropped this idea when Stevenson's aides warned the senator that it would only offend the former candidate. The meeting proved awkward. Kennedy showed impatience at Stevenson's insistence on remaining neutral in the intraparty contest, while Adlai seemed disturbed by his young rival's casual arrogance. Stevenson ignored the hints of favor that Kennedy dropped, saying only that he would not join a stop-Kennedy movement or encourage the efforts of his own friends to draft him. Arthur Schlesinger, who had helped arrange the meeting, found Kennedy angry at Stevenson for keeping him dangling, while Adlai commented, "He seemed very self-confident and much tougher and blunter than I remember him in the past." [21]

Even without Stevenson's endorsement, Kennedy held a commanding lead among the delegates chosen for the Democratic convention. He was within about one hundred of the number needed to win, and his prospects seemed bright. Yet the question marks of youth and religion and inexperience remained. The ruthless efficiency of his campaign won him victory after victory, but it also took its toll, as seasoned politicians came to resent the cool precision with which the senator forged into the lead. If all continued to go smoothly, Kennedy could win easily in Los Angeles, but if he should stumble, there were many waiting to gain their revenge.

IV

Foreign policy played little part in the political maneuvering in the early months of 1960. Despite his concern for America's declining prestige in the world, John F. Kennedy stuck almost exclusively to domestic issues in the primaries, which turned more on personalities and emotions than they did on questions of national policy. The Cold War had receded from the front pages after Khrushchev's visit to America; there were no major crises and everyone looked forward to the forthcoming summit meeting in Paris in mid-May for a peaceful settlement on Berlin and the negotiation of the long-awaited test ban agreement.

On the morning of May 1, an American pilot took off on a flight from Pakistan that would create a major international incident and bring the Cold War directly into the 1960 presidential election. Francis Gary Powers, an ex-air force officer and CIA employee, piloted his strange, bird-shaped U-2 airplane on a course that would fly him over the Soviet Union at an altitude of 80,000 feet and enable his cameras to take thousands of feet of infrared film of Russian territory. The United States had been flying these spy missions since June 1956, and though the Russians had secretly protested, the Eisenhower administration had continued them sporadically because of the extremely valuable data they provided about Soviet missile progress. Though technically the flights went on only with presidential approval, in fact the CIA had operational control of the program, and Powers' mission, only fifteen days before the summit meeting was due to open, occurred without Eisenhower's knowledge. CIA officials, worried that a summit agreement might end the flights, hoped to gain a last look at suspected new missile installations in central Russia.

Powers, who had gone on several earlier missions, had an uneventful flight until he reached the vicinity of Sverdlovsk. Suddenly a Russian surface-to-air missile, penetrating to an unprecedented altitude, either struck his plane directly or came close enough to cause an engine flame-out. As the plane lost altitude, Powers, who had been given a cyanide pellet but no instructions on what to do if he were shot down, bailed out. A Russian army patrol picked him up after he landed, and Powers became living proof of a deliberate American violation of Soviet air space for espionage purposes.[22]

The first inkling the American public had of the U-2 affair came on May 3, when the CIA released a cover story through the National Aeronautic and Space Administration, stating that an American weather reconnaissance plane in Turkey was missing. Two days later, NASA released further details and suggested the possibility that the pilot of the weather plane might have lost consciousness because of an oxygen deficiency and drifted by mistake into Soviet territory. When Nikita Khrushchev announced to the Supreme Soviet that Russia had shot down an American spy plane and accused the United States of engaging in a "bandit flight," the State Department issued an immediate denial, repeating the NASA cover story.

"There was absolutely no—N-O—no—deliberate attempt to violate Soviet air space," insisted State Department press officer Lincoln White on May 6. "There never has been."

The next day Khrushchev sprang the trap he had so carefully laid. Speaking again to the Supreme Soviet, he revealed that the Russians had captured Francis Gary Powers and had recovered the offending U-2 along with its film. To prove his point, he displayed blown-up pictures he claimed came from the U-2's cameras showing Soviet airfields and missile sites. Then, saying he still hoped to meet with Eisenhower at the Paris summit despite the American provocation, he conceded, "I am prepared to grant that the President had no knowledge of a plane being dispatched to the Soviet Union and failing to return." American militarists, he hinted, had acted without Eisenhower's knowledge.

Incredibly, the administration decided to take the escape that Khrushchev offered. On May 7, Lincoln White issued a new statement admitting the U-2 flight and justifying it on the grounds of "the excessive secrecy practiced by the Soviet Union in contrast to the free world." The flight was designed to reduce world tension, White explained, by removing the danger of a sneak attack. Then he added that, after a lengthy investigation, "it has been established that insofar as the authorities in Washington are concerned there was no authorization for any such flight as described by Mr. Khrushchev." The President, aware that this denial of responsibility suggested that he had lost control of his own administration, soon had second thoughts, and on May 9 Secretary of State Herter released a new statement in which the President took full responsibility for the U-2 overflights. The Eisenhower administration, Herter declared, would be "derelict in its duties," both to the American people and the free world, if it did not do everything possible "to overcome this danger of suprise attack." "In fact," the Secretary continued, "the United States has not and does not shirk this responsibility." [23]

Herter's statement implied that not only did the United States defend Powers' flight, but that it planned to continue overflying the Soviet Union in the future. When a reporter pressed Eisenhower on this point at a news conference on May 11, the President refused to answer directly, but he gave indirect confirmation by saying, "Our deterrent must never be placed in jeopardy." The American people apparently saw nothing wrong with the administration's plan to continue high-level aerial espionage. There was overwhelming public support for the President. In Bremerton, Washington, a high school teacher lost his job because he permitted his social studies class to telegraph Eisenhower urging him to apologize to Khrushchev; in San Antonio, another teacher was suspended for making critical comments about the U-2 flights. In Congress, Democratic Senator Mike Mansfield summed up the feelings of many when he said, "As a nation we are holding the short end of the stick, but this is the place where politics stops." Lyndon Johnson went further, calling for national unity and warning Khrushchev not to "use this incident in such a way as to divide the American people and to weaken our national strength." Of all the candidates, only Adlai Stevenson spoke out to criticize the administration. In a speech in Chicago, Stevenson said he had no quarrel with the need to gain intelligence about Russia, but he did question the timing of such a flight on the eve of the summit conference. "One could say with the cynical diplomat: 'Sir, it was worse than a lie, it was a blunder,'" Stevenson chided.[24]

Several perceptive columnists raised an even more crucial question—the implication that the United States would continue spy flights in the future. "To *avow* that we intend to violate Soviet sovereignty is to put everybody on the spot," commented Walter Lippmann. "It makes it impossible for the Soviet government to play down this particular incident because now it is challenged openly in the face of the world." James Reston made the same point in a dispatch from Paris on the eve of the summit conference. The only way the meeting could proceed, Reston predicted, would be for Eisenhower to withdraw his claim to continue intruding on Soviet air space. But Richard Nixon, appearing on David Susskind's *Open End* television talk show on May 15, defended the overflights and advocated their continuation. The Powers' flight was necessary to avoid "an intelligence gap" at the time of the summit conference, he said, and repeated the administration's position that defense against surprise attack took precedence over all other considerations, adding, "Such activities may have to continue in the future." [25]

In Paris, the summit conference appeared to be on the verge of collapse. Eisenhower arrived on May 15, a day early, to confer with other Western leaders. Khrushchev came on the same day, refusing to speak to reporters. When Cyrus Sulzberger asked a Russian official his feelings, the man replied by pointing out that May 1 was a national holiday and by asking "how we would feel if a Russian plane had been shot down in Texas on Christmas Day." Secretary of Defense Thomas Gates, in Paris to advise Eisenhower, added greatly to the sense of tension by ordering a worldwide alert for American armed forces in the early morning hours of May 16, the day the conference was to begin. [26]

The summit meeting was never held. Khrushchev boycotted the first session, and then appeared at a public meeting that afternoon to demand that Eisenhower condemn the Powers' mission and promise that the United States would discontinue further overflights as a price for holding the conference. Then, in a particularly blatant political move, Khrushchev canceled the invitation for Eisenhower to visit Russia later in the year and suggested it would be best to postpone the summit conference for six or eight months, when a new administration in Washington might be willing to negotiate peacefully. [27]

Eisenhower spoke next. With prefect composure, he ignored Khrushchev's taunts and refused to apologize for the U-2 missions. He then revealed, for the first time, that "these flights were suspended after the recent incident and are not to be resumed." The President had issued this order on May 11, apparently without informing Richard Nixon; he hoped that by making this concession in person to Khrushchev, he could demonstrate his good faith and save the conference. But Ike's peaceful gesture came too late. Khrushchev, apparently aware that the Western nations were adamant on Berlin, decided to use the U-2 incident to scuttle the summit meeting. In a mass press conference to three thousand reporters the next day, he renewed his attacks on the United States and on Eisenhower personally. Despite his invective, however, he refrained from imposing any new deadlines on Berlin, the most sensitive issue facing the world. Instead he flew to East Germany, where he said only that he expected to reopen the Berlin issue in six to eight months with the next American President, and returned to Moscow. Eisenhower left Paris for Portugal, where he had planned a brief tour, and then returned to the United States, his hopes for world peace ruined. Despite his failure, a huge crowd lined the streets in Washington to welcome him home and symbolize the way the American people rallied behind their leaders in time of grave crisis. "The cruel reality of the anger-flushed Nikita Khrushchev smashed the Western world's hope of a sturdy peace," commented *Newsweek*. ". . . Hope had faded far, but, in place of hope, came resolution." [28]

V

At home, the politicians realized that the U-2 incident and the summit breakup had created, as the *New York Times* reported, "a new political imponderable in the Presidential campaign." The Republicans, hoping to campaign in 1960 on Eisenhower's record of peace, seemed to be hurt the most, but the Democrats realized that, in the short run at least, the American people were likely to rally strongly around the President in the face of Khrushchev's insulting attacks. Lyndon Johnson was the first contender to try to turn the crisis to his advantage. On May 17, when the fate of the Paris summit was still unclear, he took the lead in answering Khrushchev's suggestion that the conference be postponed until after the American elections. In a telegram to Eisenhower which Speaker Sam Rayburn, Senator William Fulbright, and Adlai Stevenson joined him in signing, Johnson asked the President to inform Khrushchev that the Democrats "urge that he reconsider his suggestion for a postponement of the summit conference until after the national elections in this country." When it became clear the next day that the summit meeting was off, LBJ once again appealed for national unity. There might have been mistakes, he admitted, "but one mistake that we cannot afford to make right now is to weaken the free world by division within our own ranks." [29]

Adlai Stevenson refused to let the U-2 affair die so quietly. In a speech at a Cook County Democratic fund-raising dinner on May 19, he accused the Eisenhower administration of trying to sweep "this whole sorry mess under the rug in the name of national unity." The events of the past two weeks, he asserted, meant that "this year's campaign will be waged under the darkest shadows that ever hovered over the world —the mushroom clouds of a nuclear war that no one wants." He then proceeded to list the mistakes Eisenhower had made: sending the U-2 over Russia on the eve of the summit conference; denying, then admitting, the spy flight; suggesting that the missions would continue; and permitting Secretary Gates to order a worldwide alert of American military forces. He agreed that the Russian leader had actually destroyed the summit conference with his impossible demand that Eisenhower apologize, but Stevenson bitterly concluded, "We handed Khrushchev the crowbar and sledgehammer to wreck this meeting."

Stevenson's attack touched off a hectic partisan debate. The

Democratic Advisory Council, a group formed by Stevenson's supporters after the 1956 election to offset the tendency of the Democrats in Congress to work with the Eisenhower administration, issued a statement echoing Adlai's charge and contending that the administration's foreign policy had "collapsed." All the Democratic contenders except Johnson endorsed the statement, though Symington tried to take a separate position by arguing that the recent events simply underscored the need to build up America's lagging defenses.[30]

Republicans in Congress rushed to the administration's defense. In the House, Representative Everett McKinley Dirksen claimed that Stevenson had fired a "well-placed, well-timed torpedo" with his criticism of the U-2 affair prior to the Paris summit meeting. Senator Hugh Scott of Pennsylvania, citing a remark John Kennedy had made in a press conference while campaigning in the Oregon primary, accused both Stevenson and Kennedy of advocating appeasement of the Soviet Union. Later the same day, an angry Kennedy arrived back in Washington and immediately went to the Senate floor to reply to the Republican attack. A student in Portland had asked him on May 19, Kennedy explained, what he would do if he had been in Ike's place at Paris. The senator had answered that he would have rejected Khrushchev's demand that the United States publicly punish those involved in the U-2 program, but he admitted that "an apology" might have been in order, adding, "If he had merely asked that the U.S. should express regret, then that would have been a reasonable term." Scott refused to be mollified, calling Kennedy a "turnquote" and insisting, "it would be appeasement to apologize to Khrushchev." [31]

In an effort to stop this unseemly partisan infighting on the Senate floor, William Fulbright announced on May 24 that his Foreign Relations Committee would conduct an investigation of the whole affair. Nelson Rockefeller joined in the call for an impartial hearing, saying that the U-2 raised serious questions about America's foreign policy that required a full airing. Two days later, the governor announced that he would be available for the Republican nomination, a sure sign that he felt the recent events had weakened Nixon's position.[32]

The Vice-President carefully refrained from entering into the political controversy surrounding the U-2. He told reporters on May 17 that Khrushchev had simply exploited the U-2 incident to sabotage a meeting he realized he could not turn to Russia's advantage. Nixon refrained from any direct comment on Stevenson's charges; he let Press Secretary Klein state that while the Vice-President was "shocked" at the attack on Eisenhower, he did not want to drag foreign policy into the campaign. "Whether foreign policy is an issue or not will be up to the Democrats," Klein explained.[33]

The political uproar over the collapse of the summit meeting gradually died away. On May 25, President Eisenhower delivered a calming report to the nation, in which he reiterated his belief that the demands of national security justified the U-2 flight, even on the eve of the conference. "The plain truth is this: when a nation needs intelligence activity, there is no time when vigilance can be relaxed," Eisenhower declared. He blamed the summit breakup on Khrushchev's intransigence, and then reassured the American people, telling them that the Western allies had stood steadfastly behind the United States in this crisis. "The zigs and zags of the Kremlin," he concluded, "cannot be allowed to disturb our worldwide programs and purposes." In June, Fulbright's committee released its report, which was surprisingly mild in tone. Avoiding any partisan charges, the Senate Foreign Relations Committee only regretted the way in which the administration had clumsily tried to cover up the U-2 affair before Eisenhower took full responsibility.[34]

As the crisis began to recede, political analysts tried to measure its impact on the forthcoming election. On the surface it appeared that the Republicans had lost their best issue

—the claim to peace and security. "The issue of peace had been blown right out of the Eisenhower Administration's hands," commented *Newsweek.* ". . . The picture of Vice President Richard Nixon as heir apparent to a successful world policy had been fragmented." Yet Nixon in fact emerged from the crisis in a relatively strong position. His shrewd practice of avoiding public statements earlier in the year gave him considerable flexibility. Undoubtedly he had planned to stress his ability to continue Ike's peaceful policies, but now, in view of the deteriorating world situation, he could just as easily shift to the line that he, and he alone, had the experience and courage to stand up to Nikita Khrushchev. Though the Vice-President remained silent, his supporters began boosting him as an advocate of a hard line against Russia. "The argument that seems to be gaining momentum is that because Khrushchev hates Nixon," commented the *Nation,* "it is the duty of the embattled voter to spit in Mr. Khrushchev's eye and vote for Mr. Nixon." The polls bore out this analysis. Nixon, who had slipped behind Kennedy by a margin of 46 to 54 percent in April, now regained the lead in June, 51 to 49 percent. Probing into the reasons behind this sudden shift, Samuel Lubell found that 49 percent of the people wanted Nixon to represent the United States at the next summit conference, compared to only 37 percent who chose Kennedy.[35]

The Democratic front runner was clearly the leading victim of the U-2 affair. The machinelike precision of his primary drive had been geared to domestic issues, to a contrast between Republican lethargy and his own dynamic activism. The foreign crisis suddenly raised new issues—not energy but wisdom, not charm but judgment on matters of national security. Kennedy's youth and inexperience, always his greatest handicaps, were underlined by Khrushchev's rude threats and the resulting fear of nuclear war. How well could a young senator who had never dealt face to face with world leaders represent American interests in a dangerous world crisis? This question, raised by even friendly commentators, brought a new element of uncertainty that slowed Kennedy's drive for the nomination. In an effort to provide an answer, he gave a major Senate speech on June 14 in which he claimed that the "real issue" of American foreign policy was not the U-2 but rather "the lack of a coherent and purposeful national strategy backed by strength." He then outlined a twelve-point program stressing increased defense spending and stronger ties with allies abroad as a way to defeat the "determined Soviet program for world domination." In essence, Kennedy claimed that he could wage the Cold War more effectively than Eisenhower or Nixon, and though experts praised his speech, he had yet to convince the American people that he possessed the maturity, judgment, and skill to handle world affairs effectively.[36]

The other Democratic contenders gained from the events of May. Lyndon Johnson, though still not a declared candidate, tried hard to exploit the setback Kennedy had received. Relying on his power in the Senate, LBJ tried to line up support at the national convention, only to find that Kennedy operatives, working on the state level, had beaten him time after time. In near-desperation, Johnson began touring the nation in search of votes. Much of his effort was private, but in public speeches he bore down hard on Kennedy's Oregon statement on the U-2 affair. "I am not prepared to apologize to Mr. Khrushchev—are you?" he would ask, and then wait for the audience to boom back, *"No!"* He tried to cover up his own lack of experience in international affairs by citing his record of cooperation with Eisenhower and calling for national unity in a time of grave crisis. Though he still lagged far behind Kennedy in delegates, he began to advance in the public opinion polls.[37]

Adlai Stevenson made the greatest gains. Though many Americans reacted strongly against his criticism of Eisenhower's handling of the U-2 affair, his dedicated supporters rallied to his side, convinced that Adlai alone had the wisdom and experience that the nation needed in the renewed Cold War. Old friends like Eleanor Roosevelt and Thomas Finletter urged him to declare his candidacy, and staunch backers, led by Oklahoma Senator Mike Monroney, began a new movement to draft him for the Democratic nomination. In private conversations, Stevenson revealed his own misgivings about all the other Democratic contenders, but he refused to seek the nomination actively, telling those close to him that he would run only if the party freely chose him. Yet even without his participation, a growing Stevenson boom developed that threatened to halt the Kennedy bandwagon.[38]

Amid the heightened political speculation that followed the U-2 incident, one point was clear: the Cold War had become a major factor in the presidential race. "The cold air mass from the Soviet created an entirely new atmosphere in U.S. political life," commented *Time*. Nikita Khrushchev had intruded himself squarely into the American electoral process, raising questions of national will and prestige that no candidate could afford to dismiss. Though Stevenson had re-emerged as a serious contender as a result of the foreign crisis, the American people seemed to favor those who took a strong stand against Soviet bullying. "National security will be the major issue," predicted Senator Henry Jackson, a Kennedy supporter. "The public is going to expect a hard, tough line." [39]

VI

The Cold War, intensified by the U-2 affair, continued to permeate American politics in June. Early in the month, Nikita Khrushchev held a mammoth press conference in Moscow in which he ridiculed Eisenhower, calling him "spineless" and claiming that the President had deliberately wrecked the summit meeting. Mixing threats with enticements, the Soviet leader hinted that he would renew the Berlin crisis unless the

United States agreed to a new summit conference in six to eight months, and suggested that he would prefer to meet with a Democratic President. Then, saying that he had heard that Russian opposition was helpful to an American candidate, he slyly commented, "To follow this reasoning, I would say that I believe the best candidate is Nixon." The Republicans ignored this blatant attempt to interfere in American politics, while all the Democratic contenders except Stevenson condemned the Russian leader for meddling in the presidential race.[40]

President Eisenhower refused to engage in a long distance shouting match with Khrushchev. Instead, he set out to rebuild his image as a constructive world leader by embarking on a goodwill trip to the Far East, with scheduled stops in the Philippines, Taiwan, and South Korea prior to a major three-day visit to Japan. Even before Eisenhower left the United States, Communist-led students in Tokyo began to demonstrate against him, causing concern in the State Department and speculation that he might omit the Japanese stop to avoid embarrassment. The damage to American prestige from such a change, coming on top of the President's failure to make the trip to Russia after the summit blow-up, seemed too great to risk and thus Eisenhower's advisers urged him to stay with his original itinerary.

Ike flew to the Philippines in mid-June, where he was given a warm and friendly greeting. Meanwhile, a crowd of ten thousand chanting students in Tokyo blocked the motorcade of presidential advance man James Hagerty outside the airport, forcing the Japanese government to rescue him from the mob by helicopter. Frightened by this turmoil, Prime Minister Nobusuke Kishi informed the American government that since he could no longer guarantee the President's safety, he must withdraw the invitation. Hagerty announced the cancellation of Eisenhower's visit to Japan on June 16, blaming the riots on "a small organized minority, led by professional

Communist agitators acting under external direction and control." The President offered the same explanation in a report to the American people after his return, accusing the Communists of going "to great lengths and expense to create disorders in Tokyo." Despite this attempt to blame the Soviets, the administration could not hide the stunning blow to American pride. "[N]ever before in the history of America had a U.S. President been so humiliated while traveling abroad," commented *Newsweek*. Ike's popularity plunged from 68 percent in the Gallup poll to 61 percent, as *Time* explained that he had "lost some of his once vast, global personal authority." Hurt and perplexed by this turn of events, the President retreated to a cottage in Newport, Rhode Island, for a month's vacation, leaving the impression, according to *Time,* "that he has resigned himself to a caretaker's role during the remaining half-year of his presidency." [41]

Before he left for Newport, the President took one decisive and long-anticipated action. For several months, Fidel Castro had been waging an increasingly virulent propaganda attack on the United States, accusing Americans of plotting to overthrow his revolutionary regime and deny Cuba its hard-won freedom from capitalist exploitation. In early July, the Cuban government acted more provocatively by seizing two American-owned oil refineries which refused to process crude oil imported from the Soviet Union. The administration, which had displayed remarkable restraint in the face of Cuban attacks, retaliated by asking Congress for authority to adjust the Cuban sugar quota. In the early morning hours of July 3, Congress gave Eisenhower the power he requested, and the President then proceeded to reduce the quota by 700,000 tons, virtually ending any further import of Cuban sugar in 1960. Though most experts warned that the loss of the American market would simply drive Cuba further into the arms of Russia, Eisenhower justified his action as necessary "to reduce our reliance for a major food product upon a nation which has embarked upon a deliberate policy of hostility toward the United States." [42]

Castro responded with further seizures of American property in Cuba, but a far more ominous reply came from Moscow. In the course of a Kremlin speech on July 9, Khrushchev promised Cuba economic assistance, then added, "If need be, Soviet artillerymen can support the Cuban people with their rocket fire should the aggressive forces in the Pentagon dare to start intervention against Cuba." This Soviet missile threat immediately led Eisenhower to warn the Russians not to meddle in the New World. Citing Khrushchev's provocative remarks as a sign of the close ties between Cuba and Russia, the President declared that the United States would not "permit the establishment of a regime dominated by international Communism in the Western Hemisphere." Democrats, preparing for their convention in Los Angeles, tried to avoid comment, though John Kennedy did call Khrushchev's remarks "the first real attack on the Monroe Doctrine in the last century." Most Americans applauded Ike's firm response to the Soviets, but many also saw the growing Russian influence in Cuba as a major defeat for American diplomacy. The challenge to American supremacy in the New World, coupled with the embarrassing U-2 incident, the summit fiasco, and the forced cancellation of Ike's trip to Japan, undercut Republican claims to peace and security and gave the Democrats an opportunity to exploit foreign policy failures in the coming election. [43]

VII

The leading Democratic contenders were too busy trying to block John F. Kennedy's drive for the nomination to pay much attention to Eisenhower's setbacks abroad. The Massachusetts senator had not only swept the primaries; he had carefully cultivated enough local leaders to win broad support among the delegations chosen by state conventions. By the end of June, Kennedy was within 100 votes of the 761 he needed, and he had regained the lead over Nixon in the Gallup poll, 52 to 48 percent. In a desperate move, Harry Truman, Senator Symington's chief backer, called a televised news conference in Independence to announce his resignation as a delegate to the Los Angeles convention because it was rigged for Kennedy. He then asked the young senator to step aside for another candidate, "someone with the greatest possible maturity and experience," mentioning Symington and Johnson as fitting this description. The next day, in an impressive performance, Kennedy gave his answer. Stressing his fourteen years of service in Congress, Kennedy said he would not step aside. "It is time," he declared, "for a new generation of leadership to cope with new problems and new opportunities." [44]

Two days later, on July 5, Lyndon Johnson belatedly made his formal entrance into the race. He had just adjourned Congress until after the conventions, a move designed to put pressure on congressmen and senators attending the Los Angeles convention, and he now announced that instead of attacking Eisenhower he would concentrate on offering "cures" for the nation's problems. Though Johnson claimed to have more than five hundred votes committed to him on the first ballot, Kennedy was much more concerned about the strong liberal movement to draft Adlai Stevenson. On June 10, Eleanor Roosevelt gave the Stevenson supporters a great lift when she wrote, "The people seem to want a man of maturity with proved administrative ability and experience in dealing with the heads of government in all parts of the world, and this man is quite obviously Adlai E. Stevenson." Kennedy, she added, was a man of great promise, but the times required proven leadership, so she suggested a ticket of Stevenson for President and Kennedy for Vice-President. Despite Mrs. Roosevelt's efforts, however, Stevenson refused to enter the race, saying only, "I will serve my country and my party whenever called upon." This was not enough. Adlai's equivocal stand doomed his semi-candidacy to failure at Los Angeles, where the galleries displayed enormous affection for Stevenson but the delegates held steadily to their commitment to Kennedy.[45]

Though crises overseas dominated the headlines during the week of the convention, the Democrats virtually ignored foreign policy in their deliberations. Senator Frank Church gave only passing mention to the Cold War in his keynote speech, noting the "tide of suspicion and hostility" in the world reflected by the U-2 affair and the riots against Ike in Japan. The party's platform, written by a committee chaired by Kennedy adviser Chester Bowles, offered little in the way of alternatives to the policies of the Eisenhower administration abroad. The foreign policy plank pledged a firm stand on Berlin, support for Chiang Kai-shek against the Chinese Communists, and continued backing for NATO in Europe. There were brief references to the "mishandling" of the U-2 affair and to Republican laxity in permitting Soviet penetration of Cuba, but the only really full attack came on the defense issue. The Republicans, claimed the platform, had surrendered the military superiority they had inherited from Truman in 1952. "As a result, our military position today is measured in terms of gaps—missile gap, space gap, limited-war gap," the Democrats charged, and then asserted that they would build up the balanced forces needed "to deter both limited and general aggressions." [46]

The blandness of the foreign policy plank ruled out any controversy over its adoption. To Chester Bowles's disappointment, John Kennedy gave the whole platform only a cursory glance, letting his brother Bobby go over it in detail. Neither Kennedy seemed at all interested in the clauses and phrases Bowles had worked months to produce; apparently they were far too absorbed in the struggle for the nomination to worry about the platform. Most commentators found it a routine document. "[I]t reads as though two dozen precocious political science majors had pooled all their 'bright' ideas," commented Carey McWilliams. "Implicit throughout is the assumption that the basic goals of present policy are sound," noted the *New York Times,* pointing out that the only issue raised was the call for a renewed effort to achieve victory in the Cold War.[47]

The real drama at Los Angeles unfolded in the hotel suites and meeting rooms, as Kennedy and Johnson maneuvered for the final showdown on the convention floor. Despite spirited attacks on Kennedy, including suggestions that he suffered from Addison's disease, and thinly veiled references to the isolationism of Joe Kennedy prior to Pearl Harbor, Johnson failed to shake the smoothly efficient machine that Bobby Kennedy, Larry O'Brien, and Pierre Salinger had put together. Kennedy aides communicated with each other quickly through a special telephone network and even by walkie-talkies in the convention hall; Salinger broke precedent by publishing a daily Kennedy newspaper and delivering it to each delegate's hotel room every morning. The senator went into seclusion as the balloting began, watching on television as state after state gave him precisely the number of votes his aides had predicted. Wyoming put him over; then, to everyone's surprise, he selected Lyndon Johnson as his running mate in a move calculated to hold the wavering South and offset the charge of inexperience. Foreign policy considerations did not enter into his choice of Johnson. Adlai Stevenson and Chester Bowles had been mentioned as men who would add strength to the ticket at a time of world crisis, but Kennedy wanted the one man who could unify the party for the fall election.[48]

In nominating John Kennedy, the Democrats had broken sharply with the past, even though the Massachusetts senator would not depart radically from the Cold War positions of Harry Truman and Adlai Stevenson. As the *New York Times* noted, "His difference seems rather one of tactics, methods and style." With his nomination, the party had turned its back on both the big-city bosses and the post–New Deal liberals. "The old generation is gone—Mrs. FDR, Truman, Stevenson," commented Larry O'Brien to Cyrus Sulzberger. "Look around you and you will see the new generation that will be running the party." "There was an impressive atmosphere of youth," Sulzberger admitted as he surveyed the Kennedy camp, "with the kids taking over from the old party bosses." To accentuate the change, the candidate chose Senator Henry Jackson of Washington, a hawk on the missile gap and a man without ties to the old party establishment, as chairman of the Democratic National Committee.[49]

Kennedy was quick to sound the theme of change which he symbolized. "After eight years of drugged and fitful sleep," he declared in his acceptance speech, "this nation needs strong, creative Democratic leadership in the White House." Setting forth his New Frontier theme, he said again it was time for "a new generation of leadership—new men to cope with new problems and new opportunities." The world stood at one of the decisive turning points in history, ready to choose either aggressive Communism or the democratic way of life. "All mankind waits upon our decision," Kennedy concluded. "A whole world looks to see what we will do. We cannot fail their trust; we cannot fail to try." Youth, fervor, enthusiasm, dedication—these were the qualities Kennedy offered the nation as he began his formal quest for the presidency. To be successful, he would have to convince the nation that the times demanded such a call to action rather than a continuation of the cautious, restrained, and sober Republican leadership that had kept the peace for the last eight years.[50]

VIII

While the Democratic convention was in progress, violent events abroad strengthened Kennedy's assertion that all was not well in the world. The most serious threat to peace came in the Congo, which had been given its independence by Belgium on July 1. Lacking an educated class to administer the new nation and preserve order, the Congo soon became the scene of anarchy. The black troops in the army rebelled against their white officers and began a reign of terror in Leopoldville, attacking Belgians and other Europeans. The Belgian government sent in a detachment of paratroopers to protect its citizens. President Joseph Kasavubu and Premier Patrice Lumumba appealed to the United Nations to intervene in the Congo to help end the chaos and remove the Belgians. In a hurriedly called Security Council meeting, the United States and the Soviet Union both supported a resolution authorizing Secretary General Dag Hammarskjöld to form a peace-keeping force from among the African nations to replace the Belgians in Leopoldville.

Within a week, UN forces, composed of soldiers from Ghana, Ethiopia, Tunisia, and Morocco, began to end the disorder in the Congo, but Premier Lumumba, charging that the Belgians were still occupying his country, invited the Soviet Union to send in troops if all European forces were not withdrawn within three days. Speaking for the United States, Ambassador Henry Cabot Lodge announced that his country would "do whatever may be necessary to prevent the intrusion of any military forces not requested by the United Nations." A possible Soviet-American showdown in the Congo loomed briefly, but quick action by the UN force led to the rapid evacuation of the Belgians and an easing of tension. By July 21, the UN had restored order in the Congo in what *Time* called "the greatest accomplishment of its short, 15-year history." The crisis was far from over, however, since Moise Tsombe now threatened to detach the mineral-rich province of Katanga from the Congo, and thus deprive the new country of an area crucial to its economic well-being.[51]

At the height of the Congo crisis, Nikita Khrushchev renewed American fears over Communist influence in Cuba. Speaking at a Kremlin press conference attended by three hundred journalists from around the world, the Russian leader declared, "We consider that the Monroe Doctrine has outlived its time, . . . has died, so to say, a natural death." The State Department immediately issued a statement reaffirming the validity of the Monroe Doctrine, and when the Cuban government aired charges of American aggression in a special Security Council meeting on July 18 and 19, Ambassador Lodge denounced the Russians for "shedding crocodile tears about Cuba" while they denied freedom to the peoples of Eastern Europe. "All we say very simply is this," Lodge told the Soviet delegate: "Don't touch us; don't touch those with whom we are tied; don't seek to extend Communist imperialism. That's very simple and ought to be easily understood by everybody." [52]

An even more serious Soviet-American confrontation developed on July 11, when the Soviet Union announced that it had shot down an American RB-47 reconnaissance plane over Russian territorial waters in the Barents Sea. The plane had been missing since July 1, but, mindful of the U-2 affair, the American government had kept silent until the Russians finally broke the story. On July 12, President Eisenhower replied for the United States. The Soviets, he charged, had committed a "wanton" act in shooting down the reconnaissance plane "in international waters." He demanded the immediate release of the two surviving fliers and threatened to call the attention of the Security Council to "the lawless actions and reckless threats of the Soviet Government." The

American government admitted that the plane, filled with sensitive electronic equipment, was on an espionage mission, but insisted that it had never violated Soviet air space.

Once again, Lodge waged a vigorous defense of the American position in the ensuing UN debate. In a series of biting speeches, he accused the Russians of engaging in "an act of piracy over the high seas." With the wives of the dead and captured airmen sitting in the gallery, the ambassador dismissed the Soviet claim of overflight as "a pretty revolting bit of hypocrisy," and then proceeded to excoriate the Soviets for the "cold-hearted," "cynical," and "brutal" way they waged the Cold War. On July 26, the Security Council refused by a vote of 9 to 2 to condemn the United States.[53]

The heated exchanges between Lodge and the Soviet spokesmen during the Congo, Cuba, and RB-47 crises accentuated the deep shadow that had fallen across the world since the U-2 affair. The Cold War had never been colder, and though Lodge won nearly universal praise for his tough talk, Americans began to feel that the Russians had thrown them on the defensive around the globe. Everywhere they looked, the Soviets were pushing ahead to turn unstable situations to their advantage. The political repercussions of the heightened tension seemed clear. The Republicans could no longer stand on their record, claiming that they had kept the peace and contained the Soviet Union. Instead, as *Time* pointed out, the next administration would be called on to "build defense and foreign policies designed not to settle the Cold War but to win it." [54]

IX

One Republican moved to take the national security issue away from the Democrats. Nelson Rockefeller, who had declared his availability for a draft after the U-2 affair, emerged as the most vocal critic of the Eisenhower administration's defense policies. On June 10, after a White House conference with the President, Rockefeller released a 2,700-word statement to the press, criticizing Nixon for his failure to speak out on major national issues. The governor's manifesto, written by Emmet John Hughes and Henry Kissinger, hit hardest on the Vice-President's refusal to call for stepped-up defense spending. Proposing a $3 billion increase in the Pentagon budget, Rockefeller declared, "I believe that our national defense needs great strengthening to meet the physical danger in which America lives." Rockefeller kept up his pressure in the weeks preceding the GOP convention, adding a demand for the immediate resumption of underground nuclear tests and telling a National Governors' Conference, "The relative military power of the United States compared with the Soviet Union has steadily and drastically declined over the past fifteen years." [55]

With commitments from more than enough delegates to insure his nomination, Nixon refused to be drawn into a debate with Governor Rockefeller over national defense. He met the call for a $3 billion increase in defense spending with a polite "No comment," though he did tell reporters that he would respect Rockefeller's "oft-expressed desire that he not be drafted as a candidate for Vice President." In his frequent appearances before Republican audiences around the country, Nixon liked to remind his listeners of his experience in world affairs by beginning, "I once had a little discussion with Mr. Khrushchev. . . ." The Vice-President avoided interviews with the press, but his aides told reporters that he planned to make foreign policy a central issue in the fall campaign. "I've been through it," Nixon was quoted as saying, "especially in my South American travels and my kitchen debate with Khrushchev." Standing up to the Russians, not building up American military forces, with the implication that Eisenhower had allowed them to become weakened, became the basis of Nixon's foreign policy strategy. The roars of approval that greeted him every time he spoke of his success at face-to-face confrontations led *Newsweek* to conclude, "In a Presidential campaign, a hostile Nikita Khrushchev could be a candidate's best friend." [56]

The one place where Nixon could not duck the defense issue was in the party platform. GOP Chairman Thruston B. Morton had appointed Charles Percy, a young Illinois business executive with political ambitions, to head the platform committee. Eager to bring new ideas into the political arena, Percy had held a series of meetings with leading intellectuals from Harvard and M.I.T. and planned similar sessions with Stanford and Berkeley faculty members. Percy also solicited suggestions from the outgoing Eisenhower administration and, in an effort to achieve party unity, asked Governor Rockefeller for any ideas he wished to submit.

On July 9, when Percy and his vice-chairman, Representative Melvin Laird of Wisconsin, were preparing a first draft of the platform, Rockefeller handed in his suggestions—a 6,000-word statement that covered every major issue facing the party in 1960. The emphasis was on the grave world situation. Rockefeller called for a series of regional political federations, beginning with a North Atlantic group linking the United States to Western Europe, and he bore down hard on the need for both a "second-strike nuclear retaliatory power" and "a capacity for limited warfare that can deter or check local aggression." He set no price tag on his proposals, but experts quickly estimated that the new weapons and strategy he advocated would cost far more than the extra $3 billion he had mentioned in June.[57]

A week before the GOP convention was due to open, Rockefeller went to Chicago to make a personal appeal to the platform committee. He told Percy's group that the world balance of power was shifting toward the Soviet Union as he argued for his proposals. At the same time, advance groups of Rockefeller delegates arrived in Chicago and began parading around the convention hotels with placards reading, "Nixon Can't Win." The governor maintained a discreet silence about his own candidacy, but he told the press that he was "deeply concerned" about the mild foreign policy and defense planks that Percy's committee had approved. At the very least, the Rockefeller forces hinted at a floor fight over the platform, if not a full-fledged attempt to deny Nixon the nomination.[58]

In Washington, the Vice-President became increasingly concerned over Rockefeller's maneuvers. Kennedy's choice of Lyndon Johnson as his running mate made Nixon realize that he might have great difficulty in duplicating Eisenhower's success in the South. To offset the loss of southern support, he would have to carry one of the major northeastern states, ideally New York, with its forty-five electoral votes. Since Rockefeller's backing was crucial for this new strategy, Nixon decided to approach the governor directly and try to win him over. He asked Herbert Brownell to arrange a meeting on neutral ground in New York City, but when Rockefeller insisted that they confer at his Fifth Avenue apartment, Nixon gave in. On Friday, July 22, only three days before the convention was due to open, Nixon flew to New York and had dinner with Governor Rockefeller. Then for the next six hours the two men hammered out a joint statement of views on the platform, amid hurried telephone conversations with Percy and his aides in Chicago.

In the morning, Rockefeller released the text of the agreement to reporters, who quickly dubbed it the "Treaty of Fifth Avenue." The Rockefeller-Nixon statement dealt with both domestic and international issues, calling for greater emphasis on civil rights and economic growth at home and a major effort to strengthen America's defenses against the menace of Communism abroad. The statement echoed Rockefeller's earlier appeals for a resumption of underground nuclear testing, regional political confederations, and, above all, increased military spending. Though Nixon carefully kept out any mention of specific figures, the agreement advocated both a second-strike nuclear capacity and "a modern, flexible and balanced military establishment." "The United States can afford and must provide the increased expenditures to implement fully this necessary program," the statement declared, and then, in an implied criticism of Eisenhower's policies, added, "There must be no price ceiling on America's security." [59]

The President, still vacationing at Newport, became furious when he read the text of the Rockefeller-Nixon statement. He felt that the section on national security reflected very unfavorably on his policies, and remarked with astonishment that neither man had ever "voiced any doubt" about "the adequacy of America's defense" while serving in his administration. He quickly informed Charles Percy of his disagreement with Rockefeller and Nixon on national security, and instructed his convention representative, White House aide Robert E. Merriam, to block any defense plank which suggested a state of national weakness. In Chicago, conservative Republicans were equally indignant. Arizona Senator Barry Goldwater, emerging as the spokesman of the GOP right wing, claimed that the agreement would "live in history as the Munich of the Republican party," while the Chicago *Tribune* headlined its story, "GRANT SURRENDERS TO LEE." Though Nixon tried to play down the idea of giving in to Rockefeller, even the *New York Times* concluded, "On balance, the Nixon-Rockefeller pact seemed weighted on the side of Mr. Rockefeller's views, including his implied criticism of Eisenhower's defense and foreign policies." [60]

Nixon moved quickly to restore party unity. He flew to Chicago on the opening day of the convention and met with Percy and Laird to work out a new platform midway between the first draft and the Nixon-Rockefeller statement. Then the Vice-President quelled the incipient rebellion among the old guard by meeting with small groups of delegates for two days, denying any surrender to Rockefeller and persuading them to accept the new platform. The defense plank proved to be the trickiest proposition, given Eisenhower's stern interest. The platform committee finally squeezed out a compromise that promised a more vigorous effort in the future without condemning the policies of the Eisenhower administration in the past. At the President's insistence, the platform writers omitted Rockefeller's demand for a resumption of underground nuclear tests and watered down the Nixon-Rockefeller wording by saying there "is," rather than there "must be," no price ceiling on security. Other parts of the platform called for regional federations as Rockefeller requested, without ever stating their precise nature; praised Eisenhower for his successful quest for peace; and reaffirmed American support for NATO, foreign aid, and the United Nations. There was no mention of Cuba, or Berlin, or the Congo. Instead, the Republicans stood on Eisenhower's record. "Since 1954 no free nation has fallen victim behind the Iron Curtain," the platform boasted. "We mean to adhere to the policy of firmness that has served us so well." [61]

All in all, Nixon had won a notable political victory. Rather than being used by Rockefeller, he had exploited the governor's criticism of administration policy to take an independent stand on the defense issue, one which freed him from blind support of Ike's policies yet did not force him to break with the President. Nixon could now stand on the platform and call for greater military spending without alienating Eisenhower, whose support was still crucial for his candidacy. At the same time, by embracing Rockefeller's views on domestic as well as foreign policy issues, he had a good chance to carry New York in the fall. "With brilliant timing and tactics," gushed *Time*, "Richard Nixon has used the meeting with Rockefeller to position himself on the side of new departures for the 1960's." A more skeptical Robert Bendiner expressed his admiration for Nixon's ability "to leave the Eisenhower cocoon while doing classical Chinese reverence to his aged political parent," and thus to enhance his appeal "in the vote-rich states where elections are decided." [62]

X

After the platform fight, the rest of the convention was anticlimactic. Congressman Walter Judd of Minnesota belabored the Democrats as appeasers in a highly partisan keynote speech ("It wasn't under the Republicans that 600 million people disappeared behind the Iron Curtain"). Former nominee Thomas Dewey delighted the delegates by attacking Kennedy for his suggestion that Eisenhower should have apologized to Khrushchev over the U-2 ("In my opinion, the President of the United States owes no apology to anybody for protecting his country and the free world from another Pearl Harbor"). President Eisenhower spoke for an hour defending his defense policies without ever mentioning Richard Nixon ("In the sum of our capabilities we have become the strongest military power on earth"). Nelson Rockefeller ended any lingering suspense over the nomination by endorsing Richard Nixon on July 26, and when the balloting began the next day, the Vice-President received 1,321 votes to 10 for Senator Goldwater, who then asked that his name be withdrawn and the nomination be made unanimous. [63]

Later that evening, Nixon met with thirty-six Republican leaders—governors, senators, state leaders—to discuss his choice of a running mate. Actually, Nixon had already made his decision. In the spring he had approached Henry Cabot Lodge, who said he would accept the vice-presidential nomination if the convention offered it to him, and the two men had left it at that. Eisenhower had strongly endorsed Lodge in a private talk with Nixon before the convention; and the very favorable publicity Lodge received in the UN debates on Cuba, the RB-47, and the Congo crises, appearing frequently on national television as the networks covered major portions of the Security Council debates, undoubtedly reinforced Nixon's original inclination. But knowing how important it was to permit party leaders to play a role in the selection process, Nixon kept silent as the discussion ranged over a broad list of candidates, finally narrowing down to Lodge and Thruston Morton, the popular GOP chairman and senator from Kentucky. Middle Westerners favored Morton, but Thomas Dewey helped swing the balance to Lodge by arguing, "He would make a superb Vice-President, and he would put the emphasis on foreign policy, where it should be." Though many party regulars viewed Lodge as too cool, aloof, and aristocratic, as well as the man who had engineered the defeat of Robert Taft in 1952, they reluctantly went along when Ohio Senator John Bricker endorsed his selection.[64]

Liberal critics were quick to point out that Lodge had built up his popular reputation by talking tough to the Russians at the UN, often at times when more reasoned and less emotional responses would have better served the cause of world peace. "But then, of course," admitted Marya Mannes, "the quick draw is in the Western tradition and we are back in the glass saloon again, where Cabot Lodge slugged it out for seven and a half years." After the U-2 affair renewed the sense of world crisis, Lodge had emerged as the foremost American Cold War spokesman. He came through on television at the UN as "handsome, articulate, forceful, urbane," commented *Newsweek,* and, as TRB noted, Nixon chose him "to build up what he considers his trump suit—toughness to Moscow." Lodge realized his value to the ticket, and in his acceptance speech he dealt exclusively with world affairs. Praising Nixon's experience in foreign policy, Lodge stressed the critical nature of the Cold War. "The basic contest is the life and death struggle between the Communists on the one hand and those who insist on being free on the other," he declared. "This is what gives this election of 1960 its compelling, overwhelming importance to us and to the world." [65]

Nixon stressed the same somber theme in accepting the nomination. He discussed domestic affairs briefly and promised to visit all fifty states in the campaign, but he spent most of his time on the world crisis. He denied charges of American weakness, suggesting that those who downgraded U.S. prestige were playing into the hands of the Communists and affirming that "America is the strongest nation militarily, economically and ideologically in the world." The United States was ahead "in the race for survival," but the nation could not afford to relax its guard, nor "tolerate being pushed around by anybody, any place." Instead, he wanted America to take the initiative away from the Communists—to pursue a "strategy of victory for the free world," so that when Khrushchev boasts of our grandchildren living under Communism, "let us say his grandchildren will live in freedom." Above all, he called upon the American people to sacrifice and work to make the American dream come true, concluding, "I can only say tonight to you that I believe in the American dream because I have seen it come true in my own life." [66]

"When all is said and done," commented the *Nation*, "Richard M. Nixon came out looking a good deal better than when he went in." The months of quiet maneuvering and hedging on the issues had ended. Nixon had now demonstrated his deftness as a political leader and had seized on the Cold War as his primary issue in the forthcoming campaign. Even the usually hostile *New Republic* admitted that his acceptance speech was "one of the most impressively effective political 50 minutes we ever witnessed." *Time* was certain that Nixon and Lodge had hit the right theme for a triumphant election. "The Eisenhower years have matured them and fitted them uniquely to face the big issue of U.S. policy in the tense world—the issue on which they will wage the Republican campaign of 1960." [67]

Nearly all observers agreed that foreign policy would be the central issue in the election. A *Newsweek* survey of voter sentiment found that the international situation "towers above all others as the No. 1 issue of the coming Presidential campaign." George Gallup arrived at the same conclusion, commenting that the outcome "may well be decided not so much by the campaigns as it will by changes in the world situation." Khrushchev thus became a major factor in the American electoral process. *Time* believed that further blows to American prestige, such as the U-2 incident and the cancellation of Ike's trip to Japan, would hurt the Republicans, but any sudden crisis would work to their advantage. "Nixon stands to gain from any sharp increase in tension," the editors wrote, "that prompts a demand for experience in office." [68]

Kennedy's supporters realized that inexperience was their candidate's greatest handicap in regard to foreign policy. They countered that the senator's keen intelligence and obvious concern about international affairs more than made up for his lack of direct contact with foreign crises. "He is one of the most experienced politicians of the day," argued the *New Republic*. "And as for the world, he is closer in touch with realities overseas than either Mr. Truman or General Eisenhower dreamed of being when they stepped into the White House." Yet as Ernest Lindley noted, Kennedy lacked the authority of Adlai Stevenson when he spoke out on foreign problems; he would still have to demonstrate to the American people his potential for world leadership.

Perhaps even more significant was Kennedy's lack of any alternative to Republican policies. Nixon had preempted the most popular stand by stressing a hard line against Khrushchev and embracing Rockefeller's call for increased military spending. Neither the Democratic platform nor Kennedy's speeches revealed a willingness to challenge the Cold War policies of the Eisenhower administration. Indeed, Kennedy's principal argument was that he could wage the Cold War more effectively than the Republicans. Commenting on Democratic rhetoric at the convention, the editors of the *Nation* wrote,

"There was no suggestion that Eisenhower's foreign policy has been wrong, only that it hasn't been 'strong'—*i.e.,* it hasn't been backed by enough military muscle." It will be "sloganeer against sloganeer," they concluded, as each candidate tried to outdo the other in taking a hard line on foreign policy "and, above all, stepped-up arms spending." [69]

Thus once again there seemed little prospect of a meaningful public debate on the goals of American diplomacy. Each side would try to manipulate foreign policy issues for its own partisan advantage, instead of seeking to educate the American people on the realities of international affairs. By background, training, and conviction, John Kennedy was as ardent a Cold Warrior as Richard Nixon. He sought to discredit the Republicans for weakness and laxity, and offered himself to the electorate as a man who could restore the nation's declining prestige and move America once again toward victory in the continuing struggle against the Soviet Union. Since Richard Nixon promised to achieve essentially the same objective, the election would ultimately turn on the question of credibility—which man the voters believed could better provide the leadership necessary to win the Cold War.

6

"The main point about these two men is not that they are so different but that they are so similar," James Reston wrote about Nixon and Kennedy in mid-July. Both represented the new generation that came of age after the great depression and World War II. "Neither of these men is burning with ideological zeal," Reston wrote in a later column. "They are the organization men of politics." Eric Sevareid made the same point, calling them "tidy buttoned-down men," junior executives on the make who lacked passion and conviction. Kennedy resented being equated with Nixon, a man he thought had "no taste," but he recognized its political significance. In the coming campaign, he would have to demonstrate to the American people that he was different from his opponent, that he possessed distinctive qualities of leadership the nation desperately needed.[1]

The Democratic candidate spent the month of August preparing for the ordeal that lay ahead. His first task was to organize his campaign staff. Without hesitation, he kept his brother, Robert Kennedy, in the position of campaign manager and sent Larry O'Brien to the Democratic National Committee to coordinate the party's national efforts. Archibald Cox, a Harvard Law School professor, headed up a research team in Washington that took the many ideas coming in from intellectuals and reworked the most promising ones, sending them on to Theodore Sorensen and Richard Goodwin, who drafted Kennedy's formal speeches. Two veteran journalists, John Bartlow Martin and Joseph Kraft, served as advance men, scouting out the local problems in areas where Kennedy planned to appear and suggesting how he could address himself to them effectively. All in all, it was a smooth, well-oiled team, already proven in the primaries, that ensured an efficient fall campaign.[2]

Kennedy devoted much of his time to the delicate job of uniting all Democrats behind his candidacy. While Lyndon Johnson concentrated on dissident southerners, JFK sought out the liberals who had opposed his nomination. After an exchange of telephone calls with Harry Truman, Kennedy flew out to Independence to announce that the former President would participate actively in the campaign. He made an equally significant pilgrimage to Hyde Park in mid-August to confer with Eleanor Roosevelt, who now graciously gave him her endorsement and promised to speak in his behalf. Adlai Stevenson, still the most influential liberal spokesman, flew to Hyannis Port to see Kennedy in late July and announce his "vigorous support" for the Democratic ticket. Kennedy appointed Stevenson, along with Chester Bowles, as a principal foreign policy adviser, and the two men declared their determination to rally the free world against the Soviet challenge "without war or surrender."[3]

When President Eisenhower offered to brief the Democratic candidate on international issues, Kennedy appointed Stevenson and Bowles to serve as his liaison men with the administration on foreign policy. The President refused to disclose classified information to these intermediaries, however, and finally CIA Director Allen Dulles flew to Cape Cod to give Kennedy a personal rundown on the world situation. Dulles spent over two hours describing all aspects of American policy, though he failed to include the secret preparations taking place in Guatemala for an exile invasion of Cuba. Kennedy, he reported to Eisenhower, was "particularly interested in developments that might arise during the campaign, particularly with regard to Berlin, Cuba, and the Congo," and he wanted a special report from Pentagon officials on the state of America's defenses. Eisenhower at first refused this last request, but finally he agreed to permit Lieutenant General Earle G. Wheeler, director of the Joint Chiefs of Staff, to provide Kennedy with the same information he had furnished to the Senate Armed Services Committee.[4]

Kennedy's concern with military preparedness reflected his decision to make America's position in the world a central campaign issue. A memorandum Arthur Schlesinger had prepared in 1959 helped persuade Kennedy that Eisenhower's passive policies had damaged the nation's standing in the eyes of other peoples. "When we are a nation on the move, our foreign policy is effective," Schlesinger had written; "when we are mired in complacency and indifference, our foreign policy impresses no one." Schlesinger's conclusion, that "we get moving again in our national society," was attractive to Kennedy, since it fitted in with his own belief in the need for active, dynamic national leadership. At the same time, an elaborate computer-assisted study of public attitudes indicated that foreign policy was "the area of greatest weakness" for Kennedy. The "people machine," a mathematical model of the American electorate based on poll data, indicated that most Americans distrusted Kennedy because of his inexperience with world affairs. The social scientists compiling this report suggested that Kennedy might alter the pattern by "talking and acting about foreign affairs in a way which conveys a sense of knowledge and power," and above all by blaming the Republicans for America's declining world prestige.[5]

Kennedy indicated the trend his campaign would take in a

late August speech in Alexandria to 15,000 loyal supporters. In biting tones, he ridiculed the Republican claim to experience in foreign policy. "Never before have we experienced such arrogant treatment at the hands of our enemies," he declared. "Never before have we experienced such a critical decline in our prestige. . . ." "Mr. Nixon is experienced," he scoffed, "experienced in policies of retreat, defeat and weakness." Citing such setbacks as the U-2 incident, the chaos in the Congo, and increasing Soviet influence in Cuba, Kennedy denied that the real issue was who could best stand up to Khrushchev, as Nixon had so often asserted. "The real issue," Kennedy declared, "is who can stand up and summon all the resources of this land to the defense of freedom, to restore our nation's strength and leadership." [6]

Astonishingly, Kennedy had revealed that he planned to attack the Republicans on their strongest point. For eight years, the Eisenhower administration had kept the nation at peace, ending the war in Korea and preventing the outbreak of any new conflicts. Eisenhower stood as the very symbol of a successful world policy, yet the Democratic candidate boldly asserted that under the General's leadership the nation had passed from a position of strength and respect to one of weakness and shame. Gambling that the nation's sense of confidence had been undermined by the U-2 affair and the rise of Castro, Kennedy sought to burden Nixon with Eisenhower's mistakes and thus neutralize the peace issue, which had served the GOP so well in the last two elections.

In contrast to Kennedy's well-organized campaign team, Richard Nixon waged a lonely quest for the presidency. By instinct a secretive individual, the Vice-President in effect served as his own campaign manager, refusing to delegate the making of basic decisions. Leonard Hall bore the title "campaign chairman" and Robert Finch was "campaign director," but neither man had overall responsibility for the election effort. Hall worked with GOP Chairman Thruston Morton, coordinating the Nixon drive with the national party movement, while Finch headed up the Vice-President's personal staff. Several prominent members of the Eisenhower administration served as advisers to Nixon, notably Secretary of Commerce Fred Seaton and Attorney General William Rogers. James Shepley, the former *Life* editor who had written the Dulles "brinkmanship" article in 1956, headed up the team of speechwriters. But Nixon alone would determine the nature of the campaign.[7]

He announced his first decision in his acceptance speech to the Republican convention—he would campaign in all fifty states, including the newly admitted ones of Hawaii and Alaska as well as several small states usually skipped over by presidential candidates. Kennedy, in contrast, decided to focus his campaign in the urban states of the Northeast, Pacific Coast, and Middle West. Though Nixon also spent most of his time in these big states, his acceptance-speech promise forced him to dilute his efforts and engage in a killing travel schedule.

Nixon gave the nation a preview of his campaign tactics in a trip to Hawaii in early August, with stops along the way at Nevada and Washington to help fulfill his fifty-state commitment. Reporters commented on his restrained rhetoric and determined effort to strike a statesmanlike pose. Nixon found that his audiences reacted most enthusiastically when he talked about what he and Eisenhower were doing to keep the peace. "Let us never forget that we are the strongest nation on earth—militarily and economically," he asserted, and promised to achieve "a just peace for the whole world without surrender of freedom or territory." The old Nixon, the partisan campaigner who spent his time denouncing the Democrats, was gone, and in his place was a humble, earnest man trying his best to imitate Eisenhower.[8]

Nixon's strategy depended heavily on the President's support. The Vice-President planned to campaign as the General's logical heir, defending Ike against all Kennedy's attacks and promising to continue the record of Republican peace and prosperity. Yet Nixon, who for eight years had chafed under Eisenhower's shadow, felt it was essential to step out on his own. Consequently, in early August he asked the President to play a passive role during the campaign, confining himself to a handful of speeches to nonpartisan audiences. Nixon would run on the President's record but the General would be carefully kept in the background so that he would not outshine his protégé.

At first, Eisenhower seemed content to play the quiet role Nixon had assigned him. In a press conference on August 10, he told reporters that he preferred to let Nixon and Lodge carry the weight of the campaign, saying, "I think these two fellows can take care of themselves pretty well and I think they are tops." He brushed aside a question about consulting Nixon on vital national issues more often than in the past. Ike would make the decisions himself until January 20, 1961, but he added that Nixon had always been involved "in every important meeting of which I can remember." Two weeks later, however, Ike responded to a question about the "big decisions" Nixon had participated in by saying, "No one can make a decision except me if it is in the national executive area." Puzzled by this answer, journalist Charles Mohr of *Time* wanted to know what part Nixon had played in the Eisenhower administration. He had participated in "all of the consultative meetings that have been held," Ike replied, but he himself, as President, had made the final decisions. "I just wondered if you would give us an example of a major idea of his that you had adopted in that role," Mohr persisted. "If you give me a week, I might think of one," the President snapped, ending the conference on a highly negative note.[9]

"With characteristic candor, the President has gutted the claim that Vice President Nixon has shared the responsibility for decision-making in the Eisenhower Administration," commented Ernest Lindley. In a televison interview with Jack Paar, Nixon said Eisenhower was correct in his description of how presidential decisions were made, but inwardly he must have resented Ike's cutting remark deeply. His whole campaign was based on carrying on Eisenhower's policies; the suggestion that he had played a minor role in shaping them made his claims sound foolish. Yet Nixon had brought this embarrassment on himself by his deliberate refusal to let the General play an active part in his campaign. Nixon wanted to exploit Eisenhower's popularity to achieve his own election, but without being overshadowed by it. It was at best a delicate relationship, and one that Ike's ambivalence toward Nixon could easily undermine.[10]

I

While the two candidates planned their fall campaigns, the world crisis continued to simmer. In the Congo, the UN police force gradually restored order, but Tsombe encouraged the Belgians to stay on in Katanga as he insisted that his province should remain independent. Prime Minister Patrice Lumumba, backed by the Soviet Union, called upon the UN to force the Belgians to leave and end the attempted secession of Katanga. Secretary General Hammarskjöld finally convened another special meeting of the Security Council in early August and, despite Soviet objections, won support for a resolution ordering the Belgians to leave and authorizing him to have UN forces enter Katanga without prejudicing Tsombe's right of secession. On August 12, Hammarskjöld personally led a UN detachment into Elizabethville, Katanga's capital, and for the time being the Congo again quieted down. The potential for danger remained, however, as the Soviets made it clear they intended to support Lumumba's efforts to unite the Congo around his increasingly radical leadership.[11]

American relations with Castro's Cuba deteriorated further

during August. Raoul Castro returned from a trip to Moscow on August 4 to tell a screaming Havana audience that the Russians would use "rockets" to defend his brother's regime against any American attack; two days later, Fidel announced the seizure of $700 million worth of American property, virtually all that was left on the island. Citing Eisenhower's suspension of the sugar quota in justifying this extreme step, Castro included thirty-six American-owned sugar mills in his order and offered to compensate the owners with Cuban bonds redeemable in fifty years. The United States responded by asking the Organization of American States to condemn Cuba for permitting Soviet penetration of the Western Hemisphere at a forthcoming foreign ministers' conference in San José, Costa Rica. At this meeting, Secretary of State Herter charged that "the Cuban government is walking hand in hand with the Sino-Soviet bloc" and accused Castro of "spreading communism in the rest of the hemisphere." The Latin-American delegates refused to go as far as the United States wanted. Instead, they adopted a vague resolution opposing "intervention or the threat of intervention . . . by an extracontinental power in the affairs of the American republics." Though Herter called this Declaration of San José "a clear indictment of the Castro government of Cuba," the United States had failed to get a specific OAS condemnation of Cuba and was forced to settle for what one observer called "a bland resolution open to many possible interpretations." Castro showed his contempt by publicly tearing to pieces the 1952 Cuban-American mutual defense treaty and announcing his plans to establish formal diplomatic relations with Communist China.[12]

The most disturbing news of all came from Moscow, where in early August Nikita Khrushchev proposed that he, Eisenhower, and the other major world leaders all attend the General Assembly meeting in New York in September and thus hold a summit conference. Henry Cabot Lodge termed this suggestion "specious and frivolous," and the State Department quickly rejected it. On September 1, however, Khrushchev shocked the American people by announcing that despite U.S. objections, he planned to come to New York later that month to represent the Soviet Union personally at the General Assembly. The Eisenhower administration countered by announcing that Herter, not the President, would head the American delegation and that Khrushchev, for his own safety, would be restricted to Manhattan Island.

The Russian leader's visit meant that he would be in the United States during the fall campaign, underlining the grave world problems that would face the next President. Observers were unsure of the political implications, but most agreed with James Reston's comment that "every crisis overseas is generally believed here to help Mr. Nixon." William Carleton came to the same conclusion after a trip around the nation sampling voter sentiment on foreign policy issues. The American people, he reported, were in a "get tough" mood and they admired Nixon for his proven ability to "talk back" to the Communists. The heightened sense of world tension engendered by events in the Congo and Cuba and by Khrushchev's surprise visit thus seemed to be working in favor of the Republicans.[13]

II

Throughout August, John Kennedy remained in Washington, trapped by the continuing session of Congress that Johnson had arranged back in June. Despite Democratic majorities in both houses, the candidate was unable to secure adoption of any of his domestic measures, failing most notably with bills to raise the minimum wage and to establish medical care for the aged. Except for a quick trip to Detroit to address the Veterans of Foreign Wars, he had to stay in Washington until Congress finally adjourned on September 1. Then he left for a two-week swing around the nation by air, visiting twenty-seven states from New England to California; it was climaxed by a dramatic speech to a group of Protestant ministers in Houston, where he declared that his religion would not influence his actions as President.[14]

On the stump, Kennedy proved to be an energetic but erratic performer. His speaking style lacked polish—his high, strident voice, strong New England accent, awkward gestures and too-rapid delivery often weakened the impact of his words. Reporters complained of "the monotonous poke, poke gesture of his right forefinger as though punching holes in a stream of invisible doughnuts," and the poor timing that so often led him to kill the applause his words began to bring. Yet they also noted the tremendous emotional response he evoked; his very presence seemed to create a sense of excitement and passion. Women particularly reacted to his winning smile. Everywhere he went, girls jumped up to get a glimpse of him or reached out to touch him as he walked by. And despite his choppy delivery, Kennedy's sense of mission and intense conviction often brought a restless crowd to life and infused it with a great emotional fervor. He was at his best when he discarded the formal speech that Sorensen or Goodwin had prepared and launched into extemporaneous remarks with growing enthusiasm. More and more, as the campaign went on, he spoke without a text, ad-libbing variations on a set speech built around his theme of "getting the nation moving again." After following him for two weeks, a *Time* reporter became convinced that "he can be as tough, skillful, and attractive as any other candidate currently on the stump—and worthy of Dick Nixon's wariest respect." [15]

In his early campaign speeches, Kennedy avoided specific foreign policy issues. Instead, he tried to deal broadly with world problems as part of his general charge that the Eisenhower administration had allowed the nation to stagnate in the 1950's. Thus he told the Veterans of Foreign Wars "that our security and leadership are both slipping away from us— that the balance of world power is slowly shifting to the Soviet-

Red Chinese bloc." He mentioned the Soviet penetration of Cuba, but he did not dwell on it. Rather he harped on the fact that the Russians were "moving faster than we are." His solution, he told the veterans, was to overhaul American defense policy to make us "first" once again. "I do not mean 'first, but,' " he declared in a line he repeated constantly. "I do not mean 'first, and.' I do not mean 'first, if.' I mean 'first—period.' "

As he crisscrossed the nation, Kennedy elaborated on the theme of national weakness. He accused Eisenhower of taking "a vacation" in the White House while American prestige slumped in the world. "I don't want historians writing in 1970," he told a Labor Day crowd in Detroit, "to say that the balance of power in the Nineteen Fifties and the Nineteen Sixties began to turn against the United States and the cause of freedom." He wanted people to "feel that in the year of 1961 the American giant began to stir again, the great American boiler began to fire up again, this country began to move ahead again." Again and again he charged that the Republicans had no foreign policy beyond "swapping threats and insults with the Russians," and belittled Nixon's claim that he had stood up to Khrushchev in the famous kitchen debate in Moscow. "We cannot convince Mr. Khrushchev by smiling at him or by exchanging insults," Kennedy declared. "The only thing that will deter Mr. Khrushchev from loosing his hounds of hell on us will be a strong America." [16]

Kennedy sought to create a sense of crisis that would persuade the American voter that it was time for a change. Instead of dealing with such concrete issues as the Congo, Berlin, or the U-2 affair, the Democratic challenger developed the broad theme of declining prestige and military weakness. Thus he did not harp on the missile gap or Castro's dealings with the Soviets, nor did he challenge the basic Republican premise that the United States was engaged in a deadly struggle with the Soviet Union. "In effect," commented the Nation,

"Kennedy said that the devil theory of communism is a sound one and the policies based on it are the only ones conceivable, but their implementation has been too little and too late." Sensing an underlying public concern with America's position in the world, Kennedy responded by offering himself as the complete Cold Warrior, the man better able than Nixon to rebuild American strength and defeat the Russians in the contest for world control.[17]

III

As Vice-President, Nixon found it much easier to break away from Washington during the August session of Congress. He made forays into New England and the South and delivered a major address to the Veterans of Foreign Wars in Detroit. Nixon seemed much more mature and confident than in past campaigns, and he did everything he could to enhance his new nonpartisan image. Like Kennedy, he developed a standard speech which he gave every place he went with only slight variations. He spoke slowly and clearly, displaying a much more polished style than Kennedy's, yet one lacking in emotional fervor. Nixon studded his speech with lines certain to trigger applause at strategic points, and with skillful timing he was able to win a favorable response from his audiences. He soon found that people burst into cheers when he chided Kennedy about the suggestion that Eisenhower should have apologized for the U-2 flight by saying, "May no President of the United States ever feel it necessary to apologize for attempting to protect this country." He tried to counter the Democratic challenger's security argument by stating flatly, as he did to the veterans, that "the United States is first in the world militarily, economically, scientifically, and educationally." [18]

Bad luck dogged Nixon at the outset. On August 17, he banged his knee while getting out of a car in Greensboro,

North Carolina. It began to swell, but Nixon went ahead with his campaign, enjoying a triumphal reception in Atlanta, until doctors finally warned him that he had a serious infection requiring immediate hospitalization. He entered Walter Reed Hospital on August 29 and stayed there for the next twelve days while Kennedy dominated the headlines with his early campaign. When Nixon was finally discharged, his knee had healed, but he was ten pounds lighter and looked pale and drawn.[19]

Henry Cabot Lodge took over the brunt of the Republican campaign while Nixon convalesced. Traveling with Nelson Rockefeller through the vacation resorts of the Catskills, Lodge was billed as "the man who held the line for peace in the world" at the UN for the past seven years. He munched on lox and kosher egg rolls at Middletown and then moved down to Coney Island, where he displayed a new folksiness, eating hot dogs and shaking hands with the holiday bathers. In his speeches, Lodge stuck almost exclusively to foreign policy, telling a Pennsylvania audience, "We will win the Cold War by ending it—and thus reduce the danger of a hot war." He ducked reporters' questions on just how he would win the Cold War, but in other appearances he stressed the years of experience he and Nixon had had "in the front line of the battle against communism." He spoke continually about the dangers posed by the Soviets, and he won standing ovations with his punch line, "Now, my friends, no one is going to take over the U.S. and no one is going to take over the world." As *Time* observed, "Lodge campaigns, not against Kennedy or Johnson, but against Khrushchev." [20]

Nixon reentered the campaign on September 12. Eisenhower and Lodge went to Friendship Airport outside Baltimore to help see him off on a whirlwind tour of twenty-one states in the next seven days. Responding to Ike's praise of his ability to handle foreign affairs, Nixon promised to continue the record of peace that the President had established. At each stop across the country, the Vice-President emphasized his own qualifications in the Cold War and belittled Kennedy as a naïve and immature amateur who felt it was necessary "to apologize for trying to defend the United States." Again and again he asserted that the United States was ahead of the Soviet Union in military strength. "I know Mr. Khrushchev," Nixon would begin, alluding to the kitchen debate. The great issue was peace, he declared, asking a Dallas audience which candidate they thought "offers to America and the free world the type of leadership that gives the best chance to keep the peace in the world without surrender." Associating himself with Eisenhower, he boasted, "We have ended one war, we have kept out of other wars and we have kept the peace without surrender for eight years." "Five and six times a day, six days a week with metronomic regularity," commented Russell Baker, Nixon contrasted Senator Kennedy with himself, the mature leader who alone could guide the nation safely on the course Eisenhower had set in the 1950's.[21]

The issue was thus clearly joined. Each candidate claimed he alone could supply the world leadership that the times demanded. Kennedy promised to arrest declining American prestige and put the nation back on the right track; Nixon pointed to eight years of peace as the great Republican accomplishment, insisting that he and Lodge had the experience and maturity to continue Ike's wise policies. The way the American people would respond to these rival contentions depended largely on the course of world events for the remainder of the campaign. In that sense, Nikita Khrushchev could play as vital a role in the election as either Nixon or Kennedy.

IV

In early September, Khrushchev, on his way to New York aboard the *Baltika* for the General Assembly meeting, had become an acknowledged factor in the presidential election. Before he left Moscow, the Russian leader had denied having any preference, dismissing the candidates as "a pair of boots." "Which is better, the right or left boot?" Khrushchev asked. "It would be difficult to distinguish between them." Kennedy and Nixon tried to avoid any comment on the forthcoming visit, and both men, as William Lawrence pointed out, "were anxious to avoid a 'kiss of death' from the Communist leader." Khrushchev's presence in the United States during the campaign was likely to intensify the foreign policy debate, since each candidate would strive to prove he could outdo the other in standing up to the Russian. "The rival presidential candidates will be under great pressure," commented the *New Republic,* "to compete in rhetorical responses that can only be harmful and diversionary to a rational consideration of issues." Others worried that Khrushchev would dominate the headlines and thus "steal the show from two Presidential campaigners." "He might even," suggested the *Reporter,* "decide who our next President will be, just by gently hinting which of the two candidates he dislikes the less." [22]

While Khrushchev was still at sea, the unstable Congo once again flared up. President Joseph Kasavubu, disturbed by the increasingly radical stance of Lumumba, removed the prime minister from office on September 5. But instead of stepping aside, Lumumba challenged Kasavubu's authority and continued to hold office. When the Soviet Union sent fifteen airplanes to aid Lumumba, President Eisenhower issued a somber warning, telling a press conference that the United States "takes a most serious view of this action." He urged the Soviet Union "to desist from its unilateral activities" and instead support the UN peace-keeping efforts. Meanwhile there was no improvement in the Congo. "We are madmen here," one Congolese politician burst out. "We have two Presidents, two Premiers, two governments." On September 14, the army chief of staff, Colonel Joseph Mobuto, suddenly seized power in a move that doomed Lumumba, who now became a fugitive.

Mobuto supported Kasavubu when the president ordered Russian and other Communist diplomats to leave the country. The outcome still remained uncertain, but the threat of a Communist takeover began to diminish.

Dag Hammarskjöld continued his search for order in the Congo in the face of growing Russian opposition. When the Soviets vetoed a Security Council resolution enlarging the Secretary General's authority to keep peace in the Congo, Hammarskjöld convened an emergency meeting of the General Assembly in mid-September, several days before the regular session was to begin. With strong support from the neutralist nations of Asia and Africa, the General Assembly adopted a resolution backing Hammarskjöld's efforts in the Congo and asking all members of the UN to refrain from unilateral steps which "tend to impede the restoration of law and order." This unanimous vote, taken on the day Khrushchev arrived in New York, stood as a condemnation of the clumsy Soviet effort to extend the Cold War into the Congo.[23]

The rival presidential candidates ignored the volatile Congo in their campaigns, but they displayed increasing concern over Khrushchev's presence in the United States. On September 16, three days before the Soviet leader was due to arrive in New York, Senator Kennedy warned him not to try to divide the American people. "Democrats, Republicans and independents alike are united in our opposition to your system and everything it means in our stand for peace, in our hatred of war and in our refusal to tolerate appeasement," he informed Khrushchev. In a nationally televised address on September 20, JFK defended his constant emphasis on national weakness, saying, "In times such as this, I say it is wrong—and dangerous—for any American to keep silent about our future if he is not satisfied with what is being done to preserve that future." Citing the summit breakup at Paris, the cancellation of Ike's trip to Japan, and growing Russian influence in Cuba, "only ninety miles from the coast of Florida, only eight minutes by jet," Kennedy accused the Republicans of letting Russia get ahead of the United States. "This is no time to say we can out-talk or out-shoot Khrushchev," he declared. "I want to outdo him—to outproduce him." Above all, Kennedy asserted that the Soviets would continue to outstrip the United States "unless we have a President and a country in the Sixties that acts first and fast." [24]

Nixon responded with charges that his opponent was using "calculated distortion" to frighten the American people during Khrushchev's visit to the United States. The day after the Soviet leader arrived, Nixon called upon Kennedy to avoid any "resort to statements which tend to divide America, which tend to disparage America and which in any way would encourage Chairman Khrushchev and his fellow-dictators to believe that this nation . . . is weak of will, is indecisive, is unsure of and hesitant to use her vast power." GOP National Chairman Thruston Morton followed up Nixon's attack by claiming that Kennedy's constant assertion of American weakness amounted to "giving aid and comfort to the Communist enemies of the U.S." In other speeches, Nixon harped on Kennedy's suggestion that Eisenhower should have apologized to Khrushchev over the U-2 flight, to warn voters against electing "a rash and immature" President. Kennedy's lack of experience in world affairs, Nixon explained, would lead him to make concessions to Khrushchev "that would serve not the cause of freedom but would work toward the cause of surrender." In contrast, the Vice-President reminded his audiences that only a firm policy could restrain the impulsive Russian leader. "I know this man," Nixon asserted. "A policy of softness, a policy of rashness, a policy of immaturity would play directly into his hands and would not serve the cause of peace." [25]

An angry John Kennedy indignantly rebutted Nixon's charge that his criticisms were helping Khrushchev. "I want to make it clear that nothing I am saying will give Mr. Khrushchev the slightest encouragement," he told a Tennessee audience, claiming that instead the Democrats would "discourage him" by rebuilding "national strength and vitality." "Personal attacks and insults will not be enough to win the peace," Kennedy informed Nixon, "and they will never be enough to win this election." Kennedy denied he was running down America. "I say that we are a great country that can be greater," he retorted. Only those content with the existing situation, "those who are afraid to ask the American people for greater effort and sacrifice," were "selling America short." Again and again he pointed to Cuba, "a Communist satellite ninety miles off the coast of the United States"; Democratic National Chairman Henry Jackson backed him up by claiming that instead of rolling back the Iron Curtain in Europe, the Republicans let it advance "westward to Havana." "Those who say they will stand up to Mr. Khrushchev," Kennedy commented dryly, "have demonstrated no ability to stand up to Mr. Castro." But Kennedy preferred not to exchange insults with Nixon, and he rested his case with the confident assertion that "the most ominous sound that Mr. Khrushchev can hear this week is not of a debate in the United States, but the sound of America on the move, ready to move again." [26]

The candidates' charges and countercharges reflected an almost desperate effort to avoid being overshadowed by the opening of the General Assembly in New York. Khrushchev drew big headlines when the *Baltika* docked in New York on September 19. He was followed by an impressive number of other world leaders, including Tito of Yugoslavia, Nasser of Egypt, Sukarno of Indonesia, Nkrumah of Ghana, and even Fidel Castro, who noisily moved from a midtown hotel to take up residence in Harlem for the next two weeks. "The eyes of history could scarcely encompass the spectacle of so many potentates, Presidents and dictators," commented *Time,* explaining that many had heeded Khrushchev's call to turn the General Assembly meeting into a summit conference at a time when twelve new African countries would make their entrance into the United Nations. Khrushchev made certain that he was the center of attention, complaining constantly to the press over the restrictions placed on his movements and even holding a memorable impromptu press conference from the balcony of the Soviet UN mission on Park Avenue.[27]

President Eisenhower flew to New York to give the opening address at the UN session. In somber tones, he reiterated American support for the world organization, reminding the new African members that "it is the smaller nations that have the greatest stake in the effective functioning of the United Nations." He backed Hammarskjöld's peace-keeping efforts in the Congo, offered to place American naval and air forces at the UN's disposal, and promised to funnel American aid to Africa through the world body. "As we enter the decade of the 1960's," Eisenhower declared, "let us launch a renewed effort to strengthen this international community; to forge new bonds between its members in undertaking new ventures on behalf of all mankind." Then, after a luncheon with all the Latin-American leaders save Castro, and private conferences with Tito and Nkrumah, Eisenhower returned to Washington.

The next day, Nikita Khrushchev gave a fiery speech to the UN which contrasted sharply with Eisenhower's calm endorsement. For two and a half hours the Soviet leader attacked the United States and Dag Hammarskjöld, calling finally for a "troika" to replace the Secretary General, a three-man directorate made up of one member from the West, one from the Communist world, and one neutral. Khrushchev's attack shocked many Americans; more significantly, it alarmed most Third World representatives who viewed the UN as a beneficial agency which they now rallied to support.[28]

John Kennedy appeared to be the chief victim of Khrushchev's pyrotechnics at the United Nations. Trailing in the Gallup poll in the summer, he had gone slightly ahead of Nixon in mid-September. But a poll taken on September 25, after Khrushchev's speech to the General Assembly, showed him behind once again by a narrow margin, 46 percent to Nixon's 47 percent, with 7 percent still undecided. When Gallup probed into voter attitudes, he found that while Kennedy had a slight edge on domestic issues, 51.7 percent felt that Nixon was better able to deal with foreign affairs, compared to 30.1 percent for Kennedy. A *New York Times* survey made after Khrushchev's arrival revealed intense voter concern with foreign policy and a noticeable drift toward the Republican candidate. "I do not like Nixon," one man told the *Times* interviewer, "but I am voting for him because of his experience and on account of the foreign situation." The *Newsweek* survey of political correspondents around the nation showed a similar gain for Nixon, and the gambling line in Las Vegas, originally 6–5 on the Vice-President, went up to 2–1 for a Republican victory.[29]

His youth and inexperience remained Kennedy's greatest handicap. "Probably not since Hitler has the average American been more concerned about the course of world affairs," commented Robert G. Spivack in the *Nation,* noting that many voters were not yet convinced that the young senator had the maturity to deal with the crisis. Bobby Kennedy scoffed at such reports, telling journalists that his brother "had been to 30 foreign countries before Nixon had been to five." "But the Kennedys know," a skeptical *Time* writer observed, "that Khrushchev's presence in the U.S. is helping Nixon and hurting Kennedy—'a slow hurt.'" Even the staunchly liberal *Nation* had doubts about Kennedy's foreign policy competence, and the editors finally endorsed him only because Chester Bowles and Adlai Stevenson served as his principal advisers on world affairs. In the few weeks that remained before the election, Kennedy's primary task would be to convince the American people that he possessed the wisdom, the tact, and the sound judgment to preside over American diplomacy in the midst of a grave world crisis. Unless he could do so quickly, Richard Nixon, with his boast of standing up to Khrushchev, was likely to preempt the foreign policy issue, which could prove decisive in a close race.[30]

V

The 1960 campaign underwent a fundamental change on the evening of September 26, when Nixon and Kennedy engaged in the first of four nationally televised debates. The three networks had been pressing for a direct exchange between the candidates, and the Vice-President had made it possible on July 24, the eve of the Republican convention, when he gave his approval. Kennedy, eager for any chance to extend his national exposure, quickly accepted, and representatives of the two leaders worked out the details. They agreed on four hour-long debates in which each candidate would make an opening statement and then give two-and-a-half minute answers to questions posed by a panel of newsmen, with an even shorter period for rebuttals. The result would not be a genuine debate, where a man could probe in depth to explore an issue or show up flaws in his opponent's logic, but rather a series of brief exchanges with a premium on fast, almost hairtrigger, mental reactions.

Nixon agreed to debate Kennedy because of intense public pressure, and even more because he was confident of his own mastery of the medium. It was television that had enabled him to stay on the ticket in 1952 with his Checkers speech, and it was the televised exchanges with Khrushchev which had given him his reputation as a man who could stand up to the Communists. A debater since high school, Nixon apparently felt that he could use his proven skill to overwhelm a nervous and inexperienced challenger. Convinced that his greatest asset lay in foreign policy issues, Nixon decided to save the one debate devoted exclusively to international affairs until the last, when his advisers thought it would have the maximum impact. The opening debate would cover only domestic issues, while the middle two would include both.

Kennedy prepared for the first television encounter with deadly seriousness. He took two days off from active campaigning to conserve his energy and bone up on the issues. On Sunday, September 25, his three chief aides, Ted Sorensen, Dick Goodwin, and Mike Feldman, began assembling the latest facts and figures on every conceivable question the candidate could be asked and proceeded to boil the information down to a tightly packed fifteen-page summary. Kennedy spent four hours Monday morning going over this material. Then, after a noontime speech and a brief nap, he met again with his advisers, who threw him question after question to test his knowledge and reflexes in an invaluable warm-up for that evening's debate.

Nixon, by contrast, arrived in Chicago on Sunday evening without any advance preparations. Tired from two weeks of hectic campaigning and still underweight after his recent hospitalization, the Vice-President spent most of Monday studying the issues alone, cut off from his aides and from any chance to sharpen his responses to trial questions. He went to the studio early, and, though he had just shaved, his heavy beard showed through the layer of pancake makeup an assistant dabbed on his face. Kennedy, tanned and fit, arrived a little later, and after a few last-minute adjustments in lighting and set arrangements, the long-awaited debate got under way before an estimated 80 million Americans, by far the largest political audience in history.[31]

From the outset, Kennedy took the initiative, giving a variation of his set campaign speech in his opening remarks. Though this debate was confined to domestic issues, Kennedy sneaked foreign policy in by comparing this election to that of 1860, saying that the question now was whether the world, not just the nation, "will exist half-slave or half-free." The outcome depended on what the United States did. "If we do well here, if we meet our obligations, if we're moving ahead," Kennedy asserted, "then I think freedom will be secure around the world. If we fail, then freedom fails." Nixon countered by agreeing that the United States could not stand still while locked in "a deadly competition . . . with the men in the Kremlin," and went on to claim that under Eisenhower the nation had advanced steadily at home and abroad. In the questions from the panel that followed, both candidates stuck to domestic themes in giving the short, oversimplified answers dictated by the time restrictions. Kennedy displayed a retentive memory and a quick intelligence in his rapid, fact-studded replies; Nixon proved uncharacteristically accommodating, agreeing often with Kennedy's statement of goals while disputing his proposed remedies. As a result, there were no sparks, no heated exchanges in what the New York *Daily News* disdainfully called a "powderpuff performance." [32]

Nearly all observers concluded that Kennedy had made a stunning breakthrough in the first debate. Still relatively unknown and unproven, he had displayed a remarkable degree of maturity, remaining calm and unruffled as he rattled off answer after answer with machine-like rapidity. "Kennedy was alert, aggressive and cool," summed up *Time*. Viewers realized that he was not the green, immature challenger of the GOP stereotype, but rather a gifted man with remarkable poise and polish. "Kennedy did not show that he was Nixon's master," *Newsweek* acknowledged grudgingly, "but he did show that he was Nixon's match." The Vice-President, on the other hand, "was strangely nervous, perspiring profusely," as *Time* noted, "under the baleful glare of floodlights" that made him look "ill as well as ill at ease." His haggard face, sagging jowls, and pallid complexion gave him the air of a losing candidate, a man on the way down, not up. Those who listened on the radio instead of TV came away much more favorably impressed by Nixon's performance; his appearance, more than his words, created the impression that he had suffered a major setback.[33]

Surveys of public opinion confirmed that Kennedy had bested his rival. A local New York canvass reported that viewers felt Kennedy had outpointed Nixon decisively, while George Gallup found that across the nation 43 percent of those interviewed believed Kennedy had won the first debate, to only 23 percent naming Nixon. Even the Republican research service concluded that the first debate had "resulted in the undisputed public relations victory for the Democrats"; the conservative Manchester *Union Leader* put it more bluntly, telling Nixon in a front-page editorial that he had been "clobbered." The *New Republic* expressed the relief of many Democrats who had feared that Kennedy "might not be able to stand up to Nixon"; the *Nation* rejoiced in the image Kennedy projected of "a bright, knowledgeable young man of great earnestness, energy and integrity." Above all, the debate seemed to remove any doubt of Kennedy's ability to perform effectively under great pressure. Irving Brandt pointed up the foreign policy implications of this revelation in the following syllogism: [34]

NIXON: I can handle Khrushchev.
TELEVISION VERDICT: Kennedy can handle Nixon.
CONCLUSION: Kennedy can handle Khrushchev.

Democrats were jubilant at their candidate's fine showing. Ten southern governors, hitherto cool toward Kennedy's candidacy, sent him a telegram on the day after the first debate, congratulating him on his performance and pledging their support for his election. When Kennedy toured Ohio the next day, Governor Frank Lausche joined his motorcade and gave him an enthusiastic endorsement. "Lausche always waits until he sees the winner," commented *Newsweek* dryly. The crowds lining the streets seemed to have the same feeling. People turned out in huge numbers to cheer Kennedy in Ohio, calling out, "Keep after him, Jack," and "You really got him last night."

Kennedy realized that the debate was "an enormous break" for him; he told Cyrus Sulzberger that Nixon "was a damn fool to agree to debate with me on an equal-time TV basis." Buoyed by his achievement, Kennedy let loose with a full-scale attack on the Republican record in foreign policy in a speech at Syracuse, New York, on September 29. Reciting the litany of defeats—the U-2, the Paris summit meeting, Soviet penetration of Cuba—Kennedy declared, "I am tired of reading every morning what Mr. Khrushchev is doing, and what Mr. Castro is doing. I want to read what the President of the United States is doing." Then he derided Nixon's qualifications, based on trips abroad and standing up to Khrushchev. "Peace takes more than talk, more than effort, more than 'experience,' " Kennedy declared, "particularly if that 'experience,' in Oscar Wilde's words, is 'the name that everyone gives to their mistakes.' " [35]

Eisenhower was furious when he heard of Kennedy's attack on his administration's policies. "Listen, dammit," *Time* reported him telling a visitor in his White House office, "I'm going to do everything possible to keep that Jack Kennedy from sitting in this chair." Republican strategists, searching for ways to counter the trend toward Kennedy, urged Nixon to rely more heavily on the President. Eisenhower did give his Vice-President a boost in a fund-raising speech in Chicago on September 29, saying that he had found Nixon's counsel "invaluable" over the past eight years and concluding, "As a man qualified to enter on the duties of the presidential office, Dick Nixon has the broadest and deepest preparation and experience of any man I know." But despite the favorable response these words evoked, Nixon refused to depart from his decision to wage his own campaign and keep Eisenhower on the sidelines. [36]

At the United Nations, meanwhile, Nikita Khrushchev continued to divert attention away from the presidential race. Angered by Ike's refusal to meet with him, he kept calling for a face-to-face encounter with the President until finally five neutral leaders, headed by India's Nehru, asked Eisenhower to hold such a meeting "as an urgent first step" toward reducing world tensions. When Ike politely turned down the request, citing Soviet intransigence, Khrushchev blew up. In a long, angry speech to the General Assembly, he denounced the United States as a "disgrace to civilization," and then began attacking other Western nations until the presiding officer stopped the simultaneous translation of his remarks because of their insulting nature. Khrushchev astounded the Assembly and the entire world by heckling British Prime Minister Harold Macmillan during his reply to the Russian's attacks and by taking off his shoe in the midst of a speech by a Philippine spokesman and pounding it repeatedly on his desk. Unmoved by the outrage his actions provoked, Khrushchev continued his erratic and aggressive behavior; he condemned Dag Hammarskjöld as "a creature of the imperialists" and warned ominously that missiles were pouring out of Russian factories "like sausages."

Khrushchev's rhetoric could not hide the series of defeats he suffered in the General Assembly. After voting 70–0 to sustain Hammarskjöld's Congo operations, the body rejected Russian demands for seating Communist China, for censure of the United States over the U-2 flight, and for immediate UN debate on world disarmament. His only victory came on the passage of a Soviet resolution condemning colonialism. On October 3, he finally left the United States. He had failed to secure his stated objectives—removing Hammarskjöld and meeting with Eisenhower—but his stormy twenty-five-day visit had succeeded in arousing the American people to the seriousness of the world crisis and underlining the importance of foreign policy in the presidential campaign.[37]

VI

The second televised debate took place in NBC's Washington studios on October 7. This time Richard Nixon prepared carefully for the session, drinking milk shakes four times a day to regain five pounds of lost weight and using a professional makeup man to cover up his sallow complexion with a heavy layer of cosmetics. When Kennedy arrived at the studio, he found it freezing cold as a result of Nixon's request for maximum air-conditioning to keep him from perspiring heavily in front of the cameras. At the Democratic candidate's insistence, the thermostat was turned up, though the studio temperature was still under 70 degrees at broadcast time.[38]

The second debate was much livelier than the first. Ranging over both foreign and domestic policy, Nixon proved far more aggressive in an effort to seize the initiative and put Kennedy on the defensive. There were many more sharp exchanges, and at times both men came close to losing their tempers. Kennedy hammered away at the failures of the Eisenhower administration, especially in Cuba, to argue that American prestige had fallen drastically in the world. "I believe this Administration has not met its responsibilities in the last eight years," Kennedy declared, ". . . and unless the United States begins to move here—unless we start to go ahead—I don't believe that we're going to meet our responsibility to our own people or to the cause of freedom." Nixon responded by stressing Kennedy's suggestion that Eisenhower apologize for the U-2 flight, declaring, "We all remember Pearl Harbor. . . . We cannot afford an intelligence gap." He claimed that Kennedy wanted to return to the outmoded Truman policies which lost 600 million people to Communism.

Nixon drew the first real blood in the debates during the next-to-last exchange. Newsman Edward P. Morgan asked Kennedy about a statement he had made in a television interview several days earlier, when he said he thought that the Eisenhower administration had been unwise in drawing the line against Communist China at the offshore islands of Quemoy and Matsu. Kennedy replied that while he was prepared to defend Chiang Kai-shek on Formosa, he thought the administration ought not to extend its commitment to the offshore islands. "I think it is unwise to take the chance of being dragged into a war which may lead to a world war over two islands which are not strategically defensible." Instead, he thought the United States should encourage Chiang to withdraw from the islands to avoid such an unfortunate contingency.

"I disagree completely with Senator Kennedy on this point," Nixon declared in his rebuttal. Comparing his opponent's suggestion to Dean Acheson's abandonment of Korea in 1950, Nixon said such a step would invite Communist attack. Matsu and Quemoy were "unimportant" in themselves, he admitted, but a vital principle was at stake. "These two islands are in the area of freedom," he asserted, and to give them up would start a "chain reaction" that would end in the conquest of Formosa. "In my opinion, this is the same kind of woolly thinking that led to disaster for America in Korea," Nixon concluded. "I am against it. I would never tolerate it as president of the United States." [39]

Most observers felt that the second debate was a standoff. "In Round 2 Kennedy came through on foreign affairs with considerable strength," commented *Time*. "But Nixon topped him with a sureness on Cold War specifics." Gallup registered another victory for Kennedy, but local surveys indicated a narrow triumph for Nixon. Nearly everyone agreed that Nixon had scored heavily in the brief exchange on Quemoy and Matsu. "In the minds of many voters," concluded *Newsweek*, "Kennedy appeared to favor surrendering the islands to Communist China; Nixon appeared determined to hold them, even if that meant a nuclear war." Arthur Krock summed up the feelings of most foreign policy experts when he expressed regret that such a delicate issue had entered into the campaign. Kennedy, he complained, should never have challenged Eisenhower's stand on Quemoy and Matsu.[40]

In fact, both men had taken positions that conflicted with the administration's policy. The offshore islands had first become an issue in 1955, when Eisenhower and Dulles asked Congress for authority to defend Formosa and "closely related localities." There was no debate over Formosa, but several senators, including John Kennedy, wanted Eisenhower to exclude Quemoy and Matsu from the resolution. Chiang's retention of these two rocky islands, only a few miles from the coast of China, seemed to them to be a provocative act, since the islands were much more likely to be used to launch a Nationalist invasion of the mainland than to become stepping-stones for a Communist attack on Formosa. The administration refused to clarify its stand, preferring to keep the Communists guessing as to whether the United States would aid Chiang in resisting an attack on the islands, and the original resolution won overwhelming Congressional approval. Three years later, the mainland Chinese reopened the issue by bombarding the two islands. Once again, despite urging from Dulles for a firm stand, Eisenhower refused to clarify American policy, and after several months of tension the Communists eased their pressure on Quemoy and Matsu. Thus the administration policy remained ambiguous. Unlike Kennedy, Eisenhower did not want to give up the islands, but in contrast to Nixon, neither did he wish to make a firm commitment to defend them as a matter of principle. The defense of Quemoy and Matsu, the President had stated in 1958 in a letter to Senator Francis Green, was a tactical question that depended on whether the United States believed an attack on the islands endangered the security of Formosa.[41]

Though the State Department wanted both candidates to drop the offshore island issue, neither felt that he could let it go. Kennedy's aides expressed concern over the way Nixon made it appear that their candidate advocated a policy of surrender, but the senator overruled their suggestions that he reverse his stand. Instead, on October 10, three days after the second debate, the Democratic candidate issued a formal statement accusing Nixon of wanting to commit the United States "to the defense of every rock and island around the world" and thus "to involve American boys in an unnecessary and futile war." Nixon responded the next day by calling Kennedy's proposals on the islands "dangerous to world peace." Declaring that he would never surrender "one inch of free territory," he asked Kennedy if he would also give up West Berlin, an area equally indefensible. "We left the policy of retreat and defeat behind us in 1953," Nixon asserted, "and we're not going back to it in 1960."

Kennedy devoted an entire foreign policy address to the problem of Quemoy-Matsu on October 12, the day before the third debate was to take place. With impeccable logic, Kennedy pointed out that Nixon had extended the administration's commitment dangerously. In biting tones, he argued that Nixon's policy "invites war" and indicated that he would be "a trigger-happy President." The ironclad promise to defend Quemoy and Matsu meant risking American lives and exposing American cities to nuclear attack, Kennedy charged, simply to ensure that Chiang Kai-shek had a base from which to invade the mainland sometime in the future. "I do not think the American people will sustain such a position," he predicted. "I do not think they will support such trigger-happy leadership." Kennedy ended up by citing Admiral Yarnell, identified as a "former commander of our Asiatic fleet," as saying "these islands are not worth the bones of a single American." [42]

Republicans jumped to Nixon's defense. Governor Rockefeller told an upstate New York audience that Kennedy's position was "dangerous," while Henry Cabot Lodge reminded the Democratic candidate that "he who retreats often gets shot in the back." Matsu and Quemoy were far more than mere rocks, Lodge contended. "They symbolize much for both the free and Communist worlds." The GOP National Committee warned Kennedy that his words had "major policy implicatons," contending that the Democratic challenger's position was "an open invitation to Chicoms to take these islands the day Kennedy takes office—if he does." Admiral Arthur Radford, former chairman of the Joint Chiefs of Staff, claimed that Kennedy's views "could certainly start a war if they are believed by the Red Chinese." After several days of digging, GOP officials revealed in *Battle Line,* the party's newsletter, that the Admiral Yarnell Kennedy cited was an eighty-year-old retired officer who had last seen active service in the 1930's! [43]

Richard Nixon, realizing he had Kennedy on the defensive, prepared to exploit his advantage in the third debate. Robert Merriam, a White House aide, searched the State Department files on Quemoy and Matsu and then sent his findings to Nixon's staff in Los Angeles, where the Vice-President was campaigning. Merriam told Nixon that while it was true that the administration had always hedged its commitment to defend the islands with the qualification that it would do so only if an attack was seen as a prelude to an invasion of Formosa, the Chinese Communists had made no secret of their intention of seizing Quemoy and Matsu "as part of [their] overall plan to retake Formosa." He reminded Nixon that Kennedy had voted to exclude the offshore islands from the Formosa resolution in 1955, and he supplied a full summary of the Democratic candidate's past statements on the issue. "In the case of Quemoy and Matsu, the argument is made that this is a 'bad' place to stand," Merriam concluded. "The fact is there never is a 'good' place to stand," he pointed out in urging Nixon to portray the islands as a test of "the integrity of the free world's collective security system." [44]

Nixon hammered away repeatedly on Quemoy and Matsu

in the third debate on October 13, in which he [was in a] Los Angeles studio while Kennedy and the pane[l] appeared in New York. The Vice-President qu[alified his ear]lier stand by saying he would defend the island[s only if] an attack on them "was a prelude to an attack on Formosa," thus bringing himself in line with Eisenhower's position. But again and again he charged that Kennedy advocated a policy of retreat and surrender, "something that would lead, in my opinion, to war." "We tried this with Hitler," Nixon continued, "and it didn't work." The Chinese Communists, he asserted, "don't want just Quemoy and Matsu; they don't want just Formosa; they want the world." In his rebuttals, Kennedy stressed that Nixon had extended the administration's commitment by advocating the defense of the islands for their own sake, as part of "the area of freedom." He kept denying that he favored giving up territory to the Communists in other parts of the world and made clear his determination to defend Berlin. Accusing Nixon of distorting the record, Kennedy pointed out that several times the Eisenhower administration had tried and failed to get Chiang Kai-shek to evacuate the islands. Finally, his temper fraying, the Democratic candidate burst out, "Mr. Nixon would add a guarantee to islands five miles off the coast of the Republic of China when he's never really protested the Communists seizing Cuba, ninety miles off the coast of the United States." [45]

President Eisenhower became disturbed over the way the delicate Quemoy-Matsu issue had become embroiled in the campaign. The Chinese Nationalists, enraged over the idea of giving up the islands, had announced that they would "fight to the death" to defend them, and there was increasing speculation that Peking might well interpret a Kennedy victory as a green light for an invasion of the islands. Still convinced that the United States ought not to disclose its intentions in advance, Eisenhower conferred with Nixon on the day after the third debate and then announced that he and the Vice-Presint were in full agreement on Quemoy and Matsu. In releasing Eisenhower's statement to the press, James Hagerty included a copy of the President's 1958 letter to Senator Green, in which he had said that the United States would not act "merely in defense of Quemoy and Matsu," but only "for the defense of Formosa." Reporters interpreted the presidential statement as an attempt to close off debate on the islands by forcing Nixon back to the administration's original position. Kennedy reacted immediately, praising Eisenhower for rejecting Nixon's rash views "committing us in advance to the defense of every inch of another nation's territory." On *Meet the Press* the next day, Kennedy said that he supported the administration's policy and that in the "interests of bipartisanship" he would drop the issue from the campaign.[46]

Nixon, confident that he had Kennedy "over the barrel on an issue which was turning sour on him," was reluctant to let go. He released a statement saying he would agree to drop Quemoy and Matsu from the campaign only if Kennedy "makes it clear he no longer favors surrendering the islands." The next day, speaking in Buffalo, he linked Kennedy's stand on the offshore islands with his suggestion that Eisenhower apologize for the U-2 flight, to accuse him of playing "directly into the Communists' hands." "How can the American people have confidence in a man who shoots from the hip on matters that gravely affect the security of our country?" Nixon asked. In a speech to the American Legion in Miami, he again resorted to a rhetorical question: "Why are we concerned about a couple of worthless rocks? You recall the same arguments for Danzig, the Sudetenland, Austria, and all the rest." [47]

Despite Nixon's efforts to keep it alive, the Quemoy-Matsu issue gradually faded out of the campaign in mid-October. In the final televised debate on October 21, Nixon claimed that the islands would remain in the campaign as long as "Senator Kennedy persists in what I think is a fundamental error." The error, Nixon went on to explain, was announcing in advance that the United States would not defend the islands. Kennedy heatedly replied that he now agreed with the administration's view that the islands should be defended if the attack on them threatened Formosa. "That's not the position you took, however," Kennedy reminded Nixon. "The first position you took . . . was that we should draw the line and commit ourselves, as a matter of principle, to defend these islands." Then the two men turned to other matters, letting the islands, as *Time* noted, "float back out of the center of U.S. debate and back to their rightful place in ambiguity along the China coast." [48]

There is little doubt that Nixon exploited the Quemoy-Matsu issue effectively. In his memoirs, he claims that he abandoned it only after Chester Bowles told Secretary of the Interior Fred Seaton that Kennedy wanted to drop the dispute lest the Chinese Communists get the idea they could seize the islands with impunity. Without mentioning Eisenhower's intervention, Nixon claims he let the issue go "except for continuing to point to the whole 'shoot first, think later' approach as indicative of his lack of experience in the foreign policy area." Theodore Sorensen denies that Bowles ever made such a request, and in Bowles's own memoirs, though he refers to regular meetings with Secretary of State Christian Herter during the campaign, he makes no mention of Quemoy and Matsu. Bowles played a relatively insignificant part in Kennedy's campaign, conferring with the candidate infrequently by telephone, and it thus seems unlikely that he intervened on the Quemoy-Matsu debate. The offshore islands finally dropped out of the campaign because Kennedy realized his initial position was "too sophisticated" for the electorate. Once the Democratic challenger had drawn back to the administration's policy, President Eisenhower compelled Nixon to make a similar retreat. [49]

The result was a serious setback for Kennedy's campaign. Nixon's adroit use of the Quemoy-Matsu issue gave him a decided edge in the third debate; for the first time, viewer reactions indicated that he had outpointed Kennedy decisively. Samuel Lubell found that 47 percent of the voters he interviewed agreed with Nixon's argument that "we cannot give in anywhere to Communists," compared to 29 percent who supported Kennedy's view that the islands were not worth fighting for. The Gallup poll showed that Nixon had come back strongly in mid-October; he now drew even with Kennedy after trailing him by three percentage points following the first two debates.

Above all, the furor over Quemoy-Matsu indicated how the televised debates could create an artificial issue. The offshore islands represented a minor and obscure aspect of American foreign policy; yet once they came into dispute between Nixon and Kennedy, they were blown up all out of proportion. As a skilled debater, Nixon seized upon them, the *New Republic* commented, in his search "for perches from which to proclaim with absolute finality the rightness and patriotism of his position." Kennedy, who had set out to clarify what he felt was a dangerous ambiguity in American foreign policy, ended up in a debate over principle in which he was cast in the role of appeaser. When he realized what was happening, Kennedy tried to back away as gracefully as possible, but Nixon insisted on taking full political advantage of his opponent's mistake. The episode confirmed Eisenhower's wisdom in refusing to clarify the American commitment to defend Quemoy and Matsu, and taught Kennedy how risky it was to try to deal candidly with substantive international issues in a presidential campaign.[50]

VII

In mid-October, Cuba replaced Quemoy and Matsu as the leading foreign policy issue. Castro had helped quicken concern about his regime with a four-and-a-half-hour speech to the United Nations, in which he aligned himself with the Soviet Union on all major world questions. The State Department responded by urging Americans in Cuba to leave the country and by warning against travel to the island. Kennedy kept referring to the ominous Soviet influence over Castro in his speeches, as he discovered a growing public discontent with Eisenhower's restrained Cuban policy. In Cincinnati on October 6, Kennedy devoted a whole speech to Cuba, which he termed "the most glaring failure of American foreign policy." Calling Castro's rise to power "a disaster which threatens the security of the whole Western Hemisphere," the Democratic candidate condemned Eisenhower and Nixon for permitting "a Communist menace" to "arise only ninety miles from the shores of the United States." Kennedy failed to offer any constructive alternatives to administration policy, but the strong applause which greeted this attack led him to refer to "Cuber," as he pronounced it, in nearly all his subsequent campaign talks.[51]

Reacting to Kennedy's criticism, Nixon disclosed in the course of his October 18 American Legion speech in Miami that he had urged the State Department to place an economic quarantine on Cuba "to counter the economic banditry being practiced by this regime against our country and our citizens." The next day the Eisenhower administration invoked the embargo that Nixon had advocated. The State Department announced a ban on all exports to Cuba except food and medicine, in retaliation for "the discriminatory, aggressive and injurious economic politics of the Castro regime." This step, which *Time* called "the most severe trade embargo imposed on any nation except for Red China," was followed by the recall of Ambassador Philip Bonsal, who had tried patiently for twenty-one months to prevent a breach between Cuba and the United States.[52]

Kennedy, still smarting from the defeat he had suffered on the offshore islands, decided to attack the administration's embargo as too little, too late. Busy preparing for the fourth debate with Nixon, he allowed his aides to release on October 20 a statement on Cuba under his name but written by Dick Goodwin. Calling the embargo "a dramatic but almost empty gesture," the statement blamed the administration for failing to secure a specific OAS condemnation of Castro and thus prevent his becoming a major threat to the peace of the hemisphere. Kennedy promised that, if elected, he would work with our neighbors to keep Communism from spreading to other parts of Latin America. In addition, the statement continued, "we must attempt to strengthen the non-Batista democratic anti-Castro forces in exile, and in Cuba itself, who offer eventual hope of overthrowing Castro. Thus far these fighters for freedom have had virtually no support from our Government." [53]

Kennedy's statement incensed Richard Nixon. The CIA plan to sponsor an invasion by Cuban exiles was now well along; refugees from the Castro regime had been recruited in the Miami area and were undergoing training at secret bases in Guatemala. Nixon believed that the Democratic candidate had been briefed on this operation by Allen Dulles, and he asked Fred Seaton to check with the White House. When Seaton reported back that Kennedy had been informed of the CIA plan, the Vice-President became convinced that his rival was deliberately advocating a plan of action which the administration was pursuing secretly and which Nixon could not acknowledge publicly. In fact, Kennedy had no knowledge of the invasion plan. The White House aides Seaton had consulted apparently misunderstood the nature of Dulles' briefing. In 1962, Dulles stated that he had withheld information on this highly classified operation from the Democratic candidate.[54]

Instead of avoiding the Cuban situation, Nixon decided to take issue with Kennedy's proposal to encourage the exiles to overthrow Castro. In the final television debate on October 21, Nixon declared, "I think that Senator Kennedy's policies and recommendations for the handling of the Castro regime are probably the most dangerously irresponsible recommendations that he's made during the course of this campaign." The Vice-President went on to cite the American commitment in the OAS charter not to intervene in the internal affairs of member states. He then suggested that the U.S. should "do what we did with Guatemala," implying that it was the Guatemalans themselves who had removed a Communist regime in 1954. Kennedy, already regretting the October 20 statement, gave a weak reply in which he ignored the issue of an exile invasion of Cuba, claiming that Castro's real danger was to the other nations of Latin America. Incredibly, he did not challenge Nixon's Guatemalan example, which was widely known to be a CIA achievement.[55]

The liberal press came down hard on Kennedy for advocating the use of force to overthrow Castro. The *New Republic* called his proposals "deeply disappointing," while the *Nation* warned darkly against "an American Hungary in the Western Hemisphere." When both Walter Lippmann and James Reston wrote columns critical of Kennedy's Cuban policy, the Democratic candidate sent Arthur Schlesinger to explain to these influential journalists that he proposed using only moral, not military, force against Castro. Kennedy made this explanation public in a statement released in Minneapolis on October 24. "I have never advocated, and I do not advocate, intervention in Cuba in violation of our treaty obligations," Kennedy announced, adding that he only wanted to "let the forces of freedom in Cuba" know that "the United States sympathized with them." [56]

Nixon refused to let Kennedy escape so easily. For the next two days, he kept referring to his opponent's Cuban proposal as "rash," "impulsive," and "shockingly reckless." The Democratic candidate was calling for "United States Government support for a revolution in Cuba," Nixon charged, claiming that his statement was "a direct invitation for the Soviet Union to intervene militarily on the side of Castro." Nixon apparently saw no inconsistency in making this public attack on his opponent while privately he gave his full endorsement to the CIA plan designed to achieve the same objective. In *Six Crises,* he simply notes that he was "in the ironic position of appearing to be 'softer' on Castro than Kennedy—which was exactly the opposite of the truth, if only the whole record could be disclosed."

In retrospect, Nixon believed that Kennedy had outmaneuvered him on Cuba. "I got little comfort, politically, out of his change of position," he wrote two years later. "At least 60 million people had seen and heard him on television demanding a tougher stand against Castro than the Administration and I were advocating publicly." This is a dubious judgment. In the debate, Kennedy failed to repeat his call for an American-sponsored exile invasion of Cuba, and his subsequent reversal of position highlighted his immaturity and inexperience. The *New York Times* called it "a second major blunder in the dangerous area of foreign policy," and coming so soon after Kennedy's turnabout on Quemoy and Matsu, it raised a fundamental question of his ability to handle difficult and complex problems of world affairs. Kennedy wanted to get the nation moving again, but observers now began to wonder about the direction in which his unquestioned vitality and energy would take the United States.[57]

VIII

Besides Cuba and Quemoy-Matsu, only one other foreign policy issue emerged in the televised debates—the question of American prestige. In the third debate, Kennedy cited a Gallup poll showing that people in eight of the nine foreign nations surveyed thought that by 1970 the Soviets would have surpassed the United States as the world's leading power. "So I would say our prestige is not so high," Kennedy commented. "No longer do we give the image of being on the rise." In his rebuttal, Nixon cited the recent 70–0 UN General Assembly vote in favor of the American position on the Congo, then suggested that statements like the one Kennedy had just made would not help lift America's position in the eyes of the world.

Just before the last debate, reports appeared in the press that the administration had suppressed a United States Information Agency poll which confirmed Kennedy's charge of America's declining prestige in the world. When Walter Cronkite asked Nixon about this rumor, the Vice-President claimed it was an outdated survey taken just after the Russians launched their first earth satellite, but said he had no objection to the poll's being made public. Then Nixon accused Kennedy of running down the United States position in the world, charging that "America's prestige abroad will be just as high as the spokesmen for America allow it to be." Kennedy angrily denounced Nixon for trying to tell him "what my responsibilities are as a citizen." "What I downgrade, Mr. Nixon," the Democratic candidate explained, "is the leadership the country is getting, not the country." In his closing remarks, Kennedy again spelled out his major theme, saying, "I want people all over the world to look to the United States again, to feel that we're on the move, to feel that our high noon is in the future." Nixon agreed, in an unfortunate choice of words, that America "can't stand pat" in the race with the Communists, but he closed by asserting that under the Republicans America had been forging ahead. "What I am trying to indicate," he concluded, "is that the tide of history's on our side, and that we can keep it on our side, because we're on the right side. We're on the side of freedom." [58]

Most experts breathed a sigh of relief when the debates were over. The leading question in his mind, commented Max Ascoli, was "Why has such punishment been inflicted upon so many of us?" He compared the two candidates to computers, "each conditioned to recite a pre-taped message in answer to a foreseeable challenge." Douglass Cater thought the debates were like "a bastardized version of Art Linkletter's 'People Are Funny' in which the contestant had to tell how he would deal with Castro in 150 seconds flat." The surveys indicated that most viewers thought Nixon had won the last debate, but his resurgence did not change the overall impression that Kennedy could more than hold his own with Nixon. Kennedy had persuaded millions of Americans who had been uncertain about his candidacy that he apparently had the ability and the maturity to guide the nation in the difficult days that lay ahead.[59]

By the last week in October, victory was in the air for Kennedy. Though the Gallup poll showed the two candidates running evenly, all three major news magazines reported a definite Democratic trend. Kennedy continued to draw huge crowds everywhere he went, which contributed to the bandwagon effect. The nation's most influential columnists, including James Reston, Joseph Alsop, and Walter Lippmann, declared for Kennedy; Lippmann summed up the reasons in saying that the Democrat would "make much the better President." The *New York Times* agreed, though the editors admitted the choice was extremely difficult. They finally backed Kennedy because they felt his basic outlook was "more reasoned, less emotional, more flexible, less doctrinaire, more imaginative, less negative than that of the Vice President." Among the mass circulation magazines, only *Life* openly dissented, endorsing the Republican candidates because "with Nixon and Lodge in charge of U.S. world policy we shall feel both safer and more helpful." [60]

A sense of gloom and foreboding permeated the Nixon camp. "Barring truly spectacular developments," the candidate's media analysts predicted, "present trends clearly point more and more to a Kennedy victory." Searching for a way to stem the Democratic tide, Nixon met with Lodge, Fred Seaton, and William Rogers in Hartford in mid-October for a long strategy conference. Then, just before the last debate, the

Vice-President broke off his active campaigning to confer in a day-long series of meetings at the Waldorf-Astoria with Herbert Hoover, Thomas Dewey, Nelson Rockefeller, and newspaper publisher Roy Howard. Nearly all these advisers urged Nixon to abandon his nonpartisan stance and come out swinging at Kennedy on domestic issues. The Vice-President, however, still convinced that foreign policy was his strongest point, kept giving his set speech which stressed his experience in world affairs—complete with a dramatic account of how 250,000 Poles turned out in Warsaw to greet him in 1959, tears streaming down their faces. Reporters marveled how Nixon could get the same emotional catch in his voice as he told audience after audience that this incident made him realize what freedom really meant. "He reduces foreign affairs to locker-room pep talk," commented Douglass Cater, pointing out that Nixon would cite the UN vote on the Congo to his listeners and then declare, "Seventy to nothing is a pretty good score in any football game." Day after day, he won his greatest ovation for the punch line, "Eisenhower got us out of one war and kept us out of others without surrender," followed by a solemn pledge to continue the President's wise policies.[61]

Lodge also stressed foreign policy in his vice-presidential campaign, but as the race reached a climax, he became more and more of a liability to Nixon. He traveled at a leisurely pace, insisting on time for rest and naps each day. He faithfully testified to Nixon's experience in standing up to the Communists, but he embarrassed the President in a Harlem speech in which he called for more blacks in the foreign service and promised that Nixon would choose a Negro for a Cabinet post. The Vice-President, intent on a southern strategy, immediately repudiated Lodge's statement, but even after a hastily called conference between the two men, the former UN ambassador kept repeating his belief that Nixon would appoint Negroes to ambassadorial and Cabinet positions. In contrast, Lyndon Johnson subordinated his campaign to Kennedy's, concentrating on the South in a massive effort to halt Republican inroads. Johnson rarely discussed international affairs, but his folksy appeal to the party loyalty of southern Democrats proved highly effective.[62]

"On two things Vice President Nixon and Senator John F. Kennedy are fully agreed," commented a *New York Times* analyst, "—that foreign policy is the paramount issue in the Presidential campaign and that leadership is the first essential in foreign policy." Other commentators concurred, noting that for all the campaign rhetoric, there really was no conflict on diplomacy between the two candidates. Both men expressed the same Cold War philosophy, and both, in the words of Ernest Lindley, "genuinely believe that we must wage this global struggle with greater vigor." The squabbles over Cuba and the offshore islands dealt only with minor tactical questions; Nixon and Kennedy agreed that victory in the Cold War was the unquestioned goal of the United States in world affairs.[63]

The issue thus turned on which man could provide the more effective leadership, and here Kennedy gained his advantage. "Like Ike, who is 27 years his senior," commented *Time,* "he projects a kind of conviction and vigor even when talking of commonplace things in a commonplace way." Cyrus Sulzberger saw the same quality in Kennedy: "a charismatic aura of popular leadership, the kind of aura emitted by Franklin Roosevelt and by Eisenhower when they campaigned for office." Some commentators dismissed talk of "charisma" and "style" as public relations stereotypes that detracted from the substantive issues of the campaign. But James Reston thought it was legitimate for the voters to focus on "the overriding question of personality—the question of which man would provide the best leadership in a troubled period." For many, the choice was between the lesser of two evils, with the *Nation* finally choosing Kennedy because "to the end, Mr. Nixon remained the more obnoxious in his tactics and tirades." Reston, on the other hand, thought that if Kennedy won, it would not be by default, "but because of the urgency and spirit, the daring and grace of his appeal." In essence, the slight lead that Kennedy had opened up seemed to reflect a growing preference, based largely on his performance in the televised debates, for the quality of personal leadership he offered the nation.[64]

IX

During the last two weeks of the campaign, Richard Nixon turned to the highly partisan tactics that had served him so well in the past. In a whistle-stop tour of the Middle West, he launched a series of personal attacks on his opponent, suggesting that he lacked the experience and wisdom to guide the United States in world affairs. Speaking in small cities with solid Republican majorities, Nixon elicited shouts of approval as he cited Kennedy's stands on the U-2 affair, Cuba, and the offshore islands, charging, "He's been up three times, he's struck out three times and now he wants to be made the clean-up batter." Again and again he portrayed his rival as a novice in world affairs, "the kind of man Mr. Khrushchev will make mincemeat of." He pointed out the way Kennedy had reversed himself on Cuba and Quemoy and Matsu and warned voters that "we cannot afford to have as President of the United States a man who does not think first before he speaks or acts." The next President, Nixon affirmed, had the responsibility "never to lose his temper and never to shoot from the hip where the peace of the world is concerned." [65]

Nixon worked particularly hard to hold the votes of ethnic groups which had been attracted to the Republican party by the liberation theme in 1952. Aware that many Americans of Eastern European descent were Catholics, drawn to Kennedy out of religious sympathy, the Republicans created the American Nationalities for Nixon-Lodge Committee, which tried to remind ethnic groups that it was during "the Roosevelt-

Truman era when the freedom of millions of people in Europe and Asia was turned over to Communist slavery." The Nationalities Committee distributed some 48,000 foreign-language campaign buttons, held freedom rallies in cities with large Polish populations like Buffalo and Chicago, and printed tens of thousands of postcards picturing Nixon debating Khrushchev, his finger thrust in the Russian leader's face. The Republicans found the Quemoy-Matsu issue particularly effective in charging the Democrats with softness toward Communism. National Chairman Thruston Morton claimed that Kennedy's call for withdrawal from the islands was "reminiscent of the spirit of Yalta," while the Nationalities Committee termed it "part and parcel of the disastrous 'appeasement and retreat' policy advocated for many years by the pro-Soviet Hiss-Acheson clique in the U.S. Department of State." This effort to win over minority groups reached its climax with the celebration of Operation Freedom Week, from October 23 to 29, commemorating the abortive Hungarian rebellion of 1956. Nixon kicked off the ceremonies with a statement denouncing "Soviet brutality and imperialism" and promising never to accept "the status quo of Soviet and Communist domination over the peoples of the Captive Nations." Former freedom fighters from Hungary spoke at meetings around the country, where audiences watched a GOP film showing "Richard Nixon and Henry Cabot Lodge fighting for freedom at home and abroad; in Greece, Italy and even in the heart of Communism, the Soviet Union." [66]

Nixon made the appeal to ethnic groups a central theme in his final round of campaigning. He told a freedom rally in New York City on October 31 that the U.S. must not allow Khrushchev and Mao to have "a privileged sanctuary behind the Iron Curtain from which to wage their aggressive struggle for world domination." Instead, Nixon continued, "we must skillfully use every political, economic and psychological weapon at our command to weaken that tyrannical system."

In Michigan he went even further, promising a Polish audience that, if he were elected, he would go to Eastern Europe in person "to carry the message of freedom into the Communist world." Though commentators saw this as a desperate effort to imitate Ike's "go to Korea" pledge, Nixon made an even more astonishing proposal in a nationally televised speech from Los Angeles on the Sunday night before the election. In order to stimulate and nourish the desire for freedom, he planned to invite leaders of the satellite countries to visit the United States and then to reciprocate by sending President Eisenhower to Eastern Europe. He had talked with the President about this idea, Nixon added, and Ike was ready to go, suggesting only that Herbert Hoover and Harry Truman accompany him on this mission. In solemn tones, Nixon promised that, if elected, he would ask these three former Presidents to spread the message of freedom behind the Iron Curtain.[67]

Most Republicans felt that Eisenhower could be used much more effectively at home to rescue Nixon's sagging candidacy. In late October, prominent GOP leaders began pressuring Ike to play a more active role in the campaign. Barry Goldwater, claiming that Nixon's position was "precarious," told Ike on October 25 that "your full assistance will be needed to win." "Your record and achievements are at stake," the Arizona Senator declared. "This country cannot risk four years of Kennedy." Governor Nelson Rockefeller persuaded publisher Henry Luce to telegraph Ike and ask him to accompany Nixon when he campaigned in New York City in early November. William FitzGerald, in charge of analyzing the media for the GOP, warned Senator Hugh Scott on October 21 that Nixon's refusal to exploit Ike's great popularity was a serious mistake. "Failure to use this matchless asset to maximum use," FitzGerald prophesied, "might even cost the Republican party the 1960 election." The only way Nixon could win, FitzGerald told White House aide Robert Merriam, was for Eisenhower to "throw the weight of his own personality and sincerity directly into the fray, with no attitude of nonpartisanship." [68]

Ike needed little urging. Kennedy's attack on his foreign policy achievements angered him, and he was eager to strike back, but he did not want to step up his efforts without Nixon's approval. On October 26, he sent telegrams to GOP state chairmen across the country urging them to redouble their efforts for the Nixon-Lodge ticket. Two days later, he gave his first overtly political speech of the campaign at a Republican rally in Philadelphia. With obvious relish, he declared that the United States "is today militarily the strongest nation in the world, and then went on to accuse Kennedy of showing "amazing irresponsibility" in having "cruelly distorted the image of America." "The Nation's prestige," Ike affirmed, "is not measured by the stridency of a politician's voice; it is measured by proved accomplishment." [69]

On October 31, Richard Nixon, impressed by the effectiveness of the President's Philadelphia speech, came to the White House to lunch with Eisenhower and ask him to campaign actively during the last week of the election. The President quickly agreed, and the next day he attracted huge crowds as he barnstormed through New York City with Nixon and Lodge, stressing the maturity of the Republican candidates in contrast to Kennedy's inexperience. He described Nixon and Lodge as men who "know the problems that come up when the crises are developed by the Communists," men "in whom you can have confidence that they will never do anything that is rashly risking the cataclysm of war," men who "will always be proudly standing for every principle that has made the United States great." He received the greatest applause when he reminded audiences that the Republicans had ended the Korean War and kept the nation at peace during the last eight years. "Since that time we have had no single battle casualty in our Nation," he stated proudly. "Richard Nixon and Cabot

Lodge have advised and helped me well for eight years," he concluded. "They have my respect, my admiration, my friendship." [70]

Eisenhower went on to make similar appearances in Pennsylvania and Ohio, big industrial states where the outcome was in doubt. He drew the same big crowds, and he kept hammering away at the experience theme. "When the push of a button may mean obliteration of countless humans, the President of the United States must be forever on guard against any inclination on his part to impetuosity; to arrogance; to headlong action; to expediency; to facile maneuvers." In an election eve telecast from the White House, Eisenhower spoke of "the countless hours" he had spent in consultation with Nixon during moments of grave international crisis, and how impressed he had been with the Vice-President's judgment. He urged the voters to insure the continuation of his policies of peace by voting for Nixon, who, he promised, would give the nation "the most experienced and the most responsible leadership that we can produce." With these words, Ike helped remove the doubts raised in August when he so casually undercut Nixon's claim of being his righthand man. Eisenhower's intervention in the campaign, far more than Nixon's strident attacks or his appeals to ethnic minorities, stopped the drift to Kennedy and gave the Republican candidate the lift he so badly needed. [71]

X

Kennedy responded to the experience argument by focusing on the one foreign policy issue where he had the advantage— prestige. Ever since Sputnik, Americans had worried about their world image, and the events of 1960—especially the U-2 fiasco, the summit blow-up, and Khrushchev's aggressive conduct at the United Nations—had intensified this concern. The Harris poll showed that Kennedy had scored heavily in the televised debates when he charged that America's prestige in the world was declining; 62 percent of the viewers agreed with his position, compared to 38 percent who supported Nixon's contention that the U.S. was still the most respected nation in the world. When the Eisenhower administration refused to make public the USIA poll that Kennedy alluded to in the last debate, the Democratic candidate declared, "It is dangerous to hide the truth about our position abroad and to hide it for political purposes."

Sometime in late October, Kennedy aide Mike Feldman acquired copies of USIA polls showing that in fact American prestige had been slipping steadily throughout 1960. When Feldman informed Kennedy of his coup, the candidate decided not to risk charges of releasing classified information, and so, instead of presenting the information to the public directly, he passed the data on to the *New York Times*. The *Times* published the information in a series of articles beginning on October 25, and Kennedy then cited the newspaper articles to prove his case. The results of the first poll released simply confirmed Kennedy's earlier charge that people in nine of ten countries surveyed thought that within ten years the Soviet Union would surpass the United States as the world's leading power. Subsequent *Times* stories cited USIA analyses of both public opinion polls and foreign newspaper editorials which warned of a deepening "loss of confidence in American capacity for world leadership." In speech after speech, Kennedy referred to the USIA polls and analyses to accuse Nixon of misinforming the American people about the nation's standing in world opinion. "This deterioration abroad threatens our bases, our alliances, our security and the peace itself —and it is time we were respected once again throughout the world as a good neighbor," Kennedy declared. Though the Democratic candidate risked some backlash from those who resented the way he harped on national weakness (in Boston, a "Kennedy cocktail" was "America on the rocks"), his adroit exploitation of the prestige issue helped offset his reversals on Cuba and the offshore islands.[72]

Kennedy stayed away from other foreign policy issues in the last two weeks of the campaign. With Eisenhower taking an active part, he realized that foreign policy had become a Republican asset, and that he could only lose votes by engaging the President in debate on world affairs. Instead, Kennedy focused on the domestic issues of unemployment and economic stagnation, as he kept calling for the nation to begin moving again. The relative calm on the international scene played into Kennedy's hands. From the time Khrushchev left the United States in mid-October until election day, the world was quiet. The UN forces achieved temporary order in the Congo and Khrushchev refrained from making any new threats against the West. Castro provided the one moment of tension by claiming that an American invasion of Cuba was imminent when some 1,450 marines engaged in maneuvers at Guantanamo Bay; the incipient crisis quickly died down after Eisenhower stated that the United States was concerned only with defending its naval base and did not mean to threaten Cuba.[73]

Fearing a loss of public support once Ike entered the race, Kennedy campaigned virtually around the clock during the last few days before the election. Huge crowds came forth to greet him as reporters marveled at the enthusiasm he brought out, especially among women. In every gathering, there were the "jumpers" who leaped up to catch a glimpse of their hero (squealing, "I seen him, I seen him!" if they were successful) and the "grabbers" who burst through the cordons to touch him or squeeze his hand. People waited until the early hours of the morning to hear him; in Waterbury, Connecticut, a crowd of 20,000 was on hand at 2 A.M. when Kennedy arrived three hours behind schedule. But despite the frenzy, those around Kennedy could sense the tide turning back toward Nixon. "It was a strange, impalpable ebbing away," commented Arthur Schlesinger. Some attributed it to Ike, some to the end of the debates, some even to a reaction against the intense emotions Kennedy had aroused. The Gallup poll, which had had Kennedy leading by 6 percentage points, now indicated that the election was too close to predict a winner, with Nixon only one point behind. Gallup showed only 3 percent undecided, but the buttons that read "Neither" and the bumper stickers urging, "For President—Vote No," indicated that many Americans found both candidates left something to be desired "at a time of world tension such as mankind had seldom known, when two mighty coalitions . . . faced each other with weapons at the ready—the most frightful weapons of all times." [74]

In his last appearances, Kennedy stressed the crucial nature of the choice confronting the American electorate. The issue of this campaign, he told a Chicago audience, is "world freedom or world slavery, world peace or world war." He spoke of his desire to demonstrate to Khrushchev that "a new generation of Americans has taken over in this country—men who are committed to the maintenance of freedom in the 1960's." He dismissed Nixon's plan to send Eisenhower, Hoover, and Truman behind the Iron Curtain as a propaganda stunt and insisted that "words and gestures, talks and visits, will not bring peace in the future, just as they have failed to bring peace during the last eight years." In his final television speech to the nation, Kennedy referred to the United States as "the sentinel at the gate of freedom around the world." "If we succeed, freedom succeeds," he argued. "If we fail, freedom fails." Raising his Cold War rhetoric to its highest pitch, Kennedy confidently declared, "I believe that we can check the Communist advance, that we can turn it back, and that we can, in this century, provide for the ultimate victory of freedom over slavery." [75]

XI

On election day, Richard Nixon, just back from a last-minute trip to Alaska to fulfill his fifty-state promise, voted in his home town of Whittier, California, and then drove down to Tijuana for a Mexican meal while waiting for the returns to begin coming in. The early reports from the East could only depress him. Kennedy swept through the industrial states and seemed to be on the verge of a landslide triumph. Shortly after midnight, Pacific Coast time, Nixon appeared before his supporters in Los Angeles' Ambassador Hotel to admit that "if the present trend continues, Senator Kennedy will be the next President of the United States." Kennedy's aides, watching the returns on television with the Senator in Hyannis, grumbled at the Vice-President's refusal to concede, but the candidate commented, "Why should he? I wouldn't under these circumstances." By the early hours of the morning, Nixon's caution seemed justified. Though the Democrats held on to most of the South, they fared badly in the Middle and Far West. By the time Kennedy went to bed at four in the morning, his popular vote margin had dropped to less than one million and was fading rapidly.

When Kennedy awoke in the morning, the outcome was still in doubt, though the Secret Service had begun protecting him as the likely winner. At twelve-thirty, final returns from Minnesota gave Kennedy the state, and with it a clear majority in the Electoral College. Fifteen minutes later, Nixon sent Kennedy a congratulatory telegram and prepared a statement of concession that Herbert Klein read to reporters at the Ambassador Hotel. Watching on television, Kennedy agreed with his aides that Nixon showed poor form in refusing to appear in person to thank his supporters and concede defeat gracefully. "He went out the way he came in . . . no class," JFK commented.[76]

The full election returns revealed how close Kennedy's victory had been. He carried only 23 states with 303 electoral votes, to 26 states with 219 votes for Nixon (Mississippi and some electors in other southern states cast 15 votes for Virginia Senator Harry Byrd). Kennedy failed to win a majority of the popular vote, receiving 49.71 percent for a paper-thin lead of 113,000 over the Vice-President in a record turnout of more than 68 million voters. Even though Kennedy polled eight million more votes than Stevenson did in 1956, he ran behind his party by five million votes, trailing Nixon in 228 of the nation's 437 Congressional districts. The Democrats maintained their control in Congress despite the loss of 21 seats in the House and two in the Senate, demonstrating that they were still the majority party in the country. Political scientists analyzing the returns found it hardly surprising that the majority party had won; the remarkable fact was "that its return to power was accomplished by such a narrow margin." [77]

In such a close election, virtually any factor can be cited as the difference between victory and defeat. In the broadest sense, Kennedy won because he succeeded in rebuilding the old New Deal coalition that Eisenhower had shattered in 1952. JFK carried the big industrial states of the Northeast, and, thanks to Lyndon Johnson, held on to most of the South. Ethnic and religious factors were crucial. Kennedy won back two-thirds of the Catholics who had defected to Eisenhower in the 1950's, and he made impressive gains among Jewish and Negro voters with his liberal domestic program. A Republican postelection study revealed how effectively Kennedy appealed to Polish voters, who had voted Democratic in the past but had split evenly between Eisenhower and Stevenson. Attracted both by Kennedy's religion and his fervent anti-Communism, Polish voters in Buffalo, Chicago, and Detroit voted for him by margins ranging from 2–1 to as high as 9–1. Only the farmers failed to return to the Democratic fold, as Kennedy won just six states in the Middle and Far West. [78]

Most commentators focused on the religious issue in seeking an explanation for the election's outcome. The *New York Times, Newsweek,* and the *New Republic* all viewed Kennedy's ability to win nearly four out of every five Catholic votes as decisive. Louis Bean admitted in the *Nation* that Kennedy's religion cost him support in the predominantly Protestant West, but he felt that this loss was more than offset by Catholic gains in the states with large electoral votes, concluding that it was a case of "Catholic pride winning over Protestant prejudice." A more thorough survey by University of Michigan political scientists indicated that Kennedy may well have lost more than he gained from his religion. While nearly 80 percent of the Catholic vote went to Kennedy, they attributed part of this return to normal voting behavior helped by Eisenhower's absence from the ballot. The remaining Catholic votes that Kennedy attracted were canceled out by a nationwide dropoff of over 18 percent in normally Democratic Protestant votes.[79]

The controversy over the religious issue had obscured the influence of foreign policy on the outcome. Theodore White discounts the impact of international issues in his otherwise comprehensive account of the election. He barely mentions Khrushchev's visit to the United Nations, and he attributes Kennedy's victory entirely to domestic considerations. Contemporary analysts also ignored the world crisis in explaining why Nixon lost; only *Time* noted that Khrushchev's wild antics at the General Assembly meeting reduced the effectiveness of Nixon's boast that he alone could handle the Soviet leader. "It got so that anyone could wag a finger at Khrushchev," *Time* concluded. Ted Sorensen cites foreign policy as one of the seven reasons for Kennedy's victory, and he stresses that American defeats abroad, from the U-2 flight to the rise of Castro, cast doubt on Republican claims that all was well in the world. "Nixon, dependent on Eisenhower's goodwill, and defensive of the Republican record," Sorensen writes, "was required to make rosy assertions about American leadership and prestige abroad which Kennedy continually exploded."[80]

An even stronger case can be made for the argument that Kennedy nearly lost the election by his inept handling of foreign policy issues. At the outset, he rightly sensed that the deepening global crisis contradicted Republican claims of peace in the world, and as long as he stuck to the generalized charge of declining American prestige, he had an effective point. But once he became specific, as he did on the offshore islands and Cuba, he immediately faced a blistering counterattack from Nixon, who welcomed the chance to debate concrete world issues. In postmortems on the election, Kennedy's aides admitted that his stand on Quemoy and Matsu had been a "mistake." It would take months, they said, to explain Kennedy's sophisticated position compared to Nixon's "emotional" stand on the offshore islands. The reversal Kennedy was forced to make on this point, together with his similar turnabout on Cuba, boosted the impression of Kennedy that Nixon sought to develop—as a callow, inexperienced politician who could not give the nation the wise leadership that the crucial times demanded. In the debates, generally conceded to be Kennedy's most successful form of campaigning, Nixon came out ahead in the last encounter, the only one devoted exclusively to foreign policy. Nixon's resurgence dated from the time he exploited Kennedy's stand on Quemoy-Matsu and Cuba. The falloff in support for the Democratic candidate during the last week can be traced to the effective way Eisenhower questioned his ability to lead the nation in world affairs. Foreign policy, rather than contributing to Kennedy's victory, cost him votes and transformed a nearly certain triumph into a cliffhanger.[81]

In retrospect, the most astonishing thing about the foreign policy debate in 1960 is how little difference there was between the two candidates. Both men offered themselves to the voters as ardent Cold Warriors, differing only in their assessment of how well the United States was doing in the mortal contest with the Soviet Union. Neither candidate offered a clear-cut alternative to the prevailing hard line, and Kennedy in particular called for intensified efforts to halt the Communist tide. For all the rhetoric of a new generation of leadership, Kennedy offered no new departures in American foreign policy. Instead, he simply expounded the doctrines of Dean Acheson and John Foster Dulles in his constant description of a world divided between freedom and slavery and in his relentless hammering at the need to get the nation moving again in world affairs. The *Nation,* which had reluctantly supported his candidacy, urged him "to forget the political garbage of a sorry campaign and to resolve to deal with the problems of the United States in an adult fashion." As President, he would face the realities of a grave world crisis, not the stereotypes of the past. Like Roosevelt, Truman, and Eisenhower, he would have to learn to turn his back on the myth of a world torn between good and evil which had been foisted on the American people in every election since 1940.[82]

NOTES

List of Abbreviations Used

BAS   *Bulletin* of the Atomic Scientists
DDE   Dwight David Eisenhower
RNCP   Republican National Committee Papers

Chapter 1

1. Foster Rhea Dulles, *America's Rise to World Power, 1898–1954* (New York, 1954), pp. 262–66; Walter LaFeber, *America, Russia, and the Cold War, 1945–1971,* 2d ed. (New York, 1972), pp. 77–78, 104–5; Barton J. Bernstein, "Election of 1952," in Arthur M. Schlesinger, Jr., and Fred L. Israel, eds., *History of American Presidential Elections: 1789–1968,* 4 vols. (New York, 1971), IV, 3223–24.
2. LaFeber, *America,* pp. 108–14, 118–22; David Rees, *Korea: The Limited War* (New York, 1964), pp. 310–20; Ronald J. Caridi, *The Korean War and American Politics: The Republican Party as a Case Study* (Philadelphia, 1968), pp. 176–86; *Time,* LIX (March 10, 1952), 21; *ibid.* (May 5, 1952), 30; *Newsweek,* XXXIX (May 19, 1952), 37; *Public Papers of the Presidents: Truman, 1952,* p. 321.
3. Harry S Truman, *Memoirs,* 2 vols. (Garden City, N.Y., 1956), II, 306–13; Richard G. Hewlett and Francis Duncan, *Atomic Shield, 1947–1952* (University Park, Pa., 1969), pp. 535–37, 542–45.

4. LaFeber, *America,* pp. 93–94; Robert Griffith, *The Politics of Fear: Joseph R. McCarthy and the Senate* (Lexington, Ky., 1970), pp. 52–74, 123–31.

5. Cabell Phillips, *The Truman Presidency: The History of a Triumphant Succession* (New York, 1966), pp. 402–14; *Time,* LIX (February 18, 1952), 18–19.

6. William S. White, *The Taft Story* (New York, 1954), pp. 83–87, 97–104, 143–45, 158–62.

7. Robert A. Taft, *A Foreign Policy for Americans* (Garden City, N.Y., 1951), pp. 6–7, 17–18, 48–60, 64–67, 72–78, 117–19.

8. *Time,* LIX (February 25, 1952), 24; *ibid.* (June 2, 1952), 17–20; *New York Times,* November 25, 1951; *Vital Speeches,* XVIII (March 15, 1952), 332; *U.S. News and World Report,* XXXII (March 14, 1952), 50–61; *New Republic,* CXXVI (April 7, 1952), 13–15.

9. *Time,* LIX (January 7, 1952), 12; *ibid.* (March 31, 1952), 22; Joseph W. Martin, *My First Fifty Years in Politics* (New York, 1960), pp. 168–69.

10. *New Republic,* CXXVI (March 17, 1952), 3; *Newsweek,* XL (July 20, 1952), 23; William J. Miller, *Henry Cabot Lodge* (New York, 1967), p. 208.

11. *New York Times,* November 7, 1951; Arthur Krock, *Memoirs: Sixty Years on the Firing Line* (New York, 1968), pp. 267–69; Arthur Krock, *The Consent of the Governed and Other Deceits* (Boston, 1971), p. 148.

12. Miller, *Lodge,* pp. 216–22; John Mason Brown, *Through These Men: Some Aspects of Our Passing History* (New York, 1956), p. 161; Merlo J. Pusey, *Eisenhower the President* (New York, 1956), pp. 6–8; Lucius Clay memoir, Columbia Oral History Project.

13. Murray Kempton, "The Underestimation of Dwight D. Eisenhower," *Esquire,* LXVIII (September, 1967), 108; Cyrus L. Sulzberger, *The Last of the Giants* (New York, 1970), p. 323; C. L. Sulzberger, *A Long Row of Candles: Memoirs and Diaries, 1934–1954* (New York, 1969), p. 672.

14. Dwight D. Eisenhower, *Mandate for Change, 1953–1956* (Garden City, N.Y., 1963), pp. 17–18, 25; Arthur Larson, *Eisenhower: The President Nobody Knew* (New York, 1968), p. 68; Dwight D. Eisenhower, *At Ease: Stories I Tell My Friends* (Garden City, N.Y., 1967), pp. 371–72; Eisenhower to Clay, December 27, 1951, Dwight D. Eisenhower Papers, Dwight D. Eisenhower Li-

brary, Abilene, Kansas, Pre-Presidential Files, Box 22; Sulzberger, *Long Row,* pp. 700–703.

15. Pusey, *Eisenhower,* p. 10; Miller, *Lodge,* p. 228; *Time,* LIX (January 14, 1952), 15.

16. *New York Times,* January 7, 1952; *New Republic,* CXXVI (February 18, 1952), 7; *Nation,* CLXXIV (January 19, 1952), 51; Hoffman to Eisenhower, March 4, 1952, DDE Papers, Pre-Pres. Box 52; Roberts to Eisenhower, February 5, 18, and 19, 1952, and Robinson to Eisenhower, February 18, 1952, DDE Papers, Pre-Pres. Box 91.

17. Eisenhower to Hoffman, February 9 and April 1, 1952, DDE Papers, Pre-Pres. Box 52; Eisenhower, *Mandate,* p. 21.

18. *Newsweek,* XXXIX (March 10, 1952), 25; *ibid.* (March 24, 1952), 33; *ibid.* (March 31, 1952), 19–20; *Time,* LIX (March 10, 1952), 23; *ibid.* (March 24, 1952), 19; *ibid.* (March 31, 1952), 19–20.

19. Sulzberger, *Long Row,* pp. 735, 736; *Time,* LIX (March 31, 1952), 20; Hoffman to Eisenhower, April 18, 1952, DDE Papers, Pre-Pres. Box 52; Roberts to Eisenhower, March 26, 1952, and Eisenhower to Roberts, April 1, 1952, DDE Papers, Pre-Pres. Box 91.

20. *Newsweek,* XXXIX (April 14, 1952), 23, 27; *ibid.* (April 21, 1952), 27; *Time,* LIX (April 21, 1952), 21.

21. *Ibid.* (May 12, 1952), 27; *ibid.* (May 26, 1952), 24; *Newsweek,* XXXIX (April 28, 1952), 25–26; *ibid.* (May 26, 1952), 30.

22. Truman, *Memoirs,* II, 489–91; Walter Johnson, *How We Drafted Adlai Stevenson* (New York, 1955), pp. 18–19; George Ball, "With AES in War and Politics," in Edward P. Doyle, ed., *As We Knew Adlai* (New York, 1966), p. 147.

23. Joseph Bruce Gorman, *Kefauver: A Political Biography* (New York, 1971), pp. 118, 128–29; *Public Papers of Presidents: Truman, 1952,* pp. 132, 137, 225; *Time,* LIX (March 24, 1952), 20–21; *ibid.* (April 7, 1952), 19–20.

24. Gorman, *Kefauver,* pp. 132–33; *Time,* LIX (March 24, 1952), 20–24; Charles Bartlett, "The Crusading Kefauver," *Nation,* CLXXIV (May 3, 1952), 427–28; Kefauver to William Randolph Hearst, Jr., April 2, 1952, Estes Kefauver Papers, University of Tennessee Library, Knoxville, Tennessee, Series 1, Box 22.

25. *Time,* LIX (April 28, 1952), 21, 23; *ibid.* (May 19, 1952), 29, 31; *Newsweek,* XXXIX (May 26, 1952), 27–28; Harry Conn, "What's Behind the Handshake?" *New Republic,* CXXVI (June 9, 1952), 12–14; *Nation,* CLXXIV (May 3, 1952), 414.

26. *Newsweek,* XXXIX (April 28, 1952), 25; Johnson, *How We Drafted Stevenson,* pp. 20–30.
27. *Newsweek,* XXXIX (April 14, 1952), 35; *Time,* LIX (January 28, 1952), 16–19; Adlai E. Stevenson, "Korea in Perspective," *Foreign Affairs,* XXX (April 1952), 349–60.
28. Kenneth S. Davis, *The Politics of Honor: A Biography of Adlai E. Stevenson* (New York, 1967), pp. 253–70; *Time,* LIX (May 12, 1952), 26; Ball, "With AES," p. 148; Stevenson to Eric Sevareid, June 20, 1952, Eric Sevareid Papers, Library of Congress, Box 25.
29. *Newsweek,* XXXIX (March 10, 1952), 27; *New Republic,* CXXVI (April 28, 1952), 5; *ibid.* (June 9, 1952), 5; William V. Shannon, "Averell Harriman—The Cold Warrior," *New Republic,* CXXVI (June 16, 1952), 13–14.
30. Louis L. Gerson, *John Foster Dulles* (New York, 1967), pp. 56–62, 79; *Time,* LIX (March 31, 1952), 23; Ferdinand Mayer to Dulles, December 3, 1951, Dulles Papers, Box 143.
31. John Foster Dulles, "A Policy of Boldness," *Life,* XXXII (May 19, 1952), 146, 148, 151–52; *Vital Speeches,* XVIII (June 1, 1952), 494; *Time,* LIX (May 19, 1952), 23.
32. John Foster Dulles, *War or Peace* (New York, 1950), p. 243; Dulles, "Policy of Boldness," pp. 152, 154, 157, 160; text of Dulles speech at Baltimore, June 10, 1952, Dulles Papers, Box 21.
33. Hughes memoir, Dulles Oral History Project.
34. Gerson, *Dulles,* pp. 68–70; Richard Goold-Adams, *The Time of Power: A Reappraisal of John Foster Dulles* (London, 1962), p. 63; Eustace Seligman memoir, Dulles Oral History Project; Eisenhower to Dulles, April 15, 1952, Dulles Papers, Box 144; Eisenhower, *Mandate,* p. 23.
35. Gerson, *Dulles,* pp. 75–77; Eisenhower memoir, Dulles Oral History Project; Sulzberger, *Long Row,* p. 746.
36. Gerson, *Dulles,* pp. 81–82; Dulles to Eisenhower, May 20, 1952, DDE Papers, Pre-Pres. Box 33.
37. Eisenhower to Roberts, May 19, 1952, DDE Papers, Pre-Pres. Box 91; *New York Times,* June 2 and 5, 1952; *Vital Speeches,* XVIII (June 15, 1952), 515; *Time,* LIX (June 16, 1952), 19–22; *New Republic,* CXXVI (June 16, 1952), 3–4.
38. *New York Times,* June 6, 1952; *Newsweek,* XXXIX (June 16, 1952), 25.
39. Eisenhower, *Mandate,* pp. 36–37; *New York Times,* June 12 and 15, 1952; *Time,* LIX (June 23, 1952), 17.

40. *New York Times,* June 16, 1952; Edwin A. Lahey, " 'Ike,' an In-nocent at Home," *New Republic,* CXXVI (June 30, 1952), 15–16; Joseph C. Harsch, "One View of Eisenhower," *Nation,* CLXXIV (June 7, 1952), 542–43; David Schoenbrun, "Five Weeks That Made a Politician," *Reporter,* VII (August 5, 1952), 7–10; *Time,* LIX (June 16, 1952), 23; *Newsweek,* XXXIX (June 9, 1952), 26; *ibid.* (June 30, 1952), 27.

41. *New York Times,* June 2, 1952; *Vital Speeches,* XVIII (June 15, 1952), 517–19.

42. *Ibid.* (July 1, 1952), 549–50; *New York Times,* June 20, 25, and 30, 1952.

43. *Ibid.,* June 24, 1952; *Newsweek,* XXXIX (June 30, 1952), 62; *ibid.,* XL (July 7, 1952), 18; *Time,* LIX (June 30, 1952), 15.

44. Dulles to Eisenhower, June 17, 1952, Dulles Papers, Box 483; Dulles memorandum, June 24, 1952, Eisenhower to Dulles, June 20, 1952, unsent draft letter, Dulles to Eisenhower, June 23, 1952, and Dulles to Eisenhower, June 24, 1952, Dulles Papers, Box 483; *New York Times,* June 25, 1952.

45. *Time,* LX (July 7, 1952), 13; *New York Times,* June 27, and July 2 and 3, 1952; *New Republic,* CXXVII (July 7, 1952), 5.

46. *Newsweek,* XXXIX (June 23, 1952), 21; *Time,* LIX (June 30, 1952), 13; Eisenhower, *Mandate,* pp. 37–38.

47. *Vital Speeches,* XVIII (July 15, 1952), 578–81; *ibid.,* 584–86; *New York Times,* June 11 and July 10, 1952; *Time,* LX (July 14, 1952), 23; *ibid.* (July 21, 1952), 14; *Newsweek,* XL (July 21, 1952), 22.

48. Dulles to Millikin, June 20, 1952, Dulles platform drafts, June 20, July 1, 3, 4, and 8, 1952, Dulles Papers, Box 483; *Time,* LX (July 21, 1952), 14; *New York Times,* July 8, 1952.

49. Kirk H. Porter and Donald Bruce Johnson, eds., *National Party Platforms, 1840–1956* (Urbana, Ill., 1956), pp. 497–99.

50. Sulzberger, *Long Row,* p. 771; *New York Times,* July 9, 1952; *New Republic,* CXXVII (July 21, 1952), 5.

51. *New York Times,* July 11, 1952; *Newsweek,* XL (July 21, 1952), 30; Sulzberger, *Long Row,* pp. 767–70; Porter and Johnson, *National Party Platforms,* p. 499.

52. White, *Taft Story,* pp. 174–78; *Time,* LX (July 14, 1952), 17; *ibid.* (July 21, 1952), 18; *New York Times,* July 10 and 12, 1952; Richard Rovere, *Affairs of State: The Eisenhower Years* (New York, 1956), p. 32.

53. Sherman Adams, *Firsthand Report: The Story of the Eisenhower*

Administration (New York, 1961), p. 34; *Time,* LX (July 21, 1952), 19–20; *Vital Speeches,* XVIII (August 1, 1952), 610–11.

54. *New York Times,* July 12, 1952; *Newsweek,* XL (July 21, 1952), 31; White, *Taft Story,* p. 183; Rovere, *Affairs of State,* pp. 31–32.

55. *Time,* LX (July 21, 1952), 21; *Newsweek,* XL (July 28, 1952), 18–20; *New York Times,* July 13, 17, 21, and 22, 1952.

56. *New York Times,* July 24, 1952; Porter and Johnson, *National Party Platforms,* pp. 475–76.

57. *Vital Speeches,* XVIII (August 1, 1952), 613–15; *Time,* LX (July 28, 1952), 8–9; *New York Times,* July 22 and 23, 1952; *Newsweek,* XL (August 4, 1952), 24.

58. Truman, *Memoirs,* II, 496; *Time,* LX (August 4, 1952), 10–11; *Newsweek,* XL (August 4, 1952), 16–19; *New York Times,* July 26, 1952.

59. Adlai E. Stevenson, ed., *Major Campaign Speeches of Adlai E. Stevenson, 1952* (New York, 1953), p. 10; *New Republic,* CXXVII (August 4, 1952), 1, 4; *Newsweek,* XL (August 4, 1952), 24.

60. Dean Acheson, *Present at the Creation: My Years in the State Department* (New York, 1969), p. 686; *New York Times,* July 27, 1952.

61. *Newsweek,* XL (August 4, 1952), 15; *New York Times,* July 27, 1952; McGeorge Bundy, "November, 1952: Imperatives of Foreign Policy," *Foreign Affairs,* XXXI (October 1952), 1–14.

Chapter 2

1. Dwight D. Eisenhower, *Mandate for Change: 1953–1956* (Garden City, N.Y., 1963), pp. 49–53; *New York Times,* July 23, 1952; *Time,* LX (August 11, 1952), 16; *Newsweek,* XL (August 11, 1952), 20–21; Vandenberg to Adams and others, August 27, 1952, DDE Papers, GF 109–A–6.

2. Harold Lavine, *Smoke-Filled Rooms: The Confidential Papers of Robert Humphreys* (Englewood Cliffs, N.J., 1970), pp. 34–35, 37, 38, 44–45, 55, 69; Weekly Report No. 21, President Research Service, undated, Sherman Adams Papers, Box 37.

3. *New York Times,* August 9 and 12, 1952; *Time,* LX (August 18, 1952), 14.

4. "Vote for Ike," pamphlet, DDE Papers, GF 109–A–6; untitled pamphlet, Adams Papers, Box 37; *Newsweek,* XL (August 25, 1952), 21.

5. Dulles speech draft, August 16, 1952, and Dulles to Vandenberg,

August 16, 1952, Dulles Papers, Series IX, Korea Folder; Pinkley to Hoffman, July 29, 1952, DDE Papers, OF 138–C–4; Dahlfred to Adams, August 26, 1952, DDE Papers, GF 109–A–6.

6. Dulles to Eisenhower, August 21, 1952, Dulles Papers, Box 483; *New York Times,* August 22, 1952; *Newsweek,* XL (September 1, 1952), 14.

7. Stevenson to Baruch, July 29, 1952, Baruch Papers, Box 108; *New York Times,* July 31, 1952.

8. *Newsweek,* XL (August 11, 1952), 19–20; *Time,* LX (August 11, 1952), 17; *New York Times,* August 2 and 9, 1952; memorandum by Stephen A. Mitchell, August 7, 1952, Stephen A. Mitchell Papers, Truman Library, Box 36.

9. *Newsweek,* XL (August 18, 1952), 18; *ibid.* (September 22, 1952), 33; Kenneth S. Davis, *The Politics of Honor: A Biography of Adlai E. Stevenson* (New York, 1967), pp. 277–78.

10. *New York Times,* August 3 and 21, 1952; *Newsweek,* XL (August 11, 1952), 22.

11. Truman to Benton, August 12, 1952, Oscar Chapman Papers, Harry S. Truman Library, Box 87; *New York Times,* August 7 and 13, 1952; Cabell Phillips, *The Truman Presidency: The History of a Triumphant Succession* (New York, 1966), p. 425; *Newsweek,* XL (August 25, 1952), 19–20.

12. *New York Times,* August 13 and 15, 1952; *Public Papers of Presidents: Truman, 1952,* p. 517; *Time,* LX (August 25, 1952).

13. *New York Times,* August 17 and 22, 1952; *Public Papers of Presidents: Truman, 1952,* p. 530.

14. *New York Times,* August 26, 1952; *Newsweek,* XL (September 1, 1952), 19; *Time,* LX (September 8, 1952), 21.

15. *New York Times,* August 26, 1952.

16. Thruston B. Morton memoir, Dulles Oral History Project; Dulles speech, August 27, 1952, Dulles Papers, Speech File; *New York Times,* August 27 and 28, 1952.

17. *Ibid.,* August 26, 27, 30 and September 7, 1952; Jean-Jacques Servan Schreiber, "Europe Views Our Campaign," *Reporter,* VII (October 14, 1952), 39.

18. *New Republic,* CXXVII (August 25, 1952), 6; *Time,* LX (September 1, 1952), 9.

19. Adlai E. Stevenson, ed., *Major Campaign Speeches of Adlai E. Stevenson, 1952* (New York, 1953), pp. 53–56; *Public Papers of Presidents: Truman, 1952,* pp. 550–51.

20. *New York Times,* September 4 and 5, 1952; *Vital Speeches,* XVIII

(September 15, 1952), 708–10; *Time,* LX (September 15, 1952), 22–23.

21. Thruston Morton memoir and Dwight D. Eisenhower memoir, Dulles Oral History Project; Louis L. Gerson, *The Hyphenate in Recent American Politics and Diplomacy* (Lawrence, Kans., 1964), pp. 189–90; Louis L. Gerson, *John Foster Dulles* (New York, 1967), p. 88; *New Republic,* CXXVII (September 15, 1952), 3.

22. Emmet John Hughes, *The Ordeal of Power: A Political Memoir of the Eisenhower Years* (New York, 1963), pp. 29–31, 36–37, 70; Jackson to Vandenberg and others, September 10, 1952, DDE Papers, OF 138–C–4; *New York Times,* October 12, 1952; Jackson to Gabriel Hauge, October 3, 1952, Stephen Benedict Papers; Gerson, *Hyphenate,* p. 190.

23. *Ibid.,* pp. 192–93; *New York Times,* September 8, 18, and October 6, 1952.

24. Gerson, *Hyphenate,* pp. 195–96.

25. Dwight Eisenhower to Earl Eisenhower, August 30, 1952, DDE Papers, Pre-Inaugural Files, Box 12; Merlo J. Pusey, *Eisenhower the President* (New York, 1956), 26; Hughes, *Ordeal,* pp. 19–21; Robert Cutler, *No Time for Rest* (Boston, 1966), p. 272; *Newsweek,* XL (October 6, 1952), 33; *New York Times,* September 17, 1952.

26. Cutler, *No Time,* pp. 275–78, 282–84; Richard Rovere memoir, Dulles Oral History Project; *New Republic,* CXXVII (October 13, 1952), 3; *Newsweek,* XL (October 27, 1952), 35; *Time,* LX (September 1, 1952), 11; *ibid.* (November 3, 1952), 23–24; Richard Rovere, *Affairs of State: The Eisenhower Years* (New York, 1956), 38.

27. *Time,* LX (August 18, 1952), 11; *ibid.* (September 15, 1952), 21; *Newsweek,* XL (September 29, 1952), 28.

28. William S. White, *The Taft Story* (New York, 1954), pp. 184–93; Eisenhower, *Mandate,* p. 64; *Time,* LX (September 22, 1952), 24; *Newsweek,* XL (September 22, 1952), 24; *New York Times,* September 13 and October 11, 1952; Gerard Lambert to Sherman Adams, September 18, 1952, DDE Papers, GF 109–A–6.

29. *New York Times,* August 23, 1952; *Newsweek,* XL (September 1, 1952), 16.

30. Lodge to Eisenhower, August 21, 1952, and Pulliam to Frank

Carlson, August 4, 1952, DDE Papers, Pre-Inaugural Files, Boxes 5 and 6; Kohler to Adams, August 28, 1952, DDE Papers, OF 138–C–4.

31. *New York Times,* September 10, 1952; Adams to Kohler, September 9, 1952, DDE Papers, OF 138–C–4.

32. *New York Times,* October 4 and 18, 1952; Cutler, *No Time,* pp. 287–88; Sherman Adams, *Firsthand Report: The Story of the Eisenhower Administration* (New York, 1961), pp. 31–32.

33. *New York Times,* August 1, October 11, and November 3, 1952; *Newsweek,* XL (August 11, 1952), 24; *Nation,* CLXXV (October 4, 1952), 284.

34. Joseph W. Martin, *My First Fifty Years in Politics* (New York, 1960), p. 170; MM to Mr. J., October 2, 1952, and Edwin Clark to Eisenhower, October 28, 1952, DDE Papers, OF 138–C–4; Eisenhower-Nixon Research Service to Adams, October 28, 1952, Adams Papers, Box 37.

35. Barton J. Bernstein, "Election of 1952," in Arthur M. Schlesinger, Jr., and Fred L. Israel, eds., *History of American Presidential Elections, 1789–1968,* 4 vols. (New York, 1971), IV, 3243; Richard M. Nixon, *Six Crises* (Garden City, N.Y., 1962), pp. 85–86; Hughes, *Ordeal,* p. 39; *New York Times,* September 20, 1952; *Newsweek,* XL (September 29, 1952), 23; memorandum of conversation with Bernard Baruch by Tex McCrary, September 21, 1952, and Eisenhower-Nixon Research Service to Adams, September 21, 1952, Adams Papers, Box 37.

36. Cutler, *No Time,* pp. 284–86; Elmo Conley to Adams, September 23, 1952, DDE Papers, OF 138–C–4; *Time,* LX (October 6, 1952), 20–21.

37. Nixon, *Six Crises,* pp. 120–24; Garry Wills, *Nixon Agonistes: The Crisis of the Self-Made Man* (Boston, 1970), pp. 97–114; *New York Times,* September 25, 1952.

38. *Ibid.,* September 28, October 9, 12, 14, 15, 17, and 22, 1952; *Time,* LX (October 20, 1952), 24.

39. *Newsweek,* XL (October 13, 1952), 27; Stevenson to Baruch, August 18, 1952, Baruch Papers, Box 110; George Ball, "With AES in War and Politics," in Edward P. Doyle, ed., *As We Knew Adlai* (New York, 1966), p. 150.

40. David E. Lilienthal, *The Journals of David E. Lilienthal,* 4 vols. (New York, 1964–1970), III, 337; *New Republic,* CXXVII (Septem-

ber 22, 1952), 3; John Mason Brown, *Through These Men: Some Aspects of Our Passing History* (New York, 1956), p. 31; *Time,* XL (October 27, 1952), 31–33; *New York Times,* October 7, 1952.

41. *Ibid.,* August 28 and September 19, 1952; Stevenson, *Campaign Speeches,* pp. 21, 37, 127–28.

42. *Ibid.,* pp. 91–99.

43. *Newsweek,* XL (September 22, 1952), 120; Royal to Eisenhower, August 19, 1952, DDE Papers, Pre-Inaug. Files, Box 11; *Reporter,* VII (October 14, 1952), 5; *New York Times,* September 14, 1952; *Nation,* CLXXV (October 18, 1952), 341–42.

44. State Department, *Bulletin,* XXVII (September 22, 1952), 423–27; *ibid.* (October 20, 1952), 595–99; Phillips, *Truman Presidency,* p. 425 n; Dean Acheson, *Present at the Creation: My Years in the State Department* (New York, 1969), pp. 699–700; *New York Times,* October 27, 1952.

45. *Newsweek,* XL (October 13, 1952), 25; *New York Times,* September 30, 1952; *Public Papers of Presidents: Truman, 1952,* pp. 569, 590, 636, 708–9.

46. *Ibid.,* pp. 634, 709–11; *New York Times,* October 18, 1952.

47. *Time,* LX (October 13, 1952), 21; *ibid.* (October 27, 1952), 23; *Newsweek,* XL (October 20, 1952), 23; Eisenhower-Nixon Research Service, Weekly Report No. 30, October 22, 1952, Adams Papers, Box 37; *New Republic,* CXXVII (September 22, 1952), 3.

48. Lambert to Adams, September 18 and October 30, 1952, DDE Papers, GF 109–A–6; *Time,* LX (September 15, 1952), 21; *ibid.* (September 22, 1952), 25.

49. *Vital Speeches,* XVIII (September 15, 1952), 708–10; *New York Times,* September 23, 1952; *Time,* LX (October 6, 1952), 22.

50. *New York Times,* October 3, 4, and 6, 1952; Jackson to Hauge, October 3, 1952, Benedict Papers.

51. *New York Times,* October 9, 1952.

52. *Ibid.,* October 7, 1952; *Time,* LX (October 27, 1952), 35; *New Republic,* CXXVII (November 17, 1952), 3; *Newsweek,* XL (October 20, 1952), 132.

53. *Nation,* CLXXV (October 11, 1952), 315; *New York Times,* September 28, 1952; Stevenson, *Campaign Speeches,* pp. 182–85.

54. *New York Times,* October 16 and 17, 1952; Stevenson, *Campaign Speeches,* pp. 254, 261–62; *Public Papers of Presidents: Truman, 1952,* pp. 979, 980, 1033.

55. *Ibid.,* pp. 813, 831, 848–51, 929–30.

56. *New York Times,* October 25, 1952.
57. Adams, *Firsthand Report,* p. 44; *Newsweek,* XL (November 3, 1952), 26; *New Republic,* CXXVII (November 10, 1952), 5–6; Marquis Childs, *Eisenhower: Captive Hero* (New York, 1958), p. 159.
58. Eisenhower, *Mandate,* p. 72 n; Lavine, *Smoke-Filled Rooms,* p. 5; Royal to Eisenhower, October 22, 1952, DDE Papers, Pre-Inaug. Files, Box 11; Zanuck to George Murphy, October 24, 1952, DDE Papers, OF 138–C–4; Adams, *Firsthand Report,* pp. 42–44; Burroughs to Eisenhower and Adams, October 22, 1952, Benedict Papers; Hughes, *Ordeal,* pp. 33–35.
59. *New York Times,* October 26, 27, and November 1, 1952.
60. Stevenson, *Campaign Speeches,* p. xxvii; *New York Times,* October 26, 1952; *Newsweek,* XL (November 3, 1952), 27.
61. *Public Papers of Presidents: Truman, 1952,* pp. 945–46, 1011, 1044, 1046.
62. *New York Times,* October 28 and 30, 1952; *Newsweek,* XL (November 10, 1952), 27–28; Stevenson, *Campaign Speeches,* pp. 298–304.
63. David Rees, *Korea: The Limited War* (New York, 1964), pp. 385–86.
64. Bernstein, "Election of 1952," pp. 3246–47; *Time,* LX (November 3, 1952), 21.
65. *New York Times,* October 28, 29, and 30, November 1 and 4, 1952.
66. *Ibid.,* October 27 and November 3, 1952; *Time,* LX (October 27, 1952), 27; *ibid.* (November 10, 1952), 26; *Newsweek,* XL (November 3, 1952), 25, 35.
67. *New York Times,* October 25, 1952; Dulles to Clay, November 3, 1952, and Dulles to Eisenhower, November 3, 1952, Dulles Papers, Box 483.
68. *New York Times,* November 5 and 9, 1952; *Time,* LX (November 10, 1952), 21; *Newsweek,* XL (November 17, 1952), 28.
69. *Time,* LX (November 17, 1952), 24; Louis Harris, *Is There a Republican Majority?: Political Trends, 1952–1956* (New York, 1954), pp. 5, 93, 160–61; Samuel Lubell, *Revolt of the Moderates* (New York, 1956), p. 272; Murray Kempton, *America Comes of Middle Age* (Boston, 1963), p. 245.
70. *Time,* LX (November 10, 1952), 26–27; *New Republic,* CXXVII (November 17, 1952), 3.
71. *Newsweek,* XL (November 10, 1952), 3; Stuart Gerry Brown,

Conscience in Politics: Adlai E. Stevenson in the 1950's (Syracuse, 1961), p. 20; Harris, *Republican Majority?*, pp. 25–31; Ronald J. Caridi, *The Korean War and American Politics: The Republican Party as a Case Study* (Philadelphia, 1968), pp. 209–14; Richard L. Neuberger, "The West—Eyes on Korea," *New Republic,* cxxvii (November 17, 1952), 7; Kenneth N. Waltz, "Electoral Punishment and Foreign Policy Crises," in James N. Rosenau, ed., *Domestic Sources of Foreign Policy* (New York, 1967), pp. 278–82.

72. *Nation,* clxxv (November 15, 1952), 438, 445; *ibid.* (November 22, 1952), 466; Angus Campbell, Gerald Gurin, and Warren E. Miller, *The Voter Decides* (Evanston, Ill., 1954), pp. 56–58; *Newsweek,* xl (November 17, 1952), 26.

73. Gerson, *Dulles,* p. 86; Gerson, *Hyphenate,* p. 199; Lubell, *Revolt,* p. 80.

74. *Ibid.,* p. 25; Henry Luce memoir, Dulles Oral History Project.

75. *New York Times,* October 23, 1952; *New Republic,* cxxvii (October 27, 1952), 3.

Chapter 3

1. Malcolm Moos, "Election of 1956," in Arthur M. Schlesinger, Jr., and Fred L. Israel, eds., *History of American Presidential Elections, 1789–1968,* 4 vols. (New York, 1971), iv, 3341–42; William S. White, "What Bill Knowland Stands For," *New Republic,* cxxxiv (February 27, 1956), 7–10; Gordon Harrison, "The New Conservatism," *Nation,* clxxxii (June 2, 1956), 466–68.

2. Bill Lawrence, *Six Presidents, Too Many Wars* (New York, 1972), pp. 207–99; Sherman Adams, *Firsthand Report: The Story of the Eisenhower Administration* (New York, 1961), pp. 183–92.

3. *Ibid.,* pp. 221–28; *Time,* lxvii (January 2, 1956), 10; *ibid.* (February 20, 1956), 15.

4. *Public Papers of Presidents: Eisenhower, 1956,* pp. 265, 273–79; Dwight D. Eisenhower, *Waging Peace, 1956–1961* (Garden City, N.Y., 1965), pp. 4–5.

5. *Public Papers of Presidents: Eisenhower, 1956,* pp. 266, 287, 303; *Newsweek,* xlvii (March 12, 1956), 30–31; *ibid.* (March 19, 1956), 31–32; *Time,* lxvii (March 26, 1956), 21; *ibid.* (May 7, 1956), 35; Lawrence, *Six Presidents,* pp. 212–18.

6. Memorandum by Mitchell, November 8, 1958, Stephen A. Mitchell Papers, Harry S. Truman Library, Box 36; Mitchell to Hyman

Raskin, February 18 and June 3, 1955, Mitchell Papers, Box 38; Kenneth S. Davis, *The Politics of Honor: A Biography of Adlai E. Stevenson* (New York, 1967), pp. 295–301; Adlai E. Stevenson, *The New America*, Seymour E. Harris, John Bartlow Martin, and Arthur Schlesinger, Jr., eds. (New York, 1957), p. xiii.

7. Stevenson to Truman, July 5, 1955, Mitchell Papers, Box 36; Davis, *Politics of Honor*, p. 318; Charles A. H. Thomson and Frances M. Shattuck, *The 1956 Presidential Campaign* (Washington, 1960), pp. 25–28; *Life*, xxxix (November 28, 1955), 118.

8. Joseph Bruce Gorman, *Kefauver: A Political Biography* (New York, 1971), pp. 216–23; *Reporter*, xiii (December 29, 1955), 6–7; *Nation*, clxxxii (January 28, 1956), 61–62; *ibid.* (February 18, 1956), 131.

9. Gorman, *Kefauver*, pp. 224–30; *Time*, lxvii (February 6, 1956), 19; *ibid.* (April 2, 1956), 17–18; Wilma Dykeman, "Only Voters Like Him," *Nation*, clxxxii (April 21, 1956), 334–36.

10. David Rees, *Korea: The Limited War* (New York, 1964), pp. 402–5, 418–20; Ronald J. Caridi, *The Korean War and American Politics: The Republican Party as a Case Study* (Philadelphia, 1968), 246–47; Walter LaFeber, *America, Russia, and the Cold War, 1945–1971*, 2d ed. (New York, 1972), pp. 161–63, 168–69.

11. *Ibid.*, pp. 184–86; Dwight D. Eisenhower, *Mandate for Change, 1953–1956* (Garden City, N.Y., 1963), p. 527.

12. Stephen E. Ambrose, *Rise to Globalism: American Foreign Policy Since 1938* (Baltimore, 1971), pp. 219–33; Louis L. Gerson, *The Hyphenate in Recent American Politics and Diplomacy* (Lawrence, Kans., 1964), pp. 202–12.

13. James Shepley, "How Dulles Averted War," *Life*, xl (January 16, 1956), 70–80.

14. *Time*, lxvii (January 23, 1956), 15; *Life*, xl (January 30, 1956), 30; State Department, *Bulletin*, xxxiv (January 30, 1956), 155–58; *Public Papers of Presidents: Eisenhower, 1956*, p. 163.

15. Gerald W. Johnson, *"Life* and Mr. Dulles," *New Republic*, cxxxiv (February 6, 1956), 16; Douglas to Dulles, January 18, 1956, and Adams to Douglas, January 27, 1956, DDE Papers, OF 116–R.

16. Richard P. Stebbins, *The United States in World Affairs, 1956* (New York, 1957), pp. 36–51; *Time*, lxvii (February 27, 1956), 28; *ibid.* (March 26, 1956), 30; Alexander Werth, "Unsmiling Co-existence," *Nation*, clxxxii (March 3, 1956), 173–74.

17. *Time*, lxvii (March 5, 1956), 18; *New Republic*, cxxxiv (March

5, 1956), 2; State Department, *Bulletin,* xxxiv (March 5, 1956), 363–67; *ibid.* (April 16, 1956), 637–38; *ibid.* (April 30, 1956), 707–8.

18. *Newsweek,* xlvii (March 5, 1956), 31; *Time,* lxvii (March 5, 1956), 24; *New Republic,* cxxxiv (March 5, 1956), 3–4.

19. *New York Times,* April 22, 1956; Stevenson, *New America,* pp. 17–27.

20. *Public Papers of Presidents: Eisenhower, 1956,* pp. 411–23.

21. *New York Times,* April 22, 1956; *Newsweek,* xlvii (April 30, 1956), 94.

22. Ralph Lapp, *The Weapons Culture* (New York, 1968), pp. 63–66, 93–97; Ralph Lapp, "Radioactive Fall-out, III," *Bulletin of the Atomic Scientists* (hereafter *BAS*), xi (June 1955), 206–9; Ralph Lapp, "Global Fall-out," *ibid.,* xi (November 1955), 339; Ralph Lapp, "The 'Humanitarian' H-Bomb," *ibid.,* xii (September 1956), 261–64; Gene Marine, "The Delayed U-Bomb and the N.Y. *Times,*" *Nation,* clxxxii (January 28, 1956), 67–68.

23. William R. Frye, "The Disarmament Dilemma," *BAS,* xii (March 1956), 83; William R. Frye, "The Disarmament Turning Point," *ibid.* (May 1956), 166–68; *Vital Speeches,* xxii (January 15, 1956), 198; *Nation,* clxxxii (February 25, 1956), 149.

24. State Department, *Bulletin,* xxxiv (January 23, 1956), 122; *Time,* lxvii (April 9, 1956), 29; *BAS,* xii (May 1956), 181.

25. *Vital Speeches,* xx (June 1, 1956), 492–93; Stevenson, *New America,* p. 24.

26. *New York Times,* April 24 and 25, 1956; *Newsweek,* xlvii (April 16, 1956), 35.

27. *Public Papers of Presidents: Eisenhower, 1956,* pp. 428, 433, 434–35.

28. Clarence Pickett to Eisenhower, May 3, 1956, and Frederick J. Libby to Eisenhower, May 2, 1956, DDE Papers, GF 155–B; State Department, *Bulletin,* xxxiv (April 2, 1956), 566–67; *BAS,* xii (May 1956), 182; *New York Times,* April 21 and May 21, 1956; *Newsweek,* xlvii (May 28, 1956), 27–29; *ibid.* (July 30, 1956), 28; *New Republic,* cxxxiv (July 23, 1956), 3–4; *Public Papers of Presidents: Eisenhower, 1956,* pp. 523–24.

29. *New York Times,* June 13, 1956.

30. State Department, *Bulletin,* xxxv (July 30, 1956), 204, 207; *New Republic,* cxxxv (July 9, 1956), 4–5; *BAS,* xii (June 1956), 187, 198–99.

31. *New York Times,* June 29, 1956; *Newsweek,* XLVIII (July 9, 1956), 26–27.

32. *New York Times,* July 20, 1956; *New Republic,* CXXXV (July 30, 1956), 3–4; *BAS,* XII (September 1956), 234, 262–63.

33. *New Republic,* CXXXIV (June 4, 1956), 3; *BAS,* XII (September 1956), 275; *Nation,* CLXXXIII (August 18, 1956), 130.

34. Mitchell to Stevenson, March 22, 1956, Mitchell Papers, Box 36; Stephen A. Mitchell, "Adlai's Amateurs," in Edward P. Doyle, ed., *As We Knew Adlai* (New York, 1966), 90–91; *Time,* LXVII (April 16, 1956), 21.

35. *Ibid.* (February 13, 1956), 17; Gorman, *Kefauver,* pp. 234–39; *New York Times,* May 22, 1956; transcript of television debate, Kefauver Papers, 1956 Political File.

36. Thomson and Shattuck, *1956 Campaign,* pp. 56, 60–62; *Time,* LXVII (May 21, 1956), 24; *ibid.* (June 11, 1956), 29; Bert Collier, "Florida Beachhead," *Nation,* CLXXXII (June 9, 1956), 483; C. L. Sulzberger, *The Last of the Giants* (New York, 1970), p. 308; *Time,* LXVII (June 4, 1956), 24.

37. *Newsweek,* XLVII (March 26, 1956), 23–24; *ibid.* (June 11, 1956), 31; *Reporter,* XIV (June 14, 1956), 1.

38. *Time,* LXVII (May 21, 1956), 21; *ibid.* (May 28, 1956), 17.

39. State Department, *Bulletin,* XXXIV (May 28, 1956), 880; *ibid.,* XXXV (July 2, 1956), 3–5; *Newsweek,* XLVII (May 28, 1956), 42; *Time,* LXVIII (July 2, 1956), 9.

40. *Public Papers of Presidents: Eisenhower, 1956,* p. 554.

41. *Ibid.,* p. 556; *Nation,* CLXXXII (June 23, 1956), 521–22; *Newsweek,* XLVII (June 18, 1956), 57; State Department, *Bulletin,* XXXIV (June 18, 1956), 999–1000; *Vital Speeches,* XXII (August 1, 1956), 611–12.

42. *Time,* LXVII (June 18, 1956), 19; *ibid.* (July 23, 1956), 9; *Newsweek,* XLVII (June 18, 1956), 35; *ibid.* (July 23, 1956), 19; *Nation,* CLXXXII (June 30, 1956), 541–42; Sulzberger, *Last of the Giants,* p. 319; *Reporter,* XIV (June 28, 1956), 7.

43. *Newsweek,* XLVIII (July 9, 1956), 36; *Time,* LXVIII (July 9, 1956), 20; *ibid.* (July 23, 1956), 12; Stebbins, *U.S. in World Affairs, 1956,* pp. 179–80.

44. *Time,* LXVII (January 9, 1956), 15; Mrs. Ellija Druva to Eisenhower, December 31, 1955, and William R. Mathews, December 31, 1955, DDE Papers, GF 122–B; A. B. Hermann to Leonard Hall, March 24, 1956, and Hermann to Pyle, May 1, 1956, Re-

publican National Committee Papers, Cornell University Library, Box 4 (hereafter RNCP).

45. Hermann to Mrs. Hanny Cohrsen, June 8, 1956, and Hermann to Howard Pyle, July 26 and August 2, 1956, RNCP, Box 4; Gerson, *Hyphenate*, pp. 217–19.

46. State Department, *Bulletin*, xxxv (July 30, 1956), 188; Stebbins, *U.S. in World Affairs, 1956*, pp. 251–57.

47. LaFeber, *America, Russia, and the Cold War*, pp. 188–89; State Department, *Bulletin*, xxxiv (February 20, 1956), 285–86; *Newsweek*, xlvii (April 2, 1956), 33; *ibid.* (April 9, 1956), 46; *Time*, lxvii (April 23, 1956), 30, 32.

48. *Ibid.* (May 28, 1956), 26; *ibid.* (June 4, 1956), 24; *ibid.* (July 2, 1956), 18; *Newsweek*, xlvii (June 25, 1956), 44–45; *New York Times*, July 21, 1956; Thruston B. Morton memoir, Dulles Oral History Project.

49. *Newsweek*, xlviii (July 30, 1956), 20; *Time*, lxviii (July 30, 1956), 7; Eisenhower, *Waging Peace*, p. 33.

50. Dwight D. Eisenhower memoir and Allen W. Dulles memoir, Dulles Oral History Project; Harold Macmillan, *Riding the Storm, 1956–1959* (New York, 1971), pp. 102–3, 128.

51. Anthony Eden, *Full Circle* (Boston, 1960), p. 477; Eisenhower, *Waging Peace*, pp. 36–39, 664–65; Robert Murphy, *Diplomat Among Warriors* (Garden City, N.Y., 1964), p. 378; *Public Papers of Presidents: Eisenhower, 1956*, p. 635.

52. Murphy, *Diplomat*, pp. 381–84; *Newsweek*, xlviii (August 13, 1956), 43–44.

53. State Department, *Bulletin*, xxxv (August 13, 1956), 260–61; *Public Papers of Presidents: Eisenhower, 1956*, pp. 660–61, 670; Sulzberger, *Last of the Giants*, pp. 319–21.

54. Albert Rothblatt to Eisenhower, August 13, 1956, Michael F. Tamer to Eisenhower, August 12, 1956, "Ilene" to Sherman Adams, August 8, 1956, and Robert Lorry to Eisenhower, August 10, 1956, DDE Papers, GF 122–BB.

55. *Newsweek*, xlviii (August 20, 1956), 40; Adams, *Firsthand Report*, pp. 251–52; *Public Papers of Presidents: Eisenhower, 1956*, pp. 687–89; *New York Times*, August 13, 1956; Eisenhower, *Waging Peace*, p. 44.

56. Sulzberger, *Last of the Giants*, p. 326; *New York Times*, August 8, 10, and 15, 1956; *BAS*, xii (September 1956), 268.

57. Kirk H. Porter and Donald Bruce Johnson, eds., *National Party*

Platforms, 1840–1956 (Urbana, Ill., 1956), pp. 524–27, 541; Sulzberger, Last of the Giants, p. 327; New York Times, August 18, 1956; New Republic, cxxxv (August 27, 1956), 5.

58. New York Times, August 1, 1956; Robert Bendiner, "Notes on the Harriman Campaign," Reporter, xv (August 9, 1956), 36.

59. New York Times, August 11 and 12, 1956; Time, lxviii (August 20, 1956), 9; New Republic, cxxxv (August 20, 1956), 2.

60. Newsweek, xlviii (August 20, 1956), 20–21; New York Times, August 13 and 15, 1956; New Republic, cxxxv (August 20, 1956), 5.

61. New York Times, August 17, 1956; Davis, Politics of Honor, pp. 332–35.

62. New York Times, August 18, 1956; Stevenson, New America, pp. 3–7.

63. New Republic, cxxxv (August 27, 1956), 2; Frederic W. Collins, "Stevenson's Next Task," ibid. (July 9, 1956), 13.

64. Newsweek, xlviii (August 20, 1956), 19; ibid. (September 3, 1956), 34; Hughes, Ordeal, pp. 177–78; State Department, Bulletin, xxxv (August 27, 1956), 336–38; Time, lxviii (August 13, 1956), 16–17; New Republic, cxxxv (September 3, 1956), 7.

65. Draft platform, January 6, 1956, Dulles Papers, Box 484; Dulles to Bush, July 11, 1956, and Dulles to Adams, July 16, 1956, Howard Pyle Papers, Eisenhower Library, Box 44; John W. Hanes, Jr., to Dulles, July 31, 1956, Dulles Papers, Box 484; Pyle to Adams, August 15, 1956, Pyle Papers, Box 44.

66. New York Times, August 22 and 26, 1956; Porter and Johnson, eds., National Party Platforms, pp. 545–58.

67. Time, lxviii (August 6, 1956), 15; New York Times, August 20 and 23, 1956; Public Papers of Presidents: Eisenhower, 1956, pp. 623, 693, 698.

68. Time, lxviii (September 3, 1956), 9; I. F. Stone, The Haunted Fifties (New York, 1963), pp. 160–63; New York Times, August 21, 22, and 23.

69. New Republic, cxxxv (September 3, 1956), 2; Public Papers of Presidents: Eisenhower, 1956, pp. 711–13; Murray Kempton, America Comes of Middle Age (Boston, 1963), pp. 256–57.

70. George Dangerfield, "Cult of Ike," Nation, clxxxii (June 16, 1956), 504–5; Newsweek, xlviii (July 9, 1956), 23; Hughes, Ordeal by Power, p. 177; Robert Murphy memoir, Dulles Oral History Project.

Chapter 4

1. Kenneth S. Davis, *The Politics of Honor: A Biography of Adlai E. Stevenson* (New York, 1967), pp. 336–39; *New York Times,* August 28 and September 9, 1956; *Newsweek,* XLVIII (September 3, 1956), 30; *ibid.* (September 10, 1956), 32; *New Republic,* CXXXV (September 10, 1956), 2.

2. Adlai E. Stevenson, *The New America,* Seymour E. Harris, John Bartlow Martin, and Arthur Schlesinger, Jr., eds. (New York, 1957), p. xv; Herbert J. Muller, *Adlai Stevenson: A Study in Values* (New York, 1967), p. 190; *New York Times,* September 17, 1956; *Reporter,* xv (October 4, 1956), 2; Norman Moss, *Men Who Play God* (New York, 1968), p. 111.

3. Stevenson, *New America,* p. xvi; Muller, *Stevenson,* p. 179; *Newsweek,* XLVIII (September 24, 1956), 33; *New Republic,* CXXXV (September 24, 1956), 2; *New York Times,* September 16, 1956.

4. Eisenhower to Virgil Pinkley, October 13, 1956, DDE Papers, OF 138–C–4; *Newsweek,* XLVIII (August 20, 1956), 31, 43–44; *ibid.* (September 10, 1956), 21; Nixon to Eisenhower, September 14, 1956, DDE Papers, OF 138–C–4; Robert L. Branyan and Lawrence H. Larsen, eds., *The Eisenhower Administration, 1953–1961: A Documentary History,* 2 vols. (New York, 1971), I, 615; Sherman Adams to Dulles, September 17, 1956, Dulles Papers, Box 484; memorandum by John W. Hanes, Jr., October 8, 1956, Dulles Papers, Box 485.

5. Campaign leaflet, DDE Papers, OF 138–C–4; *New Republic,* CXXXV (October 8, 1956), 10–11; campaign pamphlet, James W. Lambie Papers, Eisenhower Library, Box 61.

6. Emmet John Hughes, *The Ordeal of Power: A Political Memoir of the Eisenhower Years* (New York, 1963), pp. 174–79.

7. *New York Times,* September 13 and 23, 1956; *New Republic,* CXXXV (October 8, 1956), 2.

8. *New York Times,* September 7, 10, 21, and 23, 1956.

9. Davis, *Politics of Honor,* pp. 340–41; *New York Times,* September 6, 7, and 27, 1956.

10. *Ibid.,* September 7 and 18, 1956; *Reporter,* xv (September 20, 1956), 2; *Newsweek,* XLVIII (October 29, 1956), 32; Stevenson, *New America,* pp. 64–65; Stuart Gerry Brown, *Conscience in Politics: Adlai E. Stevenson in the 1950's* (Syracuse, 1961), pp. 190–91.

11. *Washington Post*, September 6, 1956; *New York Times*, September 7, 1956.

12. Stevenson, *New America*, p. xviii; State Department, *Bulletin*, xxxv (September 10, 1956), 424–25; *BAS*, xii (October 1956), 318; *New York Times*, September 1 and 4, 1956; Adlai E. Stevenson, "Why I Raised the H-Bomb Question," *Look*, xxi (February 5, 1957), 23–25.

13. *New York Times*, September 15, 1956; Hughes, *Ordeal*, pp. 185–86.

14. *Public Papers of the Presidents: Eisenhower, 1956*, pp. 782–84, 786; *New York Times*, September 20, 1956; *Newsweek*, xlviii (October 1, 1956), 22–23; *Nation*, clxxxiii (September 29, 1956), 257; Hughes, *Ordeal*, p. 181.

15. *Public Papers of the Presidents: Eisenhower, 1956*, pp. 833, 842, 884.

16. *Ibid.*, pp. 760, 867–70; *New York Times*, September 12, 1956.

17. Hughes, *Ordeal*, p. 186; Dwight D. Eisenhower, *Waging Peace, 1956–1961* (Garden City, N.Y., 1965), pp. 17–18; *Public Papers of the Presidents: Eisenhower, 1956*, pp. 858, 863–67.

18. *Ibid.*, pp. 881–82; *New York Times*, October 7 and 9, 1956.

19. *New York Times*, September 26, 1956; State Department, *Bulletin*, xxxv (October 8, 1956), 544–45; *Public Papers of the Presidents: Eisenhower, 1956*, pp. 807–8; Eisenhower, *Waging Peace*, p. 17.

20. *New York Times*, October 2, 3, 7, and 11, 1956; *Reporter*, xv (October 18, 1956), 4; *Time*, lxviii (October 15, 1956), 27; *Nation*, clxxxiii (October 20, 1956), 317.

21. Marquis Childs, *Eisenhower: Captive Hero* (New York, 1958), p. 233; Richard Goold-Adams, *The Time of Power: A Reappraisal of John Foster Dulles* (London, 1962), p. 216; Hughes, *Ordeal*, pp. 210–11; *New York Times*, September 2, 1956; *New Republic*, cxxxv (September 24, 1956), 3.

22. Richard P. Stebbins, *The United States in World Affairs, 1956* (New York, 1957), pp. 263–65; State Department, *Bulletin*, xxxv (September 3, 1956), 374–75; *New York Times*, September 7, 8, 9, and 10, 1956; Eisenhower, *Waging Peace*, pp. 50, 669–70; *Public Papers of the Presidents: Eisenhower, 1956*, pp. 756–57, 761.

23. *Time*, lxviii (September 17, 1956), 23; *New York Times*, September 11 and 13, 1956; Anthony Eden, *Full Circle* (Boston, 1960), pp. 538–39; State Department, *Bulletin*, xxxv (September 24, 1956), 476–83.

24. *New York Times*, September, 15, 16, 22, and 23, 1956.

25. Goold-Adams, *Time of Power*, pp. 228–29, 232; *Time*, LXVIII (October 1, 1956), 26–28; *Newsweek*, XLVIII (October 1, 1956), 38–41; *Nation*, CLXXXIII (September 29, 1956), 258–59.

26. *New York Times*, September 1, 15, and 18, 1956; *Public Papers of the Presidents: Eisenhower, 1956*, p. 732; Schlesinger memorandum, September 24, 1956, Kefauver Papers, 1956 Campaign File.

27. Hauge to Adams, October 9, 1956, DDE Papers, OF 138–C–4; Jackson to Adams, October 8, 1956, Adams to Jackson, October 10, 1956, and Minnich to Adams, October 11, 1956, DDE Papers, OF 193; Hughes, *Ordeal*, p. 193.

28. *Public Papers of the Presidents: Eisenhower, 1956*, pp. 852, 883, 903; *New York Times*, October 13 and 14, 1956; Stebbins, *U.S. in World Affairs, 1956*, pp. 271–73.

29. *New York Times*, October 16 and 20, 1956; Stevenson, *New America*, pp. 27–30.

30. *New York Times*, October 3, 4, and 11, 1956.

31. *Ibid.*, September 22 and October 8, 1956; Price to Stevenson, October 4, 1956, Kefauver Papers, 1956 Campaign File; David E. Lilienthal, *The Journals of David E. Lilienthal*, 4 vols. (New York, 1964–1970), IV, 114; Brown, *Conscience*, pp. 202–3.

32. *New York Times*, October 10, 13, 14, 15, and 16, 1956; Newton E. Minow, "Marching to the Beat of Mankind," in Edward P. Doyle, ed., *As We Knew Adlai* (New York, 1966), p. 185; *Time*, LXVIII (October 29, 1956), 16.

33. Stevenson, *New America*, pp. 44–49; *New York Times*, October 12 and 16, 1956.

34. *Ibid.*, October 24 and 27, 1956; *Time*, LXVIII (November 5, 1956), 24.

35. *New York Times*, October 17, 21, and 28, 1956; *Newsweek*, XLVIII (October 29, 1956), 70; staff memos, October 19 and 20, 1956, press release, October 20, 1956, Kefauver Papers, 1956 Campaign File.

36. *New York Times*, October 13, 15, 21, and 25, 1956; list of endorsements, undated, Kefauver Papers, Series I, Box 7; broadcast summaries, October 30, 1956, Citizens for Eisenhower Papers, Eisenhower Library, Box 6; *BAS*, XII (October 1956), 287–89, 312–17; *ibid.* (November 1956), 322, 374; *ibid.*, XIII (December 1956), 19–20.

37. Murray Snyder to Sherman Adams, October 16, 1956, and draft

statement by Dulles, October 17, 1956, DDE Papers, OF 108–A; *Newsweek*, XLVIII (October 29, 1948), 29; *Public Papers of the Presidents: Eisenhower, 1956*, pp. 959, 962, 976, 1022.

38. *New York Times*, October 17, 18, and 20, 1956.

39. State Department, *Bulletin*, XXXV (October 29, 1956), 662–64; *Public Papers of the Presidents: Eisenhower, 1956*, pp. 983–84; *New York Times*, October 20, 21, and 22, 1956.

40. *Ibid.*, October 22 and 23, 1956; Davis, *Politics of Honor*, pp. 342–43.

41. *New York Times*, October 22 and 24, 1956; mimeographed copy of Nixon speech, October 29, 1956, Kefauver Papers, 1956 Campaign File.

42. Brown, *Conscience*, pp. 206–9; *Public Papers of the Presidents: Eisenhower, 1956*, pp. 997–1002; Baruch to Eleanor Roosevelt, October 23, 1956, Baruch Papers, Box 134; *New York Times*, October 17, 23, and 26, 1956; *New Republic*, CXXXV (October 15, 1956), 5; *Reporter*, XV (November 1, 1956), 8; *Nation*, CLXXXIII (October 27, 1956), 337.

43. *Newsweek*, XLVIII (October 29, 1956), 31; memos by Roland Machman, Jr., October 19, 24, and 25, 1956, Kefauver Papers, 1956 Campaign File; Austin Cravath to Eisenhower, October 21, 1956, Evelyn and Jack Alloy to Eisenhower, October 22, 1956, and Virginia Mynick to Eisenhower, October 26, 1956, DDE Papers, GF 155–B.

44. *Newsweek*, XLVIII (October 29, 1956), 42–44; *Time*, LXVIII (October 29, 1956), 24–25; Stebbins, *U.S. in World Affairs, 1956*, pp. 313–14.

45. *Public Papers of the Presidents: Eisenhower, 1956*, p. 981; C. L. Sulzberger, *The Last of the Giants* (New York, 1970), p. 335; *New York Times*, October 21 and 22, 1956.

46. A. C. Trimble to A. B. Hermann, September 6, 1956, Bernard Shanley to Hermann, September 29, 1956, Hanny Cohrsen to Hermann, October 10, 1956, RNCP, Box 4; Hermann to Eisenhower, October 5, 1956, DDE Papers, OF 138–C–4; Andrew H. Berding, *Dulles on Diplomacy* (Princeton, N.J., 1965), p. 116.

47. Eisenhower, *Waging Peace*, pp. 63–64; Sulzberger, *Last of the Giants*, pp. 334–35; *Public Papers of the Presidents: Eisenhower, 1956*, pp. 994–96; *New York Times*, October 21, 1956.

48. *Ibid.*, October 24, 25, 26, and 27, 1956; Stebbins, *U.S. in World Affairs, 1956*, pp. 315–16.

49. Sulzberger, *Last of the Giants*, p. 336; *Public Papers of the Presi-*

dents: *Eisenhower, 1956*, pp. 1018–19; Eisenhower, *Waging Peace*, pp. 67, 70–71; State Department, *Bulletin*, xxxv (November 5, 1956), 697.

50. Eisenhower, *Waging Peace*, pp. 81–83; *New York Times*, October 29, 30, 31, and November 1, 1956.

51. *Time*, LXVIII (November 5, 1956), 21, 30–33; *Newsweek*, XLVIII (November 5, 1956), 51; *New York Times*, October 27, 30, and November 2, 1956; Eisenhower, *Waging Peace*, p. 68; *Public Papers of the Presidents: Eisenhower, 1956*, p. 1061.

52. Memoirs of Allen W. Dulles, William Macomber, and Dwight D. Eisenhower, Dulles Oral History Collection; Eisenhower, *Waging Peace*, pp. 56, 69–70, 676–77; *Public Papers of the Presidents: Eisenhower, 1956*, p. 1034.

53. *Ibid.*, pp. 1042–45, 1053; Murray Snyder memoir, Eisenhower Library Oral History Project; Murray Kempton, *America Comes of Middle Age* (Boston, 1963), p. 260.

54. *New York Times*, October 30, 1956; Adams, *Firsthand Report*, p. 256; Eisenhower, *Waging Peace*, p. 72; Hughes, *Ordeal*, p. 212.

55. *New York Times*, October 31, 1956; Eisenhower, *Waging Peace*, pp. 75–78.

56. Arthur Larson, *Eisenhower: The President Nobody Knew* (New York, 1968), p. 54; Hughes, *Ordeal*, pp. 215–22; Louis L. Gerson, *John Foster Dulles* (New York, 1967), p. 347; Goold-Adams, *Time of Power*, p. 238; Herman Finer, *Dulles over Suez* (Chicago, 1964), pp. 370–71.

57. Hughes, *Ordeal*, pp. 219–21; Eisenhower, *Waging Peace*, pp. 80–81; *Public Papers of the Presidents: Eisenhower, 1956*, pp. 1064–66.

58. Stebbins, *U.S. in World Affairs, 1956*, pp. 332–35; Eisenhower, *Waging Peace*, pp. 83–84; *New York Times*, November 1 and 4, 1956; Gerson, *Dulles*, p. 296; State Department, *Bulletin*, xxxv (November 12, 1956), pp. 751, 755.

59. *New York Times*, October 30 and 31, November 1 and 3, 1956; Stevenson, *New America*, pp. 36–38.

60. Hughes, *Ordeal*, p. 195; Eisenhower, *Waging Peace*, p. 74.

61. *New York Times*, October 31, November 1, 2, and 3, 1956; Ralph de Toledano, *One Man Alone: Richard Nixon* (New York, 1969), p. 213; draft speech, November 2, 1956, Dulles Papers, Box 484.

62. *New York Times*, November 1 and 2, 1956; Francis Case to Sherman Adams, November 3, 1956, DDE Papers, GF 122–BB;

George Craig to Eisenhower, November 3, 1956, DDE Papers, OF 138 C–4; Royal broadcast text, November 2, 1956, Citizens for Eisenhower Files, Box 6.

63. Earl Chudoff to Dulles, November 2, 1956, DDE Papers, OF 116–R; Robert Cutler to Dulles, October 26, 1956, Dulles Papers, Box 485; Elmer Berger to Eisenhower, November 2, 1956, DDE Papers, GF 122–BB; David Wolper to Eisenhower, November 2, 1956, DDE Papers, GF 122–BB; James Hagerty memoir, Dulles Oral History Project.
64. *BAS*, XII (November 1956), 354; *New York Times*, November 2, 1956; Stevenson, *New America*, pp. 49–58; Muller, *Stevenson*, p. 196.
65. Stevenson, *New America*, pp. 248–49, 273, 277–78; text of Boston speech, October 29, 1956, Kefauver Papers, Stevenson Speech File; Davis, *Politics of Honor*, p. 348; Sulzberger, *Last of the Giants*, pp. 335–36.
66. *Newsweek*, XLVIII (November 5, 1956), 27, 29; *Time*, LXVIII (November 5, 1956), 22.
67. *Ibid.* (November 12, 1956), 31; *New York Times*, November 4 and 5, 1956; Collegial Society of Hungarian Veterans to Eisenhower, October 26, 1956, and Association of Free Hungarian Journalists to Eisenhower, October 28, 1956, DDE Papers, GF 122–B–1; Berding, *Dulles*, p. 115.
68. Eisenhower, *Waging Peace*, pp. 86–89; *Public Papers of the Presidents: Eisenhower, 1956*, pp. 1080–81; Stebbins, *U.S. in World Affairs, 1956*, pp. 348–49.
69. *Ibid.*, pp. 337–38; *New York Times*, November 5 and 6, 1956; *Newsweek*, XLVIII (November 12, 1956); Nikita S. Khrushchev, *Khrushchev Remembers* (Boston, 1970), p. 479.
70. *New York Times*, November 7, 1956; Hughes, *Ordeal*, p. 223; *New Republic*, CXXXV (November 19, 1956), 3; State Department, *Bulletin*, XXXV (November 19, 1956), 795; Eisenhower, *Waging Peace*, pp. 89–90.
71. *New York Times*, November 7, 1956; Eisenhower, *Waging Peace*, pp. 90–92.
72. *New York Times*, November 7, 8, and 11, 1956; *Time*, LXVIII (November 12, 1956), 17; *ibid.* (November 19, 1956), 23.
73. Louis H. Bean, "Analyzing the Vote," *Nation*, CLXXXIII (November 24, 1956), 446–47; *New York Times*, November 8, 1956; *Newsweek*, XLVIII (November 12, 1956), 61–62; *Reporter*, XV (November 15, 1956), 4.

74. *New York Times*, November 8 and 25, 1956; Stevenson to Sevareid, November 9, 1956, Sevareid Papers, Box 25; Allan Nevins, *Herbert H. Lehman and His Era* (New York, 1963), p. 366.
75. Stevenson, *New America*, p. xi.
76. *Ibid.*, p. xix; *Nation*, CLXXXIII (November 17, 1956), 421.

Chapter 5

1. Walter LaFeber, *America, Russia, and the Cold War, 1945–1971*, 2d ed. (New York, 1972), pp. 212–13; Richard P. Stebbins, *The United States in World Affairs, 1959* (New York, 1960), pp. 149–57.
2. *Ibid.*, pp. 352–54, 370–71; Dwight D. Eisenhower, *Waging Peace, 1956–1961* (Garden City, N.Y., 1965), p. 533.
3. Stebbins, *U.S. in World Affairs, 1959*, pp. 51–55.
4. *Ibid.*, pp. 27–36, 163–64; Eisenhower, *Waging Peace*, pp. 442–48.
5. *Ibid.*, pp. 476–81; Richard P. Stebbins, *The United States in World Affairs, 1960* (New York, 1961), pp. 68–72.
6. Hans Meyerhoff, "The Case of the Missing Purpose," *Nation*, CXCI (August 20, 1960), 85–87; *Newsweek*, LV (March 7, 1960), 24; *Time*, LXXV (March 7, 1960), 11.
7. *Ibid.* (January 11, 1960), 14; *ibid.* (February 1, 1960), 14–15; *ibid.* (March 28, 1960), 22; C. L. Sulzberger, *The Last of the Giants* (New York, 1970), p. 636; *New Republic*, CXLII (January 11, 1960), 2.
8. *Time*, LXXV (January 25, 1960), 20, 21; *ibid.* (April 25, 1960), 20–23; *Newsweek*, LV (May 9, 1960), 31.
9. Theodore C. Sorensen, *Kennedy* (New York, 1965), pp. 134–36; Pierre Salinger, *With Kennedy* (Garden City, N.Y., 1966), pp. 29–32; Evelyn Lincoln, *My Twelve Years with John F. Kennedy* (New York, 1965), pp. 128–29.
10. Arthur M. Schlesinger, Jr., *A Thousand Days: John F. Kennedy in the White House* (Boston, 1965), pp. 9–14; Sorensen, *Kennedy*, pp. 139–41; *New Republic*, CXLII (February 15, 1960), 3–4.
11. James MacGregor Burns, *John Kennedy: A Political Profile* (New York, 1960), pp. 259–64; Victor Lasky, *J.F.K.: The Man and the Myth* (New York, 1963), pp. 217–19.
12. Sulzberger, *Last of the Giants*, p. 623; John F. Kennedy, *The Strategy of Peace*, Allan Nevins, ed. (New York, 1960), pp. 38, 45, 201; *Time*, LXXV (January 25, 1960), 20.

13. Richard M. Nixon, *Six Crises* (Garden City, N.Y., 1962), pp. 301–3; Earl Mazo and Stephen Hess, *Nixon: A Political Portrait* (New York, 1968), p. 220; Ralph de Toledano, *One Man Alone: Richard Nixon* (New York, 1969), pp. 292–93.

14. Nixon, *Six Crises*, pp. 237, 247, 250–58; Mazo and Hess, *Nixon*, pp. 189–91.

15. *Time*, LXXV (January 4, 1960), 16; *Nation*, CXC (January 9, 1960), 21.

16. *Time*, LXXV (January 18, 1960), 17; *ibid.* (February 8, 1960), 20; *ibid.* (February 29, 1960), 23; Eisenhower, *Waging Peace*, pp. 590–91; *Newsweek*, LV (April 11, 1960), 34–35.

17. *Ibid.* (April 11, 1960), 35; *New Republic*, CXLII (February 15, 1960), 4–5.

18. William J. Miller, *Henry Cabot Lodge* (New York, 1967), p. 310; *Newsweek*, LV (June 13, 1960), 33–34; Nixon, *Six Crises*, pp. 306–9; de Toledano, *One Man*, pp. 299–300.

19. *Time*, LXXV (March 21, 1960), 13; *ibid.* (April 18, 1960), 16–17; *Reporter*, XXII (March 17, 1960), 28–30; *Newsweek*, LV (March 28, 1960), 29; *ibid.* (April 18, 1960), 31.

20. Sorensen, *Kennedy*, pp. 156–57; Victor Lasky, *J.F.K.: The Man and the Myth* (New York, 1963), pp. 338, 343, 347–48; *Time*, LXXV (May 9, 1960), 20; *New York Times*, May 11, 1960; *Newsweek*, LV (May 23, 1960), 56; *Nation*, CXC (May 21, 1960), 435; *New Republic*, CXLII (May 23, 1960), 2.

21. *Newsweek*, LV (April 4, 1960), 32; *ibid.* (April 25, 1960), 30; Schlesinger, *Thousand Days*, pp. 17, 23–25; Chester Bowles, *Promises to Keep: My Years in Public Life, 1941–1969* (New York, 1971), pp. 285–89; *Time*, LXXV (April 25, 1960), 24; Kenneth S. Davis, *The Politics of Honor: A Biography of Adlai E. Stevenson* (New York, 1967), p. 415.

22. Francis Gary Powers, with Curt Gentry, *Operation Overflight* (New York, 1970), pp. 70–82; David Wise and Thomas B. Ross, *The U-2 Affair* (New York, 1962), pp. 7–11, 178–79, 256–60; Sulzberger, *Last of the Giants*, p. 924.

23. Wise and Ross, *U-2 Affair*, pp. 72–115; State Department, *Bulletin*, XLII (May 23, 1960), 816–18; Eisenhower, *Waging Peace*, pp. 550–51.

24. *Public Papers of the Presidents: Eisenhower, 1960*, pp. 403–5; *New York Times*, May 11, 13, and 21, 1960; *Newsweek*, LV (May 16, 1960), 27; Wise and Ross, *U-2 Affair*, p. 131.

25. *Ibid.*, pp. 132, 147–48; *New York Times*, May 13 and 15, 1960.

313

26. Sulzberger, *Last of the Giants*, p. 669; *New York Times*, May 16, 1960.

27. Wise and Ross, *U-2 Affair*, pp. 150–58; *Time*, LXXV (May 23, 1960), 18–19; *Newsweek*, LV (May 23, 1960), 32–34.

28. *Public Papers of the Presidents: Eisenhower, 1960*, pp. 427–29; Sulzberger, *Last of the Giants*, p. 669; *Time*, LXXV (May 30, 1960), 16; *Newsweek*, LV (May 30, 1960), 22.

29. *New York Times*, May 17, 18, and 19, 1960; *Time*, LXXV (May 30, 1960), 9.

30. *New York Times*, May 20, 22, and 23, 1960; Stuart Gerry Brown, *Conscience in Politics: Adlai E. Stevenson in the 1950's* (Syracuse, 1961), pp. 282–85.

31. *New York Times*, May 24, 1960; *Nation*, CXC (June 4, 1960), 481; *New Republic*, CXLIII (August 8, 1960), 2.

32. *New York Times*, May 24, 1960; *Newsweek*, LV (June 6, 1960), 31–32.

33. *New York Times*, May 18 and 21, 1960.

34. *Public Papers of the Presidents: Eisenhower, 1960*, pp. 437–45; *Newsweek*, LVI (July 11, 1960), 38.

35. *Ibid.* (May 30, 1960), 31–32; *ibid.* (June 20, 1960), 42; *ibid.* (June 27, 1960), 35; *Nation*, CXC (June 11, 1960), 501; *Time*, LXXV (June 20, 1960), 12.

36. *Ibid.* (May 23, 1960), 14–15; *ibid.* (June 27, 1960), 16–17; Sorensen, *Kennedy*, p. 168; Schlesinger, *Thousand Days*, pp. 27–28; *Vital Speeches*, XXVI (July 15, 1960), 580–83.

37. Rowland Evans and Robert Novak, *Lyndon B. Johnson: The Exercise of Power* (New York, 1966), pp. 279–81; *Time*, LXXV (June 13, 1960), 25; Lasky, *J.F.K.*, p. 358.

38. Davis, *Politics of Honor*, pp. 420–24; Brown, *Conscience in Politics*, pp. 258–60; *Newsweek*, LV (June 6, 1960), 33; A. S. Mike Monroney, "The Plot Against Adlai," in Edward P. Doyle, ed., *As We Knew Adlai* (New York, 1966), pp. 250–51; Monroney to Estes Kefauver, June 27, 1960, Kefauver Papers, Box 20.

39. *Time*, LXXV (June 13, 1960), 22.

40. *Ibid.* (June 13, 1960), 19; *Newsweek*, LV (June 13, 1960), 28.

41. *Ibid.* (June 13, 1960), 27–28; *ibid.* (June 20, 1960), 46; State Department, *Bulletin*, XLIII (July 25, 1960), 131; *Public Papers of the Presidents: Eisenhower, 1960*, pp. 532–33; *Time*, LXXVI (July 4, 1960), 9; *ibid.* (July 11, 1960), 17.

42. *New York Times*, July 1, 2, 4, and 7, 1960; *New Republic*, CXLIII

(July 25, 1960), 8–9; *Public Papers of the Presidents: Eisenhower, 1960*, pp. 562–63.

43. *Newsweek*, LVI (July 11, 1960), 36–37; *ibid.* (July 18, 1960), 39; *Time*, LXXVI (July 18, 1960), 26; *Public Papers of the Presidents: Eisenhower, 1960*, pp. 567–68; *New York Times*, July 10, 1960.

44. Sorensen, *Kennedy*, pp. 170–72; *New York Times*, July 3 and 5, 1960; *Newsweek*, LVI (July 11, 1960), 22–23.

45. *New York Times*, July 6, 1960; *Time*, LXXVI (July 18, 1960), 9–11; *Newsweek*, LV (June 20, 1960), 34; Joseph P. Lash, *Eleanor: The Years Alone* (New York, 1972), pp. 288–89; *New Republic*, CXLII (June 20, 1960), 3; Lasky, *J.F.K.*, pp. 390–91.

46. *New York Times*, July 12, 1960; Arthur M. Schlesinger, Jr., and Fred L. Israel, eds., *History of American Presidential Elections, 1789–1968*, 4 vols. (New York, 1971), IV, 3471–80.

47. Bowles, *Promises*, pp. 289–90; *New York Times*, July 13, 1960; Carey McWilliams, "The Kennedys Take Over," *Nation*, CXCI (July 23, 1960), 43.

48. Salinger, *With Kennedy*, pp. 38–42; *Newsweek*, LVI (July 18, 1960), 19–20; Lasky, *J.F.K.*, p. 395; Schlesinger, *Thousand Days*, pp. 39–56; Sorensen, *Kennedy*, p. 184.

49. *New York Times*, July 14, 1960; Sulzberger, *Last of the Giants*, pp. 680–81.

50. *Vital Speeches*, XXVI (August 1, 1960), 610–12.

51. Stebbins, *U.S. in World Affairs, 1960*, pp. 175–81; *New York Times*, July 5, 8, 13, 14, 21, and 22, 1960; *Time*, LXXVI (July 25, 1960), 22–23.

52. *New York Times*, July 13 and 15, 1960; State Department, *Bulletin*, XLIII (August 1, 1960), 203–4.

53. *New York Times*, July 12 and 23, 1960; *Newsweek*, LVI (July 25, 1960), 36–37; *Public Papers of the Presidents: Eisenhower, 1960*, p. 578; State Department, *Bulletin*, XLIII (August 15, 1960), 235, 238, 240–44.

54. *Time*, LXXVI (July 25, 1960), 8.

55. *Newsweek*, LV (June 20, 1960), 29; *ibid.* (July 11, 1960), 25–26; *Time*, LXXV (June 20, 1960), 10–11; *New York Times*, July 4 and 8, 1960.

56. *Newsweek*, LV (June 20, 1960), 30; *ibid.* (July 4, 1960), 24; *ibid.* (July 11, 1960), 31.

57. Percy to Hal Short, June 1, 1960, Morton to Percy, June 18, 1960, and Morton to William Prendergast, July 9, 1960, RNCP,

Box 34; *Time*, LXXVI (July 18, 1960), 14; *New York Times*, July 10, 1960.

58. *Ibid.*, July 20, 21, 22, and 23, 1960.

59. *Ibid.*, July 24 and 27, 1960; Nixon, *Six Crises*, pp. 313–16; *Time*, LXXVI (August 1, 1960), 9–12; *Newsweek*, LVI (August 1, 1960), 16–20.

60. Eisenhower, *Waging Peace*, pp. 595–96; *New Republic*, CXLIII (August 8, 1960), 5; *New York Times*, July 24, 1960.

61. *Ibid.*, July 25, 26, and 27, 1960; *Time*, LXXVI (August 8, 1960), 11; *Newsweek*, LVI (August 8, 1960), 17; *Reporter*, XXIII (September 1, 1960), 32–33; Schlesinger and Israel, eds., *History of Presidential Elections*, IV, 3510–16.

62. *New York Times*, July 24, 1960; *Newsweek*, LVI (August 8, 1960), 24; *Time*, LXXVI (August 1, 1960), 12; Robert Bendiner, "Rockefeller to the Rescue," *Reporter*, XXIII (September 1, 1960), 30.

63. *Vital Speeches*, XXVI (August 15, 1960), 646–51; *Public Papers of the Presidents: Eisenhower, 1960*, pp. 589–98; *New York Times*, July 27 and 28, 1960.

64. Miller, *Lodge*, pp. 318–20; Nixon, *Six Crises*, pp. 317–18; *New York Times*, July 29, 1960.

65. Marya Mannes, "Candidate from the U.N.," *Reporter*, XXIII (October 27, 1960), 23–25; *Newsweek*, LVI (August 1, 1960), 25; *New Republic*, CXLIII (August 8, 1960), 2; *New York Times*, July 29, 1960.

66. *Vital Speeches*, XXVI (August 15, 1960), 642–46.

67. *Nation*, CXCI (August 6, 1960), 64; *New Republic*, CXLIII (August 8, 1960), 2; *Time*, LXXVI (August 8, 1960), 16.

68. *New York Times*, July 30, 1960; *Newsweek*, LVI (August 1, 1960), 26; *Time*, LXXVI (July 18, 1960), 14; *ibid.* (July 25, 1960), 9.

69. *New Republic*, CXLIII (July 25, 1960), 3; *Newsweek*, LVI (July 25, 1960), 47; *Nation*, CXCI (July 23, 1960), 41; *ibid.* (August 6, 1960), 61.

Chapter 6

1. *New York Times*, July 15 and 31, 1960; Arthur M. Schlesinger, Jr., *A Thousand Days: John F. Kennedy in the White House* (Boston, 1965), pp. 64–65.

2. Theodore H. White, *The Making of the President, 1960* (New

York, 1961), pp. 282–84; Theodore C. Sorensen, *Kennedy* (New York, 1965), p. 199; Schlesinger, *Thousand Days*, p. 69.

3. *Time*, LXXVI (August 29, 1960), 15; *New York Times*, July 30, August 1, 11, and 15, 1960; Evelyn Lincoln, *My Twelve Years with John F. Kennedy* (New York, 1965), p. 169; Chester Bowles, *Promises to Keep: My Years in Public Life, 1941–1969* (New York, 1971), pp. 295–96.

4. *New York Times*, July 17, 18, and 24, 1960; Dulles to Eisenhower, August 3, 1960, David Kendall to Kennedy, August 8, 1960, and Eisenhower to Kennedy, August 19, 1960, DDE Papers, OF 138 D–8.

5. Arthur Schlesinger, "The Shape of National Politics to Come," RNCP, Box 1; Victor Lasky, *J.F.K.: The Man and the Myth* (New York, 1963), pp. 428–29; Thomas B. Morgan, "The People-Machine," *Harper's*, CCXXII (January 1961), 54.

6. *New York Times*, August 25, 1960.

7. *Ibid.*, July 29, August 2 and 16, 1960; Ralph de Toledano, *One Man Alone: Richard Nixon* (New York, 1969), p. 304; Emmet John Hughes, *The Ordeal of Power: A Political Memoir of the Eisenhower Years* (New York, 1963), pp. 319–20.

8. Earl Mazo and Stephen Hess, *Nixon: A Political Portrait* (New York, 1968), pp. 229–30; *Newsweek*, LVI (August 15, 1960), 26; *Time*, LXXVI (August 15, 1960), 15–16.

9. Dwight D. Eisenhower, *Waging Peace, 1956–1961* (Garden City, N.Y., 1965), p. 597; *Public Papers of the Presidents: Eisenhower, 1960*, pp. 621–22, 653–54, 657–58.

10. *Newsweek*, LVI (September 5, 1960), 26; *New York Times*, August 26, 1960.

11. *Ibid.*, August 9 and 15, 1960; *Newsweek*, LVI (August 15, 1960), 31; *ibid.* (August 29, 1960), 35; *Time*, LXXVI (August 15, 1960), 21; Richard P. Stebbins, *The United States in World Affairs, 1960* (New York, 1961), pp. 184–85.

12. *New York Times*, August 5, 7, and 29, September 3, 1960; *Time*, LXXVI (August 15, 1960), 28; *Newsweek*, LVI (September 5, 1960), 42–43; State Department, *Bulletin*, XLIII (September 12, 1960), 400, 407–8; *Nation*, CXCI (September 10, 1960), 123.

13. *New York Times*, August 2, 3, and 17, September 2 and 3, 1960; *Time*, LXXVI (September 12, 1960), 21; William G. Carleton, "The People Have Decided," *Nation*, CXCI (September 10, 1960), 124.

14. *Time*, LXXVI (September 5, 1960), 9–10; *ibid.* (September 26,

1960), 20–21; *Newsweek*, LVI (September 5, 1960), 16; *New York Times*, September 19, 1960.

15. *Newsweek*, LVI (October 10, 1960), 24–26; *New Republic*, CXLIII (November 7, 1960), 2; Sorensen, *Kennedy*, p. 201; Lincoln, *Twelve Years*, p. 174; *Time*, LXXVI (September 19, 1960), 22–23.

16. *New York Times*, August 27, September 3, 4, 6, 7, 12, and 14, 1960; *Time*, LXXVI (September 12, 1960), 24.

17. *Nation*, CXCI (October 1, 1960), 189.

18. *Newsweek*, LVI (September 5, 1960), 16; *ibid.* (October 10, 1960), 26; *New York Times*, August 11, 25, and 27, 1960.

19. *Time*, LXXVI (September 12, 1960), 22; White, *Making*, pp. 309–10.

20. *New York Times*, September 4, 7, and 15, 1960; William J. Miller, *Henry Cabot Lodge* (New York, 1967), pp. 323–24; *Time*, LXXVI (September 26, 1960), 23–25.

21. *New York Times*, September 13, 15, and 18, 1960.

22. *Ibid.*, August 31 and September 4, 1960; *Newsweek*, LVI (September 12, 1960), 24; *New Republic*, CXLIII (September 12, 1960), 4–5; *Reporter*, XXIII (September 29, 1960), 4.

23. *New York Times*, September 6, 15, and 19, 1960; *Public Papers of the Presidents: Eisenhower, 1960*, p. 679; *Newsweek*, LVI (September 19, 1960), 47–50; *Time*, LXXVI (September 26, 1960), 30–31; State Department, *Bulletin*, XLIII (October 10, 1960), 588–89.

24. *New York Times*, September 17 and 21, 1960.

25. *Ibid.*, September 18, 20, 21, and 22, 1960; *Time*, LXXVI (October 3, 1960), 17.

26. *New York Times*, September 22 and 24, October 4, 1960.

27. *Ibid.*, September 20, 21, and 22, 1960; *Time*, LXXVI (October 3, 1960), 11.

28. *Public Papers of the Presidents: Eisenhower, 1960*, pp. 707–20; *Newsweek*, LVI (October 3, 1960), 22; *Reporter*, XXIII (October 13, 1960), 21–22.

29. Answer Desk *Bulletin*, September 19 and 24, 1960, RNCP, Box 2; *New York Times*, September 17 and 26, 1960; *Newsweek*, LVI (October 3, 1960), 37; *ibid.* (October 10, 1960), 27.

30. Robert G. Spivack, "It's Up to Kennedy," *Nation*, CXCI (October 8, 1960), 220–21; *ibid.* (October 15, 1960), 237–38; *Time*, LXXVI (October 10, 1960), 26; Sorensen, *Kennedy*, p. 192.

31. White, *Making*, pp. 317–24; *New York Times*, July 25 and Sep-

tember 25, 1960; Richard M. Nixon, *Six Crises* (Garden City, N.Y., 1962), pp. 323–24; Mazo and Hess, *Nixon*, pp. 234–35.

32. Sidney Kraus, ed., *The Great Debates* (Bloomington, Ind., 1962), pp. 348–51; *Nation*, CXCI (October 8, 1960), 218.

33. *Time*, LXXVI (October 10, 1960), 20; *Newsweek*, LVI (October 10, 1960), 23; Sorensen, *Kennedy*, p. 225; Mazo and Hess, *Nixon*, pp. 235–36.

34. White, *Making*, pp. 332–33; Elihu Katz and Jacob J. Feldman, "The Debates in the Light of Research: A Survey of Surveys," in Kraus, *Great Debates*, pp. 190–202; *Reporter*, XXIII (October 13, 1960), 2; National Media Analysis Weekly Report No. 26; Robert Merriam Papers, Eisenhower Library, Box 8; *New Republic*, CXLIII (October 3, 1960), 6; *ibid.* (October 10, 1960), 5; *Nation*, CXCI (November 5, 1960), 344.

35. *New York Times*, September 28, 29, and 30, 1960; *Newsweek*, LVI (October 10, 1960), 23; Pierre Salinger, *With Kennedy* (Garden City, N.Y., 1966), p. 47; C. L. Sulzberger, *The Last of the Giants* (New York, 1970), p. 696.

36. *Time*, LXXVI (October 10, 1960), 20; *Public Papers of the Presidents: Eisenhower, 1960*, pp. 735–36; *New York Times*, September 30, 1960.

37. *Ibid.*, September 30, October 1, 4, 9, 12, and 14, 1960; *Public Papers of the Presidents: Eisenhower, 1960*, p. 743; *Time*, LXXVI (October 10, 1960), 29; *Newsweek*, LVI (October 24, 1960), 56, 61.

38. Mazo and Hess, *Nixon*, pp. 235–36; *New York Times*, October 8, 1960; *Time*, LXXVI (October 17, 1960), 17–18.

39. Kraus, *Great Debates*, pp. 369–72, 376–77, 380–82, 385–87.

40. *Time*, LXXVI (October 17, 1960), 17; Katz and Feldman, "Debates in Light of Research," pp. 196–97; *Newsweek*, LVI (October 17, 1960), 27; *ibid.* (October 24, 1960), 37; *New York Times*, October 8 and 14, 1960.

41. Foster Rhea Dulles, *American Foreign Policy Toward Communist China, 1949–1969* (New York, 1972), pp. 154–60, 174–82; *New York Times*, October 16, 1960.

42. *Ibid.*, October 11, 12, 13, and 14, 1960; *Time*, LXXVI (October 24, 1960), 26.

43. *New York Times*, October 13 and 14, 1960; Answer Desk *Bulletin*, October 13 and 14, 1960, RNCP, Box 2; *Battle Line*, October 21, 1960, Merriam Papers, Box 9.

44. Merriam to Bryce Harlow, October 12 and 13, 1960, Merriam Papers, Box 8.
45. Kraus, *Great Debates*, pp. 391–99.
46. *New York Times*, October 15 and 16, 1960; *Newsweek*, LVI (October 24, 1960), 38; Lasky, *J.F.K.*, p. 44.
47. Nixon, *Six Crises*, p. 348; *New York Times*, October 16, 17, and 18, 1960; *Newsweek*, LVI (October 31, 1960), 22.
48. Kraus, *Great Debates*, pp. 426–27; *Time*, LXXVI (October 24, 1960), 25.
49. Nixon, *Six Crises*, p. 348; Sorensen, *Kennedy*, p. 231; Bowles, *Promises*, pp. 295–97; Sulzberger, *Last of the Giants*, p. 699.
50. Katz and Feldman, "Debates in Light of Research," pp. 196–97; Answer Desk *Bulletin*, October 15, 1960, RNCP, Box 2; *Time*, LXXVI (*October 24, 1960*), *25; New Republic*, CXLIII (October 24, 1960), 3.
51. *Time*, LXXVI (October 10, 1960), 45; *Newsweek*, LVI (October 10, 1960), 59; Lasky, *J.F.K.*, p. 447; *New York Times*, October 7, 1960.
52. *Ibid.*, October 19, 1960; State Department, *Bulletin*, XLIII (November 7, 1960), 715–16; *Time*, LXXVI (October 31, 1960), 26.
53. Schlesinger, *Thousand Days*, pp. 72–73; *New York Times*, October 21, 1960.
54. Nixon, *Six Crises*, pp. 353–54; Sorensen, *Kennedy*, pp. 231–32; Lasky, *J.F.K.*, p. 452.
55. Kraus, *Great Debates*, pp. 417–18; Sorensen, *Kennedy*, p. 232.
56. *New Republic*, CXLIII (October 31, 1960), 5–6; *Nation*, CXCI (November 5, 1960), 337; *New York Times*, October 22 and 23, 1960; Schlesinger, *Thousand Days*, p. 73.
57. *New York Times*, October 23 and 25, 1960; Garry Wills, *Nixon Agonistes: The Crisis of the Self-Made Man* (Boston, 1970), pp. 138–39; Nixon, *Six Crises*, pp. 355–56.
58. Kraus, *Great Debates*, pp. 407–9, 419–20, 428–30; Answer Desk *Bulletin*, October 20, 1960, RNCP, Box 2; *New York Times*, October 21, 1960.
59. *Reporter*, XXIII (November 10, 1960), 18; Katz and Feldman, "Debates in Light of Research," pp. 196–97; *Newsweek*, LVI (October 31, 1960), 19.
60. *New York Times*, October 27 and November 1, 1960; *Time*, LXXVI (October 24, 1960), 33; *ibid.* (October 31, 1960), 9; *ibid.* (November 7, 1960), 55; *Newsweek*, LVI (October 31, 1960), 22.
61. National Media Analysis, Weekly Report No. 8, Merriam Papers,

Box 8; *New York Times*, October 30, 1960; *Time*, LXXVI (October 31, 1960), 13–17; *New Republic*, CXLIII (October 31, 1960), 2; Douglass Cater, "En Route with the Candidates," *Reporter*, XXIII (October 27, 1960), 19–20.

62. *New York Times*, October 8 and 15, 1960; *Newsweek*, LVI (October 24, 1960), 42; *ibid.* (October 31, 1960), 23.
63. *New York Times*, November 1, 1960; *Newsweek*, LVI (October 31, 1960), 36.
64. *Time*, LXXVI (November 7, 1960), 26–27; *Nation*, CXCI (November 12, 1960), 357; *New York Times*, November 6 and 7, 1960.
65. Nixon, *Six Crises*, pp. 360–61; *New York Times*, October 25, 26, and 30, 1960; *Newsweek*, LVI (November 7, 1960), 32–33.
66. Press releases, American Nationalities for Nixon-Lodge, September 19, October 14, 23, and 24, 1960, RNCP, Box 4; *Battle Line*, October 14, 1960, RNCP, Box 4; A. B. Hermann to Members of Congress, October 4, 1960, RNCP, Box 4.
67. Press release, American Nationalities for Nixon-Lodge, October 31, 1960, RNCP, Box 4; *New York Times*, October 28 and November 7, 1960; *New Republic*, CXLIII (November 14, 1960), 2.
68. Goldwater to Eisenhower, October 25, 1960, and Luce to Eisenhower, October 20, 1960, DDE Papers, OF 138 C–4; FitzGerald to Scott, October 21, 1960, and FitzGerald to Merriam, October 28, 1960, Merriam Papers, Box 8.
69. Eisenhower to Republican state chairmen, October 26, 1960, DDE Papers, OF 138 C–4; *Public Papers of the Presidents: Eisenhower, 1960*, pp. 816–19; *New York Times*, October 29, 1960.
70. *Ibid.*, November 1, 1960, Eisenhower to Walter Williams, October 31, 1960, DDE Papers, OF 138 C–4; *Public Papers of the Presidents: Eisenhower, 1960*, pp. 824–28, 831–34. Nixon's friendly biographers, Earl Mazo and Stephen Hess, claim that the Vice-President refrained from asking Eisenhower to go all-out in campaigning during the last week at the request of the President's wife and his physician. They warned Nixon that too much activity on Ike's part could be "disastrous" to his health. Mazo and Hess claim Ike was hurt and disappointed by Nixon's attitude, but the active role Ike played during the last week contradicts their assertions. Mazo and Hess, *Nixon*, pp. 239–41.
71. *Public Papers of the Presidents: Eisenhower, 1960*, pp. 836–45, 853–55; *New York Times*, November 5 and 8, 1960; *Time*, LXXVI (November 14, 1960), 21–22; Sorensen, *Kennedy*, p. 234.
72. White, *Making*, p. 359; Sorensen, *Kennedy*, pp. 229–30; *New*

York Times, October 25, 26, 27, and 29, November 2, 1960; Time, LXXVI (November 7, 1960), 30.

73. Ibid. (November 7, 1960), 47; New York Times, October 27, 28, 30, and 31, 1960; Public Papers of the Presidents: Eisenhower, 1960, p. 822.

74. White, Making, pp. 371–72; New York Times, November 7, 1960; Lincoln, Twelve Years, pp. 180–81; Schlesinger, Thousand Days, pp. 74–75; New Republic, CXLIII (November 7, 1960), 16; Newsweek, LVI (November 7, 1960), 32.

75. New York Times, November 5, 6, and 8, 1960.

76. Nixon, Six Crises, pp. 389–90, 395–98; de Toledano, One Man Alone, p. 309; Sorensen, Kennedy, p. 239; New York Times, November 9 and 10, 1960; Salinger, With Kennedy, pp. 49–50.

77. Mazo and Hess, Nixon, p. 242; "The 1960 Elections," memo of research staff of Republican National Committee, April 1961, RNCP, Box 1; Philip Converse, Angus Campbell, Warren E. Miller, and Donald E. Stokes, "Stability and Change in 1960: A Reinstating Election," American Political Science Review, LV (June 1961), 269–80.

78. Time, LXXVI (November 16, 1960), 3; New Republic, CXLIII (November 21, 1960), 8–9; Ted Lumes' memo, "Poles and Polls," October 25, 1963, RNCP, Box 4.

79. New York Times, November 13, 1960; Newsweek, LVI (November 14, 1960), EE3; New Republic, CXLIII (November 14, 1960), 7; Louis H. Bean, "Why Kennedy Won," Nation, XCXI (November 26, 1960), 408–10; Sorensen, Kennedy, pp. 244–47; Converse, et al., "The 1960 Election," pp. 275–78.

80. White, Making, passim; Time, LXXVI (November 21, 1960); Sorensen, Kennedy, pp. 243–44.

81. New York Times, November 13, 1960; Nelson W. Polsby and Aaron B. Wildavsky, Presidential Elections: Strategies of American Electoral Politics (New York, 1964), pp. 116–17.

82. Nation, CXCI (November 19, 1960), 377.

BIBLIOGRAPHY

Manuscript Collections

Adams, Sherman, Dwight D. Eisenhower Library
Baruch, Bernard M., Princeton University Library
Benedict, Stephen, Dwight D. Eisenhower Library
Chapman, Oscar, Harry S. Truman Library
Citizens for Eisenhower Papers, Dwight D. Eisenhower Library
Dulles, John Foster, Princeton University Library
Eisenhower, Dwight D., Dwight D. Eisenhower Library
Kefauver, Estes, University of Tennessee Library
Lambie, James W., Dwight D. Eisenhower Library
Lloyd, David D., Harry S. Truman Library
Merriam, Robert, Dwight D. Eisenhower Library
Mitchell, Stephen A., Harry S. Truman Library
Murphy, Charles, Harry S. Truman Library
Pyle, Howard, Dwight D. Eisenhower Library
Republican National Committee Papers, Cornell University Library
Sevareid, Eric, Library of Congress
Truman, Harry S., Harry S. Truman Library

Oral History Interviews

Dulles Oral History Collection, Princeton University Library
    Edward Corsi   Henry Luce
    Allen W. Dulles   William B. Macomber

Dwight D. Eisenhower   Thruston B. Morton
James C. Hagerty   Robert D. Murphy
Gabriel Hauge   Richard H. Rovere
Emmet John Hughes   Eustace Seligman
Eisenhower Oral History Collection, Dwight D. Eisenhower Library
    Lucius Clay
    Murray Snyder
Truman Oral History Collection, Harry S. Truman Library
    Kenneth M. Birkhead
    Jerry Hess

Government Publications

Public Papers of the Presidents of the United States: Dwight D. Eisenhower. Eight volumes, Washington, 1960–1961.
Public Papers of the Presidents of the United States: Harry S. Truman. Eight volumes, Washington, 1961–1966.
U.S. Department of State. *Bulletin* (1952–1960).

Newspapers and Periodicals

Bulletin of the Atomic Scientists (1956)
Foreign Affairs (1952)
Life (1952–1960)
Nation (1952–1960)
New Republic (1952–1960)
Newsweek (1952–1960)
New York Times (1952–1960)
Reporter (1952–1960)
Time (1952–1960)
U.S. News and World Report (1952)
Vital Speeches (1952–1960)
Washington Post (1956)

Articles and Books

A. General

Ambrose, Stephen E. *Rise to Globalism: American Foreign Policy Since 1938.* Baltimore, 1971.

Campbell, Angus; Philip E. Converse; Warren E. Miller; and Donald E. Stokes. *The American Voter.* New York, 1960.

Campbell, Angus; Gerald Gurin; and Warren E. Miller. *The Voter Decides.* Evanston, Ill., 1954.

LaFeber, Walter. *America, Russia, and the Cold War, 1945–1971.* Second edition. New York, 1972.

Lilienthal, David E. *The Journals of David E. Lilienthal.* Four volumes. New York, 1964–1970.

Polsby, Nelson W., and Aaron B. Wildavsky. *Presidential Elections: Strategies of American Electoral Politics.* New York, 1964.

Porter, Kirk H., and Donald Bruce Johnson, eds. *National Party Platforms, 1840–1956.* Urbana, Ill., 1956.

Rosebloom, Eugene H. *A History of Presidential Elections.* Third edition. New York, 1970.

Schlesinger, Arthur M., Jr., and Fred L. Israel, eds. *History of American Presidential Elections, 1789–1968.* Four volumes. New York, 1971.

Waltz, Kenneth N., "Electoral Punishment and Foreign Policy Crises." In James N. Rosenau, ed., *Domestic Sources of Foreign Policy.* New York, 1967.

B. Election of 1952

Acheson, Dean. *Present at the Creation: My Years in the State Department.* New York, 1969.

Adams, Sherman. *Firsthand Report: The Story of the Eisenhower Administration.* New York, 1961.

Berding, Andrew H. *Dulles on Diplomacy.* Princeton, N.J., 1965.

Bernstein, Barton J. "Election of 1952." In Arthur M. Schlesinger, Jr., and Fred L. Israel, eds., *History of American Presidential Elections, 1789–1968.* New York, 1971, IV.

Brown, John Mason. *Through These Men: Some Aspects of Our Passing History.* New York, 1956.

Brown, Stuart Gerry. *Conscience in Politics: Adlai E. Stevenson in the 1950's.* Syracuse, N.Y., 1961.

Caridi, Ronald J. *The Korean War and American Politics: The Republican Party as a Case Study.* Philadelphia, 1968.

Childs, Marquis. *Eisenhower: Captive Hero.* New York, 1958.

Cutler, Robert. *No Time for Rest.* Boston, 1966.

David, Paul T.; Malcolm Moos; and Ralph M. Goldman. *Presidential Nominating Politics in 1952: The National Story.* Baltimore, 1954.

Davis, Kenneth S. *The Politics of Honor: A Biography of Adlai E. Stevenson.* New York, 1967.

Doyle, Edward P., ed. *As We Knew Adlai.* New York, 1966.

Dulles, Foster Rhea. *America's Rise to World Power, 1898–1954.* New York, 1954.

Dulles, John Foster. "A Policy of Boldness," *Life,* XXXII (May 19, 1952), 146+.

Eisenhower, Dwight D. *At Ease: Stories I Tell My Friends.* Garden City, N.Y., 1967.

———. *Mandate for Change, 1953–1956.* Garden City, N.Y., 1963.

Goold-Adams, Richard. *The Time of Power: A Reappraisal of John Foster Dulles.* London, 1962.

Gorman, Joseph Bruce. *Kefauver: A Political Biography.* New York, 1971.

Griffith, Robert. *The Politics of Fear: Joseph R. McCarthy and the Senate.* Lexington, Ky., 1970.

Harris, Louis. *Is There a Republican Majority?: Political Trends, 1952–1956.* New York, 1954.

Hewlett, Richard G., and **Francis Duncan.** *Atomic Shield, 1947–1952.* University Park, Pa., 1969.

Hughes, Emmet John. *The Ordeal of Power: A Political Memoir of the Eisenhower Years.* New York, 1963.

Johnson, Walter. *How We Drafted Adlai Stevenson.* New York, 1955.

Kempton, Murray. *America Comes of Middle Age.* Boston, 1963.

———. "The Underestimation of Dwight D. Eisenhower," *Esquire,* LXVIII (September 1967), 108+.

Lavine, Harold. *Smoke-Filled Rooms: The Confidential Papers of Robert Humphreys.* Englewood Cliffs, N.J., 1970.

Lubell, Samuel. *Revolt of the Moderates.* New York, 1956.

Parmet, Herbert S. *Eisenhower and the American Crusades.* New York, 1972.

Pusey, Merlo J. *Eisenhower the President.* New York, 1956.

Rees, David. *Korea: The Limited War.* New York, 1964.

Rovere, Richard. *Affairs of State: The Eisenhower Years.* New York, 1956.

Stevenson, Adlai E. *Major Campaign Speeches of Adlai E. Stevenson, 1952.* New York, 1953.

Sulzberger, C. L. *A Long Row of Candles: Memoirs and Diaries, 1934–1954.* New York, 1969.

Taft, Robert A. *A Foreign Policy for Americans.* Garden City, N.Y., 1951.

White, William S. *The Taft Story.* New York, 1954.

Whitman, Alden. *Portrait: Adlai E. Stevenson, Politician, Diplomat, Friend.* New York, 1965.

Wilson, Thomas W., Jr. *The Great Weapons Heresy.* Boston, 1970.

C. Election of 1956

Branyan, Robert L., and **Lawrence H. Larsen, eds.** *The Eisenhower Administration, 1953–1961: A Documentary History.* Two volumes. New York, 1971.

Eden, Anthony. *Full Circle.* Boston, 1960.

Eisenhower, Dwight D. *Waging Peace, 1956–1961.* Garden City, N.Y., 1965.

Finer, Herman, *Dulles over Suez.* Chicago, 1964.

Khrushchev, Nikita S. *Khrushchev Remembers.* Boston, 1970.

Lapp, Ralph. *The Weapons Culture.* New York, 1968.

Larson, Arthur. *Eisenhower: The President Nobody Knew.* New York, 1968.

Lawrence, Bill. *Six Presidents, Too Many Wars.* New York, 1972.

Macmillan, Harold. *Riding the Storm, 1956–1959.* New York, 1971.

Moos, Malcolm. "Election of 1956." In Arthur M. Schlesinger, Jr., and Fred L. Israel, eds., *History of American Presidential Elections, 1789–1968.* IV. New York, 1971.

Moss, Norman. *Men Who Play God.* New York, 1968.

Muller, Herbert J. *Adlai Stevenson: A Study in Values.* New York, 1967.

Murphy, Robert. *Diplomat Among Warriors.* Garden City, N.Y., 1964.

Shepley, James. "How Dulles Averted War," *Life,* XL (January 16, 1956), 70+.

Stebbins, Richard P. *The United States in World Affairs, 1956.* New York, 1957.

Stevenson, Adlai E. *The New America.* Seymour E. Harris, John Bartlow Martin, and Arthur Schlesinger, Jr., eds. New York, 1957.

————. "Why I Raised the H-Bomb Question," *Look,* XXI (February 5, 1957), 23–25.

Stone, I. F. *The Haunted Fifties.* New York, 1963.

Strauss, Lewis L. *Men and Decisions.* Garden City, N.Y., 1962.

Sulzberger, C. L. *The Last of the Giants.* New York, 1970.

Thomson, Charles A. H., and **Frances M. Shattuck.** *The 1956 Presidential Campaign.* Washington, 1960.

Voss, Earl H. *Nuclear Ambush: The Test-Ban Trap.* Chicago, 1963.

D. Election of 1960

Bowles, Chester. *Promises to Keep: My Years in Public Life, 1941–1969.* New York, 1971.

Burns, James MacGregor. *John F. Kennedy: A Political Profile.* New York, 1960.

Converse, Philip; Angus Campbell; Warren E. Miller; and **Donald E. Stokes.** "Stability and Change in 1960: A Reinstating Election," *American Political Science Review,* LV (June 1961), 269–80.

Dulles, Foster Rhea. *American Foreign Policy Toward Communist China, 1949–1969.* New York, 1972.

Evans, Rowland, and **Robert Novak.** *Lyndon B. Johnson: The Exercise of Power.* New York, 1966.

Kennedy, John F. *The Strategy of Peace.* Allan Nevins, ed. New York, 1960.

Kraus, Sidney, ed. *The Great Debates.* Bloomington, Ind., 1962.

Lash, Joseph P. *Eleanor: The Years Alone.* New York, 1972.

Lasky, Victor. *J.F.K.: The Man and the Myth.* New York, 1963.

Lincoln, Evelyn. *My Twelve Years with John F. Kennedy.* New York, 1965.

Mazo, Earl, and **Stephen Hess.** *Nixon: A Political Portrait.* New York, 1968.

Miller, William J. *Henry Cabot Lodge.* New York, 1967.

Morgan, Thomas B. "The People-Machine," *Harper's,* CCXXII (January 1961), 53–57.

Nixon, Richard M. *Six Crises.* Garden City, N.Y., 1962.

Powers, Francis Gary, with **Curt Gentry.** *Operation Overflight.* New York, 1970.

Salinger, Pierre. *With Kennedy.* Garden City, N.Y., 1966.

Schlesinger, Arthur M., Jr. *A Thousand Days: John F. Kennedy in the White House.* Boston, 1965.

Sorensen, Theodore C. "Election of 1960." In Arthur M. Schlesinger, Jr., and Fred L. Israel, eds., *History of American Presidential Elections, 1789–1968.* New York, 1971, IV.

———. *Kennedy.* New York, 1965.

Stebbins, Richard P. *The United States in World Affairs, 1959.* New York, 1960.

———. *The United States in World Affairs, 1960.* New York, 1961.

de Toledano, Ralph. *One Man Alone: Richard Nixon.* New York, 1969.

White, Theodore H. *The Making of the President, 1960.* New York, 1961.

Wills, Gary. *Nixon Agonistes: The Crisis of the Self-Made Man.* Boston, 1970.

Wise, David, and Thomas B. Ross. *The U-2 Affair.* New York, 1962.

INDEX

Acheson, Dean, 40, 64, 121, 276, 287; Secretary of State, 4, 23, 44, 47, 48, 67; and Korea, 4, 9, 30, 70, 72, 74, 259; speeches for Stevenson, 67

ADA. *See* Americans for Democratic Action

Adams, Sherman, 14, 15, 45; Ike's campaign manager, 42-43, 44, 56, 60-61, 62, 69, 75, 76, 83-84, 85; White House chief-of-staff, 87, 89, 97, 133, 134, 148-149, 167, 168; resignation of, 183

AEC. *See* Atomic Energy Commission, U.S.

African nations, U.S. development aid to, 250

Air strike intervention, at Dien Bien Phu, rejected, 94, 95

Alamo, Stevenson's 1952 speech at, 73-74

Alaska, Nixon's campaign trip to (1960), 283

Allies, Western: collective security, 3-4, 13-14 (*see also* Collective security; NATO); shocked by

Dulles's liberation doctrine, 51-52, 53, 54, 55; shocked by Ike's neutralism statement, 111; split in Suez crisis, 150, 167-170, 171, 172, 176; and summit meetings, 185, 186, 208

Alsop, Joseph, 272

Alsop, Stewart, 65

American Legion: convention of 1952, Ike at, 50-51; and Stevenson at, 66; convention of 1956, Stevenson at, 136, 138; Nixon's 1960 address to, 264, 267

American Nationalities for Nixon-Lodge Committee, 275-276

"American party" proposal, in 1952, 50

American Society of Newspaper Editors, 98

American troops: withdrawal from South Korea, 39, 68, 72, 74, 77-78; in Europe for NATO, 3-4, 13, 30; in Korean War, 4-5, 71-72, 79, 80

Americans for Democratic Action (ADA), 47

Dewey's adherence to, in 1948 Berlin crisis, 148; after 1948, 4; threats to, in early 1950's, 3-4; Taft's departure from, 8-10, 13, 29-30, 64; Stassen support for, 10-11; Warren support for, 10-11; Ike chosen as GOP defender of, 12, 13-14, 64, 85; Dulles's reaffirmation of, 23; Dulles's departure from, 27, 64; GOP abandonment of, 44, 64, 85; in Stevenson's silence on Suez crisis (1956), 148-149, 150-151; Kennedy's retreat to, in Quemoy-Matsu debate, 264

Blair, William, 47
Bonsal, Philip, 267
Boston, 280; Stevenson's 1952 speech in, 77; Ike's 1952 speech in, 80; Stevenson's 1956 speech in, 174
Bowles, Chester, 92, 121, 199, 216, 217, 233, 251, 265
Bradley, General Omar, 48, 49
Brandt, Irving, 255
Bricker, John, 36, 58, 228
Bricker Amendment, 88
"Brinkmanship" in foreign policy, 96-97, 139; Democratic attacks on, 96, 97, 108, 121
Brown, Harrison, 153
Brown, John Mason, 65
Brown, Stuart, 83
Brownell, Herbert, 12, 16, 26, 36, 56, 62, 85, 89, 151, 224
Buffalo: Stevenson's 1956 speech in, 171; Nixon's 1960 speech in, 264; Polish vote in 1960, 276, 284
Bulganin, Nikolai, 94, 97, 103, 133, 175; test-ban proposals of, 102, 139, 157-159; in Suez crisis, 176-177
Bulletin of the Atomic Scientists, 106, 156
Bundy, McGeorge, 41

Burns, James MacGregor, 83
Burroughs, Robert P., 76
Bush, Prescott, 114, 126
Byrd, Harry, 284

Cake, Ralph, 76
California primaries, of 1956, 108, 109
Callender, Harold, 51
Camp David summit meeting (1959), 186, 187
Captive Nations Week (1959), 194. *See also* Operation Freedom Week
Carleton, William, 240
Carlson, Frank, 12, 56, 58
Castro, Fidel, 184, 213-214, 238-239, 266-270, 281; in New York at U.N., 249, 250, 266
Castro, Raoul, 239
Cater, Douglass, 271, 273
Catholic vote: in 1952, 82; won over by Ike, 82, 191, 284; Kennedy and, 191, 198, 275, 284-285; in 1960, 284-285
Central Intelligence Agency (CIA), 48, 117, 166, 167, 233; in Guatemalan coup of 1954, 269; preparations for Cuban invasion, 184, 234, 268, 270; U-2 reconnaissance flights, 200-201
Chamberlain, Neville, 159
Chapman, Oscar, 83
"Checkers" speech, of Nixon, 63, 252
Chiang Kai-shek, 4, 5, 10, 30, 94, 122, 127, 216, 259, 260, 261, 263
Chicago: Stevenson's 1956 speech in, 174; won by Ike in 1956, 178; Kennedy's campaign speech in, 282; Polish vote in 1960, 276, 284
Chicago *Daily News,* 58
Chicago *Tribune,* quoted, 28, 50, 225

Childs, Marquis, 75
China (*see also* Communist China; Formosa; Nationalist China): Communist takeover, 4, 7; "loss of," Democrats blamed for, 10, 28, 32, 34, 70
Christian Nationalist party, 61
Church, Frank, 216
CIA. *See* Central Intelligence Agency
Cincinnati: Ike's 1952 speech in, 70; Stevenson's 1956 speech in, 150; Kennedy's campaign speech in, 267
Cities. *See* Urban vote
Citizens Committee for Eisenhower-Nixon, 42, 44
Citizens for Eisenhower: in 1952, 16; in 1956, 89, 134
Civil rights, 19, 38, 224; issues in 1956, 108; Stevenson's moderate stance in South, 108, 109, 122
Clay, General Lucius D., 12, 13-14, 15, 16, 25-26, 62, 81, 89, 91, 163
Cleveland, Ike's 1956 speech in, 140
"Coexistence." *See* "Peaceful coexistence"
Cohen, Ben, 121
Cold War, 3, 38, 183; effect of loss of U.S. nuclear monopoly on, 6; public apprehensions, 7, 83; blamed on Democrats, 8-9, 33; Dulles proposals for new policy, 24-26 (*see also* Liberation, doctrine of; Massive retaliation); Stevenson's "coexistence" approach to, 66-67; Stevenson ideology on, 74; apparent detente, 94-95; "being lost by U.S." warnings by Stevenson, 98-99, 124, 135, 180; easing of tensions exploited in 1956 GOP campaign, 134, 143; sense of U.S. falling behind Soviets, 184-185, 187-188 (*see also* Prestige, U.S., charge of

decline of); hope for detente, during Ike's second term, 186, 187, 200; hope destroyed, 205; as 1960 election issue, 200, 211, 216, 217, 221, 228-231, 242-243, 244, 275-279; U.S.-Soviet confrontations in 1960, 219-221
Collective security, 4, 37, 38, 262; Ike's support for, 13-14, 26, 31; Stevenson's support for, 21-22, 72; endorsed by Republican foreign policy plank of 1952, 34, 35
Colonialism, U.N. condemnation of, 257
Commission on National Goals, 188
Communism, Communists: world aggressiveness, 3, 21, 276; spies in U.S. government charges, 7; public fear of, 7; proposals of ideological and propaganda warfare against, 9-10, 25, 30 (*see also* Liberation, doctrine of); advances of, as election issue in 1952, 34-35, 44-45, 50-52, 64, 66-67, 68, 80, 83; Stevenson called soft on, 64, 79-80, 109; triumph without war possible, 97; spread of, as issue in 1956, 124, 135; as issue in 1960, 214, 228, 243, 263, 275-278; in Cuba, 184, 214, 220, 239, 249, 263, 267; in Latin America, 239, 268, 269; danger of takeover in Congo, 238, 247; Democrats called soft on (1960), 276
Communist China, 4, 216; in Korean War, 4-5, 94; U.S. blockade and bombing proposed, 5, 10, 20; and Vietnam, 94; and Quemoy and Matsu, 94, 259-265; Egypt recognized by, 116; U.S. nonrecognition policy restated in both 1956 platforms, 122, 127; Cuban recognition of, 239; U.N. seat denied (1960), 257

Dewey, Thomas E., 11, 23, 26, 63, 85, 165, 273; 1948 campaign of, 8, 42, 43, 57, 148; supports continued bipartisanship in foreign policy, 4; supports Ike in 1952, 12, 24, 59, 62, 71; at 1952 Republican Convention, 34, 36; supports Ike in 1956, 89, 128, 137; comments on test-ban issue, 151, 157, 159; at 1960 Republican Convention, 227, 228

Dien Bien Phu, 94

Dirksen, Everett McKinley, 33-34, 58, 207

Disarmament, 101, 102, 142, 257 (*see also* Arms control; Nuclear weapons); of West Germany, proposed by Soviets, 95; 1956 negotiations in London (UN subcommittee), 102, 105; Geneva talks (1958), 186

Discrimination, 108, 124, 273. *See also* Civil rights

Domestic issues: in 1952 campaign, 57, 59; voter preference for Democrats in, 83; in 1956, 108, 124; emphasized by Democrats in 1956 campaign, 131-132; in 1960 campaign, 198, 200, 209, 224, 226, 281, 284; in Nixon-Kennedy TV debates, 253, 254

Domino theory, 73

Douglas, Lewis, 97

Douglas, Paul, 20, 38

Douglas, William O., 12

Draft: proposal for ending of, 136-138, 140, 141, 157, 179; need asserted, 137, 140, 141, 142; statistics, 141

Duff, James, 12, 15

Dulles, Allen W., 117, 167, 177, 233-234, 268

Dulles, John Foster, 286; 1949 advocacy of U.S. troop withdrawal from South Korea, 39; Japanese peace treaty negotiated by, 23; and bipartisanship in foreign policy, in 1952, 23, 27, 64; critical of passive nature of containment, 24-25, 44; and massive retaliation doctrine, 24, 33, 95-96; his liberation doctrine, 24-25, 27, 44, 46, 51; *War or Peace* (book), 25; *Life* article by, 25-26, 30, 54; Ike supported by, 26, 81; 1952 GOP foreign policy plank drafted by, 26-27, 31-32, 34, 35; "War or Peace" (speech), 45; and 1952 campaign, 44-46, 51-54, 85; and Korean War as campaign issue, 45; criticized for his liberation "scenario," 51-53, 54, 66; charges Democrats with appeasement, 53; Secretary of State, 87, 89, 95-98; hard-line policies of, 95, 110-111; liberation rhetoric dropped by, 95, 113, 162-163; implements massive retaliation, 95-96; and Quemoy and Matsu, 95, 260; "brinkmanship," 96-97, 108, 121, 139; a political liability for Republicans, 97, 108, 110-112, 121, 139, 148; response to shift in Soviet policy, 97-98, 99, 100, 110-111; rejects H-bomb test ban, 102, 156, 159; and neutralism, 111-112; withdrawal of Aswan Dam aid offer, 115, 116, 150, 171; and Suez crisis of 1956, 115-120, 125, 129, 144-150, 166, 167, 168-170, 172, 180; and 1956 Republican foreign policy plank, 126; in 1956 campaign, 133; and Polish and Hungarian "liberation," 163, 164-165, 175; speech on U.S. policy toward restive Soviet satellites, 164; Stevenson's criticism of his Suez policy, 170-171

Dunning, John, 156

East German uprising of 1953, 95, 114, 163
Eastern Republicans; internationalism of, 11, 12, 17, 48, 55, 137; role in choice of Presidential candidates, 11-12, 17, 27
Eden, Sir Anthony, 117, 118, 145, 146, 167, 177
Edwards, India, 67
Egypt: Aswan Dam financing offer withdrawn by U.S., 115, 116, 150; Soviet military aid, 115, 116, 122, 171; Suez crisis, 115-120, 125, 145-151, 166-170, 171, 176-177; 1956 fighting with Israel, 116; Israeli invasion of Sinai peninsula, 166-167, 169, 170, 173; Anglo-French bombing and invasion of, 169-170, 176-177
Eisenhower, Dwight D., 188, 194, 195, 230, 287; personality of, 28-29, 57-58; 1947 recommendation for U.S. troop withdrawal from South Korea, 39, 68, 72, 77-78; Supreme Commander of NATO forces, 3-4, 15, 16; offered 1952 candidacy by Truman, 11-12; move for draft of, by eastern Republicans, 12-17; a reluctant candidate in 1952, 12-15, 85; as symbol of continuance of bipartisanship, 12, 13-14, 64, 85; supports containment policy, 13-14, 28, 32, 40-41; supports collective security, 13-14, 26, 31, 35; in 1952 primaries, 14, 15-16, 17, 29; opinion polls on, in early 1952, 15, 17, 29, 32-33; in active quest for GOP nomination, 16-17, 22, 23-24, 27-29, 30-32; and Dulles, pre-convention meeting, 25-26; supports liberation doctrine, 26,

35, 46; rejects massive retaliation doctrine (during campaign), 26, 31, 35-36, 85; and 1952 GOP foreign policy plank, 26-27, 31-32, 34, 35; accused of neglecting Asia, 26, 30; domestic policy views, 28, 57, 59; basic agreement with Truman on Korea, 28, 46, 70; internationalism of, 31-32; campaign against Taft, 30-32; 1952 nomination of, 36; choice of running mate, 36; 1952 acceptance speech, 36; GOP party regulars' reservations about, 37, 42, 50, 58; in basic agreement with Stevenson on containment policy, 40-41; campaign organization of, 42-43, 56; speech-writers, 54, 56; campaign strategy, 43-46, 59, 82; his support given to all GOP congressional candidates, 43, 59-61; his qualifications to deal with Communists stressed, 44-45, 83-84; accused of selling out to Taft and isolationism, 48, 59, 68, 74, 77, 78; declines foreign policy briefing, 49; foreign policy speeches of, 50-51, 53, 54, 70-72, 74, 80; criticized for liberation doctrine, 51-53, 66; rejects appeasement, 53; retreat from liberation doctrine, 53-54, 55-56, 84; campaign tours and speeches, 56-58, 65, 70-72, 74, 80; popularity of, 57-58, 82, 87, 88, 110, 187; the "crusader," 57-58; compromises of his 1952 campaign, 58-64, 80, 84; post-convention poll results on, 58, 69, 70, 81; agreement with Taft, 59, 64, 80, 84; unification of GOP by, 59-62, 85; and Joe McCarthy, 59-61, 64, 80, 84; and MacArthur, 61-62, 64; and Nixon fund affair, 62-63, 64,

84; his past foreign affairs errors disclosed by Truman, 68-69, 77-78; espousal of Taft's foreign policy positions, 70, 85; Korean War becomes his major issue, 70-72, 74-76, 80, 84-85; "Asians against Asians" statement of, 71, 73, 78; "I shall go to Korea" pledge of, 74-76, 80, 82-83, 85, 94; 1952 election results for, 81-82; 178; his victory analyzed, 82-85; his coattails weak, 82, 83-84, 178; and Catholic vote, 82, 191; a skillful politician, 84-85, 91; as party leader, 87-88; first term of, 87, 94-100; adoption of massive retaliation policy by, 85, 95; relations with Congress, 88, 207; "peace and prosperity" achieved, 88, 124-125, 128, 133, 173; heart attack of 1955, 88-89, 92, 98; poll results on, in 1956, 89, 110, 133, 174-175; question of second term, 89-90; health issue, 90, 100, 112-113, 129, 154, 174, 179; abdominal operation, 112; as candidate in 1956, 90, 110, 112, 133-135; and choice of running-mate in 1956, 90-91, 127-128; foreign policy successes of, 94-95, 99, 126, 139; and defense of Quemoy and Matsu, 94, 259-260, 262, 263-264, 265, 266; and brinkmanship furor, 96-97; foreign policy speech on U.S.-Soviet relations, 98, 99; and Soviet ICBM capability, 104; H-bomb testing defended by, 104-105, 138-140, 141-142, 156-157, 159; neutralism statement of, 111; and peaceful liberation, 113-114, 162; and Suez crisis, 116-120, 125, 145, 149-150, 166-171, 176-177; its effect on his candidacy, 117, 118, 119-121, 129,

144-145, 150-151, 172, 178; his foreign policy indicted in Democratic platform, 121; renomination of, 128; Republican Convention praise for, 126, 128; 1956 acceptance speech, 128; 1956 campaign of, 133-135; campaign speeches of, 135, 139-141, 157, 163, 165-167; his military achievements as asset in crisis atmosphere, 139-143, 172; on need for draft, 140, 141, 142, 157; and Péron loans, 143; and Polish crisis of 1956, 162-163; and Hungarian uprising, 163-164, 165-166, 175-176; Stevenson's criticism of his Suez policy, 170-171, 173; 1956 election landslide win, 177-178; his victory analyzed, 178-180; second term reverses, 183-185; and Castro's Cuba, 184, 213, 239, 267, 281; personal diplomacy of, 185-186, 187; plan for visit to Russia, 186, 204, 212; reversal of his stand on H-bomb test ban, 186; arms control efforts of, 186-187; his defense policies criticized, 192, 195, 210, 221-222, 225, 231; Kennedy attacks on, 192, 235, 256, 278; proclamation of Captive Nations Week, 194; Nixon supported by, in 1960, 196, 226, 236-238, 244, 256, 277-279; and U-2 incident, 201-205, 206, 208; and planned Paris Summit, 204-205, 206, 208; Khrushchev's attacks on, 204, 211-212; trip to Japan canceled, 212-213, 214, 247; decline in popularity, 213; and RB-47 incident, 220; reaction to Rockefeller-Nixon statement, 225; and 1960 Republican platform, 225-226; defense of his defense policies, 227, 278; offer of brief-

siderations on, 285-287

Embargo, on Cuban trade, 267-268

Estonia, 34

Ethnic vote (*see also* Jewish vote; Polish Americans): GOP appeal to, with liberation policy (1952), 53, 54-55, 66, 82, 84; Democratic strategy for gaining, 55; in 1952 election, 82, 84; GOP appeal to, in 1956, 113-114, 162; East European, geographic concentration of, 114; Nixon's appeal to, in 1960, 275-277, 279; in 1960 election, 284

Europe: Western, defense of, 3-4, 5, 33, 216 (*see also* Collective security; NATO); stationing of U.S. troops in, 3-4, 13, 30; Soviet threat stopped in, 7, 9; Eastern, proposals for radio propaganda aimed at, 9-10, 25, 38, 51; Eastern, loss blamed on FDR and Truman, 10, 34, 275-276; Eastern, concept of liberation policy for, 24-26, 27, 34-35, 38, 50-51, 54-55 (*see also* Liberation, doctrine of); reaction to liberation "scenario" of Dulles, 51-52, 53, 54, 55; fallout dangers of nuclear attack, 106; Eastern, uprisings in Soviet satellites, 95, 113, 114, 161-168, 173, 175-176; U.S. economic aid offered to Soviet satellites, 163, 164; Western, U.S. missile deployment in, 185; U.S. sympathies for captive nations, 192, 194, 276-277; Eastern, Nixon pledge of mission to, 277

Fair Deal, 19

Fallout, radioactive, 101, 103, 104, 105-106, 153-154, 155, 156, 160

Farm vote: in 1952, 82; in 1956 Minnesota primary, 93; in 1960, 284

Farouk, King, ouster of, 115

Federation of American Scientists, 107, 121, 152, 155

Feldman, Mike, 25, 280

Finch, Robert, 193, 235-236

Finletter, Thomas, 92, 121, 211

Finnegan, James, 123, 130-131, 132, 152, 174, 178

FitzGerald, William, 277

Florida, 1952 vote in, 81

Florida primaries: of 1952, 20; of 1956, 107, 108

Foreign Affairs, quoted, 41

Foreign aid: by U.S., 19, 99, 111, 250; Soviet offers to underdeveloped nations, 97; U.S. economic aid to Egypt, 115, 116; Soviet military aid to Egypt, 115, 116, 122, 171; requests for arms for Israel, 115, 121, 122, 127; Republican platforms on, 126, 226; U.S. loans to Péronist Argentina, 143; offers of U.S. economic aid to restive Soviet satellites, 163, 164

Foreign Ministers Conference, Geneva (1959), 184

Foreign Policy for Americans, A (Taft), 8, 24

Foreign policy planks: Democratic, of 1952, 38; Republican, of 1952, 26-27, 31, 34-36; Democratic, of 1956, 121-122; Republican, of 1956, 126-127; Democratic, of 1960, 216-217, 230; Republican, of 1960, 223-224, 225-226

Formosa (Taiwan), 4, 212; U.S. pledge of defense, 94, 95, 259-260, 262-265. *See also* Chiang Kai-shek; Quemoy and Matsu

France: withdrawal from Indo-China, 94, 95; in Baghdad Pact, 115; in Suez crisis, 116, 117, 118, 125, 144-147, 149-150, 166, 167-170, 176-177; U.S. break with, in

Hiss, Alger, 7, 36, 64, 79, 276
Hitler, Adolf, 117, 145, 159
Hoffman, Paul, 15, 16, 32, 45, 89
Hoover, Herbert, 3, 9, 33, 35, 37, 48, 85, 273, 277
Hoover, Herbert, Jr., 126, 167, 177
House of Representatives, U.S. (*see also* Congress, U.S.): 1952 election results, 82; retained by Democrats in 1956, 178; 1958 election results, 183; 1960 election results, 284
Houston, Kennedy's campaign speech in, 241
Howard, Roy, 273
Hughes, Emmet John, 25, 54, 56, 75-76, 84, 125, 129, 134, 139, 140, 149, 168-169, 171, 177, 222
Humphrey, George, 87
Humphrey, Hubert H., 93; 1960 Presidential candidate, 189, 197-198
Humphreys, Robert, 43
Hungarian uprising of 1956, 163-166, 173, 175-176, 177; effect of crisis on U.S. election, 178; 1960 anniversary rallies, 276
Hydrogen bomb, 6-7, 100-101; tests, 100, 101, 104, 138, 186; fallout, 101, 103, 104, 105-106; test-ban proposals, *see* Nuclear weapons; underground testing, 186, 187, 222, 224, 226

ICBM (Inter-Continental Ballistic Missile), 103-104, 106, 185. *See also* Missile race
Ideological warfare: Taft proposal for, 9-10, 30; Dulles's support, 25, 51. *See also* Liberation, doctrine of
Illinois primaries, of 1952, 17
Immigration, national-origins quota system of, 55, 69, 114

Independent vote: importance of, 8, 32, 195; wooed by Republicans, 42, 43, 55, 85; Korea the primary issue for, 70; alienated by "brinkmanship," 97
India, 4, 115, 257; Soviet leaders' visit to, 97, 102; proposal for test ban treaty, 105
Indo-China: French withdrawal from, 94; U.S. intervention proposed, but vetoed, 94, 95
Inflation, 28, 57
Inglis, David R., 106, 156
Internationalism, internationalists: of eastern Republicans, 11, 12, 17, 48, 55, 137; among Republicans, v. GOP isolationism, 25, 27, 48, 50, 85; support for Ike against Taft, 11, 12, 17, 27, 32; Ike's statements for, 31-32; in 1952 GOP foreign policy plank, 35; of Nixon, 36; support of draft, 137
Interventionism, Republican, 85. *See also* Internationalism
Iraq, in Baghdad Pact, 115
Irish-Americans, 1952 vote of, 82, 84
Isolationism, isolationists: of Republicans, in past, 78, 83; among Republicans, in early 1950's, 3-4, 33, 48, 59, 68, 85; opposition to U.S. NATO forces in Europe, 3-4, 13; "new," 4, 11, 73; Taft and, 8, 10, 11, 22, 27, 30, 31, 32; Ike called a puppet of, 48, 59, 68, 74, 77
Israel: question of Western arms supplies to, 115, 121, 122, 127, 149; 1956 Gaza Strip hostilities with Egypt, 116; closing of Suez Canal to, 119; question of U.S. loan to, 148-149; 1956 invasion of Sinai peninsula, 166-167, 169, 170, 173; U.S. alignment against, in Suez votes in U.N., 169, 171

issue, 10, 30, 45; Kefauver's views on, 19, 20; Stevenson's views, 21-22, 66, 72-74, 77, 78-79; Ike's statements and views, 28, 32, 46, 70-72, 74-76, 80, 84-85; public discontent, 41, 45, 69-70, 75, 83; GOP disagreement on how to exploit issue, 45-46, 70; opinion poll results on concern, 69-70; becomes major issue, 69-72, 74-76, 80, 84-85; American casualties in, 71-72, 79; Oct. 1952 resumption of fighting in, 72, 79; decisive in 1952 election outcome, 82-84; end of, 94, 99, 134

Kozlov, Frol, 193

Kraft, Joseph, 233

Krock, Arthur, 12, 143, 159, 259

Labor, 1952 vote of, 82

Lahey, Edwin, 29, 58

Laird, Melvin, 223, 225

Lambert, Gerard, 69

Landon, Alfred M., 178

Lane, Arthur Bliss, 54, 55

Lapp, Ralph, 101, 105-106, 107, 152, 156

Latin America: Eisenhower policy, 184, 267; Communist threat, 184, 214, 239, 268, 269; Nixon's 1958 trip to, 193; Stevenson's 1960 trip to, 189, 199; OAS and Castro's Cuba, 239, 268

Lattimore, Owen, 7

Latvia, 34

Lausche, Frank, 255

Lawrence, William, 246

Lear, Edward, 13

Lebanon, U.S. intervention of 1958, 183

Lehman, Herbert, 23, 179

Libby, Willard, 156

Liberals: support for Kefauver among, 20, 93; back Stevenson over Ike (1952), 40, 65, 82; of ADA, on Stevenson's campaign staff, 47; GOP, 59 (*see also* Eastern Republicans); "peaceful coexistence" endorsed by, 67; and 1960 Democratic hopefuls, 189, 190, 218

Liberation, doctrine of: formulated by Dulles, 24-25, 27, 44; Ike's approval of, 26, 35, 46, 50-51, 53; Taft's support, 29; embodied in Republican foreign policy plank of 1952, 34-35; Democratic platform "echo" of, 38; and Stevenson, 40, 52-53, 54, 66; "scenario" revealed by Dulles, 51; European reaction to, 51-52, 53, 54; "by peaceful means" qualification, 53, 113-114; Ike's retreat from, 53-54, 55-56; used on local campaign level, 55; espoused by Nixon, 64, 275; effect on 1952 election, 82, 84; rhetoric dropped after East European uprisings, 95, 113, 162-163; exploitation by GOP in 1956, for minority vote, 113-114, 127, 162; Democratic me-too echo, in 1956, 122; Nixon echo, in 1960 campaign, 275-277

Life magazine: Dulles article on foreign policy (1952), 25-26, 30, 54; Dulles interview on "brinkmanship," 95-96, 97; endorsement of Nixon in 1960, 272; quoted, 92

Lilienthal, David, 65, 152

Limited war policy, 103, 216, 223; in Korea, 5, 46, 75, 78; v. massive retaliation policy, 95

Lindley, Ernest, 37, 98, 230, 238, 274

Lippmann, Walter, 85, 98, 188, 203, 269, 272

Lithuania, 34

Lodge, Henry Cabot, 42, 56, 60, 89;

pre-convention campaign manager for Ike (1952), 12, 14, 15, 16, 31, 36; loss of Senate seat, 82, 190; UN Ambassador, 169, 186, 219, 220, 221, 227; Vice-Presidential candidate in 1960, 227-228, 237, 239, 244, 245, 261-262, 272, 273, 278-279; acceptance speech of, 228

London: 1956 UN disarmament talks in, 102, 105; Suez conference (1956), 120, 125, 145

London *Daily Express,* 118

London *Daily Mirror,* quoted, 52

London *Times,* quoted, 37

Los Angeles, campaign speeches in: Stevenson (1956), 136, 174; Kefauver (1956), 155; Ike (1956), 157; Nixon (1956), 159, 165; Nixon (1960), 277

Los Angeles *Mirror,* 45

Louisville, Stevenson's 1952 speech in, 72

Lovett, Robert A., 188

Lubell, Samuel, 84, 209, 266

Lucas, Scott, 19

Luce, Clare Booth, 32

Luce, Henry R., 54, 96, 277

Lucky Dragon case, 101

Lumumba, Patrice, 219, 238, 246

MacArthur, General Douglas, 52, 72; Korean War commander, 4-5; proposal of escalation, 5, 10, 46; dismissal of, 5; possible GOP Presidential contender in 1952, 11; keynoter at 1952 GOP Convention, 33, 37; nominee of Christian Nationalist party (1952), 61; Ike and, 61-62, 64

McCarran-Walter Immigration Act, 55, 69

McCarthy, Joseph, 7, 60-61, 69, 80, 190; Taft and, 8; Ike and, 59-61,

64, 84, 87; criticized by Stevenson, 66; reelection of, 82; Army-McCarthy hearings, and censure, 88

McCarthyism, 7

McCormick, Anne O'Hare, 25, 38

McCormick, Colonel Robert, 50

McCrary, Tex, 15

McElroy, Neil H., 185

McGowan, Carl, 47

McWilliams, Carey, 217

Macmillan, Harold, 117, 187, 257

Malik, Jacob, 52

Manchester *Guardian,* quoted, 51-52

Manchester *Union Leader,* 255

Manchuria, 5; U.S. bombing proposed, 5, 10, 20

Mannes, Marya, 228

Mansfield, Mike, 203

Mao Tse-tung, 4, 276

Marshall, George C., 4, 30, 60, 61, 66, 78

Martin, John Bartlow, 47, 131, 132, 153, 233

Martin, Joseph W., 5, 11, 62

Massachusetts primary, of 1952, 17

Massive retaliation policy, 33, 132, 139; Taft proposal, 9, 29-30, 35; Dulles's support for, 24; rejected by Ike during campaign, 26, 31, 35-36, 85; adopted by Ike in office, 85, 95; denounced by Stevenson, 99

Mathews, William R., 114

Matsu. *See* Quemoy and Matsu

Meet the Press (TV program), 264

Menzies, Robert G., 125, 145

Merriam, Robert E., 225, 262, 277

Meyer, Eugene, 69

Miami, 1956 campaign speeches in: Stevenson, 143; Ike, 166

Middle East, 183; arms race, 115-116, 121, 122, 171; Soviet penetration, 115, 116, 150, 170; 1956 crisis, 115-120, 125, 144-151, 166-170, 176-177, 178 (*see also* Suez crisis); Arab-Israeli hostilities, 116, 126, 166-167, 169; U.S. oil interests, 119, 150; Democratic platform of 1956 on, 121, 122; Republican platform on, 126-127

Midwest: Taft's strength in, 16; GOP isolationists, 48, 59; minority vote, 55, 275-276; Nixon campaign tour of, 275-277

Mikoyan, Anastas, 161

Millikin, Eugene, 34, 35

Minneapolis, Stevenson's 1956 speech in, 137

Minnesota primaries: of 1952, 16; of 1956, 93, 107

Minority groups, 122; in 1952 election, 82. *See also* Ethnic vote; Jewish vote; Negroes

Minow, Newton, 153

Missile race, 103-104, 106, 108, 185, 214, 257; "missile gap" charged, 185, 188, 189, 191-192, 195, 216; U-2 reconnaissance, 201

Mitchell, Stephen A., 47, 67, 76, 92, 107

Mobutu, Joseph, 246-247

Moley, Raymond, 67, 72

Molotov, Vyacheslav, 161, 176

Monroe Doctrine, 214, 220

Monroney, Mike, 211

Morgan, Edward P., 258

Morse, Wayne, 67, 76

Morton, Thruston B., 223, 228, 235-236, 248, 276

Muller, H. J., 155, 156

Mundt, Karl, 151

Murphy, George, 127

Murphy, Robert, 13, 117-118

Murray, Thomas, 102-103, 152

Nagasaki, 6

Nagy, Imre, 163, 165, 175

Nasser, Gamal Abdel, 115-119, 125, 126, 144-150, 167, 170, 249

Nation, 14, 93; quoted, 67, 83, 107, 112, 140, 160, 209, 229, 230-231, 242-243, 251, 255, 269, 285, 287

National Academy of Science, 105

National Aeronautics and Space Administration (NASA), U-2 cover story of, 201

National Association of Federations of Syrian and Lebanese American Clubs, 119

National security (*see also* Defense): dependent on free Western Europe, 3-4; and nuclear testing, 138-140 (*see also* Nuclear weapons); missile gap, 185, 191-192, 195, 216, 221; as election issue in 1960, 211, 214, 216, 221-226; U-2 defended for reasons of, 202-203, 227, 243

National Security Council, 138, 142, 164, 165

Nationalist China, 4, 263. *See also* Chiang Kai-shek; Formosa

NATO (North Atlantic Treaty Organization), 20, 27, 126; formation of, 3; Eisenhower as Supreme Commander of forces, 3-4, 15, 16; U.S. forces stationed in Europe, 3-4; continued U.S. support for, 216, 226

Nebraska primary, of 1952, 17

Negroes: in 1952 election, 82; in 1956 election, 178; Nixon-Lodge disagreement on appointments for, 273; 1960 vote of, 284

Nehru, Jawaharlal, 102, 115, 257

Neutralism, 135, 137; confusion within Administration over policy, 111-112, 121

Nevins, Allan, 192

New Deal coalition: in 1952 election, 82, 284; 1956 attempt to rebuild it, 131; 1960 attempt to re-

build, 191; in 1960 vote, 284
New England, won by Ike in 1952, 81
New Frontier, 218
New Hampshire primaries: of 1952, 14, 15-16, 18, 93; of 1956, 93; of 1960, 195, 197
New Isolationism, 4, 11, 31, 73
New Jersey primary, of 1952, 16
New Republic, 14, 105, 285; quoted, 32, 35, 40, 52, 75, 98, 122, 125, 144, 159, 197, 229, 230, 246, 255, 266, 269; TRB quoted, 11, 28, 40, 57, 65, 69, 123, 124, 133, 135, 198, 228
New York City: Stevenson's 1952 speeches in, 78-79; Ike's 1952 speech in, 80; Stevenson's 1956 speech in, 154; Kefauver's 1956 speech in, 155; Nixon's 1956 speech in Harlem, 172; 1956 vote in, 178; 1960 GOP freedom rally, 276; Ike and Nixon barnstorming, 278
New York *Daily News,* quoted, 254
New York *Herald Tribune,* 60
New York *Post,* 62
New York State: 1952 vote in, 81; importance to Nixon in 1960 election, 224, 226
New York Times, The, 13, 14, 60, 61, 85, 251, 285; endorsement of Kennedy by, 272; articles on USIA polls on U.S. prestige, 280; quoted, 32, 98, 137, 158, 159, 173, 177, 205, 217, 218, 225, 270, 272, 274
Newsweek, 160, 285; forecast on 1952 GOP nomination, 17, 29; 1952 election forecast, 81; poll on need for draft, 137; 1956 election forecast, 174-175; 1960 election forecasts, 251; quoted, 75, 83, 116, 128, 165, 178, 205, 209, 213,

223, 228, 229-230, 254, 255, 259
Nitze, Paul, 121
Nixon, Richard M.: Vice-Presidential candidate in 1952, 36, 49, 60, 65, 85; personality of, 197; an internationalist, 36; predicts foreign policy as big campaign issue, 40-41; campaign speeches of, 55, 63-64; $18,000 fund and "Checkers" speech of, 62-63, 84, 252; espouses Taft-Dulles line in foreign affairs, 63-64; smear tactics against Stevenson, 79-80, 138; as Vice-President, 87, 89, 192-193, 237-238; retention as 1956 Vice-Presidential candidate, 90-91, 112, 127-128; and neutralism confusion, 111-112; Stassen's "dump-Nixon" movement, 127; as target of Democrats, in 1956 campaign, 131, 154, 170, 174, 179; in 1956 campaign, 133, 134-135, 162; on the draft, 136-137; on H-bomb testing, 138, 151, 157, 159; "hand on the trigger of the H-bomb" references to, 154, 174; on Polish and Hungarian independence moves, 165; and Suez crisis, 170, 171-172; 1960 Presidential candidate, 192-197, 208, 209, 222-227; early poll results, 193, 194, 195, 196, 209, 215; Latin American trip of, 193, 222; tour of Russia (1959), 194; "kitchen debate" with Khrushchev, 194, 195, 222-223, 242, 245, 276; in Warsaw, 194, 273; pre-convention strategy of, 194-195, 196, 226-227; supported by Ike in 1960, 196, 226, 236-238, 244, 256, 277-279; and U-2 incident, 204, 205, 208, 209; hard-liner against Soviets, 209, 228, 230, 231, 240; seen as a match for Khrushchev, 209, 222-

223, 235, 240, 252, 276; stands on foreign policy experience, 222, 228, 244-245, 256, 273, 278-279; and defense spending, 222, 224-225, 226, 230; meeting and agreement with Rockefeller, 224-225; 1960 nomination of, 227; choice of running mate, 227-228; acceptance speech of, 229, 236; world tension working in his favor, 230, 240, 250-252; compared to Kennedy, 232, 235, 245; campaign of, 235-238; staff and advisers of, 235-236; campaign strategy, 236-238; campaign tours and speeches, 236, 243-245, 248, 264, 267, 275-277; on Jack Paar show, 238; speaking style of, 243; and Khrushchev's visit to U.N., 248-252; poll results after Conventions, 250-251, 266, 272, 282; in TV debates with Kennedy, 252-255, 258-266, 268-272, 275; campaign reversal for, 255-256, 272-275; views on Chinese offshore islands, 259-265; "trigger-happy" charge by Kennedy, 261; memoirs (*Six Crises*), 265, 270; Cuban trade embargo proposed, 267; and Kennedy's advocacy of Cuban expedition, 268-270; media support limited, 272; and Lodge's statement on Negro appointments, 273; appeal to ethnic vote, 275-277, 279; personal attacks on Kennedy, 275, 279; Ike's last-minute campaigning for, 277-279, 281, 282, 286; last-minute resurgence of, 279, 282, 286; 1960 election results for, 283-284; his election loss analyzed, 285, 286
Nkrumah, Kwame, 249, 250
North Atlantic Treaty Organization. *See* NATO

Nuclear weapons (*see also* Atom bomb; Hydrogen bomb): Baruch plan for control of, 159; U.S. monopoly lost, 6-7, 100; as lever in ending Korean War, 94; Democratic platform of 1956 on, 122; fallout, 101, 103, 104, 105-106, 153-154, 155, 156, 160; test ban asked by Stevenson, 99, 100, 102-104, 107, 108, 138-139, 151-161, 173, 179, 180; Soviet test-ban proposals, 101-102, 138-139, 154, 158; need of inspection safeguards for disarmament debated, 102, 142, 153, 158, 159, 186; testing defended by Ike, 104-105, 138-140, 141-142, 156-157, 159; scientific community divided on test ban, 106-107, 121, 155-156; testing defended by Truman, 142; public reaction to test-ban debate, 160-161; Ike's relaxation of stand on testing (1958), 186, 226; U.S. voluntary suspension of tests (1958-59), 186; talks on limited test ban, 186-187, 200; second-strike retaliatory capacity asked, 223, 225

OAS. *See* Organization of American States
O'Brien, Larry, 190, 217, 218, 232
O'Donnell, Kenneth, 190
O'Dwyer, William, 19
Oil interests, U.S., in Middle East, 119, 150
Open End (TV program), 204
"Open skies" proposal, by U.S., 95, 102
Operation Freedom Week (1960), 276
Oregon *Journal*, 49
Oregon primaries: of 1952, 17; of 1960, 199, 207

Organization of American States (OAS), 239, 268, 269

Pakistan, in Baghdad Pact, 115
Palestine refugees, 171
Paris Summit failure of 1960, 187, 200, 202, 203, 204-205, 206, 208, 247, 256, 279
Parr, Jack, 328
Party enrollment statistics, 1960, 196
Patton, General George, 13
Pax Americana, 8
"Peace and prosperity," Ike's achievement, 88, 124-125, 128, 133, 173; Nixon promise, 237
Peace theme: in 1952 campaign, 53, 66 (*see also* Korean War, election issue in 1952); in 1956 campaign, 133-135, 136, 140, 161, 173, 178; in 1960 campaign, 205, 209, 214, 218, 221, 235, 236, 245, 273, 278
"Peaceful coexistence": Stevenson on (1952), 66-67; propounded by Khrushchev, 97, 111
Pennsylvania, 1952 vote in, 81
"People machine," 234
Percy, Charles, 223, 224, 225
Péron, Juan, 143
Persons, General Wilton B., 197
Philadelphia: Ike's foreign policy speech in (1952), 53, 54, 70; 1956 Nixon speech in, 151; Ike's 1960 speech for Nixon, 278
Philippines, Ike's 1960 visit to, 212
Pinkley, Virgil, 45
Poland, 34; Republican repudiation of Yalta agreement on, 34, 54, 55; Poznan riots (1956), 113, 114, 161, 163; Gomulka government crisis (1956), 161-162; "liberation," 162, 163, 165; U.S. economic aid offer to, 163; Nixon's visit to (1959), 194, 273
Polish-Americans: and liberation

doctrine, 52, 54, 55, 82, 84; GOP wooing of vote of, 54, 55; Stevenson's 1952 Labor Day Speech to, 52; 1952 vote of, 82, 84; 1960 GOP appeal for vote of, 276, 277; 1960 vote of, 284
Polls, public opinion (*see also* Gallup polls): Ike v. Taft, against Stevenson or Kefauver, 32-33; on 1952 Ike-Stevenson race, 58, 69, 70, 81; on matters of most concern (1952), 69-70; on 1956 Ike-Stevenson race, 133, 174-175; on draft, 137; Kennedy v. Nixon race, 193, 194, 196, 209, 215, 250-251, 266, 272, 282; Nixon v. Rockefeller, 195; on party enrollment (1960), 196; on Johnson in 1960, 210; foreign policy found paramount issue in 1960, 229-230; on Nixon-Kennedy TV debates, 255, 259, 265-266, 272, 279-280; on U.S. prestige abroad, 270-271, 280
Potsdam Conference, 9, 10, 28, 29, 33, 34, 38
Powers, Francis Gary, 200-202
Pravda, quoted, 52
Presidential candidates: 1952 Democratic, 39; 1952 Republican, 36; 1956 Democratic, 123; 1956 Republican, 128; 1960 Democratic, 217-218; 1960 Republican, 227
Prestige, U.S., charge of decline of, 188, 191, 213, 214, 216, 221-222, 223, 229, 231, 234-235, 241-243, 247-248, 279-281, 285-286; debated on TV by Nixon and Kennedy, 270-271, 279-280; confirmed by polls, 270-271, 279-280
Price, Charles C., 152
Primaries: Democratic, of 1952, 18, 20; Republican, of 1952, 10, 14, 15-16, 17, 29; Democratic, of

rapprochement, 58-59, 70, 84, 85; Ike's unification of, 59-62, 85; emphasis on Korean War issue, 69-72, 74-76, 80, 84-85; 1952 Presidential election results, 81-82; analysis of 1952 victory of, 82-85; Ike's coattails weak, 82, 83-84, 178; congressional election results for, 82; "peace and prosperity" achieved, 88, 124-125; 1956 candidates of, 90-91, 127-128; in foreign policy debate, 98-100; Leonard Hall as National Chairman, 91, 110; and liberation theme appeal to ethnic vote in 1956, 113-114, 162; vulnerable in Suez crisis issue, 117, 118, 119-121, 129, 144-145, 150-151; 1956 campaign strategy, 133-135; and nuclear test-ban issue, 138, 151-152, 155-159, 160; attempts to exploit Suez crisis for partisan advantage, 148-149; last-minute election forecasts for, 174-175; 1956 Presidential election results for, 178; congressional election results for, 178; 1958 congressional election losses of, 193; possible Presidential candidates in 1960, 192-197, 221-225; 1960 primaries, 195; enrolled voter statistics (1960), 196; effect of U-2 incident on pre-convention race, 205, 207-209; reaction to Rockefeller-Nixon statement, 225-226; 1960 candidates of, 227-229; world tension working in their favor as incumbents, 230, 240; Morton as National Chairman, 228, 235; reaction to Quemoy-Matsu debate, 261-262; campaign reversal in wake of TV debates, 255-256, 272, 275; appeal to ethnic vote (1960), 275-277, 279; urge Nixon to let Ike campaign,

277-278; 1960 election results, 284
Republican Policy of Liberation, 162
Reston, James, 29, 81, 93, 96, 98, 133, 159, 172, 177, 203-204, 232, 240, 269, 272, 274
Roberts, Clifford, 15, 16, 27
Robinson, William, 15
Rockefeller, Nelson, 193, 244, 261, 273, 277; as 1960 Presidential contender, 193, 195-196, 208, 221-226; foreign affairs experience, 195; and U-2 incident, 207-208; asks higher defense spending, 195, 221-222, 223, 224-225, 230; foreign policy views, 223, 224-226; meeting and agreement with Nixon, 224-225, 226; endorsement of Nixon by, 227
Rogers, William P., 197, 236, 272
Rokossovsky, Marshal Konstantin K., 161, 162
Roosevelt, Eleanor, 39, 123, 211, 215, 218, 233
Roosevelt, Franklin D., 57, 82, 83, 178, 195, 287; loss of Eastern Europe blamed on, 10, 275-276; Ike's methods and appeal compared to, 40, 58, 85; Kennedy's appeal compared to, 191, 274
Roper, Elmo, 70, 81
Rovere, Richard, 37
Royall, Kenneth, 67, 75, 172
Russell, Richard, 20, 22, 37, 39, 109

St. Louis, 1952 speech by Truman, 78
Salinger, Pierre, 190, 217
Salisbury, Harrison, 152
San Francisco: UN Conference, 21, 66; Stevenson's 1952 speech in, 66; Ike's 1952 speech in, 71
San José, Declaration of, 239
Schlesinger, Arthur, Jr., 199, 282; adviser to Stevenson, 47, 65, 92,

overt missile threat to U.S., 214, 239; shift of power to, 187-188, 214, 216, 221-222, 223, 241-242, 247-248, 270-271, 279-280; 1960 confrontations with U.S. in U.N. Security Council, 219-221; and Congo crisis, 219, 238, 246-247; and RB-47 reconnaissance flight, 220-221

Space race, 184-185, 216

Sparkman, John, 40, 77

Spies in government issue, 7

Spivack, Robert G., 251

Sputnik, 184, 188, 279

Stalin, Joseph, 32, 33, 45, 75, 79, 97, 161; death of, 94; 1956 denunciation of, 97, 98, 110, 113

Stassen, Harold, 102; Presidential contender in 1952, 10-11, 32, 36; in 1952 primaries, 16, 17; aids Ike's 1952 campaign, 56; at 1956 Republican Convention, 127

State Department, 23, 276 (*see also* Dulles, John Foster; Herter, Christian); McCarthy spy charges against, 7; and U-2 incident, 201-203; and Ike's visit to Tokyo, 212; and Cuba, 220, 266-267; reiteration of Monroe Doctrine by, 220; rejects summit meeting at UN, 239-240; and Quemoy and Matsu debate, 260, 262

Stevenson, Adlai E., 190, 217, 218, 230; background and career of, 21; personality of, 21; early service for UN, 21, 41; governor of Illinois, 18, 20, 21; as Presidential candidate in 1952, 18, 20-23, 37-38, 46; prefers independence from Truman, 18, 22, 39, 46-47, 48-50, 123; domestic policy views of, 21; foreign policy views of, 21-22, 66-67, 72-74, 77, 78-79; defense of Truman's Korean War conduct by,

21-22, 66, 72-73, 78-79; supports containment policy, 21, 40-41, 47, 66; a reluctant candidate, in 1952, 22, 37-38, 46; opinion poll results on, 33, 58, 69, 70, 81; 1952 nomination of, 39; choice of 1952 running mate, 40; acceptance speech of, 40; in basic agreement with Ike on containment policy, 40-41; labeled "Truman's candidate" by GOP, 43, 44, 47, 49; lack of experience charged, 44; 1952 campaign of, 46-48, 64-69; campaign staff of, 47; Truman's efforts for, 48, 68-69; calls Ike a captive of Taft and isolationists, 48, 59, 78; foreign policy briefing of, 48-49; criticism of GOP liberation policy concept, 52-53, 54, 66; called soft on Communism, 64, 79-80, 109; called "appeaser," 64, 67, 207; rejects appeasement, 66; people's reaction to, 64, 65, 132; the "egghead" candidate, 65, 132; speeches of, 65-67, 72-74, 77, 78-79; resurgence late in campaign, 69, 80; response to Ike's Korea strategy, 72-74, 77, 78-79; sum of his Cold War ideology, 74; his plan to visit Asia, 77; 1952 election results for, 81-82; reasons for his 1952 defeat, 83; as Democratic party leader, 91-92, 207; as 1956 candidate, 91, 92-93, 122-123; brain trust of, 92; poll results on (1955/56), 92, 133, 174; in 1956 primaries, 93, 107-109, 130; on Dulles's brinkmanship, 96; April 1956 criticism of U.S. foreign policy, 98-99, 100; call for H-bomb test ban by, 99, 100, 102-104, 107, 108, 138-140, 141-142, 151-161, 173, 179, 180; change of campaign style in 1956, 107-108, 130; civil

Supreme Court, U.S., school integration decision, 108
Symington, Stuart, 103, 153, 154, 185; possible 1960 Presidential candidate, 189-190, 198, 199, 215; and U-2 incident, 207
Syracuse, N.Y., Kennedy's campaign speech at, 256

Taft, Robert A., 48, 65, 70; as presidential contender in 1952, 8-10, 13, 23, 29-32, 228; fighting his isolationist label, 8-10, 27, 30; *A Foreign Policy for Americans,* 8, 24; criticism of containment policy by, 8-9, 12, 13, 30; condemnation of bipartisanship in foreign policy, 8-10, 13, 29-30; foreign policy proposals of, 9-10, 24, 25, 29-30, 56; opposition to U.S. troops in Europe, 9, 13, 30; Korean War his main issue, 10, 30, 45; "Truman's War" statement, 10, 21; lack of understanding of foreign policy, 11, 14; New Isolationist, 11, 22, 31, 32; rejected by eastern GOP internationalists, 11, 12, 17, 27, 32; in 1952 primaries, 10, 14, 15-16, 17, 29; opinion polls on, in early 1952, 15, 17, 29, 33; pre-convention strength of, 17, 32; Dulles and, 23, 26-27; and 1952 GOP foreign policy plank, 26-27, 34; and liberation doctrine, 29, 50, 56; Ike's attacks on, 30-32; defeat at 1952 GOP convention, 36-37; his support won by Ike, 58-59, 64, 70, 71, 80, 84; "Morningside Heights" statement of, 59, 72; defense of Nixon by, in $18,000 fund affair, 63; his foreign policy line espoused by Nixon, 63-64; and finally by Ike, 70, 85; death of, 88

Taiwan, 94, 212. *See also* Formosa
Taxation, 28, 59
Teheran Conference, 9, 10, 28, 33, 34, 38
Television, in 1952 Republican campaign strategy, 43
Television debates, Nixon-Kennedy, 252-255, 258-266, 268-272, 275, 279-280
Teller, Edward, 6
Test ban. *See* Nuclear weapons
Texas: challenge of delegation at 1952 GOP convention, 36; 1952 vote in, 81
Thermonuclear weapons, 6-7, 100-101, 102. *See also* Hydrogen bomb; Nuclear weapons
Third World nations, 144, 147, 172, 180, 247; neutralism issue, 111-112 (*see also* Underdeveloped nations); and U.N., 250, 257
Time magazine, 69, 80, 148, 237; quoted, 16, 52, 116, 127, 146, 165, 188, 211, 213, 219-220, 221, 226, 229, 230, 241, 244, 249, 251, 254, 256, 259, 265, 267, 274, 285
Tito, Marshall (Josip Broz), 115, 249, 250
Tokyo, Ike's planned visit canceled, 212-213
Trade embargo, on Cuba, 267-268
Treaty-making, Bricker Amendment, 88
"Treaty of Fifth Avenue," 224-225
Truman, Harry S., 3, 16, 23, 27, 88, 143, 195, 216, 218, 230, 277, 286; in 1948 election, 43, 82, 84; and Korean War, 4, 6, 21, 28, 46, 66, 68, 71, 72-73, 94; dismissal of MacArthur, 5; and H-bomb, 6-7; loss of public confidence, 7-8; Taft's criticism of foreign policy of, 9, 10, 29; Cold War blamed on, by Taft, 9; loss of Eastern

Europe blamed on, 10, 34, 276; decides not to seek reelection, 11-12, 18-19; and choice of his successor candidate, 11-12, 17-18, 20-21, 37-38, 39; offers 1952 candidacy to Eisenhower, 11-12; Fair Deal, 19; Republican platform attack on foreign policy of, 34-35; efforts on Stevenson's behalf, 39, 48, 68-69, 73, 77-78; as target of 1952 GOP campaign, 43-44, 64; Stevenson's disassociation from, 46-47, 48, 49-50; criticism of GOP liberation policy concept by, 53, 54; domestic policy criticized by Ike, 57; attacks on Ike for past foreign affairs errors, 68-69, 77-78; dares Ike on Korea, 74, 76; and 1956 Presidential campaign, 92, 93, 109, 123, 124, 142, 162; rejection of test-ban idea, 142; backs Symington in 1960, 189, 199, 215; efforts for Kennedy, 233

Truman Administration, scandals in, 44, 47, 49, 62

"Truman's War," Taft quote, 10, 21

Tsombe, Moise, 220, 238

Turkey, in Baghdad Pact, 115

Tydings, Millard, 7

U-2 incident, 200-205, 220, 221, 228, 279; as 1960 election issue, 205-211, 214, 216, 230, 235, 256; Kennedy suggestion of apology, 207, 210, 227, 243, 248, 258, 264; U.N. censure of U.S. defeated, 257

Ulam, Stanislaw, 6

Underdeveloped nations: Soviet aid to, 97; U.S. aid to, 99, 111; neutralism issue, 111-112

United Nations, 39, 117, 145; in Korean War, 4, 5, 22, 71; Steven-son's early service at, 21, 41; development aid, 99, 250; Disarmament Commission, 101-102, 105; mediation in Middle East, 116; Republican platforms on, 126, 226; discussions of Suez crisis, 146, 147, 148, 149, 166, 167, 169-170, 171; and Hungarian uprising, 164, 175-176; U.S. break with England and France in, over Suez, 169-170, 171, 172, 176; Mid-East cease-fire resolution, 170, 176, 177; Mid-East peace-keeping force, 176, 177; U.S.-Soviet confrontations in Security Council (1960), 219-221, 228, 270-271; peace efforts in Congo, 219-220, 238, 246-247, 250, 257, 281; Cuban debate, 220; RB-47 debate, 221; Lodge as U.S. Ambassador, 219-221, 227, 228; peace force in Katanga, 238; Khrushchev at (1960), 239-240, 247, 249-250, 257, 279, 285; 1960 General Assembly session, 250, 257, 270-271; Ike's 1960 assurance of U.S. support, 250; "troika" demanded by Khrushchev, 250; Castro at, 250, 266; refusal of U.S. censure for U-2 flight, 257; Congo vote, 257, 270-271

United States Information Agency (USIA), poll on U.S. prestige, 271, 280

Urban vote: cracked by Ike in 1956, 178; in 1960, 284

USIA. See United States Information Agency

Vandenberg, Arthur H., 4, 8, 9, 27, 68

Vandenberg, Arthur, Jr., 31, 42

Van Fleet, General James, 79, 80

Veterans of Foreign Wars: Kennedy's speech to, 240, 241-242; Nixon's speech to, 243

Vice-Presidential candidates: 1952 Democratic, 40; 1952 Republican, 36; 1956 Democratic, 124; 1956 Republican, 128; 1960 Democratic, 217; 1960 Republican, 227-228

Vietnam, Geneva settlement of 1954, 94

Vinson, Fred, 12, 17

Virginia, 1952 vote in, 81

Voice of America, 38, 51

Voter turnout: in 1948, 82; stay-at-homes a GOP target, 42, 43, 58, 59, 82, 85; in 1952, 82; in 1960, 284

Wadsworth, James, 105

War or Peace (Dulles), 25

War scares: of 1948, 3; in 1956, as boost to Eisenhower, 173, 175, 176-178

Warren, Earl, 10-11, 17, 32

Warsaw, Nixon's visit to, 194, 273

Warsaw Pact, 165

West Berlin. *See* Berlin; Berlin crises

West Coast: Stevenson's speeches on test ban (1956), 152; Ike's reply speeches on ban, 157

West Germany, 139, 185; disarma-ment asked by Soviets, 95

Wheeler, General Earle G., 234

White, Lincoln, 202

White, Theodore, 285

White, William S., 37

Williams, Walter, 16

Willkie, Wendell, 15, 42, 43, 84

Wilson, Charles E., Secretary of Defense, 87, 167

Wilson, Woodrow, Stevenson compared to, 65

Wirtz, Willard, 47, 131

Wisconsin, Ike's dilemma in, vis-à-vis McCarthy, 60-61

Wisconsin primaries: of 1952, 17; of 1960, 197-198

Wolper, David, 173

Wyatt, Wilson W., 47

Yalta Conference, 9, 10, 28, 29, 33, 34, 38; Republican repudiation of "secret understandings . . . ," 34, 54, 55; repudiation not carried out, 95

Yalu River, 5

Yarnell, Admiral, 261, 262

Yugoslavia, 115; detachment from Soviet bloc, 53

Zanuck, Darryl, 75

Zionists, American, 119, 121, 173. *See also* Jewish vote